Tarot
The Definitive Guide

Published in Australia in 2006 by

New Holland Publishers (Australia) Pty Ltd

Sydney • Auckland • London • Cape Town

14 Aquatic Drive Frenchs Forest NSW 2086 Australia

218 Lake Road Northcote Auckland New Zealand

86 Edgware Road London W2 2EA United Kingdom

80 McKenzie Street Cape Town 8001 South Africa

First published January 2005 by Eagle Spirit Ministry

10 9 8 7 6 5 4 3 2 1

National Library of Australia Cataloguing-in-Publication Data:

Porter, Tracy.

       Tarot: the definitive guide

       ISBN 1 74110 393 2.

        1. Tarot. I. Title.

       133.32424

Publisher: Fiona Schultz

Designer: Greg Lamont

Production Controller: Grace Gutwein

Printer: Griffin Press, Adelaide, South Australia

Tarot
The Definitive Guide

Tracy Porter

NEW HOLLAND

www.newholland.com.au

CONTENTS

Introduction

It is not known exactly where and when the Tarot came into existence, but some believe it originated in ancient Egypt and was brought to Europe by the Romany, or 'Gypsies', as they travelled from India to Europe. Others say the cards originated in Arabia or Asia.

The first reference to the Tarot in Europe was in 1480 by an Italian writer, who claimed that it arrived from North Africa in the late fourteenth century. The Tarot appears to have been initially used as a card game, named after the Italian town of Taro. Originally there were only 22 cards, now known as the Major Arcana, and believed to have been based on the Hebrew alphabet and the 22 pathways in the Cabala. Later that century the Minor Arcana of 56 more cards was added. Its four suits—swords, cups, disks and clubs—were said to represent the nobility, the clergy, merchants and peasants. Each suit is composed of ten numbered cards, which are believed to relate to the ten sephiram in the Cabala, and four additional cards, which are used to represent actual people.

The Tarot was never intended to be used as a card game, or even for fortune telling for that matter, but as a unique symbolic pictorial analogy of the different phases and aspects of human life. Study the cards earnestly and with pureness in your heart, and you will become aware of the universal secrets that are part of the never-ending past, present, future and parallel existences, as transcribed in the Akashic records. In essence, the Tarot was designed as an aide to spiritual development, but over time people began using them to foretell the future. Consult the Tarot with clarity of mind and a genuine desire to know the truth, and the cards will reveal the answers you seek, whether they be on a mundane or universal level.

Elements and the Tarot

The Tarot, or Book of Thoth, is believed have originated in ancient Egypt. Ancient Egyptians focused heavily on the four universal elements—fire (light), earth, air (gas, sky) and water (moisture)—which are a part of almost every abstruse thought system, both past and present.

Egyptian primary gods were representative of these four elements: Shu ruled Fire or light, Tefnut ruled Water or moisture, Geb ruled Earth or firmament and Nut ruled Air or sky.

So transcendental is the concept of the elemental forces that our earth even corresponds quite dramatically to them on a seasonal basis.

The four major astronomical events that occur on the earth each year are the spring and autumn equinox, and the summer and winter solstice.

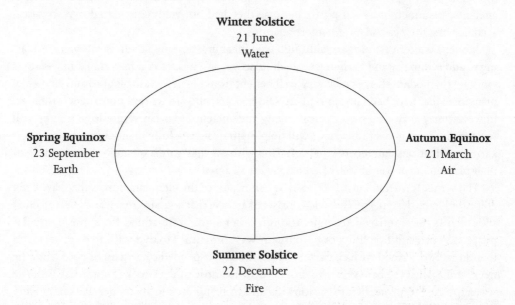

The season of Earth is associated with Aries, Taurus, and Gemini in the Northern Hemisphere, but with Libra, Scorpio and Sagittarius in the Southern Hemisphere.

The season of Fire is associated with Cancer, Leo and Virgo in the Northern Hemisphere, and Capricorn, Aquarius, and Pisces in the Southern Hemisphere.

The season of Air is associated with Libra, Scorpio and Sagittarius in the Northern Hemisphere, and Aries, Taurus and Gemini in the Southern Hemisphere.

The season of Water is associated with Capricorn, Aquarius and Pisces in the Northern Hemisphere and Cancer, Leo and Pisces in the Southern Hemisphere.

It is important to keep in mind the ancient Egyptian thought processes that formed their mythology when considering elemental compatibilities. Shu, ruler of Fire or light, mated with Tefnut, ruler of Water or moisture. Geb, ruler of Earth, mated with Nut, ruler of Air. This indicates that Earth is compatible with Air, and that Fire is compatible with Water.

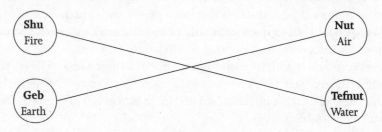

By now, students of modern Western astrology may be in a state of shocked horror, recognising that ancient Egyptian elemental analogies bear little resemblance to what has been traditionally taught by the modern Western astrological system. This is because the ancient Egyptians were concerned primarily with the seasonal changes that affected their farming methods, and they designed their astrology to work around them. The astrology of the ancients was much more simplistic because they had not yet incorporated mathematical accuracy into their calendars and interpretations.

Modern Western astrologers, although well meaning, designed their astrological reasoning to add symmetry and harmony to the horoscope, and it is for that reason that newer souls working on modern themes may very well benefit from the newer astrological and elemental principles that have been put into place. Older souls who are working on ancient themes, however, may very well benefit from using the ancient Egyptian symbologies. They will receive greater clarity of mind that will help them to successfully manoeuvre though their karmic obligations and receive their dharmic gifts, as they gain a greater understanding of their place in the universal web of which we are all a part.

The symbols used in Tarot are also an apt indicator of the elemental forces that have been employed in its design. The Pentacle consists of a circle that contains magical signs, the chief of which is the interlaced triangle, though other signs were added for some particular purpose. A piece of fine linen or parchment was sometimes folded with five corners, and then suitably inscribed with characters. Worn mostly suspended by a chain or cord from the neck, and against the bare skin, as a cross is now by those of the Greek Church, the Pentacle was supposed to protect from various ills and to bring luck to its owner. Pentacles were devised for different uses, some being employed by magicians to control the spirits, which they evoked at will during some of their magical exercises.

In the Western world we identify with the four basic elements—Fire, Earth, Air and Water—which help us relate to concepts, people, places and things. Elements were used as the principle building blocks when Tarot, astrology and other esoteric sciences were initially designed. Each element corresponds to a suit in the Minor Arcana. The element of Spirit, which is not included in the traditional grouping, corresponds with the Major Arcana, which is considered by many to be another suit entirely.

Fire

Fire is considered to be a life force, which gives zest to our lives. Fire is active, adventurous and aggressive, as well as playful, creative and loving. Fire wants to be first and it should therefore come as no surprise to discover that many people with a preponderance of Fire in their birth horoscopes tend to think primarily of their own wants, needs and desires. In matters of love, Fire is conquesting, exciting and romantic. Fire is associated with summer, and therefore corresponds with the astrological signs of Cancer, Leo and Virgo. The suit of Wands identifies most closely with this element. Because Fire is so swift, in terms of time, it relates to days. Therefore, each numbered card in the suit of Wands will equate to the number on the card multiplied by one day.

Earth

Earth is the stabilising force in our lives. It reminds us of our duties, responsibilities and obligations, and thus helps us to achieve our worldly ambitions. Earth helps us to work, earn money and advance in our careers. Because of this emphasis on materialism, Earth can at times appear boring or greedy, but it can also be very sensual and enjoys good food, drink and pleasurable entertainment. In matters of love, Earth tends to be more analytical, practical and sensual, and will choose a partner based upon what he or she can bring into the family unit rather than allow infatuation to get in the way of making a logical decision. Earth is associated with spring, and corresponds with the astrological signs of Aries, Taurus and Gemini. The suit of Pentacles identifies most closely with this element. Because Earth is somewhat slower than the other elements, in terms of time, each numbered card in the suit of Pentacles will equate to the number on the card multiplied by one month.

Air

Air is intellectual and wants to think, communicate and socialise. Air is responsible for the development of acquaintances, close relationships and marriages. Air likes to be surrounded by friends and needs a wide variety of intellectual stimulation or it will soon become bored. In matters of love, Air tends to prefer any commitments to be cemented with a legal contract because it knows all too well that verbal arrangements can easily be misunderstood. Air is associated with autumn and corresponds with the astrological signs of Libra, Scorpio and Sagittarius. The suit of Swords identifies most closely with this element. In terms of time, this element relates to the fortnight. Therefore, each numbered card in the suit of swords will equate to the number on the card multiplied by one fortnight, or two weeks.

Water

Water gives us feelings that can range from pure, to intense, to spiritual in nature. Without Water, we cannot feel, as this element is often highly intuitive and can easily escape into a fantasy world of addiction if other stabilising forces are not present. Water is an elusive element and is often responsible for delusion in our lives. In matters of love, Water seeks soul-mate relationships, which are intense and spiritual. Water is associated with winter and corresponds to the astrological signs of Capricorn, Aquarius and Pisces. The suit of Cups most closely identifies with this element. In terms of time, this element relates to the week. Therefore, each numbered card in the suit of Cups will equate to the number on the card multiplied by one week.

Spirit

The element of spirit is associated with the higher, more karmic realms of our daily lives. Spirit cannot adequately be portrayed within the confines of the four elements of Fire, Earth, Air or Water because it transcends day-to-day activities. The element of spirit normally indicates that we are going into deeper, more meaningful levels of reality. This element most closely identifies with the Major Arcana. Because matters of the spirit as a general rule tend to transcend time and space, they affect our lives in such a transformative way that in terms of time it equates to one year. Therefore, the duration of each card in the Major Arcana will equate to the number on the card multiplied by one year, as these cards take a significant amount of time to reveal themselves to us.

Fire Combined with Fire

Fire coupled with Fire usually has somewhat of a neutral effect. When the elements of Fire meet, this indicates that much energy is put into business, creative, or even spiritual matters. Although Fire, when combined with itself, is said to be beneficial, too much Fire can become explosive in nature. For this reason it is essential to properly focus the vast amount of energy inherent in the suit of Wands or the element of Fire so that it is directed into positive endeavours to achieve maximum effectiveness.

Fire Combined with Air

The element of Air tends to strengthen Fire. The creative energy of Fire coupled with the mental agility of Air brings much mental creation in the form of visions, ideas, and even prophecies. This is illustrated by the fact that when a touch of air is blown onto a burning ember, the flame will intensify and strengthen in volume and heat. However, if a huge gust of Air overpowers that same ember, it will serve to extinguish the same flames that had once been so luminous. Therefore, it is always necessary to temper Air and Fire so that these two elements can enhance each other and not falter.

Fire Combined with Earth

When Fire is coupled with Earth, these two elements have the effect of complimenting one another. The energy inherent in Fire mingled with the practicality of Earth helps us to achieve our materialistic goals through diligently applied work and effort as expressed by our very physical world. The effect that Fire has on Earth can be illustrated by the presence of periodic bushfires, which ravage our earth but are essential for the survival of the bush. The resulting ashes that result from the bushfire serve to replenish the earth with vital nutrients that are necessary for the regeneration of many species. Therefore, the very element that destroys the earth also serves to propagate new life on it.

Fire Combined with Water

When Fire is mixed with Water, much care needs to be taken to ensure these elements do not weaken one another. When emotions are mixed with creative energy, a melodramatic outburst can occur if a proper balance is not maintained. The effect that Water has on Fire can be seen when one attempts to pour water on fire. A few drops of the mist will serve to excite the fire and intensify it, but too much water will have the effect of putting the fire out altogether. The same can be reflected when one attempts to mix the element of Water with the element of Fire. A touch of emotion can create a work of art, but an overabundance of emotion or fury can escalate to all-out war. The activators inherent in Fire, therefore, can generate much creativity when combined with the sensitivity of Water.

Earth Combined with Earth

When Earth is combined with itself, it has somewhat of a neutral effect. The two Earthy elements have a tendency to reinforce each other's practical qualities so money, property and other basal concerns will tend to predominate the situation. Although Earth coupled with itself is usually neutral, too much Earth can lead to excessive materialism, possessiveness, greed or lust, which will ultimately lead to conflicts of interest and power struggles.

Earth Combined with Water

The element of Earth combined with Water has somewhat of a neutral impact. The practicality of Earth generally has the effect of stabilising Water's deeply flowing emotions and Earth helps Water to keep its emotions in check. For example, although the astrological sign of Capricorn is considered in the traditional sense to be of the Earthy element, the fact that the symbol is half fish and half goat indicates this sign, at least on an esoteric level, has deeply buried emotions that have somehow transcended to form more highly rationalised thought processes. Excavations from ancient oriental drawings also suggest the Earthly sign of Capricorn was at one time a Water element. In fact, the very first animal associated with the sign of Capricorn was the sea monster Hippocampus guttalaus, which was representative of the element of Water. Eventually the symbol was replaced with the mythological sea goat, thereby giving the sign some Earthly attributes. Some astrologers, sadly, have attempted to eradicate this sign's ancient beginnings altogether, by replacing the sea goat with that of the mountain goat, thereby intensifying the misunderstandings inherent in this sign. Additionally, our modern zodiac was not in its present form until about 2000 years ago, when it is said that Julius Caesar carved Libra and Virgo out of the former great snake-like constellation of Scorpio in an effort to make the calendar more accurate. With this in mind, Capricorn may well have been considered more emotive than present day astrologers give it credit for and these ancient influences may still lie dormant within our zodiac's most serious and ambitious sign. When Earth is combined with Water the creativity channelled through is more useful. These two elements combined tend to focus on realistic emotions and feelings toward family and possessions, thereby helping us to provide material security for those we love.

Earth Combined with Air

When Earth is coupled with Air, the influence of these two elements can be weakened. The intellectual influences of Air combined with the solid practicality of Earth can produce a conflict of material self-interest versus cerebral concerns, or analytical thought processes versus reality.

Air Combined with Air

The suit of Swords is symbolic of Air, and unfortunately many of the cards in this suit depict strife, discord and trouble. This relates to the fact that the honing of communication skills is of paramount importance in the development of relationships to prevent misunderstandings. Most wars, arguments and other such conflicts occur simply because people are not able to communicate their needs effectively. When Air is coupled with itself, it generally has somewhat of a neutral effect. Because Air is mentally agile, the combination of these two elements stimulates a great deal of cerebral activity. This mental activity can take the form of correspondence, writing, speaking, and other decision-making making processes. Since Air generally dictates verbal activity, misunderstandings and discord can sometimes occur if we don't make concerted efforts to try to understand one another.

Air Combined with Water

When Air is coupled with Water, these two elements have a tendency to strengthen one another. The intellectual characteristics of Air mingled with the emotional sensitivity of Water tend to produce many new creative ideas. It is important to remember that Water is in fact two parts of hydrogen mixed with one part of oxygen, which makes the synastry between these two elements very potent indeed. A touch of Water mixed with Air can form a fine mist, which creates refreshing coolness on a warm, sunny day. However, if that same Water becomes too heavy, the mist will give way to heavy humidity, showers, tornadoes, or hurricanes. For this reason, it is essential that just the right amount of Water should be mingled with Air to ensure a positive outcome to any given situation.

Water Combined with Water

When Water is coupled with itself, it tends to have somewhat of a neutral effect. Water mixed with itself highlights intense emotional sensitivity. If this emotional sensitivity is of a positive nature, much joy, love, fun and creativity can come from the coupling. If the emotions, however, are low, then excessive fantasy or depression can effect those involved.

Pictorial Symbology of the Tarot

The Tarot utilises archetypal symbology to get signals across to our consciousness through our supersubconscious selves. While we in the modern world take the written word for granted, supposing it is the primary means of communicating thoughts and ideas, this is not necessarily the case. This apparent contradiction is evidenced by the fact that common man has only been reading and writing for the last couple of hundred years or so, as this skill was reserved for clerics, who spent their entire lives transcribing ancient texts.

Prior to the time that reading and writing became standard practice, commoners relied heavily on word of mouth and visual perceptions, such as paintings and murals. Prior to that time, orators had superb memories, and used the technique of mind mapping to help them to remember important points while giving a speech or telling a story. In addition, pre-literate societies relied quite heavily on rote memorisation, completely memorising their tales and myths so they could relate them over and over again to subsequent generations. Storytellers were valued members of society who earned their living telling tales. Avid listeners made themselves comfortable in front of the warm fire while the skilled orator took them to another reality in their own minds, instilling in them the pleasure that only comes from completely losing oneself in an exciting story. Unfortunately, when humans became literate, they allowed the part of their mind that is responsible for extensive memory processes to atrophy, and we therefore lost a great deal of our intuitive perceptions.

The first language to be written was Sumerian, which began as simple cuneiform pictures, and can be traced as far back as 3100 BC. During the Roman occupation, about a hundred years after Julius Caesar's reign, the Roman alphabet was introduced into Britain. For several centuries only monks and other scholars practised writing, chiefly for ecclesiastical and legal documents, and always in Latin.

Because many of us read so much today, we often take literacy for granted, supposing that humans have been literate for millennia. But for centuries people passed their time in other ways; perhaps conversing with others much more than they do today. Stories would be told by travelling storytellers and bards to entertain the populace. Illiteracy was so widespread that even kings and other leaders had to employ scribes to write for them. Monks busied themselves writing original works or copying others in beautiful manuscripts, but 'ordinary' people did not need to read them, even if they could.

It was not until the printing press was invented in the mid 15th century that commoners were encouraged to write, and then eventually to read. Before that time, people received information by other means, quite often using their intuition as well as logic to acquire information and solve problems.

Cognitive psychology emphasises the mental processes that take place inside the mind. It focuses on the mental processing of information, especially the processing involved in perception, memory, language and problem solving. It is a new science, developed in the early 20th century and evolved from the work of a group of scientists in Germany known as the Gestalt psychologists. Gestalt is translated from its German origin as 'configuration' and means 'form or pattern'. It involves studying how the human mind receives information and interprets it. Perception was one of their favourite topics and they demonstrated how pieces of visual input, such as the Tarot, are organised into meaningful wholes. The approach showed the whole is more than the sum of its parts; a visual perception cannot be explained on the basis of sensory stimulus alone. While cognitive psychology has been criticised for being too materialistic and under-rating the importance of emotions in behaviour, it is one of the dominant approaches in contemporary psychology. The gestalt approach has been extended to research in areas as diverse as thinking, memory and the nature of aesthetics.

Gestalt therapy takes life situations and views them as pictures that tell us stories about ourselves, or reveals to us the stories we are telling ourselves. Long before literacy was common, there may have been a primeval science of gestalt psychology based on the conditions of human faculties in an earlier, more childlike stage when pictorial thinking was the norm. It is quite possible that the shamans and sages of old used a type of gestalt psychology to assist people who came to them for advice and healing.

Seth, the discarnate being who was channelled by Jane Roberts, briefly touched upon the concept of Gestalt psychology, although he did not call it by the name as such. He noted that in the prehistoric Lemurian civilisation, their definition of art was completely different than modern our perception. They used vast pictures and sounds as a means to communicate and convey important esoteric truths in a holistic manner. Because the Lemurians' perceptions were entirely different than that of modern humans, they was able to sense artwork differently, with the message stimulating their sensual perceptions in a way that we could never understand. After the demise of Lemuria, the Atlantean priests are said to have used a type of cuneiform, or hieroglyphic, writing that was then passed on to the Sumerians and Babylonians about 6000 years ago, which is the first evidence we have of recorded history.

The old saying, 'a picture is worth a thousand words', is an apt reflection of what we can learn from Tarot. While each card in the deck focuses on a central theme, every individual will tend to see each picture differently, concentrating holistically on issues that are pertinent to their particular lives at the time of the reading.

While our civilisation takes the written and spoken word for granted, who are we to say these methods of communication are the only ways to relate to others? The oriental languages are much more graphic than our own, with each glyph being assigned to a complete word, as opposed to the Western method of assigning a glyph to a specific sound. In fact, there is much speculation that since the oriental people's written languages require a greater visual vocabulary and are more graphic than our own, they may learn, perceive and solve problems differently than we in the west do, utilising different parts of their brain to process information and solve problems.

The widespread popularity of television and cinema proves without a shadow of a doubt that as a species, we desire visual stimulation in order to receive information. Even those in the publishing industry are well aware of this fact, including illustrations in many of their works. It is for that reason we are so drawn to Tarot: it is based almost entirely on symbolism through pictures.

Prior to literacy becoming the norm rather than the exception, humans were much more vociferous than now, relying on storytellers to pass the time of day and thereby relay traditions down from generation to generation. To a verbally oriented person, the Tarot would merely be a natural extension of his ability to tell stories, as he would only need to look at the drawing and describe an entire scene for his audience, a talent that many of us today have lost through disuse.

Tarot and Synchronicity

The use of Tarot is based on synchronicity, a term coined by physician Carl Gustave Jung in collaboration with Wolfgang Paul, which refers to a meaningful coincidence that occurs without any apparent cause. It is considered to be an acausal connecting principle between events that occur at the same time and express a shared value or meaning, but are not evidently linked by mechanical cause-and-effect. Jung poses a cross-shaped model (quarternio) in which synchronicity figures as one of the main principles of the universe, opposed to 'causality' on the horizontal arms of the cross, with 'indestructible energy' at the apex, and 'space-time continuum' at the base.

Any experience that can be attributed to 'luck', 'chance', or 'being at the right place at the right time' is an example of synchronicity. Jung, a doctor who asked religious, esoteric and spiritual questions while conducting his psychological research, felt nothing happened just by 'chance' and believed that there is an underlying principle of the universe relating to this logical reality.

When we consult the Tarot, we are taking a 'chance' that the resulting spread will reveal some meaningful information we believe can help us in some way. On a physical level, the act of shuffling and drawing the cards is a random act that has no relevant meaning to the situation, but on a spiritual or esoteric level, our higher consciousness will intuitively know the positions of the cards within the spread and thus guide the shuffling process so relevant cards are drawn and laid out in the proper sequence giving meaning to the reading.

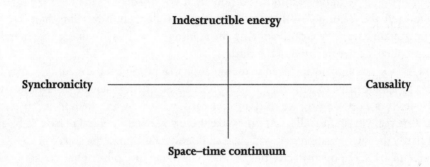

The Tarot as a Problem-solving and Creativity Tool

The Tarot is a valuable tool that enhances our creativity and problem solving capabilities. Too often we are not able to see viable alternatives or solutions to problems because we are so enmeshed in the situation we are enquiring about. The simple act of laying a spread forces us to separate ourselves from distractions and concentrate solely on the object of our enquiry. The Tarot allows us to explore alternatives we may not have originally thought of and shows the circumstances in a way that can reveal aspects of the problem we may have previously overlooked. The Tarot can show hidden agendas and solutions we may not have considered. Sometimes, when we have become so deeply involved in the problem we are seeking answers to, we are not able to see the forest for the trees, metaphorically speaking. The Tarot helps us to direct our energy in a positive direction so we can find positive solutions to any problems that we may have.

Preparing To Use the Tarot

Before using the Tarot, prepare to give an insightful reading by first centering yourself. Use meditation techniques to help intensify the mood of the reading and focus your mind, concentrating on the object of your enquiry. Find a quiet, serene place where you can perform the reading undisturbed.

After centering, hold the Tarot deck in your hands for a few moments to transfer the energy of the question into the cards. While holding the deck, picture yourself enveloped in protective white light. This white light will protect you from any negative or mischievous energy forms that may try to interfere with the card layout or interpretation. While you are imagining yourself and the Tarot inside the aura of white light, say a short prayer to your God, spirit guide or higher self to help gain insight into the circumstances that prompted the reading, thus helping you to fully interpret the spread. The entire process of preparing yourself for the Tarot reading can take up to 15 minutes, and is essential for a clear reading.

If, after attempting to centre yourself, you are still unsettled or preoccupied with outside events, put the Tarot away and try later when you feel more settled and able to focus on the reading in an objective frame of mind. Additionally, if you are depressed or sense negativity around yourself, the reading is likely to reflect such ambivalent emotions. It is therefore best to try to maintain a positive attitude during the reading, as well as about life in general, to ensure a productive interpretation of the cards.

If you feel too emotionally involved in the situation that prompted the reading, it may be a good idea to ask someone to perform a reading for you. So often, when we desire a situation to resolve itself in a certain way, we read into the cards what we want them to say instead of what they are really trying to tell us. At times like these you need a neutral person to balance out and clarify the interpretation so it will yield an honest reflection of the situation.

When embarking upon any activities that help us to tap into our higher consciousness to gain enlightenment, it is essential that our bodies are as clean as our minds. It is all the more difficult to gain enlightenment when our bodies are polluted with chemicals in the form of alcohol, tobacco, drugs and even food. Alcohol is a depressant that dulls our senses and loosens our inhibitions. When we smoke cigarettes, our etheric vision is dulled, causing us to perceive situations and events incorrectly. Even food can be used as a mind-altering drug when necessary, as certain foods, such as sugar, coffee, tea, chocolate and wheat, produce reactions that alter the body's biochemistry. Also, when you eat more than your body needs, you will be lulled into a sleepy state. It is for that reason that even the act of overeating is harmful to the body and will adversely affect readings you may give. Persons addicted to anything—food, a lack of food, drugs, alcohol, exercise, gambling, or sex, just to name a few vices—will be so focused on feeding their addiction that it will be virtually impossible to give a meaningful reading for anyone.

Refined sugar has almost exactly the same molecular structure as ethyl alcohol, and there is very strong evidence to suggest that it is not alcohol but sugar that alcoholics actually crave. It is also believed that alcoholics are hypoglycaemic, the reason being that they often trade in their desire for alcohol for sugar, and therefore consume large quantities of sugary foods as a substitute for alcohol.

It is quite common for alcoholic men to have daughters with eating disorders, thus strengthening the link between sugar and alcohol. Research has shown that people who have eating disorders have bodies that are not able to properly metabolise carbohydrates, a food they often crave. In addition, people who are depressed tend to crave carbohydrates because these foods act like endorphins, which are the body's own natural narcotics, helping people to feel happy.

Sugar is also similar in chemical composition to cocaine, thereby making it a potent drug. With all of the nutrients stripped out of it through the refining process, it has virtually no nutritive value—it is essentially empty calories. It is wise, therefore, to refrain from eating refined sugar. If hungry, you can always eat a piece of fruit, which is metabolised by the body differently and does not cause the body to produce insulin.

People who binge eat are often in an altered state of consciousness, as the huge quantities of food ingested act as a drug that induces a trance state. Binge eaters quite often have little recollection of what they ate during a binge, which is evidence of their mental blocking of the experience, and often have as little control over their actions as the alcoholic, chain smoker, drug addict, or relationship addict. To make matters worse, because food is something we need for our survival, it is not as if we can just quit 'cold turkey', as in the case of abstaining from cigarettes or alcohol. Therefore eating disorders can be quite difficult to overcome. The key, as in all avenues in this life, is achieving a balance. We need to exercise control over what we ingest to ensure that our bodies are as clean as our souls.

Laying Out the Tarot Spread

The method of shuffling and laying out a spread will vary with each individual. As you become more experienced, you will no doubt develop a technique that is 'right' for you. After you have successfully prepared yourself for the reading, you can begin laying out the cards in the spread that you and the querent have decided upon. Start by shuffling the deck to mingle the energy of the question into the cards. After shuffling, cut the deck into three even piles using your left hand. The left side of the body is considered the subconscious or intuitive side, so your subconscious will be helping you as you cut the deck. From the three equal piles, select the one you feel has the answer to your question. Using the left hand, which symbolises your subconscious self, you can begin laying the cards.

Alternatively, shuffle the deck in the manner described above and spread the entire deck face down across a table or flat surface so that each individual card can be seen and selected. With the left hand, intuitively pull each card that you will use in the reading.

When a Card 'Falls Out' While Shuffling

Generally speaking, when a card falls out while shuffling, it carries information relevant to the question being asked. The card may either answer the question or provide relevance to the reading. It can add flavour to the question being asked or refer to a different situation entirely. If it is a court card, it means a person represented by the card will hold the answer you seek.

When a card falls out during the shuffling process you have two options to choose from. If you feel the card is the answer to your question, you can study and interpret it, and then discontinue the reading. If, on the other hand, you feel the card simply adds extra insight to the situation, lay the card to the side and proceed with the reading. When you have finished with the reading, interpret the card that 'fell out'—it will provide clues to the overall theme of the reading, or add extra information that was not included in the spread.

The Major Arcana

The set of cards that makes up the Major Arcana is thought to have originally been separate from the Minor Arcana. The two were eventually combined to make up our present deck of 78 cards.

The 22 Major Arcana cards are numbered from 0 to XXI. This has direct relevance to the Hebrew Cabala because not only does the number of cards correspond to the number of letters in the Hebrew alphabet, many of the cards suggest symbolism from the Tree of Life, which forms the basis of much of the Cabalistic wisdom. The number 22 is also considered to be a master number in the science of numerology.

The Major Arcana depicts the different stages of life we must go through until our soul journey is complete. The journey begins with 0, The Fool, and ends with XXI, The World. We all, at one time or another, must go through each stage of the Major Arcana, but we won't necessarily encounter them in sequential order as portrayed by the cards. Through the nature of our existence, we will encounter several beginnings and endings, which are represented by the archetypes portrayed on the cards.

In a reading, the cards of the Major Arcana depict matters relating to the soul, spirit or destiny of our lives that often indicate karmic themes we must experience. They point out issues that are occurring within our psyche rather than the external everyday events depicted in the Minor Arcana. Take special note whenever a card of the Major Arcana appears in a spread, because it represents events that will tend to have a profound and lasting impact.

Even within the Tarot, a distinction is made between the first eleven cards and the second eleven. The Major Arcana is actually divided into two sets of eleven cards, which relate to the two departments of our physical existence. The first eleven cards, which span from 0, The Fool to X, Wheel of Fortune, relate to the physicalities of our life, those areas we cannot avoid and most of us encounter from one time to another as we go about our day-to-day activities. The second eleven cards, which are numbered from XI, Justice to XXI, World, reveal themes of a more psychological nature, themes that we must consciously explore so we can allow ourselves to ask probing questions about the meaning of our existence on this earth plane. Unless we consciously open up our mind and allow the universe to impart to us alternate ways of existing in a causative world, it will be very difficult to interpret the second half of the Major Arcana in a meaningful way. More appropriately, the first eleven cards depict that which is exoteric, while the second eleven cards represent the esoteric.

The Minor Arcana

The Minor Arcana is believed to have originally been a separate deck of 56 cards that depict the more ordinary details of our life, which form a meaningful pattern around our existence. While the Major Arcana tends to portray profound, life-changing events affecting our souls, most of the cards in the Minor Arcana seem to be less dramatic and portray day-to-day events.

The Minor Arcana consists of 56 cards divided into four suits of 14 cards. Each suit contains 10 numbered cards and four court cards. These suits correlate to the four basic elements of life—Fire, Earth, Air and Water.

The suit of Wands represents the element of Fire. It corresponds with the astrological signs of Cancer, Leo and Virgo, and the 4th, 5th and 6th houses of the horoscope. Fire brings life, love, romance and creativity into our lives. Cards in the suit of Wands tend to represent enterprise and distinction. There is generally a lot of activity and excitement in this suit by the very nature of its element. Traditionally, Wands represent energy, growth, animation, enterprise and glory. Wands is also associated with psychic and spiritual connotations because we must tap into a higher level of consciousness any time we attempt to produce anything creative.

The suit of Pentacles represents the element of Earth. It corresponds with the astrological signs of Aries, Taurus and Gemini, and the 1st, 2nd and 3rd houses in the horoscope. Earth brings practicality, materialism and a sense of service to our lives. Cards in the suit of Pentacles represent work, accomplishment, and the acquisition of wealth, materials and possessions. It governs sensuous pleasures, such as good food, drink and other indulgences we enjoy in this life. Traditionally, Pentacles represents money, material gain and industry. While some will invariably disagree, this suit is totally necessary for an expansive and fulfilling spiritual life. Many assert that we must sacrifice our possessions in order to obtain an awareness of other-world. However, if our physical necessities are not taken care of, we will direct our attentions to satisfying those needs before we can even begin to ponder the more meaningful questions that centre around our spiritual existence.

The suit of Swords represents the element of Air. It corresponds with the astrological signs of Libra, Scorpio and Sagittarius, and the 7th, 8th and 9th houses of the horoscope. Air brings mental activity and intellect into our lives. Cards in the suit of Swords tend to depict thinking, communications, messages and short journeys. Because Air is a communicative element, it can often lead to arguments, gossip and strife; and because of its propensity for conflict, the suit of Swords is generally regarded as being unsettled. Therefore, many of the cards in this suit seem to carry latent struggles and animosity. Traditionally, Swords represent aggression, force, ambition, courage, strife and misfortune, but the negative aspects of the cards can be lessened by maintaining a positive mental attitude and seeking resolutions to problems in a mature and sensible way.

The suit of Cups represents the element of Water. It corresponds with the astrological signs of Capricorn, Aquarius and Pisces, and the 10th, 11th and 12th houses of the horoscope. Water brings pure love, sensitivity and intuition into our lives. Cards in the suit of Cups tend to depict love, happiness, family, celebration, partnerships and commitment. This suit also represents intuition, emotion, fantasy and surrealism. Traditionally, Cups represent love, happiness, emotion, fertility and beauty.

Court Cards in a Reading

Although court cards in a reading can indicate abstract concepts, they normally represent real people who we will encounter during our day-to-day lives. As previously discussed, if the card in the outcome position of the reading is a court card, it very likely is an indication that the person associated with the card either has the solution, or plays an integral part in the successful outcome of the situation that prompted the reading.

When a court card appears in the outcome position, it may be necessary to perform another reading concentrating specifically on the person depicted in the card. The new reading should reflect how this person will affect the outcome and what role he or she will play.

First Celtic Cross with Kings of Cups in Outcome Position

If we perform a Celtic Cross spread with regard to a specific question, and a King of Cups falls in the outcome position, a new spread can be performed to find out more about the individual behind the King of Cups. This will be accomplished by retaining the King of Cups, re-shuffling and re-laying the Celtic Cross, placing the King of Cups in the Question position. The resulting spread will reveal more information specific to the King of Cups.

Second Celtic Cross with Kings of Cups in Question Position

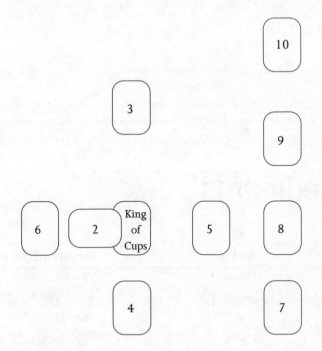

Tarot Keywords

Card	Ruler	Keyword
0 The Fool	Uranus	The Free One
I The Magician	Mercury	The Light One
II High Priestess	The Moon	The Virgin
III The Empress	Venus	The Mother
IV Emperor	Mars	The Master
V Hierophant	Taurus	Ceremony
VI Lovers	Gemini	Choices
VII Chariot	Cancer	The Victorious One
VIII Strength	Leo	The Enchantress
IX Hermit	Virgo	The Lone One
X Wheel Of Fortune	Jupiter	Luck
XI Justice	Libra	The Just One
XII Hanged Man	Neptune	The Enlightened One
XIII Death	Pluto	The Transformer
XIV Temperance	Sagittarius	Waiting
XV Devil	Capricorn	The Dark One
XVI Tower	Mars	Calamity
XVII Star	Aquarius	The Hopeful One
XVIII Moon	Pisces	Veils
XIX The Sun	The Sun	Happiness
XX Judgement	Scorpio	Healing
XXI World	Saturn	The Complete One

Wands/Rods/Fire

Card	Ruler	Keyword
Ace	Leo	Enterprise
Two	Leo	Partnership
Three	Leo	Opportunity
Four	Cancer	Prosperity
Five	Cancer	Challenge
Six	Cancer	Victory
Seven	Virgo	Defiance
Eight	Virgo	Swiftness
Nine	Virgo	Resilience
Ten	Virgo	Burden
King		Honour
Queen		Creativity
Knight/Prince		Warrior
Page/Princess		Traveller

Pentacles/Disks/Earth

Card	Ruler	Keyword
Ace	Aries	Foundation
Two	Aries	Juggling
Three`	Aries	Skill
Four	Taurus	Possessions
Five	Taurus	Poverty
Six	Taurus	Generosity
Seven	Gemini	Planning
Eight	Gemini	Learning
Nine	Gemini	Comfort
Ten	Taurus	Wealth
King		Realism
Queen		Sensibility
Knight/Prince		Practicality
Page/Princess		Prospects

Swords/Air

Card	Ruler	Keyword
Ace	Libra	Force
Two	Libra	Balance
Three	Libra	Heartbreak
Four	Scorpio	Recuperation
Five	Scorpio	Defeat
Six	Scorpio	Travel
Seven	Sagittarius	Dishonesty
Eight	Sagittarius	Restriction
Nine	Sagittarius	Cruelty
Ten	Sagittarius	Ruin
King		Loyalty
Queen		Intelligence
Knight/Prince		Confidence
Page/Princess		Eloquence

Cups/Water

Card	Ruler	Keyword
Ace	Capricorn	Love
Two	Capricorn	Commitment
Three	Capricorn	Celebrations
Four	Aquarius	Boredom
Five	Aquarius	Sorrow
Six	Aquarius	Memory
Seven	Pisces	Choices
Eight	Pisces	Seeking
Nine	Pisces	Pleasure
Ten	Pisces	Committed Love
King		Sensuality
Queen		Sociableness
Knight/Prince		Lover
Page/Princess		Gentleness

The Celtic Cross

The Celtic Cross is an ancient oracle, which has evolved through countless generations and is one of the most widely used spreads today because of its versatility and time-tested accuracy. In modern times, the Celtic Cross was mentioned by A. E. Waite in his work, *The Pictorial Key to the Tarot*. Prior to his publishing of this oracle, it had been used for many years privately in England, Scotland and Ireland. One of the reasons why the Celtic Cross has withstood the test of time is because it is such a universal spread, which can be used to answer specific questions or provide a general reading to the querent. The Celtic Cross provides insights into what the querent can expect for the upcoming half year.

Card I The Question

This card denotes the nature of the querent's question. It is important to look carefully at this card because it encompasses the entire theme of the reading. It can in fact relate to an entirely different issue, an area of life that the querent may not have previously consciously considered. In astrological terms, this position denotes the conjunction, as it synthesises the root question into something that the querent can easily understand.

Card 2 The Cross

This card reflects those circumstances that are at cross-purposes to the attainment of our goals and ambitions. It often tells the querent about an area of life that is stressful to him and is hindering him along his path in this specific part of his incarnation. Quite often the most negative qualities of the card in this placement are revealed to the reader. In astrological terms, this position can be referred to as a square, something that provides stress to the querent, but nonetheless gives him the impetus to take proactive steps to remedy any blockages that prevent him from achieving his fullest potential. In esoteric terms, the cross can depict the difficulties we have to bear in this life, the way of Christ, or it may imply a resurrection of our soul.

The cross is an ancient symbol dating back long before Christianity. It represents the incarnation of humans on earth as well as Death, Easter, new life, and liberation. There are many variations and styles, most indicating a particular belief or organisation.

Card 3 Above

The card that falls in the above position represents the querent's higher consciousness and reveals universal truths he knows to be accurate. It depicts the most beneficial influences of the situation in question. In astrological terms, this position is related to the sextile, as it shows the querent what opportunities will avail themselves to him, thus enabling him to make the best of the situation that prompted him to consult the oracle. It is a reflection of the most positive aspects relating to the card pulled.

Card 4 Below

This position represents the more negative influences of each card, and is opposed to the more positive Above placement. It reflects the querent's lower cognition and reveals unfortunate truths the querent feels he does not have the power to change at the time of the reading. In astrological terms, this position corresponds to the opposition, as it reflects those areas that are as far away as possible from the querent's true destiny in this life. The querent must nevertheless face these truths if he is to reach his fullest potential and successfully attain a positive outcome to the situation that prompted him to consult the oracle.

The Below placement is the influence in our lower level of consciousness that serves our more basal physical needs. It represents the malefic elements of this world, influences we would rather not acknowledge. Balance and harmony can only be achieved through an equilibrium of both positive and negative forces, which is why the most positive and negative card positions in the spread oppose each other, attempting to strike a balance for the reader to interpret.

Therefore, an element of evil must always co-exist with that of holiness, which is why the Bible details the ecclesiastical heights of Lucifer, God's most adored angel, and Satan, the fallen one (who were actually one and the same characters). That is simply the way of things in the world, so it does no good to think that if we deny the negativity in our lives it will simply go away, because it won't. To deny that evil exists is to deny the primal forces that compose our inner beings. All of us must battle between the forces of good and evil in this plane of existence during our earthly incarnation.

This evil can be something as minor as plucking a flower from someone else's garden when we know we shouldn't, to other more sinister activities, such as robbing a bank or committing terrorist acts.

Card 5 The Recent Past

This position represents the querent's present feelings, hopes and fears at the time of the reading. It also reveals recent events that have brought the querent to his current level of thinking. In astrological terms, this card placement relates to the 12th house of the horoscope, as it refers to the past experiences that are affecting the querent at the time of the reading and are having a deep impact on his life.

Card 6 The Near Future

This position shows what is likely to happen in the near future, usually up to three months. In astrological terms, this card position reflects the 3rd house in the horoscope, as it refers to that which is likely to occur in the near future and is at the forefront of the querent's mind.

Card 7 The Querent

This position reflects where the querent is in his soul evolution at the time of the reading. It shows his thoughts, feelings, ambitions and desires. It also reflects that which is hidden, which could be an aspect of himself that he has concealed from others as well as himself. This card indicates how he personally will affect the situation that prompted him to consult the oracle. In astrological terms, this card position refers to the 1st house in the horoscope, as it depicts the querent's true personality.

Card 8 The Environment

This position denotes the immediate surroundings of the querent at the time of the reading. It often reflects his living and working situation, as well as the attitudes of those around him, such as family, friends and colleagues. This position denotes the 7th house in the horoscope, as it refers to those individuals who we are close to and therefore have the ability to influence us in some way.

Card 9 For and Against

This position indicates the hopes and fears of the querent with regard to how the situation will progress. It gives an indication of the possible benefits and distractions of the situation that has prompted the querent to consult the oracle. It quite often denotes secret wishes, or those hoped-for events that the querent is not even consciously aware of desiring. In astrological terms, this position refers to the nodal axis, as it denotes opportunities and obstacles that will have an impact on the successful resolution of the situation that prompted the querent to consult the oracle.

After you have had an opportunity to see what you might gain or lose from pursuing the path you are currently on, you may decide it would be wise to abandon the project and pursue an endeavour that would potentially be more rewarding.

Card 10 The Next Half Year

This position depicts the probable outcome within the next six months, provided the querent continues along the path he is currently on at the time of the reading. If he decides to change his mind and embark upon a completely new path, then, of course, the outcome of the reading will change. The position includes those elements of his future that he is in many aspects destined for. Although we all can choose whatever future we would like to help us with our soul growth, we often agree to meet certain people or encounter specific situations in order to help us to resolve any karmic obligations from past, current, future or parallel incarnations. It is important, therefore, to remember that the concept of time is actually more elaborate than our three-dimensional selves can comprehend, therefore we have deemed time to be progressively linear. This is a highly simplistic analogy, but sufficient for those who choose to live in our physical reality.

In astrological terms, this position refers to the 9th house of the horoscope, as it refers to events in the long-range future.

The Celtic Cross

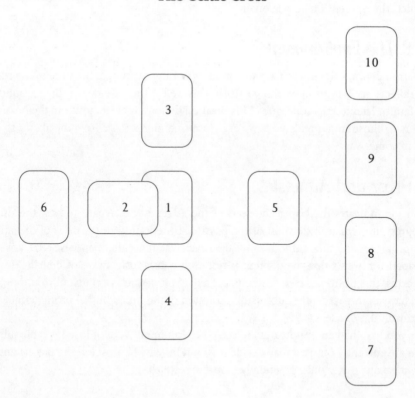

The Celtic Block

The Celtic Block is a continuation of the Celtic Cross and is used to determine the trends for the upcoming year. It can be used to answer specific questions or to provide a general reading. The spread was initially mentioned in Eileen Connolly's *Tarot: A New Handbook For the Apprentice*, and has been adapted in this work to further clarify the meanings of the three cards, called the 'triad'. The basic Celtic Block is composed of 14 cards. The preliminary procedures are identical to those used for the Celtic Cross, the first 10 cards are laid out in exactly the same manner and the positions have the same significance. They are followed by and additional three cards called the triad.

The triad placement is composed of three cards that are intended to shed more light on the situation and give the reader more information than would otherwise be revealed in the standard Celtic Cross. It reveals with clarity unexpected events, factors working behind the scenes, and what the querent should do to resolve the situation that has prompted them to consult the oracle.

The final card in the spread is the Solidifier, which sums up the reading.

Card 11 The Unexpected

This position reflects that which is totally unexpected and which the querent is unaware of at the time of the reading. The event depicted in the card is something that will take the querent quite by surprise and he will not likely be prepared for it. However, he may have to admit it isn't as unexpected as he would like to suppose. This will add flavour to the situation and give the reading greater significance. In astrological terms, this position is relates to Uranus, as it reflects that which is unique, extravagant and totally out of the ordinary.

Card 12 The Unknown

This position reflects that which is hidden from the querent or that he may have overlooked and that is hindering him from successfully resolving the issue that prompted him to consult the oracle. It represents those individuals who are working behind the scenes, often at cross-purposes with the querent. This knowledge is essential in order to effect a successful resolution to any problems that may crop up. In astrological terms, this position denotes Neptune, as it represents the area in the querent's life where his perceptive vision is veiled, thereby inhibiting him from seeing what is quite apparent to others.

Card 13 The Best Course of Action

This position suggests to the querent what he can do to bring about a successful resolution to his question. If he takes the advice the universe is giving him through the Tarot, he is one step closer to achieving the outcome he desires. In astrological terms, this position denotes the Part of Fortune, as it denotes what the querent is destined for in order to achieve the happiness and fulfilment that is his karmic right as a universal soul. It should be stressed, however, that what the querent is being beckoned to do is not necessarily going to be the path of least resistance, and will therefore require a fair amount of effort on his part to achieve.

Unfortunately, few things in life are free; even apparently unearned gifts are the result of accomplishments we have made in past, parallel and future incarnations. Just about everything else, however, we must earn through our work and other activities. And there are few lucky breaks in this life. Most opportunities that have been presented to us are the result of meticulously executed plans that have transpired in such an orderly fashion as to make it seem as if it were sheer luck. Therefore, if you would like your situation to be successfully resolved, it would be in your best interests to perform the appropriate acts to manifest that success in our physical world.

Card 14 The Solidifier

The Solidifier should serve the purpose of clarifying or verifying all previous indications uncovered in the reading thus far. This card placement solidifies the reading and formulates the previous 13 cards to provide an outcome of the reading. It is expected that many situations should resolve themselves within a year, but there are some questions, such as those relating to long-standing relationships or vocational choices, that will require more time to come to fruition. In astrological terms, this position relates to the 11th house, as it denotes our hopes, dreams and ambitions in this incarnation. With dedicated effort on our part, we just might get what we ask for.

The Celtic Block

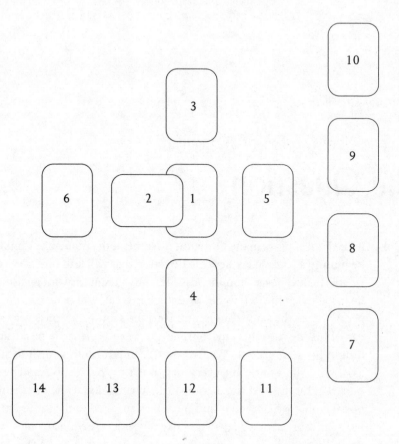

1 The Question

0 Fool   If The Fool appears in the Question placement, the querent is thinking of beginning a completely new life direction that will lead him on to experiences he had never thought possible. The querent may not realise it, but he has allowed himself to become stuck in a rut, where he sees the same people, does the same things, and feels the same emotions every single day of his life, and this environment may not necessarily be advancing him in his soul growth. We have not been put on this earth to simply exist, and die a little bit every day, but to grow, evolve and prepare ourselves for the next step in our spiritual evolution. How then, can it be possible that we can often find ourselves engaged in the same activities with the same people, day in and day out, not receiving any new stimulation that will help us to develop and grow as individuals? The querent should prepare himself, therefore, for an experience that will change his direction in life forever because a fresh start is exactly what is needed to remedy the complacent attitudes that have set in.

I Magician   If The Magician has fallen in the Question position, it is quite likely that your thoughts are centring on a young man. He may either still be studying or just graduated. If he is mature, it is likely that he is embarking upon a training programme to update his skills, or has decided to go back to school to learn an entirely new vocation. There is also the likelihood that this individual lacks the maturity his years should adequately portray, which can give him many childlike qualities. You may ask yourself if you can trust this person, and the answer is a resounding No! The reason for this is because he lacks the appropriate life experiences and stability to carry out the promises he makes. Since he is so inexperienced in certain aspects of this life, he cannot be relied upon to keep a confidence, and it is for that reason that you need to be prudent about what information you reveal to this individual. Perhaps in a year or two, after he has a bit more experience under his belt, he will make a worthy friend. In the meantime, however, it would be wise to keep this individual at arm's length until he has earned your trust and admiration.

II High Priestess If The High Priestess has fallen in the Question placement, your mind is on a young woman who could very well be yourself. This woman does not have many positive experiences with the opposite sex, and it is for that reason she often prefers the company of women. In a state of naivety, and lacking the wisdom of having dealt with the opposite sex on a regular basis, she could very well have been hurt badly by a man. The wound that remained has never properly healed, leaving a festering ulcer that psychically re-erupts on a regular basis with every triggering event. The gaping wound in this woman's soul has left her with a mistrust of men and has consequently had a detrimental effect on the relationships she has with them. If her injury was bad enough, such as in the case of rape or sexual assault, she may develop lesbian tendencies, which is her way of trying to come to terms with a violating assault against her body. This woman is somewhat of a loner and therefore spends a lot of time in her own company, reflecting on life and the universe, attempting to make sense of it all in her mediations. This time of inner solitude instils in her a knowledge that does not exist in more frivolous souls, individuals who may not have had to learn about the harsh realities of the physical world in the same manner she did. The task at hand, therefore, is getting this young woman to impart what she knows to others, as she does not normally consider her thoughts and opinions to be worthy of discussion.

III Empress If The Empress has landed in the Question placement, your question concerns a woman of childbearing age who very well could be yourself. This is a very sensual person, who loves food and drink, and therefore may have what some might consider a weight problem. She does not, however, let any excess pounds get in the way of living her life, and she certainly has no shortage of admirers. While the individual in question exudes a type of sensuality that makes her attractive to the opposite sex, she is also a very jealous person, and is somewhat territorial about what she feels is hers. She will, therefore, defend her turf and fight to the death for what she perceives to be her personal property, be it material possessions or people. It is for that reason that she can be a formidable foe when she feels threatened in any way, especially with regard to her personal relationships. Positively, the woman loves animals and has a creative streak. She may have a vocation or hobbies that she is able to use as an outlet for the many fruitful ideas that come into her mind.

IV Emperor If The Emperor falls in the Question position, a very powerful man is on your mind. You may not even consider the person in question to be that influential, but it is important you are not deceived about the level of power he has over other people. If you know or are intimate with this particular person, it is all too easy to become lulled into a false sense of security. You may know very well just what he is capable of, but for some reason, you believe he would never do to you what he has done to others. How wrong you are! As soon as he tires of your company, he will discard you just as ruthlessly and quickly as he has all the others who came before you, and there have been many others, just in case you were wondering. This individual is a very me-centred person who thinks only of his own personal gratification. Once he is no longer pleasured by your presence, you will no longer exist to him and he will deal with you accordingly. Therefore, if you dare to associate with this individual after having been forewarned, it is important to keep your wits about you and develop a contingency plan to enable a quick escape when things get hairy, which they inevitably will.

V Hierophant If The Hierophant has fallen into the Question position, you are considering embarking upon an activity that is of a life-changing magnitude. You may be considering getting married, and if so, you would like to have a huge ceremony to mark the event. It can be quite costly, so it is important you save for it and make sure the person you want to form a union with is the person you would like to spend the rest of your life with. If you are unhappily married, you may be thinking of getting a divorce, which again, can be a very costly exercise, especially if property or children are involved. You may consider taking up a vocation that will take up much of your time and entails making a major lifestyle change, such as entering into a professional field, the military, or the clergy. It is essential, therefore, that you think carefully before entering into any contractual obligations that involve your future, because they may be very difficult to rescind, should you decide that you made a mistake.

VI Lovers If The Lovers has appeared in the Question position, you are thinking about a couple who have met and have become attracted to one another. The attraction is still new and has therefore not withstood the test of time. This love affair, however, is not without difficulties because, as you will see, there are three individuals portrayed on the card. It is for this reason that an obstacle will present itself on the path to true love. We have all been put here on earth as a means to grow and develop in our soul evolution. If everything were all plain sailing, we would not have an opportunity to grow within ourselves. It is for this reason that you have come across this special someone who will help you meet the challenges that lie ahead.

VII Chariot If The Chariot has appeared in the Question position, you are contemplating making a move of sorts. You feel the need to travel, either to move house, go to school, or change your job. Whatever you decide, it will be in an attempt to improve your circumstances in life. You can be somewhat headstrong in any decisions you make, and the tenacity you show from the onset will help to strengthen your determination during those occasions when your resolve waivers and you feel like giving in to the malefic forces that have put obstacles in your path.

VIII Strength If Strength has fallen into the Question position, there is a woman who is on your mind. In ancient times, she was referred to as The Enchantress because she has the ability to spellbind people with her hypnotic and charming demeanour. This individual has certain gentleness in her being, which enables her to tame the wild beast that exists within us all. This serenity and maturity has come to her through her vast breadth of experience and the knowledge she has gained during an eventful life. Strength indicates that obstacles will be put in your path, which will help you to develop alternative ways of living and will in effect help you to achieve a greater understanding of the world that you co-exist in.

IX Hermit If The Hermit has appeared in the Question position, you or someone you know may feel somewhat alone in the world that you have incarnated into. No one can understand quite how you feel, and it is for that reason you spend time on your own, reflecting on the questions you are seeking answers to. You can be quite shy and lack the social skills necessary to formulate relationships, which will bring about further isolation. You are quite knowledgeable, but may not know how to impart that knowledge to others. You are a very spiritual being, but are non-pretentious in your primary certitude and do not even attempt to force your views onto others. In some ways you may be considered a reluctant prophet, a person who never asked for and does not want people coming to you with their questions and problems.

X Wheel of Fortune If The Wheel has landed in the Question position, you are thinking of making some major changes in your life that may very well involve money. Perhaps you are taking a risk that could improve your circumstances in this life, but as with every risk, you could stand to lose something. If the gamble you are planning on taking does not prove profitable, however, you may find you lose everything you put into the venture, if not much, much more. Great changes can come in the form of pain, so it is possible that some inner turmoil is prompting you to move on in your cycle of soul growth. When things in our lives stagnate, atrophy and loss tend to set in, which is not what the universe intended for us when we incarnated into the earth plane. It is for that reason that the need to change is an essential element of our soul evolution.

XI Justice   If Justice has appeared in the Question position, you or someone you know is involved in a situation where impartiality is needed. You may need to ask for the assistance of an outside party, such as a mediator, who will work to resolve the situation so it is favourable for all parties involved. You may find yourself embroiled in a legal battle, which is very trying and you may not be sure of the outcome, thereby compounding any uncertainty you may feel. It is for this reason you can become quite anxious when considering making plans for the future. It is important to keep in mind that life is not fair, and even if you are morally and ethically right in a particular situation, there may be a loophole in the law of the land that keeps you from getting the outcome you feel you deserve. It is essential, therefore, that you brush up on the law. Although you would expect the lawyers you employ to do a good job for you, the forces at work are of such a nature that you cannot expect these individuals to accomplish anything other than the bare minimum they can and still demand to be paid. These individuals are, after all, only looking after their own best interests. There are many things, legally speaking, that you must do for yourself, such as researching current legislation and scrutinising any legal documents. The law, just like locks, was merely designed to keep honest people honest. A dishonest person, therefore, has no regard for the law or anyone else for that matter, and will use the laws of the land for his own advantage.

XII Hanged Man   If The Hanged Man has appeared in the Question position, you or someone you know is feeling a sense of despondency right now over a situation that is beyond your control. It is for that reason that you might be quite depressed and will need all of the support you can get from others. Sadly, you will find that very little, if any, support will be forthcoming, which will further compound your feelings of isolation in this world. You are going through what could be best described as the dark night of the soul, a time when you have to find within yourself the strength to carry on and progress along the appropriate path with no outside assistance. You have turned everywhere you can think of for help, yet no salvation has come to you when you needed it the most. You may find you are at the point of giving in to the prevailing climate when suddenly, you receive a flash of insight from entities more highly evolved than yourself. There are some things, you realise, that you simply have no control over, and this is one of those occasions. This is the time when you need to put your faith in a force much higher than yourself because faith is the only thing that will see you through such a difficult time.

XIII Death If Death has entered into the Question position, you or someone you know is going through a personal crisis in which the only positive thing that can come out of it is total regeneration. You may be going through what many consider a creative illness, which is similar to a psychotic breakdown brought about by a period of intense mental activity. Sigmund Freud, Carl Jung and other contemporaries of theirs all experienced such episodes of illness, and emerged transformed, able to produce much more than had previously been imagined. Some drastic changes need to be made in your life, and there is no time like the present to evoke those forces of change.

XIV Temperance If Temperance has fallen in the Question position, what you or someone close to you is thinking about has been on your mind for quite some time now. You have reflected on it a great deal and the matter at hand is not something to be taken lightly. In many ways, you or someone close to you needs a deep inner cleansing, which will also bring about much needed healing in the process of renewal. There are very many memories, which, although not clear, need to be brought to the surface of your consciousness so balance and harmony can be restored and you can resume your soul growth after a period of stasis.

XV Devil If The Devil has appeared in the Question position, you or someone close to you is concerned about your responsibilities in the material realm of our existence. You have many obligations that may or may not wear you down, thereby causing you to temporarily forget that you are a spiritual as well as a physical being. You may have been appointed the head of the household, which means the success or failure of the material aspects of the home rests firmly on your shoulders, something that can cause you nervousness in your day day-to-day dealings with others. Because a great deal of your time and energy is spent taking care of other's material needs, you may neglect the spiritual side of yourself and take on a rather dour outlook on life. It is important, therefore, that you remember that you are a spiritual being as well as a physical being, and this can be accomplished by ensuring that you are firmly grounded to the earth.

XVI Tower   If The Tower has landed in the Question position, you or someone close to you is thinking of making some changes that are not quite so drastic as that portrayed in Death. Your environment has, however, become quite static and you may find yourself even a bit bored at times. It is for this reason the cosmos has decided to shake things up a bit, which will in effect give you the chance to experience many of the different aspects of this existence that may have previously been unknown to you. The changes that come, however, can come swiftly and abruptly, leaving you wondering exactly what has happened. It is important that you watch your step because you may have an accident that has costly repercussions that could very well have been avoided. It is also important that you pay your bills because defaults in payments could put your home in jeopardy and leave you looking for alternate accommodation.

XVII Star   If The Star has landed in the Question position, you or someone close to you is full of hope and high ideals for the future. You may be thinking of doing something that has been a lifelong dream, but are unsure of the probable outcome. You are able to look to the future with an air of optimism, even though the outcome is not yet assured. Friends will play a significant role in your life, as they will be a source of comfort and company to you during those times of loneliness, which are merely opportunities for solitude that we all feel from time to time.

XVIII Moon   If The Moon has landed in the Question position, it seems there is something on your mind that is causing you a great deal of confusion. At this point in time, you really don't know who your friends are, which could result in receiving faulty information. There are forces working outside your control and sphere of awareness, which will result in you not getting a clear picture of the situation you are in at the present. As a result, you could make decisions based upon incorrect perceptions, which could cause you a great deal of anxiety and uncertainty, inevitably leading to depression. It is important, therefore, to make decisions based upon facts, and not assumptions, which could very well be in error. It is also important that you develop an attitude of self-reliance because you cannot expect your friends to be there for you when you are desperately in need of a friendly face. Your friends, like just about everyone else in your life, will not be a source of comfort for you. This is because you need to learn the art of self-reliance.

XIX Sun   If The Sun has landed in the Question position, you or someone close to you is concerned about a young person who is very energetic and full of life. Regardless of their age, this individual is not very mature and will tend to exhibit many childlike qualities. This person may be somewhat of an exhibitionist and can have difficulty not attracting attention to themself. It is essential, therefore, that a sense of discretion is instilled in this person at a very young age. Alternatively, you may be thinking about having children yourself. Although you have thought of all the positive aspects of parenthood, have you taken into account all the responsibilities that will be involved in such a venture as well?

XX Judgement   If Judgement has found its way to the Question position, you are considering resuming an endeavour that you began long ago, but never finished for some reason. Whether this new venture is a success this time around depends upon whether it is something that is a part of your own personal destiny. As difficult as it can be to come to terms with, we are not meant to be successful at all things in this life. A look at your natal horoscope will give you guidance and subtle illumination, showing you what your true path in this life is. Even if you are not successful this time around, a deep inner healing process that comes with slowly re-visiting this sphere of your conscious awareness will help to release many of the demons from your past. Success or failure is not the issue here: what is important is how you enjoyed the trip you took to receive the much needed healing that was essential before you could go to the next step of your spiritual evolution.

XXI World   If the World has found itself in the Question position, there is something in your life that needs to be resolved before you can further develop in your soul evolution. Perhaps the matter has in fact been resolved for you, but you are reluctant to let go of a situation or relationship that has reached the final stages of its existence. When you do let go, however, you will experience a feeling of completion that will enable you to move on to other more rewarding projects, thereby resuming the circle of existence that all of us must fulfil in order to move onto higher levels of awareness.

Wands/Rods/Fire

Ace   If the Ace of Wands has appeared in the Question position, you or someone close to you is contemplating initiating a creative endeavour that may or may not be a fruitful business proposition. You may want to build a hobby into something more substantial, and are wondering if it will yield a profitable outcome. You may also be considering adding to your current household, so a baby or pet may be on the way. The prospect of such an addition is causing you a certain degree of uncertainty, as you cannot help but wonder if it is the right thing to do. The cards that follow will further clarify the situation for you so you will have a greater understanding of your next course of action.

Two If the Two of Wands has found itself in the Question placement, you or someone close to you is thinking of forming a partnership with another person that you hope will yield a positive outcome. You may find you are working with another individual on a certain venture, and you are not sure of the outcome of the endeavour you are embarking on. This union has the possibility to produce a creative result, but whether or not it will be successful will depend upon other factors, such as the current economic climate and whether it is something that would be of interest to other people.

Three If the Three of Wands has fallen in the Question placement, you or someone close to you is thinking about an endeavour that will require the co-operation of several people. You may be contemplating issues that have no relationship whatsoever to the here and now, and it is for that reason you may decide to join a mystical, spiritual or religious group in your quest for answers to questions that have no easy definition. You are beginning to realise that there is much more to this life than meets the eye, and would like to take some time out to explore the world of the unseen and unheard in an attempt to attain a greater understanding of what you can see and hear.

Four If the Four of Wands has appeared in the Question position, your concern centres on your home and what makes you feel secure in an insecure world. You are interested in establishing a firm home base, and may even consider taking a new job or moving house in order to achieve a semblance of stability in your life. You may have been given responsibilities at home, which you did not ask for and did not necessarily want, and this could cause you a feeling of consternation. Issues surrounding the family are at the forefront of your mind because they are a priority in your life at this time.

Five If the Five of Wands has found its way into the Question position, you or someone close to you is fighting unseen forces. You may very well believe you know what the core problem is, but what you are fighting is merely a symptom and not the cause of your current dilemma. Because you have not pinpointed what the actual root cause is, as soon as you have eradicated one complaint, another one will pop up almost out of the blue, it would seem. This process will continue over and over again with an increasingly greater intensity until you realise that behind all of this bad luck that seems to have befallen you is a much greater issue that needs to be addressed if you wish to eradicate the misfortune that has become so much a part of your life. Take a good look around and you will eventually find that the problem has always been right under your nose. Perhaps the root cause of all this misfortune does not come from outside sources, but within. It is for that reason that you will need to spend time in reflection, to try to come to terms with the primary event that has triggered all of the subsequent calamities that have befallen you. When you have isolated the cause, you will be able to develop a solution to the problem.

Six   If the Six of Wands has found its way to the Question position, the issue on your mind is something that on a conscious level you feel you have been successful at. But, if you had truly succeeded, would it still be so prominently on your mind? Figuratively speaking, you may have won the battle, but the war is still most definitely raging in your mind. It is time to rethink, reprioritise, and re-strategise because events will come into play that will cause you to renew your interest in this particular subject. As you will soon discover, the battle of life over death is never truly over, as you will continuously be presented with tasks that you must complete before you can go on to the next level of your soul evolution.

Seven   If the Seven of Wands appears in the Question position, you are involved in a situation that you have been struggling with for quite some time. This has resulted in your being rude and aggressive to those individuals who are not sympathetic or understanding of the situation causing you so much worry. Because you have been struggling to stay on top of the problem for such a long time, you may be wondering when it will all end, if ever. The subsequent cards that fall will yield the answer you seek, but in the meantime you must struggle on in an attempt to keep failure at bay. Even during difficult times you will need to maintain a positive mental attitude because others will be more inclined to lend a helping hand if they feel you are friendly and approachable.

Eight   If the Eight of Wands has appeared in the Question position, you or someone close to you has a very strong need to make a move in your life. Even if it is not a physical move, a change in mental scenery will do you a world of good. This card often indicates a promotion of some kind is at hand, which will mean you will leave your current situation and move on to another one that you hope will be an improvement in your life circumstances. If the move is of a physical nature, you may find you must get on an aeroplane or go to another country or state, which will ultimately enhance the level of your life experiences and broaden your perspective. This move is quite often necessary to help you advance in your work or career path, and the resulting cards in the spread will yield further illumination, as you continue on with the delineation.

Nine   If the Nine of Wands has landed in the Question position, you or some-one close to you is involved in a situation that has caused you to feel defensive. Because you are always on your guard, you often become tired quite easily and can become snappy to others, individuals who are not involved in the situation that is causing you so much worry. It is for this reason that people are not seeing you at your best because they are relating to you when you are in a condition of extreme stress. You cannot continue as you are indefinitely because you need to take a break from the pressures of this life in order to renew your physical and psychological energies. The cards that follow will give you further insight into the situation and reveal to you what needs to transpire before you can get the break you need at this time in your life.

Ten   If the Ten of Wands has found itself in the Question position, you or someone close to you may feel war torn and weary. You may have taken on more than you can handle at this time in your life, and are therefore beginning to feel the strain of all of the responsibility that has been placed upon you. The fact of the matter is that your skill level was not nearly as great as the confidence you had in yourself, and now you are beginning to reconsider your original decision to take on such a monu-mental task that you really were not adequately prepared for. The cards that follow will provide further illumination with regard to this issue and help you to decide what your next course of action should be.

King   If the King of Wands has landed in the Question position, you are think-ing about a man who has a great deal of wisdom and insight into the ways of the universe. He has a wide breath of experience and is therefore knowledgeable on a vast range of subjects. He is generally of a happy disposition, which is evident by his fiery sense of humour. The part he plays in your life will be further revealed in the cards that follow.

Queen   If the Queen of Wands has found herself in the Question position, you are thinking of a woman who has somewhat of a fiery temper. This individual has a good head for business and is not likely to allow sentimentality to get in the way of tough professional decisions that need to be made. She desires success and is not terribly bothered if she hurts another person's feelings to get it. It is for that reason that while she may be successful in business matters, at home, she may find herself somewhat lonely on occasion; the reason being self-centredness is not an attribute that is conducive to family life.

Knight/Prince   If the Knight of Wands has appeared in the Question position, you are thinking of a young man who has a rather tenacious character. He is very impetuous and has much energy, which makes him quite attractive to the opposite sex. He can be somewhat of a romantic soul, which can lead others to believe that he is in love with the object of his adoration. The fact is, however, that he is in love with the concept of being in love, and not necessarily the individual who is allowing him to fulfil his fantasy. It is for this reason that he will leave a string of broken hearts behind him before he tires of his wandering lifestyle and decides to settle down with one woman who will tolerate his wandering ways. This man is not very reliable and should therefore not be trusted, especially in matters of love, until he has proven himself to be a loyal and faithful friend.

Page/Princess   If the Page of Wands has appeared in the Question position, you are thinking about a young person, quite possibly a woman, who is astrologically one of the Fire signs. This individual is at the moment playing a very important part in your life scenario, whether you think so or not, so it is vital that you take her needs into consideration when making any important decisions that will affect her.

Pentacles/Disks/Earth

Ace   If the Ace of Pentacles has found its way into the Question position, you are thinking of beginning a venture that will be rewarding in a financial or material way, and are wondering what the probable outcome will be. You may also be considering adding to your family unit in the form of a pet or a child, which would entail an enormous expenditure of your resources, and you would like to know how such a move will affect your material prosperity at this time in your life.

Two   If the Two of Pentacles has appeared in the Question position, you are concerned about financial considerations. You are in the process of juggling your finances and are wondering if enough money will come in to pay all the bills that come in to your home. These money worries can cause you a great deal of anxiety, as you are not sure you will have the resources to do all that you need to. The cards that follow will reveal to you how best to deal with what is becoming a highly emotive situation.

Three If the Three of Pentacles has found its way into the Question position, you are considering a move that you hope will improve your material prospects in this world. You may have decided you would like to move house, which could possibly involve you building one, or at the very least, renovating it to make it more habitable. Because this card indicates success through skill is forthcoming, you may finally at long last receive recognition for your hard work and aptitude, and quite possibly receive a pay raise to go along with your elevated professional status.

Four When the Four of Pentacles finds its way to the Question position, you are thinking about spending money on one particular venture, but are not sure of the outcome of such a venture. If there were not even a shadow of a doubt about what you were doing then you would not need to consult the oracle now would you? Something is holding you back from making a wild leap of faith and you are wise to err on the side of caution. It is important, therefore, that you keep your money, emotions, thoughts, and ideas close to your chest for the time being at least. You will need to take a 'wait and see' attitude before you invest any more than you absolutely must in this endeavour. The cards that follow will reveal to you in greater detail the particular aspects of the situation at hand and how best to navigate around any possible pitfalls.

Five If the Five of Pentacles has found its way into the Question position, you are experiencing what could best be described as a poverty of the soul, which has led you to experience a depression of the soul. There are many things in your life that are not right at the moment, and it is for that reason that you have found yourself consulting the oracle in an attempt to remedy the situation. The cards that follow will yield further illumination and give you insight into exactly what the problem is.

Six If the Six of Pentacles has landed in the Question position, you have used all of your own devices to get you where you presently are in this life. It is for that reason that if you would like to progress any further, you will need outside assistance from those individuals who have the wherewithal to lend a helping hand. The cards that follow will give you guidance as to who can help you during this time of need.

Seven If the Seven of Pentacles is in the Question position, you have made some mistakes in the past and are wondering how best to minimise the damage that has been done. Although you will have to work very hard to recover what has been lost, it will take significantly longer than you had imagined to restore your losses. It is for that reason that you need to persevere even when you feel there is nothing more to struggle for. There will be a light at the end of the tunnel; you just can't see it at this point in time. The cards that follow will provide further illumination on the best way forward. It is always helpful to remember that today is the first day of the rest of your life.

Eight If the Eight of Pentacles has fallen in the Question position, you are considering doing something completely new, which will require you to go through an apprenticeship of some kind. You will be required to learn a whole new set of skills, most of which must be picked up through experience. Whether this venture is successful or not depends on how much effort you are willing to put into it. To receive further illumination, it will be necessary to delineate the cards that follow.

Nine If the Nine of Pentacles has landed in the Question position, you are considering taking a well-deserved break. You have been working exceptionally hard, and need to recharge your batteries before you can effectively continue on your path during this incarnation. You may also be expecting some money from an unknown source, and more details about this scenario will be revealed to you in the cards that follow.

Ten If the Ten of Pentacles has landed in the Question position, you are thinking of a family project. Whether you like it or not, there is a situation within your family unit that you are involved in, which has been weighing on your mind quite heavily. How the situation will progress, however, will be revealed in the cards that follow.

King If the King of Pentacles has entered into the Question position, you are thinking of a man who is wealthy in many ways. Because he has acquired confidence through experience and maturity, he can be benevolent to those who he feels deserving of his wealth. He may have a large family network, and will therefore gain a great deal of happiness through his extended family, which he is quite rightly very proud of. He may also have a large circle of friends who he has cultivated through the years, which means that he will rarely be short of company. The role this individual plays in your life will be revealed in the cards that follow.

Queen   If the Queen of Pentacles has fallen in the Question position, you are thinking of a woman who is very practical, reliable and generally down to earth. She may be financially well endowed because she is not foolish with her resources. Thinking to the future, she may very well have astutely married a man of means, which has meant that she will have little or no need to work for the money she receives in this life. Negatively, this woman can be opinionated, rude and obstinate, which can make it difficult for her to get along with others and fit into a crowd.

Knight/Prince   If the Knight of Pentacles has landed in the Question position, you are thinking of a young man. This person is quite practical and methodical, and those who don't know him well may even consider him to be somewhat boring, but this is simply because they have not yet learned what captivates his interest. When young, he may be considered a bit awkward and clumsy, but as he matures, his true potential will emerge, as metaphorically speaking as in the tale of the ugly duckling.

Page/Princess   If the Page of Pentacles has landed in the Question position, you are concerned about a young person with a stubborn streak. This individual is very practically minded and has somewhat of a no-nonsense personality, and this makes it very difficult to reason with her when she has her mind made up about certain issues. As a result, she can be quite determined in her opinions, which could even border on the obstinate. She is a late bloomer whose potential is not likely to be realised while she is young, but will develop beautifully as she matures.

Swords/Air

Ace   If the Ace of Swords has landed in the Question position, there is an issue of communication that surrounds your aura. It can be a document of some importance, such as a contract, affidavit or certificate, which carries legal connotations. You may find it necessary to write a letter, containing information that is of utmost importance to your current situation. Emails and telephone calls are also prominent in this placement, and the cards that follow will provide further revelations.

Two   If the Two of Swords has landed in the Question position, you are of two minds on one particular issue and may not know the most appropriate course of action to take. You may have reached an impasse with one particular person and have therefore agreed to disagree on one particular subject. You may have fallen out with that individual to such an extent that you may have had to part company, for a while, anyway.

Further illumination on this particular situation will be gleaned from the cards that follow.

Three   If the Three of Swords has fallen in the Question position, your heart is aching with regard to one particular person. It seems that another person, whether you realise it or not, has interfered in the course of your life. This has caused you a great deal of upset for which it will not be easy to recover, but you need to try to pick up the shattered pieces of your soul and carry on regardless. Although you are hurting greatly, time will heal the wounds and help you to see the situation in a more insightful and different light. It will be necessary, however, to identify the individual who has brought about such disarray so that you can take measures to ensure it doesn't happen again. The cards that follow will give you further illumination into the situation that prompted you to consult the oracle.

Four   If the Four of Swords has fallen in the Question position, you have entered into a period of reflection, pondering about what you should do next. Something needs to be done to resolve a certain situation, but you are not quite sure exactly what it is. It is for that reason that you have decided to sit back and wait for the unfolding of certain events before you decide to take appropriate action, which is a wise decision indeed. The cards that follow will yield more light on the unfolding of events that will soon transpire.

Five   If the Five of Swords has landed in the Question position, there is a situation that is causing you a great deal of distress, and as a result, arguments can ensue. You may find there will be no winners in this situation and compromise is not a possible option at this time. There may be hard feelings on all sides, so it will be difficult to come to a satisfactory solution to the problem. The cards that follow will reveal more as to the specifics of this situation so you will know the best way to approach it to achieve a successful resolution to the problem.

Six   If the Six of Swords has fallen in the Question position, there is something in your life that you have made the decision to walk away from. You have been embroiled in a situation that has caused you a great deal of emotional anguish, and you have made the reluctant decision to move on to new pastures. The decision has been a sad one to make, and not one that you took lightly, because you will be leaving the known and entering into the unknown. You also have no assurances that the situation you will be entering will bring you the happiness that you so desire. Nevertheless, a decision needs to be made if you are to progress in your soul development. With any luck, therefore, your environment should begin to improve when you get settled in to your new surroundings.

Seven If the Seven of Swords has fallen in the Question position, you are involved in a situation that is highly dubious in the very best of circumstances. You are not in possession of all the facts, which has affected your ability to make sound decisions on the matter. In addition, the issue of theft has arisen, so it is essential that you stay guarded in your interactions with others. Exactly what is going on will be further revealed by the cards that follow, but for the time being you should keep your confidences to a minimum.

Eight If the Eight of Swords has fallen in the Question position, you have found yourself in a situation where you feel you have no avenue of escape. You may have trusted the wrong person, which has put you in a very uncomfortable position. Because you have been left in an awkward position, it is quite likely that whatever move you make will leave someone feeling quite upset. It is for that reason that, for the time being anyway, it is permissible for you to stay where you are, gather your thoughts, and wait until the time is right to take appropriate action. The cards that follow will show you how best to proceed in a rather uncertain path.

Nine If the Nine of Swords has appeared in the Question position, you have found yourself in a situation that has caused a great deal of anxiety. You may find yourself worrying so much that you are not sleeping properly, and this will consequently affect your ability to make sound judgements. You, or someone close to you, may be in the midst of a creative illness, which will make you feel further isolated when you need all the support from others you can get. In addition, the intense anxiety you have been feeling may mean you have fallen prey to one of the many depressive illnesses that plague our society, so you may need medical attention to rectify any emotional imbalances you may be suffering from.

Ten If the Ten of Swords has landed in the Question position, you have been let down very badly by an individual and need some time to adjust to the situation you have found yourself in. It is quite possible that someone who you trusted betrayed you in some way, and you are reeling from the aftermath of the subsequent events. You need to rest, gather your strength, and reflect upon the sequence of events that have recently transpired in your life before you decide what your next course of action will be. The cards that follow will enlighten you as to how the situation will progress.

King   If the King of Swords has landed in the Question position, a man with a great intellect is weighing heavily on your mind. This individual is an intellectual and tries to use logic to come to the conclusions he makes. He is also quite manipulative, so it is always best to question his motives. If he is under stress or has experienced a traumatic event, however, he can be susceptible to neurosis or even psychosis. The role this man plays in your life will be further revealed in the cards that follow.

Queen   If the Queen of Swords has landed in the Question position, you are thinking of a woman who has a quick mind and can use it to her advantage when the need arises. If she is comfortable in her position in this world, she can act as a humanitarian and will help others who are less fortunate than her. If she is unhappy, however, she can be somewhat bitter and perceived by others as somewhat of a gossip. How she relates to you will be revealed in the cards that follow, but it is best to be cautious until you know her well.

Knight/Prince   If the Knight of Swords has landed in the Question position, you are thinking of a young man who has a swift mind and a sharp tongue. He is able to think quickly on his feet, so it is essential not to take everything he says and does at face value. Because he has not yet matured to the extent that he can take responsibility for his actions, he can be somewhat economical with the truth, especially when it is not in his best interests to be forthcoming with any unpleasant facts.

Page/Princess   If the Page of Swords has landed in the Question position, you are thinking of a young person, possibly a girl, who has a quick mind, is chatty and inquisitive. She is very talkative and as a result can unwittingly say the wrong thing at the wrong time. The part she plays in your life will be revealed in the cards that follow.

Cups/Water

Ace   If the Ace of Cups has appeared in your spread, your question regards a very happy event that could leave you feeling fulfilled in your life. There is a clear flow of emotional energy present, which indicates you may be in touch with your emotions. How this event will transpire will be further revealed in the cards that follow.

Two   If the Two of Cups has appeared in the Question position, you are thinking of a union or reunion that has a great deal of emotional intensity.
This union could involve either you or someone close to you, and it is
one of those encounters in this life that seems to have been predestined.
It is a relationship of love and harmony, and needs to be cultivated so it
can develop into something more substantial in the years to come. What
happens next will be revealed in the cards that follow.

Three   If the Three of Cups has found itself in the Question position, you are
thinking a great deal about a party or social event that has much significance to you. A great deal of socialising is indicated, which has been
occupying much of your time. How this happy event will affect you
personally will be further revealed in the cards that follow.

Four   If the Four of Cups has landed in the Question position, you are in a
situation that you feel is doubtful at best. Although logic and common
sense tell you everything is fine and you have nothing to worry about, a
little voice inside your head is whispering to you that all is not as it
should be. Whether or not your reservations are founded will be
revealed in the cards that follow, but it is important to trust that inner
voice, which is the gateway to your subconscious.

Five   If the Five of Cups has landed in the Question position, there is something in your life that is causing you to feel rather melancholy, and you
could very well be suffering from one of the many forms of depression
that prevail in our modern society. Perhaps you have discovered something that has shattered your hopes and dreams, thereby leaving you
somewhat disillusioned, as you try to come to terms with the new situation that has occurred as a result of your discovery. On any account, the
cards that follow will reveal further details of the picture that is being
painted, which should help you to rebuild what is left of that particular
aspect of your life.

Six   If the Six of Cups has landed in the Question position, you are thinking
of times past, a period when life seemed to be much simpler and you
did not have as many concerns that weighed you down. You may be
thinking of either your own or someone else's childhood, and children
may play a prominent role in your life. The following cards that are laid
out in the spread will reveal the situation in greater detail.

Seven   If the Seven of Cups has landed in the Question position, you have been
presented with several options and don't know which to choose.
Because these choices appear so rewarding, you may have difficulty

deciding which path would be the most appropriate to take. There are, however, hidden pitfalls, so it is therefore important to properly research all the alternatives before selecting one particular path to follow. Further details will be revealed to you in the cards that follow which will be able to guide you onto the correct path.

Eight If the Eight of Cups has found itself in the Question position, you are thinking of something that has caused you some sadness in your life. Perhaps you have given your all to one particular person or situation, and have done all that you can do. You have consequently made the sad realisation that it is time to give in and let go of an area of your life where you cannot possibly achieve the happiness and fulfilment you crave. In many ways, you are embarking upon the unknown because you are entering into fresh territory and don't know what the future has in store for you. The cards that follow will provide greater clarity to the situation and reveal to you the best course of action to take.

Nine If the Nine of Cups has entered into the Question position, you are thinking of a social occasion where the invitees will be expected to eat, drink and make merry. As a result of the socialising that will take place, you may find yourself putting on weight, so it is important to watch what you eat. You may very well have reason to celebrate, so it is important to retain a modest perspective and try to refrain from smugness, which would negate much of the good fortune you are so deserving of. This is a very positive card, and the cards that follow will further illuminate the situation you are presently involved in.

Ten If the Ten of Cups has appeared in the Question position, you are thinking about a family matter that is very close to your heart. There is an issue that relates to your emotional wellbeing and involves a partnership of some kind. This partnership is likely to be marital or cohabital in nature, as children are often involved in the union that will transpire. How the situation will evolve will be revealed in the cards that follow, providing you with further illumination on what is hoped will be a fortunate and prosperous time.

King If the King of Cups has appeared in the Question position, you are thinking about a man who is very emotional. At times he allows his feelings to overrule his rational reasoning processes, and this could cloud his better judgement. He is a loving person, and how he expresses this love will depend on other aspects of his character. When he becomes aroused, he has much energy that he can use either positively or negatively, which will ultimately sway the situation in his favour.

Queen If the Queen of Cups has appeared in the Question position, you are thinking about a woman who is quite reactive to the many situations in her life. She is highly intuitive and uses her emotional intelligence much more than she uses her rational senses. She can be a very caring person, but when she feels she has been wronged, may attempt to enact the vindictiveness she feels entitled to display. How this woman expresses herself will be further revealed in the cards that follow.

Knight/Prince If the Knight of Cups has appeared in the Question position, you are thinking about a very sensitive young man who has not yet learned to keep his emotions in check. He can be very loving, given the right environment, but alternatively, he can also be prone to emotional outbursts if other stabilising factors are not present to balance out his temperament. This individual is one of life's dreamers, as he contemplates the utopian ideal that can never be.

Page/Princess If the Page of Cups has landed in the Question position, you are thinking of a young person, possibly a woman, who can be very emotive in her behaviour and mannerisms. She is not restrained in showing her likes and dislikes, as this behaviour is instilled in the core of her being. As she matures, she will learn to separate her emotional responses from her logical reactions, but for the time being, people around her must be patient and allow her the space to develop through experimenting with various ways to relate to others.

2 The Cross

0 Fool   If The Fool has found itself in the Cross position, it seems that you have become embroiled in a conflict that is causing you to go through an extreme personality crisis. You may want to break free and begin a new life for yourself, but someone or something is holding you back. Alternatively, someone who you thought would be around for a while longer has decided to depart, much to your dismay. This has caused you a fair amount of unhappiness that you cannot easily shake off. On any account, you have some thinking to do. There are changes that need to be made and you would be wise to decide the best way to make the amendments to your life so that it will be fruitful and prosperous. A new beginning is beckoning you, and the resulting cards in the spread will further clarify precisely how you need to undertake such an endeavour.

I Magician   If the Magician has landed in the Cross position, there is a young person, probably a man, who is working at cross-purposes to you. This person is either currently studying or has just recently finished a course of study, and is therefore looking for work in his chosen field. He has a quick mind and uses it to his advantage, but not necessarily to your advantage. It is for that reason that you need to keep your eye on him to ensure what he does will not cause harm to you or your business activities. Although you may not be aware of it, this individual is deeply involved in the dark arts, shaping time, motion, space and physicality to meet his needs. Although he has only used his intense powers of concentration to advance himself in this life, the time will come when he may try to influence the lives of others. Although he will be expected to karmically pay for any harm he has done any other souls in his desire for dominance over others, it is important that you realise his true personality so you will know how best to deal with him.

II High Priestess

If The High Priestess has landed in the Cross position, you are concerned about a woman who seems to be working at cross-purposes to you. She is probably single, but if married, does not necessarily have a good relationship with her husband. This person has difficulty relating to men in a mature one-to-one fashion, and as a result keeps her contacts on a more immature level, which is all she is capable of at this point in time. She may be involved in magic, trying to use whatever power she has to influence people and situations in her favour. She will be expected to repay any harm she has done to any others through her attempts at manipulation: if not in this life, the next. The specifics of how she affects you will be further illuminated in the cards that follow.

III Empress

If The Empress has landed in the Cross position, a woman is on your mind. If she is not a mother already, she is of childbearing age and would like to start a family. For reasons known only to you, she is operating at cross-purposes to your life, which is causing your best laid plans to go awry. It could be that she is either your mother or the mother of someone close to you, and is making such a fuss that you cannot help but notice her. There is also the possibility that she is part of a love triangle, and she or her offspring may be adversely affecting the life you would like to have. Lastly, you may find you are in fact the person portrayed in the card, who is wrecking havoc in the well-laid plans of others. If that is the case, you are very fertile indeed, and adequate precautions will need to be taken if you do not want to increase the size of your existing family. It is also important to remember that you will be expected to atone for any harm that you do others: if not in this life, the next.

VI Emperor

If The Emperor has found itself in the Cross position, there is a very powerful individual who has the capability to wreak havoc in your life. This person is ruthless and is only interested in who is going to give him pleasure in this life. It is for that reason that it is pointless trying to get any sort of rational thought out of him because he is only interested in listening to those individuals who are prepared to agree with him wholeheartedly. The best thing to do when dealing with this person is to tread carefully and stay away from him as much as possible. The cards that follow will provide further illumination into the situation you will soon be embarking upon.

V Hierophant If The Hierophant has landed in the Cross position, you have reached a crossroads in your life where you need to make an important decision. You may be entering into a marriage for all the wrong reasons, which will in the end bring you a great deal of unhappiness and temporarily halt your soul's development. You may already be involved in a marriage that is not turning out the way you thought it would, and are therefore thinking of entering into a separation. If the issue is not one of marriage then you may be thinking of, or have already entered a contractual agreement that will bring with it some difficulties. Additionally, you may be involved in a religious ceremony that is not to your liking. Perhaps someone you know is getting married and you wish you were the one getting married instead. You may have decided to enter into a vocation or profession that you have sadly discovered is not giving you the happiness and fulfilment you desire. The cards that follow will further illuminate your current unfolding situation.

VI Lovers If The Lovers have found themselves in the Cross position, it seems there is a particular pair of lovers who are having a detrimental effect on your wellbeing. Perhaps you are involved, whether you are aware of it or not, in the midst of a love triangle, which can be frustrating for all involved partners. You may find yourself in the role of mistress, adulterer or betrayed spouse, but in any event, the situation is likely to cause you a great deal of unrest. It could be that your lover is having second thoughts about the bond he has established with you, so it is essential you observe the messages people are sending out very carefully. The cards that follow will give you greater insight into how best to proceed.

VII Chariot If The Chariot has entered into the Cross position, a certain situation with regard to travel is weighing heavily on your mind. Perhaps either you or someone close to you must commute extensively, either for professional or personal reasons. The time, effort and money used to make these trips are taking its toll on your wellbeing and you are beginning to wonder if such activities are worth all of the fuss. In addition, either you or another person close to you is not one to give up, so you may find yourself hanging in there when more mortal souls would have let go of what appears to be a very bad situation. The cards that follow will provide you with further illumination to the situation that you are currently embroiled in.

VIII Strength If Strength has landed in the Cross position, it seems you are under a great deal of stress and are susceptible to falling prey to one of the many depressive illnesses that are so much a part of our society. It seems as if the moment you get over one hurdle, another one pops up to further complicate your life. The ancient meaning of Strength is The Enchantress, so whether you are aware of it or not, there may be another woman in the picture who is operating at cross-purposes to what you would like to achieve. It is therefore essential that you exercise caution over any new people who enter your life, or any suspicious characters who are already a part of your life, because they may have a greater influence on the situation you are involved in than you would like to believe. Additionally, animals play a huge part in this situation and you may therefore find yourself falling ill due to allergies, which incidentally, are exacerbated by stress. If you simply cannot bear the thought of saying goodbye to your beloved creatures then it is vital you exercise impeccable standards of cleanliness and hygiene to prevent any unnecessary allergic reactions or illnesses.

IX Hermit If The Hermit has landed in the Cross position, you or someone close to you is feeling very isolated at the moment. This feeling of separateness may be self-imposed or ordered by a higher force, but you do not find it to necessarily be a good thing for your personal circumstances in this life. When one is unhappy, it is so easy to lock oneself away from the world in an attempt to try to resolve the problem from within, but there are some times when outside help is necessary to solve the problem that is causing you such angst. This outside assistance could be in the form of therapists, friends or family. What is important is that contact with other human beings is necessary at such a crucial time in the person's spiritual evolvement. If the creator had intended human beings to be alone, he would have made them hermaphrodites who did not need another individual to procreate. Because he made humans male and female, he intended our species to be social beings, which is what is vital to our spiritual, physical and mental development. A case in point is children who, for whatever reason, have become institutionalised. If they are not given appropriate human responses, they will soon wither up and die. In addition, children who are neglected will develop attachment disorders that will haunt them for the rest of their lives, thus affirming their need for human interaction in what can often be a very insular world.

X Wheel of Fortune If The Wheel of Fortune has found itself in the Cross position, you may have felt good luck has befallen you when in fact the reverse is actually the case. While people generally attribute The Wheel of Fortune to luck and prosperity, the Wheel does in fact have a downside, which you or someone close to you is experiencing. It should also be remembered that The Wheel has often been used as an instrument of torture, and it is for that reason this archetype should be approached with a certain element of caution. Because The Wheel is composed of a circle, it is inevitable that when one follows the perimeter of The Wheel, he will encounter high and low points. You may very well be enduring one of The Wheel's low points in the buoyancy of its rotation, but if you weather the psychological storm, you will emerge a better person for the experience. The cards that fall will reveal in greater detail the situation at hand.

XI Justice If Justice has fallen in the Cross position, you are involved in a dispute that seems to be wearing you down in some way. Whether you are right or wrong is not the issue because the law of the land is not on your side in this particular instance. Unfortunately, you will have to learn the hard way that the vast majority of the laws were not designed to protect the innocent, but the perpetrators of the many crimes in our society today. If the laws were in fact designed to protect those who are not in a position to protect themselves, we would not have so much pain, sorrow and grief in our world. Regardless of the original intent of a law when it was written, its only use is to provide limits for people to operate within. If a cunning person wants to commit a crime, however, he will be able to do it in such a way that he can escape criminal prosecution, and if possible, lay the blame on someone else. Ah, such are the circumstances that we all must come against when trying to live a just and proper life. It is for that reason, therefore, that you must rely on your wits to get by because the local authorities who have been employed to serve you will not be there in your time of need. The cards that follow will reveal in greater detail the circumstances of the situation you face.

XII Hanged Man If The Hanged Man has landed in the Cross position, you, or someone close to you are at the verge of giving up on a situation that you do not possess the necessary skills to successfully manoeuvre around. This sense of resignation could be in the form of a melancholic depression, but on a more severe note, the person involved could be in such a serious state of despair that he may actually think of taking his own life. Although there is reason for concern, there is a way out of this situation if the individual stays focused on his ultimate goal. This is not the time to sit back and allow others to make your choices for you, but a time to make proactive, life-changing decisions. How the situation unfolds will be further revealed in the cards that follow.

XIII Death If Death has made its way into the Cross position, there are some life-changing events that either you or someone close to you is having difficulty dealing with. It is for that reason that emotions of a rather intense nature are being felt, and efforts need to be made to effect the transformation with as little fuss as possible. The person in question may be encountering a creative illness or breakdown of sorts, and as a result, needs all the help he can get to help him through such a dramatic period. Control is of the essence in order to effect the changes needed to restore order in the universal scheme of your life.

XIV Temperance If Temperance has landed in the Cross position, you or someone close to you is impatient about something that is still in the gestational phase of its existence. This is an important matter you are powerless to resolve until a certain amount of time has elapsed and specific events have occurred, and you are powerless to do anything except wait for fruition. In addition, a deep inner healing is necessary before you can continue along your evolutionary path, which will be a lengthy process of transformation you are presently undergoing. As you begin to understand that where you are today would not have been possible if you had not had the life experiences that you have had in the past, the psychic wounds to your soul will begin to heal, leaving tiny, etheric scars that only one with auric vision can perceive. Time heals all wounds, and it is for that reason you must wait the allotted time for your soul to transcend through the remembrance of your past life experiences.

XV Devil If The Devil has landed in the Cross position, you or someone close to you is a bit too preoccupied with the material things of this world. You may have, shall we say, made a pact with the Devil in an attempt to acquire all of the material possessions you believe you need in order to survive. Instead of bringing you the happiness you thought they would, these possessions have become a burden that, quite frankly, you could very well do without. All of the nice things you have at your disposal have not come without a price, as you have found you must work endlessly to keep them, and you may very well have been required to deny an existential part of yourself in the process. How the situation will resolve itself will be revealed in the cards that follow, but you may decide that in the interest of your psychic development, you would rather abandon the life of amassing as much material wealth as you possibly can and pursue a more simplistic existence.

XVI Tower If The Tower has landed in the Cross position, things have been shaken up a bit and you are not amused in the least by the situation you have found yourself in the midst of. Perhaps you or someone close to you has had an accident at a most inconvenient time, which has posed a number of major problems to your present living arrangements. There is also the possibility of a house move, which may not necessarily be a welcome endeavour. In times like these, it is best to err on the side of caution because any wrong moves will take a great deal of time and effort to rectify.

XVII Star   If The Star has fallen in the cross position, you may be over-optimistic about a certain situation you have recently found yourself in the midst of, which is having the effect of clouding your better judgement. You may be on the brink of embarking on a dream you have had for such a long time that other important issues are being neglected. There is the possibility you need to seriously look at how you project yourself because your dress, appearance and mannerisms may be holding you back in some way. You may also have put your trust in a friend, who you will soon discover is an unreliable person to depend on. It is therefore essential that you appoint yourself as your own best friend because in times of crisis, you are really the only person you can truly depend on. When you make yourself your own best friend, you will be amazed at how much happier you will be and how, quite suddenly, other people will want to get to know you better. The situation will be revealed to you in the cards that follow.

XVIII Moon   If The Moon has landed in the Cross position, you or someone close to you is very depressed. This is one of those situations where you are inundated with so much stress in your life that you literally cannot see the forest for the trees. It seems the moment you solve one problem, another one will crop up, which is beginning to wear you down. You do not know who your true friends are, and as a result you will encounter many wolves in sheep's clothing. There are individuals who pretend to be nice to you, but in fact have an agenda at cross purposes to your own, quite possibly intending to use you as a pawn in the elaborate psychological game they have been playing for quite some time. It is times like these you need to keep your own counsel and exercise caution with the people you place your trust in, because you will soon discover that some of these individuals are inappropriate confidantes.

XIX Sun   If The Sun has landed in the Cross position, it seems that your disposition is not as cheerful as you would like it to be. You may have encountered a rather obstinate family member who has left you feeling somewhat unsettled. As a result, you could find yourself adopting a crabby disposition, thus leaving other people wondering exactly what the problem is. You may have received some news about a family member that is not particularly welcome. In addition, you may find you have an addition to your family at what is a most inopportune time. There may be someone in your life who, like a clown, is laughing on the outside but crying within. The cards that follow will reveal in greater detail exactly what the problem is.

XX Judgement If Judgement has landed in the Cross position, the pain that is within you, or someone close to you, is of such an intense nature that you do not know if you can bear the anguish any longer. Whether the pain is physical or emotional, you are in need of a deep inner healing that will cleanse your soul and bring you to a state where you are able to carry on living for a little while longer. If professional help is not available to you, you may tend to self-medicate in the form of food, drugs, alcohol, cigarettes, sex, shopping, or anything that will take your mind off the trauma that is buried so deep in your psyche that you can no longer even remember the event. The problem is that self-medication, while it may very well mask the symptoms that have brought you to such a state of despair, brings with it a whole new set of problems that you must inevitably deal with if you want to progress in your spiritual, emotional and physical evolution. Therefore, in addition to the problem that caused you to adopt such elaborate coping mechanisms, you will also have to overcome the coping mechanisms as well. In addition to a deep psychic healing, which you so desperately need, you would also benefit from behaviour modification training, because you will need help in overcoming your addictions.

XXI World If The World has landed in the Cross position, there is a situation that you, or someone close to you, is reluctant to let go of. As a result you and the other persons involved are not following the path you should be embarking upon. Maybe you are clinging to a stale relationship, job or social activity that you have long outgrown, but as of yet have not been able to let go of. It is therefore time to discard those things in your life you have outgrown, because new opportunities will not come to you until you open up yourself to receive them. The cards that follow will reveal more about the situation at hand.

Wands/Rods/Fire

Ace   If the Ace of Wands has landed in the Cross position, it seems you are bubbling over with creativity, but it is not being focused in the direction that will yield the most satisfactory results. It is for that reason your energies are being scattered, and while your intentions are good, you are not accomplishing much of anything of any kind of significance. You need to think about exactly what it is you would like to accomplish and then proceed in that direction. The cards that follow will yield further illumination with regard to the best way you can act.

Two   If the Two of Wands has landed in the Cross position, it seems you are embroiled in a professional relationship that is not necessarily in your best interests. If anything, this relationship could very well be detrimental to your work and business enterprises, so it is therefore important to look at any such liaisons with scrutiny before they further develop. Because of this, you need to look carefully at any relationships you forge at this time to ensure they are positive in nature and will help you to progress in the path you should following.

Three   If the Three of Wands has landed in the Cross position, you may be involved in an enterprise that may not be in your best interests. Whether it is leisure, business, or something you consider to be creative, it really has not given you the opportunity to grow and develop in a manner that is most appropriate for you. There is the possibility that you are engaging in these activities with one or more individuals, and it is for that reason you should carefully critique your associates because they very well could have agendas working against your own. In addition, the individuals who you are acquainted with very well could be intentionally using you. The cards that follow will further reveal the scenario that you are involved in.

Four   If the Four of Wands has landed in the Cross position, you may have embarked upon a certain course of action, hoping it would give you a much wanted sense of security. You may have decided to enter into a business venture or formed a relationship that, while not something you would consider ideal, was entered into in the hopes of bringing a sense of stability to what is often a rather hectic lifestyle. Because your heart was not in it, however, the likelihood of achieving the hoped for outcomes seems to be beyond your grasp. What you failed to see is that true security comes from within, and it is therefore pointless to rely on others for something you can only acquire through your own efforts.

Five   If the Five of Wands appears in the Cross position, it seems you are fighting unseen forces. You may believe you are battling a major problem that, once eradicated, will cure all that ails you. The fact is, unfortunately, you are merely fighting what is a symptom of a much greater problem. When you solve the problem that is affecting you at this point in time, another one will crop up with a much greater magnitude than the previous dilemmas you have been dealing with. It will seem to you that you will become embroiled in a vicious circle of fighting fires, never really making any apparent progression in your life, because you are trying to cure the symptoms, but not the true cause. Until you pinpoint what the problem actually is, you will find yourself perpetually involved in one trauma after another. The cards that follow will help you to get to the root of problem once and for all.

Six   If the Six of Wands has landed in the Cross position, it is highly likely that you have been set up for a fall. You have found yourself in a situation where you are so sure you will be successful, but there are hidden pitfalls that can thwart even your most stalwart of efforts. It is for that reason you would be wise not to allow yourself to become smug or complacent because if something can go wrong, it will.

Seven   If the Seven of Wands has landed in the Cross position, it seems you are continuing your uphill struggle and have very little time to rest and recharge your batteries. Whether you realise it or not, competitors and other enemies are nipping at your heels, waiting for you to lose your balance and topple. It is for that reason you need to refrain from dubious alliances and activities that can put you in a compromising position. The following cards will reveal in greater detail the scenario you have found yourself in, and how best to tackle it.

Eight   If the Eight of Wands has appeared in the Cross position, it seems you are planning on making a trip that may very well be detrimental to your wellbeing. What would be more appropriate would be for you to stay where you are for the time being, and take in all that is around you before deciding on a course of action. The time will come for you to make a move, but for the time being it would be in your best interests to take a wait and see attitude. Alternatively, you may find your affairs are being affected by someone from afar, so you need to pay close attention to your extended relationships as well as your local ones.

Nine   If the Nine of Wands has landed in the Cross position, you may find yourself in a position where you are defending yourself from the wrong people or things, which makes you vulnerable in other areas of your life. As a result, you could find yourself unduly weary of the circumstances life presents you with, and are thereby letting your guard down in times when you need to remain vigilant.

Ten   If the Ten of Wands has found itself in the Cross position you may have bitten off more than you can chew, and are having to burn the candle at both ends to take care of all of your commitments. It is for that reason that you may have lost the pep in your step and the sparkle may no longer be found in your eye. You may be ill equipped to deal with certain events that have transpired, and as a result are not sure what the correct course of action is. Although you would like to just throw in the towel, it is important you persevere because there will be a light at the end of the tunnel, eventually.

King   If the King of Wands has landed in the Cross position, a knowledgable and wise man is on your mind. He can be quite jealous, and as a result can direct his activities in other more inappropriate areas. He can also become violent when angry, and may well benefit from anger management or assertiveness courses to help tame the beast within. The part he plays in your life will be revealed in the cards that follow.

Queen   If the Queen of Wands has landed in the Cross position, you are thinking of a woman who has a great deal of energy, which she usually expends satisfying her own self-gratification. It is quite possible this woman is working in business because she has a sharp mind and directs it in a task-oriented way that enables her to get people to do what she would like them to do. If the woman is not employed in a useful capacity, she could become bitter, feeling life has passed her by in some way. This frustration could unleash itself in fits of temper, so it is best to keep your distance from her during these dark moods. The cards that follow will reveal in greater detail the role this person plays in your life.

Knight/Prince   If the Knight of Wands has landed in the Cross position, you are thinking of a young man. This person is full of energy and bright ideas for the future, but he lacks the maturity to carry them to fruition. It is for that reason he begins many projects but completes few, if any. He is not ready to settle down and romantically drifts from woman to woman, savouring the excitement of new love, but becoming bored the moment the excitement has worn off. In matters of love, this man is not very trustworthy, and it is best to give him time to tire of his propensity as a serial lover before any romantic interest is taken of him. By the same token, this man may have a habit of drifting from job to job, and will work in many vocations before he finds his true niche in this life.

Page/Princess If the Page of Wands has landed in the Cross position, there is a young person, possibly a woman, who is on your mind. You may very well be worried about her, or she could be causing you a bit of aggravation in your life. She can be something of a prankster and may be the proverbial party girl, staying out all hours of the day and night. The problem needs to be sorted out, but you may not be the right person to do it, which could cause further difficulties if you are not careful as to how you handle the situation. The cards that follow will reveal more to you.

Pentacles/Disks/Earth

Ace If the Ace of Pentacles has landed in the Cross position, you may be thinking of money matters. Instead of positive thoughts, however, you may worry to the point of distraction. You may need capital for a specific venture, but do not know how you can go about acquiring it. You may also find there is an addition to your family, but the resources needed to accommodate this new addition have been stretched to the limit. You may also be considering embarking on a venture that promises to yield income, but this activity may not necessarily turn out to be a profitable endeavour. If it proves to be financially viable at all, it may entail some unethical activities, which would have the effect of tarnishing your reputation if your involvement became public knowledge. The cards that follow will reveal in greater detail the circumstances surrounding this issue.

Two If the Two of Pentacles has entered into the Cross position, you have more money going out than you have coming in, which is causing a bit of aggravation to you. You may have decided to buy some items on credit, but the money will have to be paid back eventually, much to your dismay. The cards that follow will help you to determine how best to pay what you owe to others. Because you are not in full control of your financial situation at this time, it would be wise to live as simply as possible until your circumstances improve.

Three If the Three of Pentacles has landed in the Cross position, a property you own or are living in has some flaws you need to be aware of. There may be some structural problems that will take a great deal of expense to correct, and these faults could decrease the value of the house. If you are thinking of moving into a property, it is best to look around some more and get a second opinion because there very well could be hidden costs that you will not be made aware of until it is too late to do anything constructive about it. If you are renting, there may be a fair amount of strife between you and your landlords, which will ultimately affect your living conditions. If you are living with other family members, now may be the time to spread your wings and go it alone, getting a place of your own.

Four If the Four of Pentacles has landed in the Cross position, you or someone you know is a bit too miserly. You may worry about future security, and as a result you can be a bit too frugal with necessities for your existence. Instead of enjoying your life with the money you have, you put it all away, saving for a rainy day. What is essential for you is to try to achieve a balance between the money you spend and the money you save. It is worthwhile to save for the future, but it is also important to spend your hard earned money on leisurely pursuits from time to time, treating yourself when you deserve it. In addition, if there is someone close to you who is in need of financial assistance, it is worth assessing whether you can help them in some way. If you turn your back on people when they are in need, you will find that they will turn their backs on you at just that time when you need a helping hand.

Five If the Five of Pentacles has landed in the Cross position, you or someone you know is in the midst of experiencing difficulties of such a severe nature they are having the knock-on effect of affecting your finances. Because you are not able to focus on the things that are important to maintain your standing in the community, you are at risk of losing your job, money or other resources associated with your material livelihood. Sadly, people who you believed to be your friends will be unavailable to help you in your hour of need, thus leaving you feeling even more vulnerable and alone. Unfortunately, you will go through a period in your life when there will be no one to help you. This is one life experience you must endure all on your own, and you will have to improve what will prove to be a difficult situation all on you own. It is no doubt a difficult karmic assignment you must undertake, but you have within you the strength of character to weather such a difficult time in your life. You will get through this difficult time, but the scars that remain will colour your perspective of the world you are so much a part of.

Six If the Six of Pentacles has landed in the Cross position, it seems you may be required to ask someone for assistance, and this is something you would rather not do. Alternatively, you could find someone is taking advantage of your good nature and is asking too much of you. It is important you learn to set limits before you begin to feel used by the people who are supposed to be your friends, individuals who should not be exploiting you.

Seven   If the Seven of Pentacles has landed in the Cross position, you are involved in a situation that is going to take a fair amount of time to come to fruition. The waiting game can cause many difficulties because much emotional anguish can transpire before the desired results are achieved. The only thing you can do is make sure all the necessary tasks are complete. When all of the necessary activities have been set into place, the fruits of your labour will appear.

Eight   If the Eight of Pentacles has landed in the Cross position, you are in a situation where you are learning from your experiences. If someone is teaching you then it is very likely he is showing you how to do things incorrectly, which will cause you further problems in the long run. It is therefore essential that before you seek advice from anyone about a work related topic; you first ascertain the credibility of the individual who you are asking for assistance. If not, you may find you must re-do any projects you begin. In addition, you may find some individuals who are jealous of you and are intentionally showing you how to do things incorrectly. Although it seems bizarre that people could be so bitter and petty, it is an unfortunate fact of life you must be aware of so you can progress along your spiritual path. Sometimes, when in doubt, it is best to trust your own judgement instead of the opinions of others.

Nine   If the Nine of Pentacles has landed in the Cross position, it seems as if you have too much free time on your hands. Aside from the boredom that can result, you may also find yourself worrying and fretting over things you have absolutely no control over. It is for that reason you need to find something to do, even if it is voluntary work, to keep your hands busy and your mind active.

Ten   If the Ten of Pentacles has found itself in the Cross position, it appears certain family members are dragging you down. For reasons known only to you, you have family obligations you can't or won't relate to. It is important for you to realise you have a life of your own, and if you allow others to control you through guilt or emotional blackmail, it will ultimately detract from your own quality of life. The cards that fall will reveal more with regard to this particular issue.

King   If the King of Pentacles has landed in the Cross position, there is a man who figures prominently in your life. He is very well off, although he may feign poverty. He can also be somewhat miserly, and will withhold money from people, using it as a bargaining chip to get what he wants out of them. This man will go to any lengths to protect what he feels is his, even if it means slandering, libelling, defrauding, and other unethical acts. It is therefore important to refrain from engaging in business and financial pacts with this individual because he will use ruthless tactics that are aimed to suit only himself.

Queen   If the Queen of Pentacles has landed in the Cross position, a woman who can be very stubborn and obstinate is on your mind. This woman is somewhat affluent, but can be miserly with her possessions, using them as bargaining chips and withholding them when necessary. She may have a weight problem, as she will tend to overeat or over drink, quite often when she is upset about something.

Knight/Prince   If the Knight of Pentacles has landed in the Cross position, a young man is weighing heavily on your mind. He is somewhat down to earth and consequently can be considered by some to be rather boring. He may also be a slow and methodical learner, which can be misleading to those individuals who have swifter minds. Because he enjoys the sensual pleasures of life, including good food and wine, he may have a weight problem, which is merely a reflection of his love of the sensual pleasures this world provides.

Page/Princess   If the Page of Pentacles has landed in the Cross position, a young woman or child is weighing heavily on your mind. She may be a bit slow and have some learning difficulties, which can be somewhat frustrating when strict deadlines need to be met. She could also have a bit of a weight problem, so whatever she eats needs to be closely monitored to ensure her weight does not become a serious issue when she reaches adulthood.

Swords/Air

Ace   If the Ace of Swords has landed in the Cross position, you have had some contact of an unpleasant nature. You may have received a letter, telephone call or email you have found to be rather unpleasant, or you could even have read a book or article that has caused you to rethink some of your ideas. Your reputation may have been harmed in some way because of what was written or said, and unfortunately the onus is on you to disprove the negative opinions others have formulated because of this malicious gossip. The cards that follow will further reveal how the situation will soon transpire.

Two   If the Two of Swords has landed in the Cross position, it seems you are at odds with one particular person who is has the ability to help you in some way. This whole situation is quite upsetting to you because until your circumstances changed, you thought a lot about the individual who you are involved in a disagreement with. If you are not able to resolve the conflict, you may have to separate from the person in question, which will ultimately bring you some sadness to lose someone who you regarded as a friend. The cards that follow will reveal in greater detail the unfolding situation that has prompted you to consult the oracle.

Three   If the Three of Swords has appeared in the Cross position, someone has broken your heart. The damage done may be of such an extreme nature that your relationship with that individual may be unsalvageable. While it is admirable to forgive others, the fact is we are all mere mortals, and have a great deal of difficulty accepting others' transgressions, especially when they have had the direct effect of harming us. There is no getting around the subject and excuses cannot be made for the individual who has brought such pain to your soul. Whether you forgive is up to you, but it is doubtful you will ever forget the pain that you have felt. In situations like this, it is important to remember the words of Queen Elizabeth I when she wrote of the death of her lover, 'If you could look inside my heart, you would see a body without a soul.'

Four   If the Four of Swords has landed in the Cross position, you or someone close to you is failing to take action on an important issue. By choosing not to act with regard to a particular situation, you are in fact taking a certain course of action, which is inaction. Is inaction the correct course of action to take, however? Perhaps you are waiting for a more propitious time, but what you must realise is that until you make a move, things will not change and the situation you are in will continue to stagnate. You need to take some proactive steps to initiate the wheels of change. No matter how minor the move, in this case, something is better than nothing.

Five   If the Five of Swords has landed in the Cross position, it seems you are at odds with a particular group of people, which is causing you a great deal of frustration. It seems you are not able to see eye to eye with certain individuals, which results in inevitable conflict. Since those involved in this scenario do not mean that much to you anyway, you are not too particularly bothered if anyone's feelings are hurt. It is for that reason that you may find it appropriate to just walk away from this situation that is leaving a bitter taste in your mouth. The cards that follow will reveal more to you as to how the situation that prompted you to consult the oracle will unfold.

Six   If the Six of Swords has landed in the Cross position, you are contemplating making a move you believe will lead to a better life, but in reality you could very well be creating even more problems for yourself. It is for that reason you need to conduct research before committing yourself into any agreements that are irrevocable, because you may very well change your mind at a later date. You may be unhappy about your present situation, but believe it or not, things could get a whole lot worse. Think very carefully about any changes you make right now and ensure a contingency plan can easily be put into place.

Seven   If the Seven of Swords has appeared in the Cross position, beware of theft, which is abounding around you. Someone who you are in competition with could be taking your ideas and using them as his own. Alternatively, it could in fact be you who is doing the pinching of property or ideas. It is very important to keep your possessions secure because someone may surreptitiously sneak in and take an item that has a great deal of sentimental value to you. The theme of this card placement is that you feel wronged in some way. The best way to forestall this feeling is to keep your own counsel when it comes to matters of trust because you may have to learn the hard way that there are very few in this world who are genuinely trustworthy.

Eight   If the Eight of Swords has appeared in the Cross position, it appears you have been constrained in some way. You have found yourself in a profession, home or other situation where you have been inundated with rules and regulations, which you find difficult to uphold. Some of these regulations you have been forced to adhere to may seem quite petty, but they serve the purpose of helping you to see what is really important in this life. Alternatively, you may find it is in fact you who are placing what is considered to be unreasonable demands on others, thus causing a great deal of resentment. If that is the case, you need to look at your practices to determine if they are in fact necessary components to aid you in what you would like to accomplish. If they are not, then maybe it is time to make some much needed changes, for the benefit of you and others.

Nine   If the Nine of Swords has entered into the Cross position, it seems you have a lot on your mind. You may be worried about something, and this anxiety is affecting other parts of your life, such as sleeping, eating and working habits. It is important, therefore, to keep your problems in perspective because they really are not as bad as they seem. The cards that follow should shed more light on the situation you are enquiring about.

Ten   If the Ten of Swords has appeared in the Cross position, it appears some-one has let you down in a really big way, so much so that the experience has served to colour your outlook on life. Perhaps you trusted someone, only to find they were not a suitable confidant. Alternatively, it could be that you have unwittingly said or done something that has inadvertently caused harm to another individual. It is for that reason you really need to be careful about who you associate with for your own and others' safety and wellbeing.

King   If the King of Swords has landed in the Cross position, you have encountered a man who may very well be a powerful person, but he may suffer from an ailment, which will affect his behaviour. He may very well have accomplished significant deeds in earlier years, but time has caught up with him and the brilliance he once displayed has turned to eccentricity at the very least. Because he once was such an active thinker, he may have fallen prey to a disease of the mind, such as Alzheimer's disease, psychosis, or any of the number of depressive illnesses that affect one's thinking patterns in this modern age. This individual probably needs a thorough medical examination to pinpoint precisely what the problem is, which will be a great help to his state of mind and wellbeing.

Queen   If the Queen of Swords has landed in the Cross position, you are thinking of a woman who has a quick mind and an equally sharp wit. Although she is very intelligent, she is resentful about life's missed opportunities, and has consequently become very bitter, oftentimes taking her frustrations out on innocent victims. Perhaps she has found life has passed her by because she passed up many opportunities that had been presented to her, hoping something better would come along, only to realise that what she passed up was the best she could possibly hope for. Alternatively, she may have made some unwise decisions only to later regret them. Any of a number of life events have served to colour her personality, which can be dour at the best of times. As a result of this, she could be a bitter gossip, trying to wreak havoc on the lives of others through the power of her words. It is therefore essential you take everything this woman says with a grain of salt because her hidden agendas may not necessarily be propitious to telling the truth.

Knight/Prince   If the Knight of Swords has landed in the Cross position, you are thinking of a young man. Because he is still young, he has not yet learned to focus his energies, and they have therefore become somewhat scattered. He also has not acquired maturity of expression and often cannot relate in a manner that is most appropriate to his needs. It is for that reason this individual can lash out in violence when he does not get his own way. Because he has such an active mind, he may put it to negative use, such as revenge, theft, and other nefarious activities. The cards that follow indicate the prominent part this individual will play in the scenario that prompted you to consult the oracle.

Page/Princess   If the Page of Swords has landed in the Cross position, you are thinking of a young person, quite possibly a woman. She has not yet grown up and acquired the wisdom that comes with experience, and can therefore act in immature ways. She can at times be indiscreet, which can land her and other individuals in hot water. When she has been slighted, she can react with malice because she has not yet learned that it is more graceful to turn the other cheek than to retaliate in kind.

Cups/Water

Ace   If the Ace of Cups has found itself in the Cross position, you have found yourself to be in a position where there is a false sense of happiness in your immediate surroundings. You may not be seeing life clearly at the moment, and have therefore lulled yourself into a state of self-denial, so on the surface you appear to be happy, but are you really? You may feel as if you are the luckiest person alive, but if you look closely, you will see there are tears in the make-up of your aura. It is not necessary for you to put on a happy face all of the time. Your true friends will still like you if they see you cry or show unhappiness. After all, you are only human, as we all are.

Two   If the Two of Cups has landed in the Cross position, there is a particular relationship that is not providing all the happiness and satisfaction it should. Perhaps because you were yearning so much for that one special person to come into your life, when someone did come along, you allowed yourself to be confused as to the true nature of the union. As with all relationships, this person has come to you at a specific point in time to allow you to grow and develop in your soul evolution, but the liaison may not necessarily be long lasting or ultimately fulfilling. Enjoy your time with this individual while it lasts, but it is wise not to make any long-term plans with him because he might not be the one who you are destined to spend eternity with.

Three   If the Three of Cups has landed in the Cross position, you may become involved in a social event that is not necessarily good for your soul growth. You may find yourself involved with a group of people who exert a negative influence on you and deter you from proceeding along your chosen path in this life. The cards that follow will reveal more about the situation you have become involved in.

Four   If the Four of Cups has landed in the Cross position, your wavering is holding you back in life. You are unable to make a decision and are listening to conflicting stories from a variety of people, and don't know who to believe. Instead of relying on your intuition, you wrongly trust the opinions of others, who all have agendas of their own. When you have taken the advice of other people and found it to be unsuitable to your needs, it is not those individuals who are going to have to live with the decisions you have made. It is for that reason you need to do what you feel is best, and not take a particular course of action just because you think it will make someone else happy.

Five   If the Five of Cups has landed in the Cross position, it seems as if you are very upset because someone or something has not lived up to your expectations. The despair you feel is understandable because in many ways you feel as if you have been misled. The individuals involved did not overtly deceive you, but because they knowingly did not fill you in on some crucial information, they are at the very least guilty of complicity. There is nothing you can do now except pick up the pieces and try to re-build your life from what remains. This will take time, however, because you need to heal the wounds of your soul and put the entire situation into its proper perspective before you can move on.

Six   If the Six of Cups has landed in the Cross position, it seems you are living in the past, and this constant rumination is affecting your ability to adequately deal with the future. Our mission in this sojourn is to focus on the now. To dwell in the past or live in the future will only cause us more problems in the long run because we are not living in the present. Stop, look, listen and think of what you are doing at this precise point in time.

Seven   If the Seven of Cups has landed in the Cross position, you are presented with several choices to select from, all of which seem to be very lucrative. The catch is that not one of the options available to you is what it seems, and each and every one has hidden pitfalls that you may or may not be aware of. If you must decide on a particular course of action, get plenty of advice, conduct research beforehand, and develop a contingency plan just in case you want to gracefully remove yourself from any sticky situation.

Eight   If the Eight of Cups has landed in the Cross position, it seems you have found yourself to be in a position from which it is difficult to extract yourself. Even if you haven't found yourself in an institution such as a jail, hospital, military or government organisation, you are mentally locked into an environment where you do not see a way out of a predicament that is causing you so much frustration. There is a way out, but you have been stuck in a rut for so long that your mind is not open to alternative ways of thinking. If you ask someone for advice, he may have the answer you seek to help you out of this dilemma.

Nine   If the Nine of Cups has landed in the Cross position, you are allowing your emotions to rule your sense of taste. It is for that reason you are compensating for negative emotions by allowing your sensory percep- tions to take over. You may be overeating, overdrinking or using drugs as a way to self-medicate and push those feelings you would rather not deal with to the back of your mind. In addition, all of this substance abuse is not doing your waistline any good. Maybe you can speak to a friend about what it is that is bothering you so you won't need a crutch in the form of one of the many substances that are being made available to you.

Ten   If the Ten of Cups has landed in the Cross position, you want desperately to live in a happy family, but the circumstances that prevail are prevent- ing you from accomplishing this. You may very well live in a family environment, but there is conflict within the unit that keeps it from being happy. The cards that follow will reveal the scenario in greater detail so you will have greater clarity about the situation that you are presently involved in.

King   If the King of Cups has landed in the Cross position, there is a very ruth- less man who has the capability to harm other people who get in his way. He has had a series of life experiences that have affected him to the extent that his thinking processes have been altered such that he is no longer capable of sane thought. It is for that reason this man is not so much a danger to himself as he is to other people. The cards that follow will reveal in greater detail how this individual will affect your life.

Queen   If the Queen of Cups has landed in the Cross position, a woman who has emotional difficulties figures prominently in the picture. She in all probability has come from a dysfunctional family herself, and did not get all of the love and support she needed as a child. She may have also had some traumatic life experiences as an adult that she has not been able to come to terms with, which has served to colour her entire perspective on life. It is for that reason this woman has hysterical outbursts and is somewhat of a bully to those who are vulnerable. Because she has a personality disorder, it is very difficult for her to get along with other people most of the time.

Knight/Prince If the Knight of Cups has entered into the Cross position, you are think-ing of a young man who has a few emotional difficulties. These emotional disturbances have crossed over into other areas of his life, as he may be an inconsistent lover or friend. He may also have addictions, which include relationships, sex, gambling and substance abuse. If you become involved with this person, be prepared for a rocky ride ahead.

Page/Princess If the Page of Cups has entered into the Cross position, you are thinking of a young person, probably a girl. She has some emotional difficulties and needs help adjusting to life in general. It seems that she can cry a lot, and at times can throw a tantrum or two. She may have an eating disorder or substance abuse problem because she uses over-indulgence as a way to self-medicate in the belief that she will not have to deal with her more traumatic life experiences.

3 Above

0 Fool If The Fool has found itself in the Above position, you have completed one cycle and are ready to begin a new direction in your life. Although you do not know where this new journey will lead you or what you will do, what is important to remember is that you will be protected along your path to true enlightenment. You will find that your experiences will be higher octaves of the ones you experienced in your previous cycle of existence.

I Magician If The Magician has landed in the Above position, you or someone close to you is a very mutable soul who is able to utilise the vast powers of your mind to manifest whatever you like in the physical realms of your existence. Some people call it magic, others call it a superior mental ability, but this individual can make things happen just by thinking about what he would like to occur. Sigil magic figures prominently in this placement, so it would be propitious to keep a diary and write down exactly what it is that you would like to achieve in this lifetime. You need to be careful what you ask for, however, because you just might get it.

II High Priestess If The High Priestess has entered into the Above position, you contain much wisdom and innate knowledge, which you can express through your intuitive thought processes. You are an old soul and have utilised the knowledge you have gained during the past incarnations to help you along your present earth walk. You are one of the carers and healers of this world, looking after those who for whatever reason have no one to care for them, and in the process you in turn will be cared for by the gratitude they will show you for your selflessness.

III Empress — If The Empress has landed in the Above position, there is a woman who figures prominently in the scenario that has prompted you to consult the oracle. She is very nurturing and is able to take care of and heal those in need who are a part of her immediate environment. This woman is quite focused on her family and possessions, so it is probable that this preoccupation will prevent her from extending her sphere of awareness to those outside her immediate surroundings. It is for that reason that those who are not a part of her immediate or extended family will not feel the warmth and loving generosity this person has within her. It is also for that reason that it will be difficult for people who do not have the advantage of her affection to understand why people like her, because she isn't particularly nice to people who she considers to be outsiders. Although this woman has many good qualities, she does not possess the selflessness of character that the High Priestess does. While she is good to her family, she is not necessarily benevolent to others, and can actually be wicked, cruel and spiteful if she feels threatened or jealous. This woman, although maternal, is not impartial and is quick to take sides in any dispute that will arise within her familial setting.

IV Emperor — If The Emperor has landed in the Above position, there is a very powerful man who has a great deal of influence over your current situation. This archetype corresponds with Solomon, King of ancient Israel, second son of David and Bathsheba. When God told him he would present him with anything he would like, King Solomon said he would like wisdom. In Jewish and Muslim literature Solomon appears not only as the wisest of sages but as one gifted with the power to control the spirits of the invisible world. He is frequently noted in history and literature as the builder of the Temple. Solomon succeeded his father despite the claims of Adonijah, his older half brother. He divided Israel into 12 parts for administrative purposes, and his territory extended 'from the river [Euphrates] unto the land of the Philistines, and unto the border of Egypt'. He made slaves of the Canaanites who remained in the land and formed an alliance with Hiram, King of Tyre. In return for food, Hiram furnished him with timber, and the ships of the allies went out trading together. The Temple, completed in about seven years, was built in great splendour with Hiram's aid and dedicated with much magnificence. Solomon's distinguishing quality was as an administrator. He kept the united kingdom largely intact, strengthened its fortifications, and made alliances not only with Tyre, but also with several other nations surrounding Israel. Commerce, consisting of trade by caravan and sea, and an extensive copper-mining industry were encouraged by the international intercourse. Contact with other nations also resulted in a marked intellectual advance, and it may be assumed that genuine literary activity was carried on. Solomon himself is traditionally regarded as an author of high skill and remarkable output. The writings that have been ascribed to him are the biblical Proverbs, the Song of Solomon, Ecclesiastes, the Wisdom of Solomon, and the later Psalms of Solomon and Odes of Solomon.

V Hierophant If The Hierophant has entered in the Above position, you have reached a major crossroad in your life and have an important decision to make with regard to the path you would like the rest of your life to take. Whatever course you decide upon, only positive things are destined to transpire, although some avenues will bring you greater soul growth than others. A professional person, teacher or religious leader may be able to direct you in the path that you need to be on, but it is important to trust your intuition and do what your higher self is urging you to do.

VI Lovers If The Lovers has landed in the Above position, it seems that you are at one with and in harmony with the universe. There are forces around you that are of a very positive nature, and you will come into contact with people who will help you to expand your soul growth. You may meet one particular person who is destined to take you on an esoteric journey that will enlighten you in ways you never thought possible. Your soul is evolving in the direction that has been preordained prior to your incarnation onto this earth plane. You or someone close to you may have met your one true love in this incarnation, and this encounter will be very beneficial for you to see the more positive aspects of the physical existence that you have chosen to incarnate into.

VII Chariot If The Chariot has landed in the Above position, you are able to focus on what it is you want from this life, which means ultimately you will be successful in what you set out to achieve. This card depicts a king, in his military garb, riding through the streets of his domain, which shows very clearly he is a powerful warrior ruler who seeks to win any battles he becomes involved in. You are an ambitious soul and have a regal aura, which indicates that people will stand back and take note of your presence. You are usually on the move, which means you may take up a vocation or lifestyle choice that takes you to far away places and in contact with exotic peoples. Although the military is not necessarily an ideal vocation because of the ethics such a profession promotes, it will enable you to travel, see the world, and utilise some of your leadership abilities.

VIII Strength If Strength has landed in the Above position, you are instilled with an air of charm and grace that makes you approachable to others around you. It is for that reason you have many admirers and friends. In addition, you possess natural good looks, which you will keep even in old age. You do not wither with age as some do, but ripen and mature with each passing year. There is an inner strength in you that you have acquired through encountering and conquering the many adversities life has a way of placing in our path. Animals play an important part at this time in your life, as they can afford you valuable comfort and healing to enable you to come to terms with some of the more turbulent life experiences in your past.

IX Hermit If The Hermit has landed in the Above position, you or someone you know is a very knowledgeable soul who can impart your wisdom to others just by the sheer act of being. You have the unusual ability to lead by example, which is a lot more than can be said for many leaders of today. You maintain a simplistic lifestyle, which enables you to focus your attention on other areas of the physical realms of existence. During intense periods of meditation, you are able to get a glimpse of alternate realities that most of us only ponder the existence of, but have had no real cognisant experience of. It is for that reason you are not overly impressed by the treasures that can be found in the material world, as they pale in comparison to what exists within other realms of the higher levels of our consciousness. When Jesus said, 'In my father's house are many mansions,' he was referring to the esoteric realities that await us if we are willing to open our minds and free ourselves of the chains that have bound us to the physical world.

X Wheel of Fortune If The Wheel of Fortune has landed in the Above position, it has been decided that the wheel will turn in your favour and lady luck is smiling down upon you. Expect good things to come your way, such as money, a new job, or acclaim and recognition. What is important, however, is to keep a level head and not allow your good fortune to inflate your sense of self worth. The winds of change are fickle, and it is for that reason that everything could be taken away from you just as quickly as it was given.

XI Justice If Justice has appeared in the Above position, a judgement is very likely going to be made in your favour. There has been a matter that you have been unable to resolve using your own resources, so you have had to approach an outside source for help. This mediator has very likely decided that you are legitimate in your request, which should make you breathe a sigh of relief. On the same note, you may find you have been asked to preside over an issue of importance to another person. It is essential therefore that you act in your delegated position wisely because your reputation will be determined by how well or badly you handle yourself in this matter.

XII Hanged Man   If The Hanged Man has found itself in the Above position, you are an enlightened soul who quite often has no need for the trappings of every day life. It is for that reason you tend to take life as it comes because you want to fully experience the journey you are currently involved in to enable you to further develop your soul. This sojourn is very likely one of your final incarnations in the earth plane because you have experienced much of the physical realms on this plane of existence. You will move on to a higher plane of awareness, but in the meantime, it is important to impart your spirituality onto others so they can begin to realise there is more to this world than meets the eye.

XIII Death   If Death has landed in the Above position, there are some very transformative qualities that need to be addressed before you can proceed along your destined path to enlightenment. You have reached a point in your life where you can no longer carry on as before, and circumstances will occur that will force you to make much needed changes to your life. The situation that you will soon be entering will be nothing like the one you have known in the past. Because you have no comprehension of what is to come, words cannot describe what you will soon be experiencing. The only thing you can do is to fully live and experience every moment of the phase of the transformation you will be undertaking. This will help you to attain greater understanding of your existence before and after the major cataclysm that will accomplish nothing less than total renewal of your soul. You will be able to see with clarity why certain situations in your life have progressed in such a way, because without such an experience, you would never have been given the opportunity to step into a new world that will be much more rewarding than the old one.

XIV Temperance   If Temperance has landed in the Above position, you need to cultivate the art of patience before the good things you are deserving of will come to you. Balance is the key here because it is all too easy to view life in one particular direction, which will ultimately lead you on a trail that is not intended for you. The best course of action is to stick to the tried and true, and keep your focus on the ultimate goal, which lies far in the future. It is important to allow the universe to take its time to act because universal time is completely different from the time we perceive on earth. What to us is years could be a blink of an eye in a universe, and what to us is the blink of an eye could the amount of time necessary to see the birth, growth and death of an entire universe. The reason is that time is occurring linearly, logarithmically, forwards, backwards and laterally all at once.

XV Devil   If The Devil has entered the Above position, there is nothing to fear from this placement. While in the West, the Devil is portrayed as a malefic being who attempts to wreak havoc on the best laid plans of mice and men, other cultures do not see this being in such a way. The Native Americans have a ceremony called the sweat lodge. This ritual is of religious significance and can best be described as their 'church'. The Keeper of the Fire is one of the most esteemed positions within the ceremony because he starts the fire and keeps it burning throughout the entire process. With this in mind, the Devil is a much maligned character indeed and does have a useful purpose in our lives. He resides in the earth plane and reminds us on a daily basis that we have been put here in the physical world to experience what we would be unable to explore in other realms existence. The Devil is the practical side of ourselves, if not a little mischievous. It is the archetype that helps us to stay grounded to the earth plane.

XVI Tower   If The Tower has entered into the Above position, be prepared for opportunities to come to you that are disguised as a loss of some kind. You may lose your job only to find that a better, more rewarding one is presented to you just around the corner. You may find you have to move house, only to discover that you have found a new place that will give you a great deal more happiness and peace of mind. The important thing to remember is that when God closes a door, he opens a window, thereby allowing new opportunities to come to you. There are always alternatives available to you; you only need to use a bit of imagination to perceive them.

XVII Star   If The Star has appeared in the Above position, you are full of Aquarium ideals and therefore possess great deal of enlightenment about your present situation and hope for the future. No matter how dismal life may seem at this point in time, you still must look on the bright side and look forward to a better future. You have dreams, which you must never let go of, regardless of how strong the opposition to the attainment of your goals may be. If you keep a positive mental attitude, you will find that, even in the darkest of times, there is a light at the end of the esoteric tunnel.

XVIII Moon   If The Moon has landed in the Above position, you are a very intuitive being who is able to read people and situations in a highly perceptive manner. It is therefore essential that you go with your feelings on any particular matter because logic is not necessarily a clear indicator of signs of the times. Trust your instincts and you cannot go wrong. You will also find friends in the most unlikely of places, so it is important to keep all of your options open.

XIX Sun   If The Sun has landed in the Above position, you have a very sunny disposition and can quite often be the life and soul of any party or social gathering. There is a bright light shining over you to ensure higher beings are looking after you and making sure you are secure in this physical world. If you are planning to start a family, it is a very propitious time to do so, as children are in the offing. In order to become one with the universe, you may find the presence of plants and animals to be a soothing experience because they contain innocence and the universal life force, which you will be able to draw off.

XX Judgement   If Judgement has landed in the Above position, you are going through a major healing process that will serve to cleanse your soul to enable you to resume your karmic journey. You may spend some time in convalescence after an illness, which is break you need to undergo in order to continue your path on this earth plane. In addition, you may spend some time in hospital, but again, this is necessary to correct an imbalance that has existed in your auric makeup for quite some time. You will, however, emerge a renewed being, able to cope with the normal day-to-day stresses that had previously seemed daunting to you, after the healing process has begun.

XXI World   If The World has landed in the Above position, it seems you have become a whole being through your past experiences. Although life inevitably presents us with obstacles we must overcome in order to progress along our spiritual path to enlightenment, it seems you have managed those hurdles in a manner that has satisfactorily heightened your psychological makeup. You are a mature, well-developed being, which is quite rare in the fast paced lifestyle that most 21st century Westerners embark upon. There will be other lessons for you to learn, but they are nothing you will not be well equipped to handle. You have within yourself the skill and aptitude to achieve your destiny. You will find the only limitations you will encounter are within your own mind.

Wands/Rods/Fire

Ace   If the Ace of Wands has landed in the Above position, there are some highly creative influences at work, which are going to bring about a satisfactory resolution to any dilemmas that you may be currently encountering. You may be thinking of initiating a new project, such as a book, a business venture, a holiday, a new home, or even an addition to your family, which is taking up a great deal of your thought processes. Whatever you decide to do in relation to expanding your present sphere of awareness can only be a positive endeavour because it will bring new experiences to you and help you to fulfil your own personal destiny.

Two   If the Two of Wands has landed in the Above position, you are considering embarking upon a partnership with another person, which could very well yield benefits for the both of you. While this deed will be formed for the sole purpose of completing a specific task, you will find it to be a rewarding experience because in addition to focusing on what it is you should be accomplishing, you will find you have made a friend in the process. This friendship will be much more satisfying to you than any material successes you may have, so it is important that you nurture your contact with this person and respect the relationship the two of you will go on to develop.

Three   If the Three of Wands has appeared in the Above position, it is quite likely that you will find yourself involved with a group of people to accomplish one particular task. It could be work, social or spiritual, but you will gather together to embark upon a creative journey that would not be possible if you were to embark upon it on your own. What your group is able to accomplish with combined efforts will be a very worthwhile venture, which will enhance your reputation amongst your peers and hold you in a high esteem for some time to come. You will also learn valuable team working and leadership skills, which are a must if you wish to succeed in most ventures nowadays.

Four   If the Four of Wands has landed in the Above position, you have a very important reason to celebrate. It seems good fortune has been smiling upon you, and you will feel a renewed sense of solidity and security within yourself. You may have decided to embark upon an endeavour, such as a new house, job or programme of training that will assure you future material security. This card also indicates celebrations of some kind, most probably featuring other family members who you think fondly of, will be taking place.

Five   If the Five of Wands has appeared in the Above position, it appears you are engaged in a battle of wills with at least one other person. While you believe you know very well what the conflict you have become involved in is all about, in actual fact, you don't. There are subtle influences operating in the background, which you are only vaguely aware of. A case in point is the fact that governments all over the world send young men and women to fight and die for causes that are not necessarily their own. If these young people had even an inkling of the notion of the true realities of what they were shedding blood for, they would be horrified, and would subsequently refuse to take up arms and fight wars for other people. It is for this reason the highly effective propaganda machines all over the world use brainwashing techniques and allow their young men and women to die for highly dubious causes, such as oil, money, and world domination. Because you know other more powerful beings are at the root of your troubles, it is essential that you ensure your activities are above reproach, so that your reputation will remain intact when all is eventually revealed.

Six   If the Six of Wands has appeared in the Above position, you have a very good reason to celebrate because you have made a significant achievement in your life. You have worked hard to get where you are, and can pat yourself on the back for a job well done. What is important to remember, however, is that all of life is a series of minor and major struggles that help us to progress along our spiritual path in this world. It is therefore essential that you continue to strive for excellence beyond the success you have achieved so far because, as you will soon find out, there is so much more to come.

Seven   If the Seven of Wands has appeared in the Above position, you will need to work hard to hang onto your recent acquisitions. You may find there is a great deal of competition around you, and your competitors would love nothing better than to have some of your good fortune. It is one thing to get your heart's desire, but it is quite another to keep it. It is therefore essential that you keep this in mind when you carry on with your day-to-day activities. That which has been given to you can just as easily be taken from you, so it is up to you to keep that which is yours.

Eight   If the Eight of Wands has landed in the Above position, be prepared to go somewhere out of the ordinary. Even if you are not in a position to physically travel to a distant place, you may find you have some fascinating out of body experiences in the form of dreams or astral projections that will expand your present level of awareness. These experiences will give you renewed clarity about the meaning of your existence and help you to carry on, knowing there is so much more to the world than our primary senses can normally perceive.

Nine   If the Nine of Wands has appeared in the Above position, you rightly carry an air of vigilance in your mannerisms. You have worked very hard to get where you are today and it would be unwise to let go of well-established procedures that you have adopted at this time. In order to keep what you have, it is necessary to nurture it and guard it fiercely, thereby assuring success and stability for years to come.

Ten   If the Ten of Wands has appeared in the Above position, you have a huge task ahead of you. You may feel that you are not up to achieving what you have been presented with, but you should be aware that you have within yourself all of the skills necessary to accomplish the objective. It will entail a great deal of effort on your part to achieve satisfactory results, but any sacrifices you make now will be returned to you tenfold. Although you do not realise it at this time, you do have the situation under control, even if you do not feel it to be so. It is important to keep on keeping on and never give up because it is only at the end of your journey that you will realise just how much you have actually accomplished.

King   If the King of Wands appears in the Above position, you are thinking of a person who has a vast amount of business flair that can be used to help you to advance in your current situation. This person has much energy, which will be to your advantage, and can be used to help you to attain your goals. He is can present his ideas in such a way that people will listen to what he has to say. He is able to read people and situations and use the knowledge he has acquired to his advantage, thereby knowing when to pursue a specific course of action and when to abandon a non-productive project altogether. Success is assured if you play your cards right and make this individual your friend.

Queen   If the Queen of Wands has landed in the Above position, you are thinking of a very intuitive person who relies on flashes of inspiration to help her to achieve her goals. She has a lot of creativity to use as an outlet for the energy within. Hobbies where she can use her hands, and sports activities will help to tame the wild side of her nature, thus enabling her to aspire to ethical goals in the area of business, enterprise and social activities.

**Knight/
Prince**
If the Knight of Wands has entered into the Above position, you are thinking of a young man who is very impetuous and has much energy, which he may or may not know how to properly utilise. He has a great deal of get up and go, and will be able to achieve a great deal when he acquires more life experiences and confidence that can only be achieved by successful living and a stable relationship.

**Page/
Princess**
If the Page of Wands has entered into the Above position, you are thinking of a young person who has a great deal of energy and creativity within herself. She is happy because she has not yet encountered the dark forces that prevail in our society today, and hopefully she will not be subjected to them in this incarnation. You may at times feel you have your hands full because of the exuberant personality of this individual, but you have within yourself the ability to calm down her exuberance for life in an effective manner. Your contact with this person will prove to be beneficial, as you will be able to re-experience many of the child-like qualities that you have long forgotten and thought had faded into the distant past.

Pentacles/Disks/Earth

Ace
If the Ace of Pentacles has landed in the Above position, you have a great deal of financial acumen you can use to help build a firm foundation as a basis for your future security and prosperity. Possessions are very important to you, but only in the sense that they afford you the ability to live an affluent lifestyle, which is something that all of us aspire to whether we openly admit it or not. With your goal of material prosperity in mind, you may very well exert a great deal of skill and a high level of expertise in your chosen profession, thereby enabling you to accumulate all of the nice things you would like to be surrounded by.

Two
If the Two of Pentacles has landed in the Above position, you have money coming in from various sources and money going out to several different people. It is for that reason you need to keep a tight reign on your expenditures to make sure your financial situation stays balanced. You may find that in addition to your main vocation, which provides the bulk of your income, you have a few part time ventures that top up your earnings, thereby enabling you to purchase those extra items you would not otherwise have been able to afford. Because your financial situation is so precarious at this time, it would be wise to live simply and keep your expenses to a minimum, thereby minimising any negative influences that may surround you.

Three   If the Three of Pentacles has appeared in the Above position, you have a good head on your shoulders and are able to use it to your advantage. You are able to focus your energies in a practical manner to help to achieve the material success you aspire to in order to live a comfortable lifestyle. In order to achieve the material prosperity that you desire, you would be wise to work within the established, traditional framework of business and enterprise, which of course entails hard work, in order to build a better future for yourself and others.

Four   If the Four of Pentacles has found itself in the Above position, you are very good at hanging on to your possessions and managing your money. You would be wise not reveal a great deal about yourself and your possessions, which will keep others wondering about your true material worth. There are some people in this world who do not possess a strong work ethic and would endeavour to live off the hard work of others if they could. It is for that reason that you would be wise to live a modest lifestyle so you don't attract the wrong type of people to yourself. You are very good at utilising your resources so they produce maximum efficiency, which will come in handy during those lean times, which inevitably affect us all due to the buoyancy of the universe.

Five   If the Five of Pentacles has appeared in the Above position, it appears that you are presently going through a rough patch as an exercise in your soul development. Perhaps you need to experience first hand what it is like to be down in the dumps in order to have empathy and understanding for others because it is the only way you can truly feel the anguish of another soul. In any event, the tough times you are encountering will lighten up soon enough, giving you a fresh perspective into what it is like to be in need of a helping hand. Once you overcome this rough patch, you will find that you will have greater empathy and understanding for other individuals who seem to be having difficulty coping in our very material world.

Six   If the Six of Pentacles has appeared in the Above position, it is essential that you carry an air of benevolence because there are other individuals who are less fortunate than yourself and are in need of your assistance. The world is full of needy people, and while you surely cannot be expected to help each and every soul who crosses your path, you are morally obliged to lend a helping hand to some of those who are in need. You may feel your meagre efforts could do nothing to even put a dent into the masses of poverty that abound in our world today, but any act of kindness that you commit will not go unnoticed in the universe.

One noted English spiritualist, when thinking of how little she had to contribute to the poor and needy in her area lamented, 'All I can do is make pie!'. Years later, the same woman was in charge of distributing pies to the homeless all over England. Even though all she could do was make pie, that one small skill went a long way to ease the plight of many homeless and needy people.

Seven   If the Seven of Pentacles has appeared in the Above position, you have entered into a period of waiting. The individuals concerned in this scenario are still contemplating what it is they would like to do next, so it is essential not to push them into doing something irrevocable. If you appear too eager, you will be pre-empted in midstream before the situation has an opportunity to come to fruition. On the same note, if you appear indifferent to the circumstances, chances are that you will not get your heart's desire either, because it is felt that you will not put forth the effort required to sustain whatever it is that you wish for. It is therefore essential to maintain an eager stance while not getting too involved in the situation at hand, so you can maximise any opportunities that might come your way.

Eight   If the Eight of Pentacles has landed in the Above position, you have reached a point in your life where you need to acquire new skills along your path of soul evolution. Opportunities will present themselves to allow you to take up a new vocation or hobby, and these instances will be valuable learning times for you to show yourself and others what you are truly capable of. Because we live in a world where there are so many negativities, it would be nice to make a positive contribution and accomplish something that you previously did not have the self-confidence to embark upon. This card also indicates that it would be beneficial for you to take up a new venture that involves working with your hands, such as needlework, woodwork, craftwork or building. It is important to note that it has been observed that in less technologically advanced cultures, people do not suffer from neurosis nearly as much as those who live in Western society, and it is believed, therefore, that the reason for this is because they keep their hands busy and do not have the time to think laboriously on inconsequential subjects.

Nine   If the Nine of Pentacles has landed in the Above position, your material and physical needs are being met, which is enabling you to take a break from the world around you and relax a bit. You may be in a period of convalescence, which is a much needed time to enable you to recuperate and recharge your weary soul. This is also a period of solitary independence because the card is traditionally depicted as a lone person enjoying the garden scenery. It is for this reason you must be aware that you must take your path solely on your own, quite possibly with no one to help you accomplish your goals. You may very well encounter people on your journey, but they are not in a position to help you in the manner that you would like, which at times will be more of a hindrance than a help. With this knowledge in mind, you will be able to successfully accomplish the task being asked of you, which is becoming an independent person in the universe.

Ten   If the Ten of Pentacles has landed in the Above position, you may have inherited wealth, prosperity or some other resources from your family. It is for that reason you are very closely linked to your family, as you tend to rely upon them for support, as they do you. Even if you are not financially well off, you are rich in many other ways, thereby not feeling the need to acquire copious amounts of material wealth in this life.

King   If the King of Pentacles has appeared in the Above position, you are thinking of an affluent man who very likely works in a professional capacity. He has a good eye for business and invests his money in what he feels will bring him even more material resources. This individual is a respected member of society and has many contacts, thereby making him an exceptional ally. He is a good person to befriend, as he is generous and benevolent to those individuals who he is fond of and feels are in need of help.

Queen   If the Queen of Pentacles has landed in the Above position, you are thinking about a woman who is very well to do in her environment. It is quite likely that she is highly thought of in her milieu, perhaps because she presents a calming, sensible influence during times of transition. It is quite likely this woman has come into wealth, either through her partner or her family, and therefore has no need to work, as many of her contemporaries are obliged to do. Because of her circumstances, she has a great deal of confidence and does not worry unnecessarily about the future.

Knight/ Prince   If the Knight of Pentacles has landed in the Above position, you are thinking of a young man who is well on his way to building a substantial fortune for himself. He is slow and methodical, and takes his time in completing any projects he is given. He has a very noble character and can teach us all a great deal about the ethics in what is quite often an immoral and wicked world.

Page/ Princess
If the Page of Pentacles has landed in the Above position, you are just beginning to develop an appreciation for the materiality in the world we live in and are developing an understanding of the importance of the physical world around you. Alternatively, there may be a demure young person around you who is teaching you a great deal about your responsibilities in this world.

Swords/Air

Ace
If the Ace of Swords has landed in the Above position, you are in the midst of an intellectual experience where new ideas are coming to you at an astounding rate. You are utilising thought processes that have been residing dormant in the recesses of your mind for years, and you may not know how to handle the abundance of mental imagery that is flashing through your mind at an alarming rate. There may have been experiences that you could not fully understand at the time, so you pushed those experiences into the recesses of your mind. The time has come for you to recall those events and you may not be able to deal with the feelings and emotions that come with them. In the past you may have been able to get through life by keeping a mental agenda of the sequence of events that compose your life, but you have found now it is simply not enough. In order to help you to keep track of all of the flashes of inspiration that are coming to you, you will need to write them down, making notes of the most seemingly inconsequential of thoughts that come to mind. A notebook where you log your itinerary, obligations, thoughts, responsibilities and ideas will come in handy during this time of rapid growth and soul assessment.

Two
If the Two of Swords has landed in the Above position, you have reached a point in your life where you cannot continue any longer with your current mindset. You have been brought up to believe in certain principles, and up until very recently felt that they were accurate reflections of the way the world revolves. Events of late, however, have given you cause to re-think your primary certitude, which has given rise to a mental crisis within your psyche. You know that in order to develop and evolve as a member of the human race, you must discard biased opinions that were impregnated into your mind when you were still a young, impressionable being. You know you must change your thinking processes before you can successfully navigate through the ideological cataclysm you are currently experiencing, and the sooner you do so the easier it will be for you in the long run.

Three   If the Three of Swords has landed in the Above position, there is a situation that you are aware of and, although it causes you a great deal of anguish, is giving you the opportunity to reflect and think about your current position in life. You know you need to cut a few things out of your life, whether they are destructive relationships, addictions, or a lifestyle that no longer suits you, but as soon as you do, the good things you deserve will come to you without any effort on your part.

Four   If the Four of Swords has found itself in the Above position, you have found yourself to be in a period of inner reflection, a time where you can meditate about the true meaning of your life. As you know, now is not the time to move about in action, but to still your soul and mind, allowing yourself to listen to the gentle rustle of particles colliding just beyond the normal range of human hearing. When you are able to hear the atomic particles that result only from the stillness of your mind, it will be then that you can hear the calm, sober voice of your inner self telling you the correct action to take regarding the situation that prompted you to consult the oracle in the first place.

Five   If the Five of Swords has fallen in the Above position, you need time to reflect on a difficult situation that you have become involved in. You may be at odds with some people who are able to make or break your reputation amongst your contemporaries, so how you handle yourself is of the utmost importance. Under the circumstances it is probably best to part company with the individuals who you are in disagreement with, for the time being anyway. How you go about severing the ties, however, is just as important as your decision to cease communication with others. Therefore, it is best to stay calm and endeavour to maintain a professional attitude at all times, even with those individuals who you do not particularly care for.

Six   If the Six of Swords has appeared in the Above position, you are coming out of a very difficult situation that has been a large part of your life for quite some time. This situation has been very emotive in nature, which has had the resulting effect of causing you a great deal of mental anguish, as you may not have known precisely how to respond. Once you make the conscious decision to move on, things will improve slowly but surely. The main hurdle you must overcome is your mindset, because you must accept the fact that no matter how hard you try, you cannot change the past. No matter how traumatic your past experiences may have been, those events have formed you into the person you are today. With the help of good friends and a positive attitude, things can only get better. It is important that you realise, however, that only you can improve the situation you are currently in and move on to other areas of awareness.

Seven   If the Seven of Swords has fallen in the Above position, you need to keep your thoughts and feelings close to your heart. Maintain a surreptitious nature and trust no one with matters close to your heart. In addition, keep your assets well hidden so you can protect them from less ethical individuals who would seek to steal them from you.

Eight   If the Eight of Swords has landed in the Above position, you know you have become stagnated in your current thinking patterns and need a change of scenery. The problem is that in order to go about making changes, you need to begin a new venture that will put you in touch with different types of people and new experiences that will enhance your current level of spiritual awareness. Even the simplest move, such as beginning a new hobby or enrolling in a course of study will work wonders to expand your mind and show you alternatives that you had not previously considered.

Nine   If the Nine of Swords has landed in the Above position, you are in a self-imposed isolation and are spending a great deal of time involved in intense thought. Although some people who do not fully understand the problem would disagree, you need this time on your own to help to reflect upon how the past has made you the person you are today, and exactly what type of person you will be in the future. You may suddenly remember incidents that had long been buried within the recesses of your sleeping consciousness, which would leave you quite perplexed as you wonder if they are accurate reflections of the past or mere fantasy. These mental pictures that come into your head may very well contradict what you have been brought up to believe, which can be even more confusing to you as you endeavour to gain an understanding of them. In time, the truth will be revealed and you will have a greater understanding of exactly what those mental pictures actually mean. But for the time being, it is only necessary for you to acknowledge the thoughts that come into your mind and let them pass without note.

Ten   If the Ten of Swords has appeared in the Cross position, it seems that you have entered into a low point in your life. People who you trusted and relied upon have let you down, and this has had a knock-on effect of bringing you into a deep depression. You need to take a break to recharge your batteries and re-think the associations you have made. Perhaps you have attracted the wrong sort of people to yourself, which is part of the problem. If your relationships were healthy, you would not be feeling so low, now would you? After a time of solitude and reflection, you will know what it is that you need to do.

King If the King of Swords has appeared in the Above position, a knowledgeable man is influencing the situation that has prompted you to consult the oracle. He very likely serves in a mentor capacity because he is well educated in his area of expertise. Because he has superb communication skills, he is able to get his point across eloquently and can therefore easily sway others to his line of thinking. It is for that reason that he is a valuable ally who can help you when you need him the most. If you upset him, however, he can also be a bitter foe.

Queen If the Queen of Swords has appeared in the Above position, you are thinking of a knowledgeable woman who is a major influence on the situation that prompted you to consult the oracle. She knows a great deal about a wide variety of subjects, and when you speak to her you will be amazed about her breadth of awareness on many things. Because she is not a particularly pretentious person, you may not at first suspect her true intelligence and worth in a world that is primarily dominated by the wealth and material possessions we are often compelled to acquire. If you speak to her about what is on your mind, her words of wisdom will lead you well on the path to finding the answers you seek.

Knight/Prince If the Knight of Swords has appeared in the Above position, your mind is on a young man who is a major influence on the situation that prompted the reading. He is quite intelligent and is able to formulate his thinking patterns in a highly focused manner, which will help him to achieve a great deal when he matures. He has a lot on his mind and can appear preoccupied to those who are not aware of his many mental activities. It is likely that he has a wide social network because he is able to relate to the variety of people that exist in our culture today. It is for that reason he always has something to do and is rarely at a loose end.

Page/ Princess If the Page of Swords has appeared in the Above position, you are thinking of a young person who is witty, sociable and likes to communicate. It is likely she is quite vociferous, but if circumstances prevent her from talking, she will make her feelings known through gestures, writing, emails, art or music. She is generally a happy person and is well on her way to becoming a good conversationalist. Alternatively, this placement indicates a message of an important nature is forthcoming, so it is important to keep an eye out for any clues that will reveal the true nature of this piece of information.

Cups/Water

Ace   If the Ace of Cups has appeared in the Above position, the potential for emotional happiness and abundance exists within yourself if you maintain an optimistic attitude. There is a great deal of love that flows through your being, and it will be transferred to those close to you. Even during difficult patches you will be able to look ahead to better times that will keep you balanced and on an even keel when other, less optimistic souls would falter.

Two   If the Two of Cups has appeared in the Above position, you are engaged in a relationship with another person that is essential for your soul growth. You may be in the early stages of a courtship of sorts, which means you are still infatuated with this person who has just come into your life, and are totally in awe of everything he or she does. It is for that reason you are happy just being in this individual's presence, not yet taking any serious notice of the subtle nuances that make this individual unique. The sense of self-satisfaction you feel with your new partner will have the effect of moving into other areas of your life, and others will find you generally have a much more pleasant temperament.

Three   If the Three of Cups has landed in the Above position, you have cause to celebrate, and will in all likelihood receive social invitations that will allow you to meet new people and hopefully make a few more friends. You have a pleasant disposition, which will make you a likely candidate when invitations are being handed out. If for some reason you are short of social engagements, you may well decide to organise events yourself. Who knows who may show an interest in socialising with you? You will never know until you try.

Four   If the Four of Cups has appeared in the Above position, you are taking time out to reflect upon contradictory information you are being given from various sources close to you. Because several people are attempting to put ideas in your head that are at variance to what you believe to be true, you may at times feel confused and not know what precisely to believe. If you carefully research the situation from credible sources of information, and then trust your intuition, you will come to the correct conclusion in the end.

Five   If the Five of Cups has appeared in the Above position, you have slowly come to the realisation that a certain situation has not turned out as you had anticipated. Although the clarity of this situation has caught you somewhat by surprise, and you had not planned for events to transpire in the manner they have, you are in a position to correct any mistakes that have been made. Now is the time to take stock of many areas of your life, so you would be wise to consider those things that you feel you have failed at. If there are any aspects of your life that you are not happy with, you have within yourself the ability to make any necessary changes, thus ensuring happiness in the future.

Six   If the Six of Cups has appeared in the Above position, be prepared to encounter someone from your past. It is likely you will have fond memories of his person, and you will spend time reminiscing about past experiences you both have had together. This individual may put you in touch with some people who can help you in some capacity, so it is best to stay on good terms with him even during those turbulent times. In addition, you may find yourself in the presence of children, who will help you to see life from an entirely different perspective than what adults normally perceive.

Seven   If the Seven of Cups has appeared in the Above position, you have been presented with a number of choices, of which you can select only one. Each option available to you appears to yield highly beneficial results, but it is for you to determine which choice will be best in the long run for your own personal growth. It is therefore essential that you research each and every option available to you thoroughly, asking advice only of those individuals who are qualified to give it, and then using your intuition and best judgement to select the appropriate course of action that will help your destiny to unfold in a positive way.

Eight   If the Eight of Cups has landed in the Above position, you are walking into an area that is totally alien to you because it involves a sequence of life events you have not yet experienced. It is for that reason you are not sure of what the future has in store, and you therefore carry a feeling of foreboding, possibly expecting the worst. There is no need to worry because you will soon realise that you have within yourself all the skills necessary to accomplish the task at hand. Although you are not so sure of your abilities at this time, you will get through this uncertain time and find you can rely on a little help from your friends along the way.

Nine   If the Nine of Cups has appeared in the Above position, you are quite a popular person, as you receive many invitations to social events where food and drink are readily available. You are, as a rule, content with yourself and know very well how to have a good time, which will ultimately make you a popular person amongst your contemporaries. People only want to be around happy individuals, so the ability to uplift others is a definite asset when it comes to making friends and influencing others. The happiness you feel exudes throughout your entire being, and those around you can catch a glimpse of the satisfaction that you can aspire to if you are balanced, well adjusted, and fair in your dealings with others.

Ten   If the Ten of Cups has appeared in the Above position, you have reached a point in your life where you have good reason to be happy, contented and settled. The influences surrounding you indicate you are a very secure in your relationships with others, thereby bringing harmony and happiness to others. Your intimate relationships will flourish, as you will be drawn to your one true soul mate in this life.

King   If the King of Cups has landed in the Above position, there is a very affectionate man in the scene who has a great deal of intensity and depth in his interactions with others. He is highly perceptive and is able to tap into a kind of reality that more practical beings would only scoff at. It is for that reason he is able to impart advice and feelings to others with a sincerity that is unmatched in the other court cards.

Queen   If the Queen of Cups has appeared in the Above position, a very sensitive, intuitive woman plays a paramount part in the situation you are currently involved in. She is very aware of what is going on, both on a logical and emotional level, and can therefore suss out people and situations quickly and effectively. She may be somewhat quiet, keeping her opinions to herself, only revealing what is on her mind when she is asked directly for her assessment of the situation.

Knight/ Prince   If the Knight of Cups has landed in the Above position, you have come across a sensitive, intuitive young man. Because he has not yet become cynical as a result of the cruel ways of the world, he is still able to show love and affection in a genuine, caring manner to other individuals. He is very sincere and honest, and can become hurt quite easily. It is therefore essential to nurture the love he freely gives so it remains healthy, pure and enduring.

Page/ Princess   If the Page of Cups has landed in the Above position, a young person who is very intuitive and sensitive is clearly in the picture. She has much to teach you about unconditional love and forgiveness, which can only be perceived through the eyes of a young person. When you have learned the lessons you can learn only through this special person, you will be able to move on to your next stage of esoteric development.

4 Below

0 Fool If The Fool has landed in the Below position, you have made the conscious or unconscious decision to take a divergent path, which is not necessarily good for your soul growth. This route will ultimately lead to your own self-demise, but unfortunately you may learn this later rather than sooner. The time you spend embarking upon these new activities will show you at a much later date that you are really very naïve, and your time would be better spent focusing on more noble endeavours. Although you are somewhat misguided in your approach to the situation at this time, you are ultimately protected and hopefully will find yourself returning to the journey that was meant for you with minimal inconvenience.

I Magician If The Magician has landed in the Below position, there is an individual around you who is astutely cunning. He thinks highly of himself and prides himself on his ability to manipulate people and situations to get them to do his bidding. He is a master salesman, as he works to influence people for his own personal gain. He may be somewhat misguided and genuinely try to persuade people because he honestly believes his particular philosophy to be the one true path in this world. He sees himself as a shape-shifter, shaping time, people, objects and animals to suit his own needs. He is able to use his hypnotic powers to manipulate situations to his advantage. Because he has a friendly demeanour and a smile on his face, it is difficult for casual observers to recognise his subtle techniques of persuasion are the very early stages of the dark arts, for which much mischief has been brought down to earth. This man is very superficial and there is no love in his heart, so you need to be wary of him. You also need to search the depths of your inner being to make sure the person who the oracle is describing isn't you.

II High Priestess   If The High Priestess has landed in the Below position, there is a woman who has very strong psychic abilities, and she is not necessarily using the gift for the good that it was intended. She may very well be somewhat of a malicious gossip, relaying misinformation to others in the guise of concern. She may have difficulties in her relationships with the opposite sex, which leaves her preferring the company of women. These relationships with women, however, can be fraught with just as many, if not more, obstacles than her relationships with men, as they take on the extremes and intensities of an actual marriage. This woman has little, if any, maternal instincts and would prefer to remain childless. If this woman does have children despite her lack of nurturing skills, her offspring in all probability will be neglected and ultimately suffer from psychological problems as a result of their rather austere upbringing.

III Empress   If The Empress has appeared in the Below position, there is a woman who tends to use her status as a mother to get what she wants out of life. She may elect to have a family in the hopes that it will secure her a home, husband and food on the table, which in this day and age is a totally unrealistic reason to bring children into the world. If she already has children, she may use her children as a means to get extra benefits or acquire status by some other means. If this woman's children are grown, she may use emotional blackmail as a means to get her offspring to do what she would like. Most of the family members who this woman deals with tend to suffer in silence, never daring to assert themselves for fear that she may withdraw the little love that she has to offer. As they mature, however, they will tire of her manipulativeness and she could very well find herself all alone in the world.

IV Emperor   If The Emperor has landed in the Below position, you have come across a man who seems to be very powerful. The problem is that he abuses the power that has been bestowed upon him, which he will ultimately have to atone for in this life or the next. Because he does not care who he steps on as long as he gets what he wants, he is liable to make many enemies on his way to the top. When circumstances change and he loses his authority in the world, the people who he harmed will remember all the trouble he caused in times past, and they will consequently allow him to suffer in the same way that he allowed others to suffer.

V Hierophant   If The Hierophant has appeared in the Below position, it relates to a religious ceremony that is taking place for all the wrong reasons. It could be a couple are deciding to marry for reasons other than true love and mutual friendship, which means without a strong foundation the union is destined to wither and die. This card placement also indicates a religious leader who is using his position to exploit others. Examples of such abuses of trust abound, as one lavishly paid religious leader after another is exposed in scandal after scandal, showing them in their true light. As sad as it is, we must realise there are many people who enter into the clerical or helping professions for reasons other than a genuine desire to aid their fellow man, and these people often exploit the very people who they are responsible for serving.

VI Lovers If The Lovers has appeared in the Below position, it seems there is a struggle between vice and virtue, and vice seems to be winning. The individuals concerned may very well have come together because they have important work that needs to be conducted on a karmic level, but somehow they have lost their way in this life and are engaged in a destructive relationship, rather than a constructive one. This placement is reminiscent of love gone awry, as the individuals involved have forgotten how to love in a positive, uplifting manner. One partner in the union may have developed an obsession with the other partner, who is apathetic to the love being offered at best. Because there are three individuals in the card, the possibility exists that there may be outside influences the querent may or may not be cognisant of.

VII Chariot If The Chariot has appeared in the Below position, there is a powerful person who seems to be trying to do too much too soon. He can be likened to the bull in the china shop because he is trying to use brute force when gentleness is the key to accomplishing certain tasks. This individual is thinking like the consummate soldier, dictating orders to people who do not want or appreciate being told what to do. Because this individual is in reality a good intentioned soul, the situation becomes all the more frustrating as time goes on. He may accomplish what he sets out to do, but he needs to learn some valuable lessons about tact and diplomacy if he wants to make allies on his way to the top.

VIII Strength If Strength has appeared in the Below position, there is an individual who is using his or her grace and guile in a very destructive way. She may appear to be nice, but only because she has an ulterior motive for which she feels graciousness is the key to achieving her goals. Although this person presents a pleasant and charming appearance, inwardly she is a very disturbed individual. Her personality disorder is deeply embedded within her soul, as she has a tendency to abuse animals, children, and other vulnerable individuals.

IX Hermit   If The Hermit has found itself in the Below position, it seems someone is giving you bad advice. The individual concerned may be very well intentioned, but he is not in possession of all the facts and is therefore not able to make an accurate assessment. Alternatively, you may be choosing to act on a matter you know is against your better judgement, which will do nothing but cause you further grief in the long run and hinder you along your true path in this life.

X Wheel of Fortune   If The Wheel of Fortune has appeared in the Below position, it appears that Lady Luck is not smiling down upon you at this time in your life. The circle is considered to be an ethereal symbol of eternity, and during its cycle we will encounter fortune and misfortune. Unfortunately, you have entered a period where you must take adequate precautions in all your actions. You may feel you are being dogged by bad luck, but the fact of the matter is everything that is happening in your life at this moment in time is merely a culmination of decisions you have made in the past. It is for that reason you need to stop, take a look around, repair any damage you can, and exercise extreme caution when making future life choices.

XI Justice   If Justice has landed in the Below position, it seems there is a loophole to one particular law that affects you, and someone has found it, much to your chagrin. It seems in principle you may very well be right, but the rules have been established by the governing bodies are not on your side, which can cause you a great deal of upset. You may not have necessarily erred to find yourself on the wrong end of the law, but you are nevertheless the one who is being made to suffer. If you have legal counsel, it is best to seek a second opinion because the people who you are employing may not necessarily be working in your best interests.

XII Hanged Man   If The Hanged Man has appeared in the Below position, it seems there is an air of despondency around you. At the very least, you are surrounded by a severe depression, but the illness that is surrounding you could go much deeper than that. You may have lost your zest for life and may very well wonder why you should even bother carrying on in what you consider to be such a pointless existence. You may have allowed yourself to be lulled into a deep numbing slumber that can only come through the use of drugs or other substances that are not necessarily good for you, but you nonetheless feel you need to make it through each day. Although you are not yet aware of it, the coping mechanisms you adopted are no longer something you engage in for enjoyment, but things you have come to depend on just to help you cope with normal day-to-day activities. One day you will reach the dawning of your soul, but for the time being you need to experience the depths that come only from a state of prolonged mental dreaming.

XIII Death If Death has landed in the Below position, you are going through such profound changes and nothing short of total renewal is in store for you. Because of the nature of the transformation that must inevitably take place before you can progress onto the next step of your spiritual evolution, you may not be pleased about the events that must transpire in order for the changes to take place if you were left to your own devices. You would rather putter along your path to boredom and stagnation, too afraid to try new things or look for alternatives to any dilemmas you may have, which is ultimately a stagnating situation for you to be in. It is your lack of motivation to get up and go that is causing the cosmos to move in ways that do not necessary appeal to you. As a result of this, you may sustain a loss in the form of a relationship, job or a way of life. You may spend a time in convalescence, which you will need to help you to come to terms with the transformative process that your psyche is undergoing. During your darkest hour, when you feel as though you cannot carry on one moment longer, it is important to keep in mind that you will emerge a new being, much wiser for the war you have had to fight within yourself.

XIV Temperance If Temperance has landed in the Below position it seems you are waiting, but waiting for what? You can only actively wait for a certain course of events to transpire if you have laid the foundation to allow such gestations to occur. If you have done nothing, however, the period of waiting you are undergoing is futile, time consuming and ultimately stagnating. It may very well be that in your attempt to stay on an even keel and not rock the boat, you have forgotten there are some things in this life that are worth becoming passionate about. Your refusal to involve yourself in a world that is passing you by will not only adversely affect you, but others as well. If you see someone who clearly needs you and refuse to take any kind of constructive action, you are just as guilty of complicity in wrongdoing as the people or circumstances that put the needy person in such an awkward position. That is something to think about the next time you feign ignorance or refuse to involve yourself in a particular situation that clearly needs your active participation.

XV Devil If The Devil has appeared in the Below position, there are some very negative influences around you that can predispose you to destructive behaviour. You may have had a very difficult upbringing, and without appropriate support mechanisms set in motion, you may have developed coping mechanisms that are often more harmful than helpful. You may be somewhat obsessive, which could lead to compulsive behaviour. Because the person this card refers to is not happy with himself, he may resort to vindictive, spiteful behaviour that will only backfire on him in the long-run. In the worst-case scenario, this individual could find himself engaging in the dark arts, which really is a pity.

XVI Tower If The Tower has appeared in the Below position, there is a major upheaval affecting your life. Security and your home are paramount to you, as events you have no control over are compromising the serenity you had once had with regard to your home-life. You may have sustained a loss of some kind, which has made it difficult to carry on in the manner you have grown accustomed to. You or someone close to you may have entered into a period of convalescence, which has put your livelihood and standard of living at risk. There may also be someone who has entered into your sphere of awareness who serves as a catalyst to shake things up a bit. To be forewarned is to be forearmed, so it is best to exercise caution and discretion in all matters, especially those relating to your security and prosperity.

XVII Star If The Star has appeared in the Below position, you are overly hopeful about one particular situation that weighs heavily on your mind. Instead of taking constructive action to ensure the sequence of events that occur turn out in your favour, you have a tendency to sit back and wish for the best. In addition, the possibility exists that you have placed your faith in an unreliable friend, thereby compounding your sense of frustration over circumstances you feel you have no control over.

XVIII Moon If The Moon has been placed in the Below position, you are in an environment where those around you are highly insincere in the best of circumstances. At worst, they are setting you up for a fall. It is essential that you use your intuition to help you to determine who to associate with and who to steer clear of, because you will soon discover who your true friends are, much to your chagrin.

XIX Sun If The Sun has appeared in the Below position, it seems as if the brightness that the Sun gives us has been eclipsed. This card is traditionally thought of as the card of children because a drawing of a small child smiling gaily on a horse is often the archetypal theme of this key. Because of the elusive overtones of this placement, it indicates that children, animals and other vulnerable beings who are not in a position to defend themselves are being abused or misused in some way. You should therefore be on the lookout for any unusual activities from people who have been placed in a position of trust and authority.

XX Judgement If Judgement has appeared in the Below position, you are not in possession of all of the facts, which makes it impossible to correctly assess the situation you are currently involved in. You may also be in a period of enforced convalescence, and although you are not happy with your restricted activities, it is a necessary component in the healing and replenishing process that enables you to continue with your soul growth. If you are currently under the supervision of a doctor, it would be in your best interests to carefully research your illness on your own and seek a second opinion if you are not totally happy with the diagnoses. It is also important to note that there are some secrets deeply buried within your lineage, which are affecting you at this very moment in time, even if you are not aware they exist.

XXI World If The World has appeared in the Below position, you are having problems accepting the fact that there is a certain aspect of your life that is over. It may be that you are in an unfulfilling relationship, job or other situation you know you must step aside from and re-evaluate. Until you are able to let go of this particular aspect of your life, you will be unable to move onto higher, more fulfilling planes of awareness.

Wands/Rods/Fire

Ace If the Ace of Wands has landed in the Below position, you have many new ideas, but they are not necessarily conducive for positive soul growth. You may plan on embarking upon some mischief-making endeavours, and although you may very well receive a rush of excitement at the very beginning of such activities, you should soon realise that what you are doing is counterproductive to your ultimate advancement in this life. You may be considering embarking upon a business venture, but you need to rethink any decisions you make. It is essential you research your market and ascertain there is a valid need for the business you would like to initiate before investing any time or money into such a venture. If you are in any doubt whatsoever about the viability of any projects you are contemplating, it may be necessary to rethink your original proposal and look into alternative ventures.

Two   If the Two of Wands has appeared in the Below position, you may have entered into an agreement with another person that may not necessarily be suitable for your own personal growth. It is important to check the fine print on any contracts or documents to make sure there are not any hidden loopholes you were previously unaware of. It is important to get a second opinion before committing yourself to anything because someone may be giving you bad advice. It is also important to listen to your inner voice because the people around you may not be forthcoming in relating to you any potential problems you may encounter if you pursue one particular course of action.

Three   If the Three of Wands has landed in the Below position, you may have become involved with a group of people who do not necessarily provide positive influence for you. Your involvement with these individuals is not purely social, as you may come together in the hopes of completing a particular task, such as a business enterprise or an occult undertaking. It is very important you look at your milieu carefully to ensure your activities are above reproach.

Four   If the Four of Wands has appeared in the Below position, there are circumstances around you that are affecting the happiness and security you feel at home. Perhaps you have encountered an intruder who has threatened you in some way, making you feel somewhat unnerved. Whatever the circumstances, events that transpire will cause you to feel quite unsettled, as you struggle to return to the tenacious equilibrium you once felt that you had such a firm grasp on.

Five   If the Five of Wands has appeared in the Below position, there is a sense of futility around you because you seem to be fighting a losing battle. There is much anger within you, which has been built up from unresolved resentments over the years. Because you have so much hatred inside your core being, you tend to pick fights over things that are totally inconsequential in the grand scheme of things. You need to search your psyche for that one trauma that occurred oh, so long ago, which is at the root of the problem causing you so much angst. Once you have successfully dealt with the core trauma in your life, everything else will fall into place, thereby enabling you to live serenely with others.

Six   If the Six of Wands has appeared in the Below position, it appears you have been set up for a fall. You may have decided to embark upon one particular project but have forgotten to take into account one crucial piece of information. Because you are not in possession of all the facts and are not able to accomplish everything you should, the idea of success will be inconceivable to you at this point in time. You must also be aware of enemies disguised as friends, because some of the people you have discussed your plans with do not wish you well and are eager to see your downfall. Now is not the time to place your trust in those who have not proven themselves as loyal friends, because some of them will be the cause of your undoing.

Seven   If the Seven of Wands has appeared in the Below position, you are using your best intentions to overcome obstacles that have come to you quite unexpectedly. What makes the situation stressful is the fact that you are working on issues you have no experience of, making your attempts to stay on top of the situation clumsy at best. Because you are under a great deal of stress, you may find yourself in a dejected mood and therefore somewhat unpopular amongst your peers. You need all the allies you can get at this point in your life, and alienating yourself will only serve to prolong the difficulties you are enduring. The best you can do is to put a smile on your face and weather the hard times ahead. The difficulties you are currently experiencing will pass, and you will emerge successful for having managed the obstacles for as long as you have.

Eight   If the Eight of Wands has appeared in the Below position, it seems you are going too fast too soon. There is an old saying that we must learn how to crawl before we can walk, and that has never been truer than in this particular case. You may have taken on a project that, while you have all the confidence in the world of completing, you have not yet acquired the skills necessary to manage it. It is for that reason you need to step back and honestly assess the situation. If you lack the expertise necessary to accomplish what is being expected of you, it will be in your best interests to speak up before you embarrass yourself and others.

Nine   If the Nine of Wands has appeared in the Below position, it appears you are very paranoid and are therefore spending a great deal of time and energy fuelling your thoughts on one particular issue. It is this extreme defensiveness that is wearing you down and bringing you to a point of mental exhaustion. While it is important to remain vigilant, it is also important to dismiss any innocuous elements that also enter into your sphere of awareness. While it is certainly prudent to maintain a healthy concern for your wellbeing by paying attention to detail, it would be unwise to allow your concerns to escalate to the sphere of anxiety, depression or paranoia, which is clearly an unhealthy path to pursue.

Ten   If the Ten of Wands has appeared in the Below position, you are overwhelmed by an insurmountable burden that is causing you many difficulties. You are very angry about the fact that you do not have the skills and expertise necessary to accomplish the task you have been given, and are therefore inept at the very best. You are quite lonely because you feel you have no one to talk to about this particular matter. Perhaps it is best to abandon the project for the time being because you can always resume it when you are more confident about what procedures you would like to take in order to accomplish your goals.

King

If the King of Wands has appeared in the Below position, there is a man who figures prominently in your life. He has a great deal of energy, but since he has not accomplished what he believes to be his life purpose, he seems misguided in many of his opinions. He may have hobbies, which he can become quite obsessive about, and this will ultimately have the effect of thwarting his soul growth. He struggles with his hobbies as if they were work, and then becomes disappointed when they no longer give him the enjoyment they once did. Because he is not able to focus his energies constructively, much of it is dissipated into utter chaos, leaving a rather confused, ineffectual individual who is not really happy with himself or anyone else.

Queen

If the Queen of Wands has appeared in the Below position, there is a woman in the picture who has an abundance of energy within her being. She is very angry, possibly about the opportunities missed in her life, as well as the fact that her personal relationships are not as fulfilling as they could be. Whatever the reason, she conducts her activities in a frantic hysteria, doing lots of things at the same time, but accomplishing very little, if anything at all. Because she is so angry at life in general, she expresses this frustration to other individuals who have nothing whatsoever to do with the angst that is within her being.

Knight/ Prince

If the Knight of Wands has appeared in the Below position, there is a young man who figures prominently in the situation that has prompted you to consult the oracle. His energies are scattered and he has difficulty focusing on one particular subject. Because he is such an unsettled soul, he has difficulty staying in one place, job or relationship for any length of time. The reason for his misguided endeavours is that in his more formative years he suffered a trauma, which he has never recovered from because he has repressed the memory of the event. Once he is able to recall the incident and allow the healing process to begin, he will be much more stable and able to focus on important issues that he must face before he fully matures and becomes a celestial being of the universe.

Page/ Princess   If the Page of Wands has appeared in the Below position, there is a young person who is having a detrimental influence on the situation at hand. This person may have had early life experiences that will make her a difficult person to care for. She can be very angry and release this pent up aggression by hyperactivity and mischief making. She may also resort to attention seeking tactics, which serve only to exasperate those individuals close to her.

Pentacles/Disks/Earth

Ace   If the Ace of Pentacles has landed in the Below position, it seems there are some material concerns that are paramount on your mind, which in many ways is causing you to lose sight of your true purpose in this life. You may be considering beginning a project that involves money or other valuable resources, but this new endeavour may not necessarily be in your best interests. Before committing yourself to anything, it is best to thoroughly research the object of your interest and not allow yourself to be swayed by manipulative individuals who only have their own best interests at heart.

Two   If the Two of Pentacles is in the Below position, you or someone close to you may be acquiring money unethically. You may have found yourself in debt, as you have committed yourself to more than you can actually afford. This has subsequently put you in a very difficult position and you will have to make a few tough choices about how you intend to remedy the situation.

Three   If the Three of Pentacles has appeared in the Below position, it appears that you are not suitably qualified to perform a particular task you have been presented with. It is for that reason you appear awkward and are not confident of your own abilities. Alternatively, one particular venture that affects your material prosperity is on shaky ground. It is for this reason the venture in question may collapse sometime in the future if adequate precautions are not taken to ensure its success.

Four   If the Four of Pentacles has appeared in the Below position, you or someone close to you is being somewhat miserly. You are holding on too tightly to your worldly possessions, which is inhibiting the enjoyment that you could have in this life. You would be much happier if you would loosen up and open yourself up a bit more to the prosperity that you deserve. It is important to remember that you only receive what you give out to the universe, so if you keep all of your resources for yourself then the universe will not replenish them for you.

Five   If the Five of Pentacles has appeared in the Below position, you seem to be in a phase of despondency, which could be much more than just a material depression. It seems you are very depressed, which is affecting your ability to stay grounded and focused on what needs to be achieved at this time in your life. You may be aware of people who are much more affluent than yourself, and have a tinge of jealousy because what other people have seems to be unreachable to you. Instead of focusing on what you don't have, it is much better to reflect on that which you have, and everything else will fall into place.

Six   If the Six of Pentacles has appeared in the Below position, you are in desperate need of some help from an outside source. It seems you do not have within yourself all of the facilities you require to satisfy your immediate needs. It is best, therefore, to ask for help because people won't know what your needs are if you don't tell them. It is important to remember that you won't get what you don't ask for.

Seven   If the Seven of Pentacles is in the Below position, you are in the process of playing a waiting game. It is very difficult for you because you are filled with anxiety and trepidation about your future. You must be very careful in all of your dealings with others because any mistakes you make now can lead to accidents and mishaps. It is important to remember that others are considering you, just as you are considering them.

Eight   If the Eight of Pentacles has appeared in the Below position, it appears you do not have the skills necessary to complete a certain task that really needs to be accomplished. It may be that you lack guidance and supervision, which is leaving you inept at the very best. Unfortunately this is one of those situations when formal schooling is not going to do you any good, and you must therefore learn through experience the task that has been presented to you. There are people out there who will show you how to perform specific roles, but it is essential that you ask them because they are not going to go out of their way to help you. After you have learned through experience, you will feel much more confident within yourself.

Nine   If the Nine of Pentacles has appeared in the Below position, you are a financially sound individual who has acquired wealth from your work, an inheritance, or a windfall of some kind. Because you have not necessarily earned this money in a normal way, you see it as mad money and have therefore found yourself spending it willie nillie. While it is nice to treat yourself once in a while, it is important to exercise a bit of frugality in your spending, because you will never know exactly when you will need the nest egg that has been built up over time.

Ten   If the Ten of Pentacles has landed in the Below position, you have some family ties that are becoming quite burdensome. It may be that you are financially responsible for someone in your family, and this is dragging you down. You feel as if the whole world is on your shoulders and this is a burden that you do not necessarily want. The best you can do is tighten your belt and limit your contact with those family members who are dragging you down.

King   If the King of Pentacles has appeared in the Below position, there is a man who figures prominently in the situation that prompted you to consult the oracle. He can be a bit miserly and will therefore not give to those in need, which ultimately detracts from his overall personality. Although he may very well have money, he pleads poverty at every opportunity and insists people give to him because he has a tendency to exploit his position in the world. Because he thinks of his material comfort above all else, he has few, if any, true friends.

Queen   If the Queen of Pentacles has appeared in the Below position there is a woman who figures prominently in the situation that prompted you to consult the oracle. She is somewhat materialistic and does whatever it takes to make sure she has a reasonable standard of living. This woman is very possessive and does not like any form of competition because, deep down inside, she lacks confidence in her ability to attract people through her positive personality traits. She tends to see her relationships as a way to a better future for herself, and therefore will discard friends and partnerships when they are no longer useful to her, which is a pity because there are people who do not possess wealth and power who can teach her a thing or two about real life.

Knight/ Prince   If the Knight of Pentacles has appeared in the Below position, there is a young man who is influencing the situation in some way. He can be stubborn and obstinate, and is slow to take any kind of action. This person would like to escape from the harsh realities of this world, and will therefore immerse himself in hobbies and other pastimes. He may have a problem managing his finances, and will need to control the urge to spend money as a compensatory mechanism.

Page/ Princess   If the Page of Pentacles has appeared in the Below position, there is a young person who is weighing heavily on your mind. This individual is a slow starter, and as a result may appear not to be very intelligent as well as a bit clumsy. This is not necessarily the case, however, because this person is still in her formative years and has a long way to go until she has fully matured. She needs a little extra guidance and reassurance because she lacks confidence at this stage in her life, but once she has grown up a little, her true value will shine forth from her persona.

Swords/Air

Ace   If the Ace of Swords has appeared in the Below position, it seems as if there is a great deal of communication going on, so much so that you may find yourself somewhat confused about what is going on around you. Unfortunately, all that is being related to you is not necessarily positive. There is an element of malicious gossip involved, which has the potential to destroy reputations. This is also the card associated with karma, which means you will need to keep your wits about you to weather the storm of mental activity that will soon be coming your way. It is always important to keep in mind that we are treated the way we treat others, so if we want to be treated well, we need to treat others well.

Two   If the Two of Swords has appeared in the Below position, it seems there is a major disagreement brewing between you and another individual, and the both of you cannot see eye to eye. Because of the nature of the dispute, there is the likelihood of slander, libel and perjury. It is for that reason that sound counsel and advice will be necessary to cleverly manoeuvre yourself around the mire of dishonestly that ultimately prevails in this situation. You may find that the only positive thing you can do is to walk away from the situation because it is not likely to be resolved in a manner that you will find satisfactory.

Three   If the Three of Swords has appeared in the Below position, there is some unhappiness and heartache in your life, much of which, unfortunately, you have created. You may well be involved in a relationship that is counter-productive to your soul growth, and you know deep down inside that before you can find happiness you will need to discard this union. It is difficult, however, because you may very well feel it is better to be in a bad relationship than to be in no relationship at all, which is the reason why you are not able to move on in your life. The important thing to keep in mind, however, is that the good things you are deserving of will not come to you until you clean out the psychic rubbish from your life. There are many unsatisfactory elements in your personal relationships that need to be resolved before true happiness can be achieved.

Four   If the Four of Swords has appeared in the below position, you are clearly experiencing a great deal of anxiety while you are waiting for the outcome of one particular situation that is weighing heavily on your mind. It would probably be best to calm yourself down by going into a deep mediation, as you try to work yourself around the worry you are experiencing. At this moment in time, however, the only thing you can do is wait for further illumination to be provided to you because the universe will give you guidance when it is time for you receive it, and not necessarily when you would like to receive illumination. You will receive guidance during your meditations, but the information you receive may not be what you would like to hear, so you need to consider it very carefully before acting upon it.

Five   If the Five of Swords has landed in the Below position, you are involved in a series of disputes that is affecting your personality and causing you a great deal of anguish. You may very well end up the victor, but at what cost? Even if you do manage to achieve the upper hand, your reputation may very well become tarnished in the process. The best that you can do, therefore, is to walk away from such a destructive situation with your dignity intact. It does no good hoping for retribution for any slights that you may have incurred because the atmosphere is not propitious for your views to be heard with an open mind. There are some instances when we would be wise to cut our losses and walk away, and this situation you are currently in appears to be one of them.

Six   If the Six of Swords has appeared in the Below position, you have been through a very difficult time and have suffered a great deal of mental anguish over one particular situation. Much of the anxiety you have been feeling has been to a great extent created by your imagination, but that does not make the adverse situation created by you to be any less real in your mind. You also may have encountered relationship difficulties, which you will have to move away from if you want to achieve satisfying friendships and partnerships. Sometimes it is necessary to give something up to achieve everlasting happiness, and this may well be one of those instances.

Seven   If the Seven of Swords has appeared in the Below position, there is an element of deceit that permeates the entire situation you are presently involved in. Nothing is as it seems, and supposedly trustworthy individuals will not keep your confidences. There is a lot going on behind the scenes that you are totally unaware of, so it is essential that you place your trust in yourself and not outside sources. It is therefore best to keep your thoughts close to your heart because someone is sure to repeat what you have said at a most inopportune time. In addition, if you reveal a clever idea to anyone, the climate is such that the individual you confide in will adopt your idea as his own and take all the credit.

Eight If the Eight of Swords has appeared in the Below position, you may be stuck in a rut and have no idea how the remove yourself from it. Because you have been in such an awkward position for such a long time, it may be difficult for you to make any decisions that need to be made in order to progress in your spirituality. It seems you are also not in possession of all the facts, which makes it even more difficult for you to act in a manner that will enable you to delicately extricate yourself from what will soon become an awkward situation for you. You may feel stuck in a rut, unable to move, but if you think carefully, you will discover for yourself a way out of the situation that is causing you so much disturbance.

Nine If the Nine of Swords has appeared in the Below position, you have spent so much time fretting and worrying about the situation that has prompted you to consult the oracle that you are at the point of nervous exhaustion. You may have so many concerns that you are severely depressed and may be on the brink of a breakdown. A period of time in convalescence may be necessary to help you through this difficult period. In addition, it would be best to receive counsel from authorised individuals who can help you with some of your more tangible concerns. With the help of qualified persons, you will eventually be able to see a light at the end of the long, dark tunnel that you have found yourself in.

Ten If the Ten of Swords has appeared in the Below position, someone has let you down in a big way. It is for this reason that you have lost all faith in other people and will have a difficult time trusting others. It may be necessary for you to spend time recovering from the shock of what you see as a betrayal, but time really does heal all wounds, as you will eventually learn. You may be suffering from emotional and physical ailments that are a result of this trauma, and the only thing that you can do is to seek the appropriate medical advice and allow time to heal the wounds that have seared through your soul.

King If the King of Swords has appeared in the Below position, there is a very bitter man who is strongly influencing the situation that prompted you to consult the oracle. He may be deeply unsatisfied with the course of events that have brought him to his current position in this life, and he has therefore decided to take his frustrations and resentments out on those individuals who are not able to defend themselves. It is much easier for this man to blame other people for his failures than to work towards bettering his position with the assets he possesses. Because his dissatisfaction with life is so clearly evident, he has few, if any, friends. That, however, is just another example of the fickle world we live in, where people only want to be our friends when we are up. The problem is that when we are down is when we are in need of friends.

Queen   If the Queen of Swords has appeared in the Below position, there is a woman who is a malicious gossip and derives a great deal of pleasure out of stirring things up. She may be bitter about the life that she could have had, and therefore feels the need to put a little excitement into a rather dull existence by using the spoken word to wreak havoc on the lives of others. Any things this woman relates must be taken with a grain of salt because she has a highly fertile imagination and prefers to use it to stir up controversy rather than to benefit mankind in some way.

Knight/   If the Knight of Swords has appeared in the Below position, there is a
Prince   young man who enjoys stirring things up in the lives of others. He can be quite volatile in his speech processes, a trait that does not necessarily endear him to others when he is giving one of his tirades. Because his communication skills are not as well developed as he would like them to be, many of this frustrations are expressed through anger and vindictiveness, rather than love and compassion.

Page/   If the Page of Swords has appeared in the Below position, you will find
Princess   there is a young person involved who is a detracting influence on the situation that led you to consult the oracle. This individual may prove to be somewhat disruptive, as she tends to steal and makes up stories, not thinking about the future consequences of her actions. Before she will be a productive member of society, she will need the assistance of a mentor who can guide her on the correct path.

Cups/Water

Ace   If the Ace of Cups has appeared in the Below position, it appears there could be some emotional disorders that are wreaking havoc on a situation that would otherwise be perfectly harmonious. You, or someone close to you, could be suffering from neurosis or any of the many depressive illnesses that will affect your outlook on life. It is therefore essential to seek help and support if it appears that these emotive imbalances are unmanageable and causing you a great deal of upset.

Two   If the Two of Cups has landed in the Below position, it appears you are having some relationship difficulties that are affecting your ability to function effectively in this life. Perhaps you have got together with one particular person for all the wrong reasons, and are having second thoughts about continuing the liaison. Perhaps you or your partner is using the other for your own aims, which also cannot bode well for a happy and harmonious relationship. Good relationships are built on mutual love and respect, and this relationship may be lacking that, which will ultimately pose problems for its long-term success. Whatever the reasons for the tension in your personal life, you need to take a look at how best you can improve your ability to communicate with others so you can add meaning to the life you are currently living.

Three   If the Three of Cups has appeared in the Below position, it seems that either you are doing too much socialising or are befriending the wrong types of people whose personalities are counter-productive to your soul's destiny in this incarnation. While it is good to get out and mingle with your friends, too much of a good thing can be just as harmful to your health as too little. You may find you are eating too much or partaking of too many recreational drugs, which includes alcohol and even some foods. Such activities will only serve to ruin your health and make it difficult for you to carry out your day-to-day activities in an efficient manner. Alternatively, be prepared for an unusual situation to develop at a social event, which will cause you much consternation in the end.

Four   If the Four of Cups has appeared in the Below position, you may find yourself inclined to trust totally inappropriate individuals, who will only cause you problems in the long-run. It is all too easy to listen to the malicious gossip of others and accept hearsay as a fact. It is also important to remember there are some individuals who thrive on spreading gossip, so it is best to stay away from such individuals who will only tarnish your reputation by association. It is best to trust your intuition and only listen to reliable sources of information before making any decisions.

Five   If the Five of Cups has appeared in the Below position, you are severely deflated and let down by a certain situation in your life. You may have had your hopes high and were sure that a certain situation would transpire in the way you had hoped, only to find the opposite to be true. You have been quite dismayed and perplexed that events did not occur as you had planned, and you were totally unprepared for the resulting situation that has developed. As a consequence, you will have to go through the grieving process before you can accept the new situation that has developed. When you have accepted the course of events that has resulted, you will be in a position to plan your next course of action based upon the realisations that you have recently made with regard to the dilemma that has prompted you to consult this oracle. Although the events of our life may not necessarily be what we want, they are what we need to enable us to grow and evolve into better human beings.

Six   If the Six of Cups has appeared in the Below condition, it indicates someone has had or is currently having an unhappy childhood, which will in the end affect his adult relationships in this life. This is a very sad situation to be in, which indicates neglect, child abuse and general unhappiness that occurred in his more formative years. In order for the individual concerned to proactively grow in his psychic development, he will need to work through the many anger-inducing experiences that have affected his attitudes in adulthood. This individual needs a reliable friend, and that friend could be you. We all have traumas from the past, and it is those traumas that we must work through before we can be the adults we were meant to be.

Seven   If the Seven of Cups has appeared in the Below position, it appears that you are not in full control of your mental faculties. You may be under the influence of substances, which would affect your ability to make appropriate decisions concerning your true destiny in this life. You may also have become afflicted with addictions, compulsions and eating disorders that give you the added sense of self loathing and the need to keep formidable secrets. Because you are really not in a position to cope with your problems on your own, it would be in your best interests to seek support from someone you can trust.

Eight   If the Eight of Cups has appeared in the Below position, a sense of sadness pervades your soul because you have suffered a loss that is too great for many people to comprehend. Perhaps you gave up something that was dear to you because you had not realised just how precious it was. The whole incident has given you something to think about, as you have had to realise what is important and what is not. It is often hardest on our souls when we have to give up that which we love, but it is also those occasions that afford us the most emotional growth.

Nine　If the Nine of Cups has appeared in the Below position, you may have some difficulties with alcohol or other substances, which are affecting your ability to be a whole person. You may find your weight fluctuating, which is a result of the emotional difficulties you are currently experiencing. You may find you are engaging in solitary activities, but this is a time when you need other people around you. While it is good to be in your own company, perhaps you would benefit from the company of others from time to time to help you stay balanced.

Ten　If the Ten of Cups has appeared in the Below position, there are problems affecting the happiness and security you feel deserving of. Someone at home may very well be ill, which is creating an imbalance that is reverberating through the whole of your life. It is therefore important that you attune yourself to the feelings and motivations of others so you can ascertain any potential problems and correct them before they get out of hand. While you need to be in a stable relationship to help you to grown and evolve, if that relationship is destructive it will be very difficult for you to develop in the manner that was destined for you.

King　If the King of Cups has appeared in the Below position, there is a man who is emotionally disturbed and figures significantly in your life. Because he was never provided with adequate support mechanisms necessary to help him to become a well-adjusted individual, he has resorted to addictions and compulsions he has had to keep hidden from the rest of the world. Even though he tells himself that what he is doing is only a lifestyle choice, deep down in his heart he knows there is something wrong with his actions, or why else would he keep them so well hidden from those people who are close to him. In order to keep secrets, he resorts to bullying, harassment and other intimidation tactics to keep people who have witnessed the dark side of his soul quiet. He is a truly sad man who needs pity, not contempt, but that certainly does not help those people who have to suffer him.

Queen　If the Queen of Cups has appeared in the Below position, there is a woman who is very emotionally disturbed and figures prominently in the situation that prompted you to consult the oracle. She may have had a very difficult childhood or early adult life, and inadequate support mechanisms had the effect of corrupting her fragile mind. Because she herself was mistreated, she may resort to mistreating others, which is a pity because she could give so much love to this world that we inhabit. Because there is an emptiness inside her soul that is too omnipotent to describe by using human words, she may very well resort to perversities and other dark arts as a way to feel anything at all that can permeate the emptiness of her soul.

Knight/ Prince   If the Knight of Cups has appeared in the Below position, there is a young man who is unsure of his own abilities. He therefore tends to make up stories about his happiness and success in the world in an attempt to hoodwink the casual acquaintance who isn't really that interested in delving into his personal life anyway. He may also be uncertain about his sexuality and will therefore dabble in more austere forms of physical gratification as a way to test the waters of his psycho-development. Because he is so immature, he needs a mentor to help him leave the destructive rollercoaster of life that he has found himself on and move toward more positive forms of entertainment.

Page/ Princess   If the Page of Cups has appeared in the Below position, there is a young person who is having emotional difficulties, that are preventing her from functioning positively in this world that we inhabit. She may live in a fantasy would, which is in fact a coping mechanism that she has developed to get away from the harsh realities of a sometimes sinister world that may be too much for her to bear at times. When she matures, she may develop eating disorders and abuse substances as a way to self-medicate a disturbance that needs a deep, inner cleansing before she can grow and develop in a manner that is suitable to her ego.

5 The Recent Past

0 Fool   If The Fool has landed in the Recent Past position, you have embarked upon a new venture that has been totally alien to you. You may have, on the spur of the moment, decided to leave a job, relationship or an activity that has not been satisfying to you. While others may have found your activities to be quite abrupt, the fact is that you had been contemplating making some much needed changes for quite some time, but one particular incident gave you the impetuous needed to take the actions required to evoke the much needed change. While some may believe you behaved foolishly, that is not necessarily the case. What you do next will depend on the success or failure of your new path, so take care on your new journey in this life.

I Magician   If The Magician has landed in the Recent Past position, you may have just recently completed a course of study that should theoretically enable you to make much more of yourself in the future. This course of study may or may not have been in a formal classroom environment, but it entailed a great deal of study and reflection upon the subtle intricacies that form the invisible forces of our physical world. There may be a young person involved who plays a significant role in your learning process, which could be either positive or negative, depending on his temperament and personality.

II High Priestess   If the High Priestess has appeared in the Recent Past position, you have just come out of a period of self-imposed solitude that was intended to give greater clarity and understanding of the esoteric aspects of our exoteric existence. A period of celibacy may very well have been involved in this purifying process because the heterosexual act itself involves male energy that may interfere with the intuitive process of enlightenment that needs to be experienced in order to fully understand your place in this life.

III Empress   If The Empress has appeared in the Recent Past position, home and family have recently been very important to you. Children are highly significant, so if you do not have children of your own, you may have had contact with other people who you care for as your own. You may have recently gone through a very fertile period, which would have been propitious for procreation, if that is what you desired.

IV Emperor   If The Emperor has appeared in the past position, you have recently had contact with an individual or organisation that has put you in touch with some very real aspects of your physical world. You have had dealings with individuals who have the ability to influence your credibility in this world, and it is very important that your activities have been conducted with the utmost authority and diplomacy. Your future status depends on what you do next, so you need to think very carefully about any upcoming courses of action.

V Hierophant   If The Hierophant has appeared in the Recent Past position, you have had a very important decision to make that was crucial to your life path. You have decided to embark upon a path that is one of your life initiation events, something that is an important process of your development along this path of life. The choice you made was of such a serious nature that you had reached a crossroad in your life, a point where things would never be the same again. In astrological phraseology, The Hierophant is regarded as the YOD, which is often translated as the finger of God because, like The Hierophant, once the YOD has been activated, things will never again be the same.

VI Lovers   If The Lovers has appeared in the Recent Past position, you have recently had an experience that has been very rewarding to you. You may have come into contact with a person or organisation that somehow seemed predestined, allowing you to fulfil some of your lifelong dreams and to experience the sensation of being truly happy. This major event that was timed to enable your soul to further develop does not come without sacrifices, however, as you were no doubt asked to give something up in order to experience the bliss you craved. The path to true love is not without obstacles, which is something you will soon discover as future events unfold before your very eyes.

VII Chariot   If The Chariot has appeared in the Recent Past position, you have sustained a victory of some kind and have been seen by others as being a successful individual. You very likely had to take a trip, preferably over land, to reach a very important destination. The journey you took enabled you to gain a better perspective on your particular situation, as you have realised there are two sides to every story that both need to be taken into consideration before making any important decisions. Everyone has a specific viewpoint, which you may or may not agree with, and you will need to learn the subtle art of agreeing to disagree while still maintaining your alliances. Your recent success has given you greater confidence that has helped you to become more assertive with others, especially when you feel another's rights have been violated.

VIII Strength If Strength has appeared in the Recent Past position, you have recently been the centre of attention, exuding all of the charm and grace you have been able to muster. It is very likely animals have figured significantly in the situation that makes up your life because you have had more of an affinity to all manner of living beings other than your human counterparts. The reason for this is because you have perceived many souls have allowed their physical and sensual urges to override their esoteric destiny in this life, which has subsequently caused some of their more negative personality traits to emerge. Animals, on the other hand, are motivated for the most part by their group consciousness that drives their instincts, and their motives are pure and therefore in line with their spiritual destiny in this physical world.

IX Hermit If The Hermit has appeared in the Recent Past position, it appears that you have just gone through a period of solitude in your quest for enlightenment. Although you would have preferred to be in the company of others, you needed to be on your own to find the answers within yourself to the questions you have had. You may have been seen by others as somewhat of a loner, and these individuals therefore shied away from getting too close to you because they honestly thought that you wanted to be on your own, but what was a desire for solitude may very well have been shyness. You are leaving this period of self-imposed isolation, and the cards that follow will reveal with greater clarity your future destiny.

X Wheel Of Fortune If The Wheel has occurred in the Recent Past position, you have recently gone through a change in fortune, in many ways as a result of calculated risks you had to take in order to move on in your life. A sudden swirl of events has taken place in many aspects of your life experience, which will enable you to change in a positive direction. In many ways you have been given the freedom to accomplish many of the important goals that have been set for you, thereby enabling you to carry out your purpose for reincarnating into the earth plane.

XI Justice If Justice has appeared in the Recent Past position, you have recently gone through a period where mediation has been required so you can approach a difficult issue with a little bit more reason than has been used in the past. You may have endured some legal proceedings, and were not totally sure of the outcome. When handing your private affairs over to others to resolve, there is always the possibility that those individuals will not accede to your particular viewpoint. You have learned that it is important to keep a litigious attitude in your dealings with others because a trusting stance is not appropriate at this point in time. If we lived in an ideal world we would be able to place our trust in others unreservedly, but unfortunately we do not live in an ideal world and must therefore be cautious of who we place our faith in.

XII Hanged Man If The Hanged Man has appeared in the Recent Past position, you have recently had to make a sacrifice, which has left you with somewhat of a philosophical attitude towards life. You may have realised you would have to abandon a dream of yours, and this has undoubtedly caused you to re-evaluate your goals and what you would like to acquire in this life. Because you have been forced to relinquish some hope or dream you have held so close to your heart for such a long time, you have been forced to develop an alternate philosophy of life to accommodate some of your thwarted ambitions. As a result of your new awareness of the co-existence of beings in the universal web, of which we are merely minor fragments, you may not have the impetuousness that only comes from innocence and ignorance of the opposing forces within.

XIII Death If Death has appeared in the Recent Past position, you have recently sustained a major transformation in your life, which was needed to help you along the path of your true spiritual evolution. You may have been confronted with some information that may have surprised, dismayed or even shocked you. The event you were forced to acknowledge had such an extreme effect on your psyche that you were left with no other alternative but to make the appropriate changes to your lifestyle because it is impossible for you to carry on as if nothing had happened. Because recent events have been of such an extreme nature, you will need a period of inner healing and reflection to enable you to emerge a stronger and wiser being for the experience.

XIV Temperance If Temperance has appeared in the Recent Past position, you may have recently had a calming influence that has helped you to see more clearly the inner workings of the universe. You may have had an experience that enabled you to become a spectator of events taking place beyond the here and now, thereby intrinsically showing you our world is merely one of many parallel spheres of existence that make up the universal ebb, an energy force of which we only have the faintest awareness. During this experience you achieved a greater understanding of the concept of time, realising we only perceive the concept that we call time in a linear fashion because that is the easiest way we can piece together corresponding occurrences in our rather three-dimensional minds. For a brief period you were able to glimpse the world through the eyes of a higher dimensional soul, thereby enhancing your exoteric understanding of the universe and helping you to express this heightened insight through one of the many creative pursuits, such as art, drama, music or writing.

XV Devil If The Devil has appeared in the Recent Past position, you have recently come into contact with the dark forces that are a natural part of our physical existence. Although you very much would have liked to have stayed on the straight and narrow path of morality and ethics, circumstances have transpired to force you to decide to go the way of the physicalities of this world. You may have had so many financial obligations that the only way to take care of them was to engage in activities you would rather have steered clear of. These activities may not have been malefic, but because they were not something you would have normally chosen to attempt of your own accord, you have been instilled with a certain level of sombreness with regard to the issue. Although you may not have supposed such issues could exist, it is important to keep in mind our thoughts will manifest directly in our physical world. It is for that reason you should keep in mind that negative thoughts, projected by you or someone else, will produce negativity in our physical world. Therefore our thoughts need to be policed with just as much efficiency as the written or spoken word, because you or someone you know may have unknowingly been a victim of a psychic attack. Alternatively, you or someone you know may very well be psychically attacking others.

XVI Tower If The Tower has appeared in the Recent Past position, it seems you have recently endured some cataclysmic events that have served to change the course of your life. You may have become somewhat complacent, feeling your existence has reached a plateau, but events you were totally unaware of have served to wreak havoc on what you believed to be your safe, cosy existence. The Tower indicates your way of life has been put at risk, which means your living situation has had to change. It also indicates there may have been either an accident or a temperamental outburst that has brought about this sudden turn of events. How you handle yourself in the future will be revealed in the cards that follow.

XVII Star   If The Star has appeared in the Recent Past position, you have recently acquainted yourself with a person or group of people who have the potential to become lifelong friends. You are full of hope and high expectations for the future, which will only enhance your outlook on life and ensure your popularity in the future.

XVIII Moon   If The Moon has appeared in the Recent Past position, you have just recently been ill, which has affected your ability to function rationally in our physical world. It seems you have been somewhat confused by the contrasting influences you have been bombarded with. Because you have not been able to think with the greatest clarity, you have been unsure of your standing in this world, and this uncertainty has led you to question your own inner judgement. As a result of your impaired vision, you may have had some bad experiences with people who you erroneously believed to be your friends. In addition, people who you never counted on being there for you have given you support in your time of need. This whole experience has served to change your whole outlook in life, as you have learned who your true friends are.

XIX The Sun   If The Sun has appeared in the Recent Past position, you have gone through a period of heightened illumination where you have gained a greater understanding of why certain events in your life have transpired the way they did. The Sun is a card that represents the self, and this indicates there are some very egocentric forces at work, suggesting you or someone close to you is very focused on their own needs instead of the needs of others. Because The Sun represents the pure essence of immature exhibition, children often figure prominently because they have not yet learned restraint and control, something that usually comes with maturity and experience.

XX Judgement   If Judgement has landed in the Recent Past position, you have recently gone through a deep healing process that has changed your entire being. In many ways the experience has changed you completely to the point that you are now unrecognisable to those people who knew you before. It is possible you went through an illness that required you to spend time in convalescence, thereby allowing you to reflect on all of the incidents that brought you where you are today. Although your wounds have gone through the core of your being and transcended many incarnations, you have been given a new lease on life. Having been given a second chance, it is important to exercise prudence in your choices so you can make the most of your new existence.

XXI World If The World has appeared in the Recent Past position, you have recently come to the end of a very important cycle in your life. You have completed a task that was a required initiating process to help you develop your soul growth. In the completion of this important milestone, you have self-actualised, as you realised you are capable of much more than you have been accomplishing in the past. This apex, however, was short-lived, as it did not take you long to discover there are many more goals you would like to achieve before your present sojourn on the earth dimension has reached its natural conclusion. It is best, therefore, to record your experiences in the annals of your mind as you look for other theoretical mountains to climb.

Wands/Rods/Fire

Ace If the Ace of Wands has appeared in the Recent Past position, you have recently gone through a creative spell, where you were bombarded with thoughts and ideas about many things you would like to bring life to. Because your eyes have been opened to the many possibilities that can be experienced in the world today, some may have perceived you to be a bit crazy. You were not unstable, but a channel to other spheres of awareness has been opened to you and the experience has left you totally unable to express in words your impressions.

Two If the Two of Wands has appeared in the Recent Past position, it is likely you have been approached by another individual to participate in an activity that will help to expand the energy that both of you could collectively produce. This venture would have made it possible to build upon the creative forces and has the ability to bring about an additional income, which would have been very beneficial to the both of you.

Three If the Three of Wands has appeared in the Recent Past position, you have recently been with a group of people who are creatively minded and look for ways to express their creativity. These people may be business associates or work colleagues because they seek to earn an income through the expression of their ideas and impulses.

Four If the Four of Wands has appeared in the Recent Past position, you have recently had cause for celebration. You may have landed a job or other achievement, which has enabled you to feel somewhat more secure about your future, and this is leaving you feeling quite pleased with yourself. You may have decided to move house or make some additions to your home, which have served to give you a sense of wellbeing and optimism for your future stability and prosperity.

Five   If the Five of Wands has appeared in the Recent Past position, you have recently been in disagreement with others. This difference of opinion has been so severe that you may have had heated arguments that have resulted in physical or verbal violence, which is a totally unacceptable way to respectfully relate to other individuals. The fact is you have been lashing out, but not necessarily at what the true problem is. Because you are not yet aware of the true extent of your incompatibility or differences with another person, you will continue to squabble over irrelevant issues until the truth of the matter is revealed to you. You will be somewhat surprised when you finally realise what the root of the problem is.

Six   If the Six of Wands has appeared in the Recent Past position, you have recently been very pleased with yourself because you have had a minor victory in what is often a complex web of the drama that makes up your life scenario. You have achieved a long held ambition, which has left you smiling to yourself, gaining more and more confidence after a period of much uncertainty. It is important, however, not to become complacent after one minor achievement in a whole myriad of battles that will ultimately form the struggles you must overcome before you have completed your life's purpose. Opposing forces will continue to present themselves to you, and it is therefore essential you take great care in choosing those you place your trust in.

Seven   If the Seven of Wands has appeared in the Recent Past position, you have recently gone through a period of turbulence in your life, as malignant forces have presented themselves to you at a most inopportune time. It is for that reason you are probably a bit worn down from all the stress you have been confronted with.

Eight   If the Eight of Wands has appeared in the Recent Past position, you have recently made a significant accomplishment in your life, which has left you feeling much more confident than you have been for a very long time. It is quite likely you have been on a journey that has broadened your horizons in some way, thereby enabling you to carry on even in the face of adversity.

Nine   If the Nine of Wands has appeared in the Recent Past position, you have just recently come through a very stressful period. You have felt very defensive and have conducted your affairs accordingly, not placing your trust in others. It is for that reason you have been considered somewhat of a loner, not caring to engage in the superficial chit-chat that brings people together and formulates more substantial friendships. Because you felt you had to do everything all on your own, without the benefit of assistance from others, you have become tired and are in need of a well earned break. Such a period of relaxation will serve to recharge your internal batteries and enable you to carry on even when opposing forces present themselves to you.

Ten   If the Ten of Wands has appeared in the Recent Past position, you have just recently gone through a period of intense work, and as a result are weary from the experience. You may have taken upon yourself a particular venture you felt confident you could successfully accomplish, only to discover you did not possess all of the skills necessary, and therefore had to expend much more energy than would otherwise have been required of you. You managed to accomplish what you set out to achieve, but are much wiser for the experience. It is unlikely you will embark upon such a grand project in quite a while because you need time to recuperate and reflect on the events that have brought you where you are today.

King   If the King of Wands has appeared in the Recent Past position, a man who has a great deal of business sense has made a significant impact on your life circumstances. He is a very astute individual who is able to use his shrewdness to his advantage and earn a substantial income. It is very likely he is involved in several ventures, which allow him a fair amount of free reign in the creation of his own destiny.

Queen   If the Queen of Wands has appeared in the Recent Past position, there was a woman with a fiery temper who has figured prominently in your life situation. She has a lot of energy and therefore tries to fill her days with activities that will keep her busy. If she works in the business or professional sector, she is likely to be successful in what she does because she has a sharp eye for detail. Because she is very egocentric and opinionated in her views, she may find it difficult to cultivate harmonious relationships with others who have views that are at variance to hers.

Knight/ Prince   If the Knight of Wands has appeared in the Recent Past position, a young man has figured prominently in your life. He is rather tempestuous and has many qualities the ladies find too charming to resist. Unfortunately, he is not yet settled, and will therefore need to undergo many changes before he has the confidence to choose one vocation, home or relationship that he will be content with.

Page/ Princess If the Page of Wands has appeared in the Recent Past position, there is a young person who has figured prominently in your life. She has much energy and has a bit of a temper. Although she can be sociable, she is a very me-centred individual and therefore may find it difficult to make lasting friendships. This young person likes to be the centre of attention, which at times can be truly testing for those around her.

Pentacles/Disks/Earth

Ace If the Ace of Pentacles has appeared in the Recent Past position, you have recently been thinking of money and finances a great deal. You may have decided to make a large purchase, which will entail using your savings or taking out a loan, all of which will require a significant commitment on your part. In addition, you may have an unexpected expense you can not easily evade, which has further intensified your interest in money and possessions in general, things that you need to exist comfortably in this material world.

Two If the Two of Pentacles has appeared in the Recent Past position, you have recently had several debts that need to be repaid before your can progress any further in your physical development in this world. Your finances have been in a state of fluctuation for quite some time, and this has been somewhat of a stressful experience for you, as you have been forced to juggle very limited resources to meet your commitments. It is important, therefore, that you keep your financial situation as simplistic as possible, so your monetary worries do not become genuine problems in the future.

Three If the Three of Pentacles has appeared in the Recent Past position, you have recently been through a period of material success, where money and other physical goods have been achieved with much less effort than previously. You also may have had some work completed on your home, either in the form or a renovation or an expansion of some kind. You may have gone through a complete house move, hoping the change would improve your particular circumstances in this life.

Four If the Four of Pentacles has appeared in the Recent Past position, you have spent much time at home, reflecting on your current position in this world. You have kept many thoughts close to your heart, not revealing a great deal to those near you. You have also gone through a period of frugality, not spending the little money you have had because you did not feel it was prudent to spend extravagantly. In many ways, you have been in what can be considered a self-imposed state of impoverished confinement, not daring to venture out into the world, quite possibly fearing failure or embarrassment.

Five   If the Five of Pentacles has appeared in the Recent Past position, you have recently come through a period of deep depression and despondency. Even amongst friends, you felt like an outsider because nobody could possibly understand exactly what you were going through inside your head. Finally, you just gave up trying to get people to see the depression that had taken over your entire being because you did not even have the energy to do that anymore. Along with the depressive illness you have suffered from, you have lost a lot of stamina necessary to go out and acquire income, which has placed even greater stress on you. Because you simply have not had the energy to go out and work to maintain a reasonable standard of living, you have consequently fallen into a state of poverty, which has added to the despair you have been feeling. To put it bluntly, you have been wallowing in your own self-pity for long enough, and it is now time to pick yourself up and do something constructive about your happiness and wellbeing.

Six   If the Six of Pentacles has appeared in the Recent Past position, you have recently gone through a period of philanthropy, engaging yourself in a fair amount of unpaid work. This charitable work has been good for your soul, as you have been giving back to the universe what you have taken, thereby helping those who are less fortunate than yourself. In addition, you have picked up skills you would not have acquired within the context of your normal paid employment, so the experience has been a valuable exercise in what you can do when you set your mind to something.

Seven   If the Seven of Pentacles has appeared in the Recent Past position, you have recently gone through a period of waiting. Many important things cannot come about until a certain amount of time has elapsed to enable a predetermined sequence of events to take place. Whether or not the outcome you anticipate turns out to be successful will depend upon what preparatory work you have accomplished while you were in such a period of stasis.

Eight   If the Eight of Pentacles has appeared in the Recent Past position, you have recently been in a learning environment, where you had to pick up skills through life and work experience. This has been a period of trial and error, as you have had to make a few mistakes before you could achieve a degree of proficiency. You have by now become quite capable at this new skill and are therefore ready to ply your trade. How successful you become will depend upon how personally and professionally you conduct yourself.

Nine   If the Nine of Pentacles has appeared in the Recent Past position, you have spent some time in convalescence, a time for you to meditate on your life experiences thus far. This has been a time for you to reflect upon how your experiences of the past have brought you where you are today and where you would like the direction of your life to go from this day forward.

Ten   If the Ten of Pentacles has appeared in the Recent Past position, you have recently had a great deal of contact with your family. You may have assets tied up with other family members, which would make it difficult to extricate yourself from more difficult individuals, even if you wanted to. While your complete involvement with other family members has its uses, it is not necessarily beneficial to your growth and development, because too much family involvement will limit the other social contacts that could be presented to you. It may be time to venture outside of the confines of the support of your family because you need the contact of other individuals to help you advance your soul growth.

King   If the King of Pentacles has appeared in the Recent Past position, a wealthy man has figured prominently in your life. He is very affluent, having earned his money in either the professional or business sector. It seems he has a natural flair for creating income and is always looking for ways to increase his already substantial wealth. He is a very caring individual, but expresses it through giving practical advice he hopes the questioners will have the good sense to heed.

Queen   If the Queen of Pentacles has landed in the Recent Past position, a woman of considerable means has played a prominent role in your recent situation. She is self-assured because she has the maturity and wisdom that has been acquired through years of watching the follies of others. She has therefore determined she is not going to do anything to jeopardise the stability she has worked so hard to achieve, which is why she is reluctant to act in so many life situations presented to her. This woman is a very generous person, giving to those who are less fortunate than her, thereby accruing much spiritual wealth through her generous endeavours.

Knight/ Prince If the Knight of Pentacles has appeared in the Recent Past position, a young man has figured prominently in the situation that prompted you to consult the oracle. He can at times be quite moral, possessing a strong sense of right and wrong, thereby presenting a somewhat boring image of himself. Because the physical world is so important to him, money and material possessions figure high on his list of priorities. He has a need to amass great wealth, possessions and property, and if he is not able to achieve this, his self-esteem will suffer until his modest situation is improved.

Page/ Princess If the Page of Pentacles has landed in the Recent Past position, a young person has figured prominently in your life situation. She is likely to be a methodical and slow learner, taking her time to complete any task she is given. Even though this individual is quite young, she is very strong-minded and not easily swayed once she sets her mind on something that she wants.

Swords/Air

Ace If the Ace of Swords has appeared in the Recent Past position, you have recently had an inspiration to communicate with other beings on a much higher plane than you normally would be inclined to. It is for that reason ideas of expression are overflowing, as you work out exactly how you would like to relay the message that has been sent to you. You may very well have begun a course of study, which will equip you to say in an authoritative manner the message that needs to be relayed. You may have begun legal proceedings to resolve a certain issue that has been on your mind for quite some time. The thing to keep in mind, however, is the sword is dual edged. It therefore cuts both ways, both positive and negative. It is for that reason you need to exercise caution in all you say and do to ensure you do not incriminate yourself.

Two If the Two of Swords has appeared in the Recent Past position, you have had a disagreement with a person or a group of people, and the rift that has been created has become so great that you have been left with no other alternative but to walk away completely. The thing to keep in mind is that you may not have been in possession of all the facts, which means you may not have been able to speak with as much credibility as you would have preferred. The key here is to do your homework so you will be prepared for the next debate on a subject that means so much to you.

Three   If the Three of Swords has appeared in the Recent Past position, your heart has been aching over an emotional situation you simply cannot resolve. There have been many words uttered, and some of them have wounded you deeply. The anguish you are feeling at this time will soon fade, as you come to terms with the fact that sometimes there will inevitably be personality clashes you have no control over and cannot resolve.

Four   If the Four of Swords has appeared in the Recent Past position, you have spent a fair amount of time in reflection on the situation that has prompted you to consult the oracle. You may have decided to take up meditative practices in an attempt to quiet your mind and listen to what God has to say to you. You need a period of stillness for a time to enable you to determine your best course of action. The time has come, however, to wake up, analyse what information you have been given, and decide upon your next course of action.

Five   If the Five of Swords has appeared in the Recent Past position, you have been at odds with a particular organisation or group of people because you differed on a particular issue. It is for this reason you have a bad taste in your mouth and are somewhat bitter about the individuals concerned. You will move on, and this is one instance where it is best to put the past behind you and look to the future.

Six   If the Six of Swords has appeared in the Recent Past position, you have recently left a very difficult time, a time that caused you a great deal of distress. It was a very emotional time and you may have difficulty coming to terms with many facets of the whole situation that have transpired, leaving you quite confused as to how you could have found yourself in such a situation. The past experience that has caused you so much angst, however, is something you would like to put behind you so you can resume your karmic journey and await newer, better opportunities to be presented to you.

Seven   If the Seven of Swords has appeared in the Recent Past position, you have recently found yourself engaged in some surreptitious activities that may not necessarily be advantageous to you in the long run. For reasons known only to you, you have felt the need to be somewhat secretive in your activities, which further reveals the nefarious nature of the situation you have involved yourself in. It is important, however, to make sure all of your actions will be above reproach because the truth will one day be revealed to you, and anything you do in secret will no longer be hidden from the world.

Eight   If the Eight of Swords has appeared in the Recent Past position, you have been stuck in a rut for quite a long time. Perhaps you were not in possession of all the facts to make a decision about what you needed to do with regard to one particular situation, so you decided not to make a decision at all. The fact is your refusal to chose meant you did need to make a choice about your life circumstances, but decided to go nowhere, wasting valuable time that should have been spent working on your psychic development. It is time now to open your eyes and see with clarity the situation you have found yourself in. You will then be able to observe the opportunities that will soon present themselves to you as an avenue for much needed change and self-development.

Nine   If the Nine of Swords has appeared in the Recent Past position, you have gone through a period of intense mental anguish, which may have even resulted in an illness that required recuperation on your part. You have been under a great deal of stress and have literally worried yourself to distraction, possibly making yourself ill in the process. Because you have had so much mental anguish, it is likely you have not received a great deal of sleep, thereby prolonging the feelings of despair that have plagued you. Because you are not really in a position to solve your problems on your own, it would be in your best interest to seek help from an outside source who can give you sound advice and ease some of the burdens you have been carrying all this time.

Ten   If the Ten of Swords has appeared in the Recent Past position, you have recently been let down by someone who you trusted in a really big way. Perhaps you depended on someone for something that was very important to you, and the fact he or she turned out to be unreliable has thwarted other plans you had anticipated carrying out. It is for that reason you have reached a point of total exhaustion and need to recover sufficiently before you will be able to trust again. You will move on from this difficult time with a greater understanding of the motives of individuals who have let you down so. In all probability, you will decide to mix with a whole new set of friends, and hopefully they will be people who are not so fickle in their affections and sentiments.

King   If the King of Swords has appeared in the Recent Past position, you have recently had dealings with a mature man who has much eloquence and is able to get his point across using a variety of communicative techniques. He is very much a forward thinker and therefore takes into consideration the good of all, as opposed to the good of a select few. He is also an impartial person and is not prone to sentimentality, so it will therefore be difficult to appeal to his emotions on any particular issue.

Queen If the Queen of Swords has appeared in the Recent Past position, you have recently encountered a woman who is very knowledgeable and has a wide breadth of experience to back up her views. She is very communicative, and therefore has many people who she can speak to about a variety of subjects. It is quite likely she revealed to you one particular piece of information that will help you to resolve the specific issue that prompted you to consult the oracle.

Knight/ Prince If the Knight of Swords has appeared in the Recent Past position, you have recently had dealings with a young man who is very communicative and likes to socialise with his peer group. Although he has within himself the ability to amass a vast array of knowledge and impart what he knows to humanity, he has not yet gained the experience and maturity to be able to relate effectively to other individuals. In time, he will become a valued member of society because he has much insight and wisdom to give to the world.

Page/Princess If the Page of Swords has appeared in the Recent Past position, there has been a young person who has figured prominently in your life. She has been witty and chatty, bursting forth with new ideas because she has not yet had the misfortune to see firsthand the negative side of humanity. Because she is so communicative, she may very well have unknowingly betrayed a confidence, thereby making things a bit awkward for you or at least one other person.

Cups/Water

Ace If the Ace of Cups has appeared in the Recent Past position, you have recently gone through an emotional period that had the potential to give you a great deal of happiness and fulfilment. Perhaps someone put their hand out to you in friendship, and this one act of unselfish love and kindness was enough to restore your faith in humanity.

Two If the Two of Cups has appeared in the Recent Past position, you have recently had a harmonious encounter with another person that has left you feeling quite happy with your world. The relationship is new and therefore still in the courtship phase, thereby giving you a rush of enthusiasm whenever you think of this new person who has entered your life. How you get on with this individual will be further revealed in the cards that follow.

Three If the Three of Cups has appeared in the Recent Past position, you have recently attended a social engagement that is very crucial to your present life circumstances. It is very likely you were put in touch with people who are able to influence your current situation, thereby hastening the process of change.

Four If the Four of Cups has appeared in the Recent Past position, you have just recently gone through a period of uncertainty. You have heard several rumours and are not sure exactly who you should believe, and in what direction you need to proceed in order to achieve optimum results in your life. Even though you are doubtful and unsure of what the future holds for you, very soon all will be revealed to give you an element of clarity in what you feel is an otherwise dubious situation.

Five If the Five of Cups has appeared in the Recent Past position, you have recently been through a period of disappointment, as you have had to discover things are not always as they seem. Perhaps you have had your hopes up high with regard to one specific subject, only to realise things did not work out as you had originally anticipated. You may also have been quite chagrined to realise people are quite often not exactly as they present themselves to be. The expression, 'beauty is only skin deep' is a quite apt reflection in this particular situation, as you have had to learn you cannot take people at face value. Everyone has secrets, and it is the revelation of those closeted skeletons, which are not so deeply buried in our past, that make up who we are today. You will move on, which is the important thing to remember at those times when you seem to be in a state of despair. You do, however, need an appropriate period of grieving before you can contemplate embarking upon any new endeavours.

Six If the Six of Cups has appeared in the Recent Past position, you have recently engaged in activities that brought back many of the feelings and thoughts of your childhood. It is important to reflect upon the impressions that have recently been revealed to you because they help you to realise what is going on as an adult. When you were younger, you may not have been equipped with the reasoning ability to fully understand certain life experiences, which no doubt caused you difficulties when you set about making friendships with other individuals. As an adult, however, you can reflect on your experiences so you can build on them and become a whole human being.

Seven If the Seven of Cups has appeared in the Recent Past position, it seems you have recently been presented with several options from a variety of sources. All of the choices available to you seemed very appealing and had much potential, but you were not sure exactly what path you should follow. Some options were more suitable to your temperament than others, and at least a couple of offers would prove to be fruitless. The cards that follow will reveal to you how beneficial your selection was to your particular circumstances.

Eight   If the Eight of Cups has appeared in the Recent Past position, you have recently decided that you were going to have to make a sacrifice and walk away from a venture that was very important to you. It saddens you to have to give up on someone or something, but at this point in time you must relinquish something to continue with your soul growth. You will eventually find that you made the correct decision to walk away from the emotive situation because other more worthwhile opportunities will soon be coming your way.

Nine   If the Nine of Cups has appeared in the Recent Past position, you have recently gone through a period of happiness and contentment. You may have found yourself dining out a lot or drinking at pubs, which may have had the knock-on effect of increasing your waistline. It is therefore essential, if only for your health, that you return to a more frugal way of life by eating and drinking in moderation. Simplicity is the key that will bring you the happiness you desire and deserve.

Ten   If the Ten of Cups has appeared in the Recent Past position, you have recently been through a period of harmony and wellbeing in a sanctioned family type setting. There is nothing in this world that has given such pleasure as your time with your one true love and your children or pets. This sense of oneness with the universe, which has come about through the eternal bliss that can only be achieved with a soul mate bond with your one true love, is what will carry you through life's darker times.

King   If the King of Cups has appeared in the Recent Past position, you have very recently come into contact with a very powerful, emotive man. He can become irate quite easily over the pettiest concerns, so it is best to tread carefully when dealing with this individual.

Queen   If the Queen of Cups has appeared in the Recent Past position, you have recently had contact with a very emotional woman who has had a huge impact on your current situation. This woman is very sociable and therefore has a large circle of friends and acquaintances that can assist you on your path to true enlightenment. It is essential, however, that you guard your dealings with this woman because she is not averse to embellishing the truth if she feels it will be in her best interests to do so.

Knight/ Prince If the Knight of Cups has appeared in the Recent Past position, you have recently come in contact with a young man who has a sentimental nature and is therefore very sensitive. He can be quite thoughtful and romantic, and can therefore endear himself to his admirers. Because he is so sensitive, he can at times find his mind is caught between fantasy and reality, and it is therefore prudent to take whatever he says with a grain of salt until other verifying factors are present.

Page/ Princess If the Page of Cups has appeared in the Recent Past position, you have recently had contact with a young person who has a very emotional nature. Even at a young age, she may suffer from mental disturbances, which will make her prone to neurosis and other depressive illnesses if she does not have suitable outlet for emotions caused by situations that have disturbed her.

6 The Near Future

0 Fool   If The Fool has appeared in the Near Future position, you will soon be embarking upon a new path that will aid you in your karmic evolution. In many ways, you will experience a total rebirth because you will come across people and situations that are totally new to you, thereby allowing you to build upon your current skill base. You may suffer a loss of some kind, but this too is necessary for you to gain an understanding of the ebb and flow of universal trends. Although you will be unsure of your footing in some situations you find yourself in the midst of, it is important to remember you will be protected in whatever you do, as long as your intentions are honourable.

I Magician   If The Magician has appeared in the Near Future position, you will soon be entering into what can only be described as a magical time in your life. You will soon begin a course of study that will reveal to you knowledge you have previously been totally unaware of. This knowledge will instil in you the wherewithal to create a better future for yourself, which is something you would definitely like to have and need. You will also encounter a young person who is a very astute individual. This person is educated and can show you different ways of looking at things, which will ultimately enhance the creative impulses you have within yourself. The tools The Magician has at his disposal are the four elemental forces that are a part of the earth forces.

II High Priestess   If The High Priestess has appeared in the Near Future position, you will soon be made privy to a secret that will enable you to go about your daily activities with greater efficiency. The information that will soon be revealed to you will have such a profound impact on you that you will never view the world in the same ordinary way you had previously. You will begin to see new meaning in the most ordinary, mundane things that will begin to take on a whole new spiritual significance. It is quite likely you will begin to see auras, but if not, you should take note of the messages people will send through the clothes they wear or the body language they present.

III Empress   If The Empress has appeared in the Near Future position, you will soon be influenced by maternal instincts, which could be referring to either you or someone close to you. You may consider planning a family, which will be of great importance to you. In addition, a female figure may decide it is time to wield her influence over her offspring, which may or may not be to your liking if you are not part of her family.

IV Emperor   If The Emperor has appeared in the Near Future position, you will soon encounter some karmic influences, where you may wonder exactly who is in control of your destiny. You may have dealings with a powerful person who has much control over many aspects of your wellbeing, which means you will need to tread carefully so you do not interrupt the very fragile make-up of universal forces. The time coming is one of the making or breaking of your destiny, so it is propitious to conduct your affairs soberly at all times to ensure you use the opportunities presented to you wisely.

V Hierophant   If The Hierophant has appeared in the Near Future position, you will soon come upon a major crossroad in your life. You need to make an important decision of such magnitude that things will never be the same again. It is important you think very carefully about this choice you will be confronted with because once your mind is made up, you cannot go back to the way things were without great difficulty.

VI Lovers   If The Lovers has appeared in the Near Future position, you will soon meet an individual who is one of your soul mates who you were destined to meet in this life because the both of you have important karmic work to do. In many ways, when you get together with this individual, you will feel a true connection, as though you can look into his eyes and reminisce on the different existences you have had before, and the secret is that you have. Although you will feel you have met your one true love in this world, there are some choices you will need to make on the path to true enlightenment. In order to achieve eternal bliss with another person, you may be asked to give something up in return in order to balance out the universe. The important thing to remember, however, is before you can truly love another person, you must first love yourself.

VII Chariot If The Chariot has appeared in the Near Future position, you will soon be making a journey that will be worth your while, and it will give you a fresh perspective on your current situation. Your travels are likely to be successful and you will be wiser for the experience, thereby enabling you to lead your life with much greater clarity of purpose in this life and the destiny of the group of people who you have incarnated with.

VIII Strength If Strength has appeared in the Near Future position, you will soon be put in a situation where many of your resources will be drained. You may have some health problems, which are a result of much stress in your life that has manifested as disease. It is for that reason you need to put your best foot forward and show the world you can still shine under pressure. Animals will be a huge help to you because they will love you unconditionally and restore the harmony in what is otherwise a rather hectic world. These beings can give you the pure, simplistic love that only an animal can present to another being.

IX Hermit If The Hermit has appeared in the Near Future position, you will be spending some time on your own. This period of solitude will enable you to reflect on your current situation in this life so you will know what it is you need to do, thereby enabling you to continue on your path to true enlightenment. It is important you develop an inner calm, which you can achieve through meditation and introspection, thereby allowing you to open your mind up to possibilities you would not have otherwise perceived. If possible, it would be in your best interest to attend a sanctuary or retreat, as you will be put in touch with like-minded souls who will become best of friends in time.

X Wheel of Fortune If The Wheel of Fortune has appeared in the Near Future position, you will soon encounter a change in fortune. If things have been difficult for you in recent months, you should find that by some fluke, things will turn in your favour, thereby enabling you to embark on activities that were previously closed to you. If things have been going well for you, you can expect a hidden glitch to shake up your stability, which will ultimately keep you from becoming too complacent in this life. The Wheel has within it the four fixed astrological signs of Taurus, Leo, Scorpio and Aquarius, which correspond with the four elemental forces and give it a sense of stability and equilibrium. Because all four signs square each other, however, a feeling of tension is in the atmosphere, which needs to be released if good fortune and harmony are to be attained. It is also important to keep in mind most 'luck' is in fact hard work, which has shown a profit at the most unlikely of times.

Therefore, if you have put in the effort, you will reap the rewards of your labour.

XI Justice If Justice has appeared in the Near Future position, you will shortly encounter equilibrium of forces where there has previously been an imbalance. The reason for this is because in order for the universe to continue, it must operate in a state of co-existence, striving to balance the positive and negative forces that are an inherent part of your life. You may find yourself engaged in legal proceedings, which could be an anxious time if you are relying on an outcome in your favour. In order to assure fair dealing, it may be possible to bring your issue to an impartial party who can mediate and help you come to a decision that is suitable to all concerned parties.

XII Hanged Man If The Hanged Man has appeared in the Near Future position, you will soon find you will have to make a sacrifice and give up something dear to you. You will realise you cannot force the things that are destined to occur because as soon as the pressure is released, what you have desired will leave of its own accord. It is for that reason that you must use subtle influences to bring that which you desire into your sphere of existence. Because gentleness is the key, you may have to wait for that which is your utmost goal. In the process of waiting and slowly manipulating the cosmic forces in your favour, you may find that what you thought you wanted is not what you really need for your soul growth. When you come to this realisation, you will achieve a fair degree of enlightenment with regard to the forces of nature, thereby allowing what you need to be given to you with little or no effort on your part.

XIII Death If Death has appeared in the Near Future position, you will shortly encounter a situation that will be such a massive change that it is likely you will experience a loss of some kind. It will be a transformative time for you because you will have experiences of such an extreme nature when the dust has settled, you will have been through nothing short of a re-birth. When a woman gives birth to a child, it is in many ways a traumatic experience like nothing she has ever encountered, leaving her temporarily weakened from the birth crises. In the same vein, when Death appears, a re-birth of sorts will occur, which in all probability will entail a similar level of pain and anguish before the realisation of the new life has been acknowledged. It is important to remember the beautiful butterfly must first emerge from a cocoon; you too must endure a time of darkness before the brilliance of your new identity will emerge.

XIV
Temperance

If Temperance has appeared in the Near Future position, you will soon be entering a time where all appears to be in a period of stasis. This is not a time where you can make any magnificent achievements because the universe is in the process of harmonising and achieving a balance between positive and negative forces. Because it seems there is nothing productive you can do during this time of waiting, you may assume the best you can do is to do nothing. Doing nothing, however, is in effect doing something, because you are making the conscious decision to take no action at all. The best action you can take, therefore, is to make sure all of your affairs are in order for the more propitious time that will ultimately occur. It would be in your best interest, therefore, to work to achieve moderation in all aspects of your life.

XV Devil

If The Devil has appeared in the Near Future position, you will soon be given lots of responsibility, which will subsequently cause you to think more of the practicalities of the earth we have incarnated into. Because you will be preoccupied with work, money and responsibilities, you may not feel as carefree as you have felt in earlier times. You will focus more on the physical and material side of existence, which will in many ways weigh you down to the earth. Because you are concentrating your energies on the more basal aspects of life, you will be more susceptible to the lower, darker influences that can pervade your soul when you are thinking negatively. It is for that reason you may find yourself more sombre in temperament, perhaps even possessing more of a dark, sardonic type of humour.

XVI Tower

If The Tower has appeared in the Near Future position, expect some upheaval in your life. You may very well have made sure that all of the i's were dotted and the t's were crossed to ensure there was as little confusion as possible. Because everything in your life may have seemed to have been ticking along smoothly, you have developed an attitude of complacency, feeling you have done all you possibly can to achieve a stable, secure, and even possibly boring life. There are, however, some things you have absolutely no control over. Although you have free will over your own destiny, you do not have free will over the destiny of others, whose lives may very well overlap with yours. This interconnecting of individual destinies are at cross purposes to yours could very well bring about a sort of karmic confusion, as all parties involved try to restore equilibrium in the resulting chaos. In addition, you may need to come to terms with the fact the life you have carved for yourself may not necessarily be the life that is going to afford you maximum soul growth, which is why your subconscious has decided to shake things up a bit. You may therefore see the upcoming period as a time of loss, but this is a fine time of opportunities, a time when you can explore choices that you may not otherwise have been open to. It is always important to keep in mind that when the universal forces close a door, they open a window.

XVII Star If The Star has appeared in the Near Future position, you will soon be entering a period of optimism and hope for what lies in store for the future. You will have a happy disposition, as you try to think positively that the dreams you have will turn out to be true. It is likely you will develop a friendship with another person, and this liaison will be satisfying for the both of you. This is a time of Aquarian ideals, where science and technology will figure prominently in your day-to-day activities. If you have been considering becoming more involved in information technology, the timing would be auspicious.

XVIII Moon If The Moon has appeared in the Near Future position, you will soon be entering a period of confusion, as all is not as it appears. There are forces at work that are occurring simultaneously and at cross-purposes to the life you are currently living. You are aware that there are situations occurring simultaneously and parallel to your own, but you cannot pinpoint exactly what is transpiring right under your nose. While you are in the dream state you will be able to glimpse those worlds that are similar, but not identical to your own, making you discover there are other realities that co-exist on the earth plane, just beyond your mental grasp. There are times when you are daydreaming or lost in thought when you will receive mental flashes of lost worlds, which will make you wonder if the imagery you were presented with was a memory from this or a parallel life. All of those intrusions from other realities can make you question your own sanity, but reasonability is not an issue as long as you reveal those impressions you have received only to your most trusted friends. Your friends, however, can be deceptive, as you come to realise who your true companions in this life are. Just because a person is friendly and polite does not make that person a friend, which you will soon discover for yourself. You will be quite surprised to learn that those people who you had believed to be your allies will pass you by, but the people who you had not previously given much notice to will be worthy of merit.

XIX Sun If The Sun has appeared in the Near Future position, you will go through a period of happiness and gaiety. It seems you will have a high level of self-confidence you have not had before. Animals and children will figure prominently because they love unabashedly and are not terribly concerned about a person's outward appearance. This will also be a time of high exposure to yourself, so you will therefore need to make sure you are at your best when under public scrutiny.

XX Judgement   If Judgement has appeared in the Near Future position, you will soon be going through a deep cleansing process and the faith you had lost in humanity will be restored to some degree. You may decide to embark upon a type of therapy, which will go a long way to heal many of the wounds that still remain in your auric web. You may meet someone along your earth walk who can help you to meet the many demands that are placed upon you, thereby giving you a feeling of unity, which you have not experienced for quite some time.

XXI World   If The World has appeared in the Near Future position, you will soon be completing a major cycle in your life, which will bring you closer to unity of the soul. You may complete a course of study, which would end your sojourn as a student of life and hopefully propel you into the arena of work and professionalism. You may have decided it is time to take a personal relationship one step further in its evolution, which could be a commitment of some kind. Alternatively, if a relationship you have been involved in has been non-productive, or even destructive, dissolution of the union may be deemed more appropriate. The body plays a significant theme in the symbology of the world so that matters relating to the body will also take precedence.

Wands/Rods/Fire

Ace   If the Ace of Wands has appeared in the Near Future position, you will shortly enter into a period of creativity that may possibly yield financial or business results. You may begin to think about what you can do to expand your professional standing and therefore explore new ideas. You may decide to expand on what you already know or decide to embark upon an altogether new path.

Two   If the Two of Wands has appeared in the Near Future position, you will soon be approached by another individual to partake of an activity that should theoretically yield profits for the both of you. The reason for this is because you both possess skills independent of each other, and when these assets are used in conjunction of each other, they have the potential to produce far more than both attributes combined. What you are planning is likely to be creative in nature, but is ultimately a profitable venture so the both of you could enjoy the fruits of your labour.

Three If the Three of Wands has appeared in the Near Future position, you will shortly find yourself amongst a group of people who are engaged in achieving one common goal. This group may be comprised of work colleagues because business enterprise is often associated with the element of Fire, which governs the magical nature of the wand. The group could also be comprised of friends and acquaintances, who have gathered together for a sporting or social activity. It could also be comprised of family members who are tied together in a business venture. It is unlikely the alliances you form during this time will be lasting, as the group was formed only in pursuance of a specific task. You should form this union nonetheless because it will serve as a satisfying experience and help to build the confidence you have in yourself.

Four If the Four of Wands has appeared in the Near Future position, you will soon have cause for celebration. Events will transpire that will make you feel more secure than you have been in a long time. You may have received a professional position that would enable you to fulfil some of your personal goals, thereby enabling you to feel less vulnerable in a volatile world. Your family and home will be paramount, as you will feel greater solidarity towards those who you are close to.

Five If the Five of Wands has appeared in the Near Future position, you will soon discover you are struggling over one particular situation. This situation has been a huge source of trouble for you, and you are not able to put your finger on exactly what the root of the problem is. Because you are in the dark about the precise problem that is causing many of your difficulties, you are striking out in all directions, trying to solve one problem after another. You are probably thinking to yourself, 'just as soon as I get over this one hurdle, everything will be okay and I will be able to live normally'. The problem is, however, that just as soon as you do get over that one hurdle, another one of even greater magnitude will present itself to you. It will take much soul searching on your part to try to come to terms with the root of all your problems, but when you have, many things that had previously been inaccessible to you will seem to fall into place. If you are not able to find out what the root cause is on your own, you may want to consider outside help.

Six If the Six of Wands has appeared in the Near Future position, you will make a significant achievement in the future that is a part of your purpose in this life. This accomplishment will be of such magnitude that you will feel the need to reward yourself for a job well done. There is much to do, however, to secure your future prosperity and happiness, so it is not appropriate to sit back and relax after what is in reality only a minor victory. It is essential you make appropriate preparations for any proposed activities because one minor mistake could negate all previous successes.

Seven   If the Seven of Wands appears in the Near Future position, you will have to work very hard to maintain any successes you may have had in the past. If you have recently been promoted to a position that is higher than you had been working at, you will find you will have a steep learning curve and those around you will not be prepared to wait for you to catch up to their speed. It is for that reason you should keep any insecurities that you have close to your heart, because if you confide your doubts to inappropriate people, you will merely be perceived as weak and not up the tasks you have been given overall responsibility for.

Eight   If the Eight of Wands appears in the Near Future position, you will soon be taking a trip that will expand your level of awareness in some way. You will go somewhere that, to you, is quite far away.

Nine   If the Nine of Wands has appeared in the Near Future position, you will soon have reason to feel as if you are on the defensive. People may not see you as you really are, which could cause them to discredit you in some way. Because you feel threatened, you will tend to behave differently and people will not see the 'you' that is relaxed and would like to enjoy life.

Ten   If the Ten of Wands appears in the Near Future position, you will soon find yourself in a position where you are totally overwhelmed by certain events. You may take on a job you are not quite ready for, and because you do not possess the skills necessary to see it successfully to this end, you are filled with a sense of foreboding. Although you work tirelessly to try to complete the tasks you have been presented with, you are spinning your wheels, not accomplishing a great deal of anything. Before you reach a level of total exhaustion, you need to take a good look at the problem that this is causing you so much angst. You may need to go out and get the skills you need to see the project to completion, which will further lengthen the learning curve you will soon be embarking upon. Alternatively, you may decide it is in your best interests to abandon the pursuit altogether, leaving such endeavours to more able souls.

King If the King of Wands has appeared in the Near Future position, you will soon be influenced by a man who has a flair for business and enterprise. Whenever he happens upon a new opportunity, he instantly wonders how he can expand on it and make it useful for his particular circumstances. He has a lot of love to give, which he will lavish on children, animals, partners, or anyone he feels is worthy of his affection. This individual will stand out and the colours yellow and red will be significant to him.

Queen If the Queen of Wands has appeared in the Near Future position, you will soon be influenced by a woman who is very shrewd and astute about the ways of the world. She has much vibrancy about herself, which makes her the life and soul of any gathering. She is very wise and can impart wisdom to you metaphorically, using parables to get her message across. She is not, however, one to relate to those who do not wish to listen, and will therefore wait until she is asked to speak frankly on any given subject.

Knight/ Prince If the Knight of Wands has appeared in the Near Future position, you will soon become involved with a young man who possesses a great deal of energy. He has much charisma within himself, which makes him very attractive to others, especially those of the opposite sex. It is important to note, however, that because he has not yet experienced many of the facets of this life, he needs time to explore the world and learn from what he has been exposed to. It is for that reason he may be an able paramour to dally in the waters of romance and the fleeting feelings of love, but he is not ready for commitment and therefore will make an unsuitable candidate for lasting commitment at the moment.

Page/ Princess If the Page of Wands appears in the Near Future position, you will soon come into contact with a young person who has a lot of energy and needs to stay busy, or she will get into mischief. She is a very loving individual, but needs a great deal of attention, or she will soon feel neglected and could react inappropriately to the wrong people.

Pentacles/Disks/Earth

Ace If the Ace of Pentacles has appeared in the Near Future position, you will soon be thinking of money and material possessions. You may be considering beginning a new venture that has the possibility of bringing you greater wealth and prosperity, which would definitely improve your current standard of living. Alternatively, you may be thinking of making a major purchase that will bring more responsibility with it, as you will have to organise exactly how you will pay for those items you want.

Two   If the Two of Pentacles has appeared in the Near Future position, you will soon have some financial or material concerns that will need to be resolved before you can progress any further in your current endeavour. It appears you will need to learn how to take greater control over your financial situation, as it will be necessary for you to manage your resources more effectively so you do not find yourself swimming in a sea of debt. You may find it necessary to take on extra paid employment in an attempt to pay the people who you owe money to, and you may need to ask people to repay debts they owe you, which could be somewhat of an awkward exercise in tact and diplomacy.

Three   If the Three of Pentacles has appeared in the Near Future position, property and possessions will soon mean a great deal to you. You may consider moving into a new home, which you hope will be an improvement over your present living circumstances. You may also consider making a major renovation to your property, which will entail considerable investment and expertise on your part. A marriage, engagement or other type of commitment is likely, but this union would in all probability be based just as much on purely material concerns as the concept of true love, so it is important not to let yourself fall prey to any illusions with regard to the partnership you are considering.

Four   If the Four of Pentacles has appeared in the Near Future position, your possessions specifically relating to your personal security will shortly be very vital to you. You need to prepare for lean times by living simply and keeping your expenditures down. It is not a propitious time to invest in risky ventures because it is unlikely you will get back your initial investment, much less make a profit. You need to be discriminating about who you allow into your confidence and your home because some individuals who wish to get to know you better have interests at cross purposes to your own. It is important, therefore, to keep your doors locked because intruders will use any opportunities available to them to profit from any lapses in your own personal security.

Five   If the Five of Pentacles has appeared in the Near Future position, you would be wise to prepare for lean times ahead. You will very likely go through a period of melancholic illness because there are certain aspects of your life you are not happy with. You have a very strong desire to belong to a group, and when people snub you and deny you membership to their particular clique, you will feel the full force of their rejection. The fact that you are not exactly where you would like to be in your career and social standing is not necessarily a failing on your part, but merely a phase you must go through in the cycle of transformation that affects us all. The best that you can do is save your money, live simply, and prepare for more prosperous times.

Six If the Six of Pentacles has appeared in the Near Future position, you will soon be going through a karmic balancing act that will correct any inequalities that may have existed for quite some time. A sense of harmony in the universe is necessary to enable it to run smoothly and efficiently, allowing life to grow and thrive. It is for that reason you may be asked to perform a task that would have no apparent benefit to you. You will, however, reap the rewards of your gift at a later date, so you do not need to worry about giving without the benefit of any type of recompense. By the same token, you may find yourself in the position where you need to ask for assistance. You should not be ashamed or embarrassed at having to receive any kind of help from others because it is merely a part of the cycle of things.

Seven If the Seven of Pentacles appears in the Near Future position, you are in a period of waiting, especially with regard to the situation that prompted you to consult the oracle. You may very well have put in a fair amount of effort to see a certain project to completion, but the forces that prevail indicate there is nothing you can do about the situation for the time being but wait. Because Pentacles represents the physical aspects of ourselves, if you have been hoping to start a family, you will soon be very fertile and receptive to the influences that come about to make such an objective reality. If, however, you do not want to add to your existing family, it would therefore be wise to take adequate precautions with regard to that matter as well.

Eight If the Eight of Pentacles has appeared in the Near Future position, you will soon learn some new things either in your current vocation or a different line of work altogether. These skills you will soon be acquiring will in all probability relate to something to do with working with your hands, which can go a long way to healing some of the emotional or mental blocks that continue to reside in your psyche.

Nine If the Nine of Pentacles has appeared in the Near Future position, you shall soon be entering a hiatus, which is something you desperately need in order to recuperate from a stressful situation. During this time of rest, your physical needs will be taken care of, which will enable you to spend time in reflection so you can determine exactly what direction it is you would like to follow.

Ten If the Ten of Pentacles has appeared in the Near Future position, it is anticipated that very soon you will find yourself involved with your family in a matter that concerns property or money. It is a distinct possibility that you will be asked to work closely with older members of your family group, which should instil in you a sense of responsibility. The increased duty you may be asked to take on promises to yield greater wealth and prosperity in later years, thereby lessening some of the resentment you may feel at being denied the carefree existence you feel you deserve.

King If the King of Pentacles has appeared in the Near Future position, you will soon come into contact with a very influential man. He is somewhat of a man of means, and even if he is not instilled with a great deal of material wealth, he is a valued member of his community because his opinions are sound and considered worthwhile. This individual has a solid personality and is not prone to rash behaviour. He can be generous when it is in his best interests, but he needs to exercise caution not to become too miserly in later life.

Queen If the Queen of Pentacles has appeared in the Near Future position, you will soon meet a woman who is confident in her self, and has money of her own. She is an independent woman because she has wealth in her own right to enable her to do the things she would like. She can be kind, and helps those who are less fortunate than herself, which ultimately makes her a leader in her own community. She is very practical and level-headed, and is therefore not inclined to whimsical behaviour. When asked, she can impart sound advice to the querent.

Knight/ Prince If the Knight of Pentacles has appeared in the Near Future position, you will soon have the opportunity to come into contact with a young man who is stable and level headed. He has a good head on his shoulders and is not one to act hastily. Although he is somewhat slow and methodical, he usually gets what he wants through persistent and diligent effort. Material possessions are very important to this individual whose self-esteem is often determined by what he owns and how much money he earns. It is for that reason he will endeavour to work hard so that he can amass wealth and strive towards self-actualisation through experiencing the physicalities of our universe.

Page/ Princess   If the Page of Pentacles has appeared in the near future position, you will soon come into contact with a young person who has the potential to be affluent, but has not yet made her mark in this life. She is very practical, methodical and steadfast in her opinions. She is determined to achieve material prosperity because wealth and prosperity are very important to her sense of self and wellbeing.

Swords/Air

Ace   If the Ace of Swords appears in the Near future position, you will soon enter into a period of correspondence with regard to one specific issue. The initial sparks of an idea will flow, but this is not to be confused with the creative energies inherent in the Ace of Wands. Rather than the concept of building something new, which is part of the creation principle of Fire, you and those associated with you will have an intense desire to make your ideas and opinions known via the spoken and written word. This is also a time of deep karmic significance, where you will be forced to come face to face with the karmic influences that have been built up over various incarnations.

Two   If the Two of Swords has appeared in the Near Future position, you will soon find you are in disagreement with another individual. The both of you are not in possession of all the facts and therefore are not in a position to made an accurate assessment of the situation. As a result of you not being able to see eye to eye with this person, you may decide that, for the time being anyway, the best thing you can do is to part company until the truth is revealed in a more coherent fashion. If this individual meant nothing to you, you would have no difficulty whatsoever walking away. The fact is, however, that much emotional energy has been cultivated between the two of you, which makes it all the more difficult to depart. When all the facts come to light, it may be possible to establish a reunion, but a cooling off period is necessary if equilibrium and harmony are to be restored.

Three   If the Three of Swords has appeared in the Near Future position, you will soon go through a very emotionally tumultuous period. It seems there are individuals who mean a great deal to you, but they are not treating the relationship with the respect it deserves. Their total disregard for you and your feelings is causing you a great deal of emotional pain, as you cannot understand what you have ever done to this individual to cause him or her to treat you with such a lack of respect. The fact is you didn't do anything to bring such emotional pain to yourself.

The problem lies with the other person, who must find his own way in this life before he can wholly relate to you, and has not yet learned to treat his relationships with maturity and care that ultimately comes from mutual respect and love. Although you are in anguish at this point in your life, it is important to keep in mind you were merely caught in the crossfire of the antics of a misguided soul. The person who has hurt you so is merely not ready to be loved by you, which is why he or she has behaved in such a hurtful manner.

Four   If the Four of Swords has appeared in the Near Future position, you need to get as much rest as you can to restore any strength that has been dissipated. You need to reserve your energy for a time when things are much busier than they are at the moment. This period of rest should be used as a time of meditation and inner reflection, a time where you allow your mind to wander so new ideas can come into your head, undeterred by the hustle and bustle of an active lifestyle. New thoughts that enlighten you will come, if you let them. If you take the time to quiet your mind and open yourself up to new and wonderful impressions of other worlds that await you and anyone else who is ready for such inner adventures.

Five   If the Five of Swords has appeared in the Near Future position, you will soon be at odds with a person or group of people who you had originally felt to be your friends. There seems to be a lot of banter going on, but much of it appears to be malicious gossip intended to harm the reputation of involved participants. While some of the activity can be viewed as lively debate on the ethics of a particular topic, some of it is merely stories that have been made up in an attempt to slur the characters of others. It is not envisaged that you will stay in this environment for any length of time because you will soon tire of such destructive behaviour from other individuals. Since you will find yourself mixing with people who are morally and ethically inferior, the best you can do in such a situation is to exercise caution in all you say or write, and keep copies of any documents relating to the situation. The documents will be useful in the future if there are any intentional or accidental lapses in your or other individual's memories.

Six   If the Six of Swords has appeared in the Near Future position, you will soon be leaving a difficult time, hoping to make a new life for yourself. You may have been involved in a relationship or vocation that was not healthy for you and consequently brought you a great deal of sadness.

After much soul searching and reflection, you will decide the best you can do is to walk away from a situation that has been causing you so much grief, even if it means you will have to give up a great deal in the process. The decision to build a new life for yourself will come about with some melancholia because the fact is you would have preferred the situation you are leaving to have turned out more positively. Because you will need to make new acquaintances in the environment you will soon be entering, you will need to practise discretion so you can select only positive people who will be able to afford you harmonious relationships in your milieu. The time coming will be a period where you will need to learn from your mistakes, so you need to exercise attention to detail so you can keep any errors to a minimum. All you have experienced in the past will have been of no value to you if you cannot learn from it and then move on to better, more fulfilling relationships and situations.

Seven If the Seven of Swords has appeared in the Near Future position, you need to be guarded in your activities because there are individuals around you who are taking your ideas as their own. You need to guard your possessions because you may unknowingly invite someone into your home who may decide to take something of value, an item that means a great deal to you. Even if you take adequate precautions not to invite dubious characters into your space, an opportunist could always take it upon himself to take advantage of any locks that are not properly utilised. Alternatively, you may find yourself in a situation where stealth and secrecy is necessary. You will therefore need to ask yourself whether what you intend to do is honourable and ethical. If it isn't, maybe there is something more worthy of your efforts you can engage yourself in to achieve the same goal.

Eight If the Eight of Swords has appeared in the Near Future position, you will soon enter into a period of entrapment that has in many ways been caused by your own sense of tact and diplomacy. You may find you have become involved in something that is not beneficial for your soul growth, and this has consequently taken you off your true path to such an extent that you will not know the correct course of action to take. You will find yourself to be in a period of confinement, which may be self imposed or caused by forces more powerful than you possess at this current time. During your isolation you will not be made privy to vital pieces of information that are very important to your own wellbeing and safety, which will thus compound the problem you will soon be involved in. Although it is difficult to see, there is a way out of this predicament, but you will be required to make some tough decisions with regard to your future. The best you can do at this time is to keep your affairs legitimate and above board, thereby lessening any negative influences that come your way.

Nine   If the Nine of Swords has appeared in the Near Future position, you will soon go through a period of mental confusion, which will cause you to feel very anxious in your self. You may find you have difficulty sleeping because you have so much on your mind it is difficult for you to relax enough to sleep. You may also find that you succumb to one of the many mental illnesses, such as depressive disorders, personality disorders that are a result of past, unresolved experiences, obsessive/compulsive disorders, anxiety, panic, addictions that have come about as a result of your attempt to self-medicate, neurosis, and even psychosis. While there are many things in your present life you have no control over, there are some things you have within yourself the ability to take command of. It is for that reason the best you can do to navigate through this difficult patch is to live simply and honestly, steering clear of those individuals who will only drag you down. Above all, you need to eat properly and get plenty of rest, which will give you adequate reasoning ability to decide what is best for your particular life path.

Ten   If the Ten of Swords has appeared in the Near Future position, you will soon feel quite unhappy about a particular situation. It seems you have placed your trust in inappropriate individuals, who have only let you down. Unfortunately, there is nothing you can do but lick your wounds, nurse your damaged ego, and take stock of the situation that has developed. Upon reflection, you may see the signs of dissent were there, but you did not want to see them. It may be a good time to decide to mix with a different crowd of people who would be more appreciative of your company, thereby lessening the chance of subsequent betrayals.

King   If the King of Swords has appeared in the Near Future position, you will soon be influenced by a man who has a significant command of the power of words. He has the ability to express himself eloquently, which instils in him the ability to speak poetically and metaphorically. He needs the company of other people, which makes him a witty and pleasant conversationalist most of the time. Although he is intensely loyal to people while he is with them, when they leave his sphere of awareness, he can easily forget all about the friendship that had been developed. It is for that reason this individual has had many relationships, much to the dismay of his present partner, who is also at risk of being merely one of his past conquests.

Queen   If the Queen of Swords has appeared in the Near Future position, you will soon be widely influenced by a woman who is very articulate and able to express herself. She is very knowledgeable about many subjects, but fame may have alluded her, leaving her with the feeling life has passed her by. It is for that reason she may carry an air of self-importance that she has not really earned, thereby leaving some people perplexed by her over-the-top behaviour. She is knowledgeable about a wide variety of subjects and would like to impart the wisdom she has gleaned to others, but only needs an audience who will listen.

Knight/ Prince   If the Knight of Swords has appeared in the Near Future position, you will soon be influenced by a young man who has some very high ideals and aspires to great things. He has somewhat of a temper, however, which manifests itself through explosive outbursts and insulting remarks he makes because he does not have the maturity and strength of character to relate on a positive level. He has the potential to one day be a great thinker and communicator, but until that time he needs to mature and grow through his life experiences. Because he is able to freely express himself, he will never be short of admirers.

Page/ Princess   If the Page of Swords has appeared in the Near Future position, you will soon be influenced by a young person who is quite chatty. She has an inquisitive mind and therefore asks many questions less astute individuals would overlook. She can also be quite nervous and may be prone to biting her nails or engaging in a frenzy of activity, as she tries to release much of the energy inside of her. As she matures, many of the frenetic activities she pursues will wane, but until that time it is important she stays busy through hobbies or educational pursuits so she does not become involved in destructive activities.

Cups/Water

Ace   If the Ace of Cups has appeared in the Near Future position, you will soon enter into a situation that has the potential to bring you great happiness and fulfilment. This situation could very well be a job, school, holiday or relationship, but you will know when you come across it because it will seem right to you for the first time in a very long time.

Two If the Two of Cups has appeared in the Near Future position, you will soon become involved with an individual who can bring you a great deal of happiness and fulfilment just through your contact with him. There will be a unique bond that will keep the two of you together, as you form a partnership that is likely to be long lasting. You will find this person will be a true friend, and your relationship will in all probability withstand the test of time.

Three If the Three of Cups has appeared in the Near Future position, you will soon find you have a lively social life, full of parties and get-togethers. There is likely to be much merry-making, as the people involved would like to have a good time and enjoy themselves. You will receive invitations to social events, and it would be in your best interests to attend them because you never know what opportunities might be presented to you. Because there will be so many social outings, you may find you are eating and drinking more than what your body needs to function healthily, and you may find yourself putting on weight or experiencing a general feeling of unwellness. It is for that reason you may want to prepare for this period of intense social activity by watching your weight, getting into shape, and trying to live your life with a semblance of moderation.

Four If the Four of Cups has landed in the Near Future position, you will soon be entering into a period of uncertainty and doubt. While all outward signals appear normal, you cannot help but get an inner feeling that all is not well in paradise. You may suffer from nervousness or anxiety, which gives further rise to the misgivings you have with regard to the situation. To further confuse the issue, you will be receiving conflicting stories from various sources, leaving you rather perplexed about what the truth of the matter actually is. It is for that reason you should only be swayed by factual evidence and let your inner voice guide you toward your best course of action.

Five If the Five of Cups has appeared in the Near Future position, you will soon be entering a period of melancholia because the events you had hoped would happen have not transpired in the manner you would like. You may have had your hopes up high with regard to one particular issue, and never really believed the situation could turn out differently than what you had previously envisaged. When the unexpected occurs, it seems you will be caught totally off guard, which will only serve to add to the angst you are feeling. It is understandable you will be disheartened, but with the new knowledge you possess, you have within yourself the ability to create a new life for yourself, and the wisdom you have picked up along the way will help you to achieve true happiness.

Six   If the Six of Cups has appeared in the Near Future position, you will soon enter into a situation that reminds you of past times. You may be reunited with someone from your childhood, thereby enabling you to relive those experiences. You may also find yourself engaged with children in some capacity, which will enable you to grow as an individual. If you live far away from where you lived in your more formative years, you may find yourself travelling back to that place, which will help to renew your sense of self. You will soon be able to see with clarity where you have been, and this should help you to determine where you would like to go from there and then to visualise what your ultimate goal with regard to this particular instance is.

Seven   If the Seven of Cups has appeared in the Near Future position, you will soon find yourself in a situation where several options will be made available to you. You do not, however, know which option will yield the greatest results, and that is precisely where your challenge lies. The point to remember is some choices will be positive, while others will get you nowhere, and still others will be detrimental to your psychic wellbeing. It is for that reason you should not become bamboozled by a highly developed sales pitch that will be presented to you by a confidence artist. If you are unsure, it would be best to ask for a second opinion and shop around until you find something that feels right for you. It is crucial you do not allow others to force you into a decision you are not fully prepared to commit yourself to.

Eight   If the Eight of Cups has appeared in the Near Future position, you will soon be entering into an unknown realm of existence. There is one particular area of your life you have held onto relentlessly, but before you can progress any further in your current evolutionary path, you must learn to let go of it. Even though you know deep down in your heart this person, situation, or way of life was not a positive experience, you nevertheless clung on, hoping if you persisted in the endeavour that circumstances would change and you would be happy at last. After a great deal of soul searching, you will come to the reluctant decision that you must walk away from that which has caused you so much anguish and unhappiness. The decision to leave will be difficult because you will have to sacrifice some long-term goals that have fuelled your dreams. Better, more worthwhile experiences will come to you, but in the meantime, you must go through the grieving process of coming to terms with what you have given up.

Nine　If the Nine of Cups has appeared in the Near Future position, you will soon enter into a period where you are happy and content with yourself. You may, however, spend a lot of time on your own, so you should use this time to get to know yourself better, a time of inner reflection and attunement to your spiritual awareness. On the down side, however, you may find you are eating or drinking more than is necessary for the healthy functioning of your body, and this could consequently lead you to put on weight, which is not necessarily a good thing for your psychic development. It would be wise, therefore, to rest, eat sensibly and exercise regularly so you do not gain unwanted pounds and dull your auric web.

Ten　If the Ten of Cups has appeared in the Near Future position, you will soon find yourself in a situation that has the ability to give you a great deal of happiness and harmony. You may come face to face with your soul mate in this life, the person who you love and want to share a home and family with. It is likely you will bask in the simplest pleasures this world has to offer, such as walking in the countryside and spending time with the one you love.

King　If the King of Cups has appeared in the Near Future position, you will soon find yourself under the influence of a man who is a very sensitive individual. He is quite knowledgeable about a variety of subjects and can even be psychic at times. He is very perceptive, assessing any given situation before deciding whether he would like to involve himself in it or not. He is somewhat introverted, preferring to keep his thoughts and opinions to himself, not wishing to offend anyone with any views that might be considered controversial. He does, however, have many secrets, which you will need to uncover before you decide just how involved you would like to become with this individual.

Queen　If the Queen of Cups has appeared in the Near Future position, you will soon be influenced by a woman who is quite emotional. It is very easy for her to display her feelings, whether good or bad, thereby making it difficult for her to lie to people. It is easy to determine when she is saying something that is not true because she will tend to avert her eyes from the recipient of her communications in a somewhat coy fashion. She does, nevertheless, have something very important to impart to you, but you will need to watch her closely to glean the true meaning of her words.

Knight/ Prince   If the Knight of Cups has appeared in the Near Future position, you will soon come into contact with a young man. He can be very caring because he is such an emotive being, which instils in him a great deal of compassion for his fellow man. Because he is so sensitive, he appeals quite strongly to the opposite sex, as they feel an affinity for the more intuitive side of his nature. The dark side, however, is not something most people would like to explore because he has a depth that even he may not be aware of. When slighted, he can be petty and spiteful, which detracts from what is otherwise a delightful personality.

Page/ Princess   If the Page of Cups has appeared in the Near Future position, you will soon come in contact with a young person who is very sensitive to the moods of others. She is somewhat emotional and wears her heart on her sleeve, often becoming affected by the subtle motives of others that less sensitive souls might not pick up on.

7 The Querent

0 Fool If the Fool has landed in the Querent position, you have within your-self the wherewithal to break free from the old you and begin a new life, completely different from what you had previously imagined. Because you are undergoing a process of change, it is highly likely that your old friends will be somewhat perplexed by your new behaviours and attitudes, and will consequently stay away from you because you no longer fit into their mould of what a friend should be like. While this can be confusing and even hurtful, it will be a good opportunity for you to mix with a new set of acquaintances, people who will be more supportive of the qualities that you are striving to develop.

I Magician If The Magician has appeared in the Querent position, you are a very clever, thoughtful individual. Much of the energy you utilise is your ability to intellectualise any given situation, as you ponder the world around you. You are in awe of the universe, wondering how such a thing could have been created to work in such deep synchronisation, with only a few minor celestial mishaps occurring every several thousand years or so. As you contemplate what makes the world keep going despite insurmountable odds, you reflect upon the four elemental tools we so easily identify with; wands for light, disks for earth, swords for air and cups for water. What you will soon discover is that with those four archetypal tools that are so much a part of our earth, you can set about the creation process and build a universe of your own, if that is what you desire. When you begin to use your mind, focusing on the four archetypal symbols, you will enter into the realms of magic, which is merely the mind's ability to manifest into the physical world your creative mental processes. After a few successful attempts at this, to your astonishment, you will realise your thinking patterns can actually manifest themselves into the physical realities of this world, bestowing upon you the ability to create your own destiny. Therefore, if you think negatively, you will continuously be surrounded by what you perceive to be perpetual bad luck. Conversely, if you think positively, only good things will come to you.

II High Priestess If The High Priestess has appeared in the Querent position, you are going through a period of feminine introspection, where you are attempting to get in touch with the more receptive qualities that are an inherent part of yourself. You may decide that you would like to explore the esoteric aspects of universal awareness, which will predispose you to spending time on your own, studying astrology, tarot, numerology, the Cabala and other metaphysical subjects. While there are groups and circles you can join that will enable you to exchange ideas with other like- minded souls, the esoteric path to enlightenment is quite often a lonely one. You may find your relationships with men do not give you the satisfaction and fulfilment you desire for a variety of reasons, which will consequently cause you to seek the company of women. You feel you can trust women because you understand them. Although you are fertile and able to live in a family environment, for reasons known only to you, you do not want to pursue such a path in this stage in your soul's development.

III Empress If The Empress has appeared in the Querent position, you are seeking to utilise the receptive side of yourself. Home, family and relationships are very important to you, as you function at peak efficiency when those areas of your life are running smoothly. Your maturity gives you a calming influence over those individuals who are unruly or overbearing. Relationships are very important to you, and you are at your best when you are able to work within the confines of a stable, monogamous relationship.

IV Emperor If The Emperor appears in the Querent position, you know what you want out of life and continuously work toward that aim. You can be quite forceful, which can be somewhat off-putting to more timid souls. You are a born leader, but the problem lies in the fact that some people don't want or need to be led, and this can cause problems if you try to force your will on those who don't desire it. You have a somewhat impetuous nature, which needs to be tempered if you want to amass the great abundance that you truly deserve. As you mature you will mellow and become proficient at expressing yourself through less aggressive means, which will endow you with more endearing qualities to others.

V Hierophant   If The Hierophant has appeared in the Querent position, you are some-what of an orthodox person, preferring to express yourself through tried and true, socially acceptable channels. You aspire to the comfort and opulence that comes from following the path of the physical realms of our existence, and therefore seek to enter into the professional vocations that allow you to manifest your individual destiny through them. You were presented with a choice long ago in connection with your present sojourn in this earth plane. When presented with the choice of a life of comfortable luxury or a life of struggle, you chose the more convenient way of the pursuance of your karmic obligations. It is important to realise, however, that before your ego can develop, it must experience the more frugal aspects of our existence. Because you are so firmly grounded to the earth, you possess the qualities of a more practical, stable being, and are not that terribly concerned with the esoteric aspects of the soul. Your realm of existence is the exoteric, which is where you feel most at home in the physical realms of our universe. You are not one to rock the boat, but prefer to operate within the conventional methods that have been established in our society. It is for that reason you rarely take a stand on what you truly believe in, preferring to attune yourself with whatever system of thought is the most popular at the time.

VI Lovers   If The Lovers has appeared in the Querent position, you are being presented with a choice you must make, which will affect the entire course of your life. You may meet a person who will influence your decision. Quite often this card indicates that you are involved in a love affair, but sometimes it refers to a love triangle of sorts. The path to true love is often littered with obstacles that need to be overcome, thereby showing you the worth of your one and only soul mate. Sometimes another person may interfere in the scenario before a true union can be made. It is for that reason you need to think very carefully about what you are doing in relation to this one particular liaison. Your true soul mate is of such an enduring nature that there is no room in the relationship for other people and situations to interfere with your relationship with each other.

VII Chariot   If The Chariot has appeared in the Querent position, you strive for excellence in all you do in this life. You are not one to engage in idle pursuits, but prefer to stay active so you do not have to think about whatis bothering you. Because you are very ambitious, you will in all likelihood become successful in whatever you set out to achieve. The key to remember, however, is that you have the propensity to be more successful at some tasks than others, so you need to determine what you are really good at and then go for it. It is envisaged that you will be taking a trip that relates specifically to your query in the very near future.

VIII Strength   If Strength has appeared in the Querent position, you possess a great deal of charm and charisma that makes you a natural leader amongst your peers. You have the ability to lead by example, which makes less focused souls want to follow you naturally. Even if you have not been given an official position of authority, you have found yourself in the position of informal group leader of your peers, which instils in you a great deal of confidence in your ability to relate to others. Because people look up to you, you have been vested with a great deal of responsibility whether you desire it or not. It is therefore essential you use your gift wisely and refrain from situations where you might abuse or misuse the powers that your peers have awarded you. You also have a natural affinity with animals, as you can identify with the feralness so inherent in their personalities. Animals are such simple beings, who are motivated by primal instinct alone, drawing upon the collective consciousness of their species. They do not allow petty personality differences and squabbles to get in the way of their need for security, shelter and sustenance. You can sense the majesty of those animals that share this earth with us.

IX Hermit   If The Hermit has appeared in the Querent position, you are very much an old soul, possessing much wisdom through eastern philosophies. Although you enjoy the company of others, you spend a lot of time on your own, reflecting upon the laws that make up the universe. You will receive much universal knowledge through meditation or dreams, as you will be given visions and other flashes of inspiration that show you more of the grand scheme of the universal knowledge the vast majority of us are not open to. It is also during periods of illness, when you wonder about your own mortality, that you are able to gain a greater understanding of the progression of the collective cosmic consciousness.

X Wheel of Fortune   If The Wheel of Fortune has entered the Querent position, it seems you are somewhat of a risk taker, wanting to take a chance to better your odds in life. Because you are not one to take life as it comes, you tend to create your own scenario, which is manifested by the calculated risks you take. Although you are somewhat of a gambler, you are nonetheless philosophical about what your lot in life might be. The rapid spiral of events you are a part of is typical of the fact that the four fixed astrological signs are portrayed in this card. The friction that is inherent in the astrological grand square composed within the archetype is what drives you to heed a continuous flow of variance, thereby giving you a fluctuation of fortunes.

XI Justice   If Justice has appeared in the Querent position, you have a strong sense of right and wrong, and can at times be somewhat judgmental in your assessment of others. There is very much a polarity in your way of seeing things, which presents somewhat of a dichotomy to your sensual awareness. Sometimes you only see that an individual partook of an activity that is against society's moral and ethical codes, but you fail to take into consideration any mitigating circumstances that may be presented to you. You have an inability to see that in between the dualistic world of black and white we live in there are varying shades of grey, which differentiate the moral sense of right and wrong we are confronted with on a daily basis. It is the grey areas that you would be wise to analyse because they define the true character of a living being's consciousness.

XII Hanged Man   If The Hanged Man has appeared in the Querent position, you tend to take life as it comes, and do not necessarily go to any great lengths to change the course of events that seem to be occurring along your journey. You have a 'whatever will be, will be' attitude, and allow your destiny to unfold before your very eyes. You have somewhat of a philosophical perspective on life, tending to analyse events as they occur, attempting to master your future through a dedicated application of retrospective hindsight, which will later be used as introspective forethought. You may have had to make a huge sacrifice in your more formative and ideological years, which has affected your current personality. You have so much wisdom in your essence, which is a result of having had to give something up that was very important to you. When someone looks into your eyes, they can see the ember of life that exists within, an ember that was once a flame. If you want to carry on in such an existence, you need to re-ignite that ember so it will burn and illuminate the glory of your soul.

XIII Death   If Death has appeared in the Querent position, you are going through a major change in your life that is nothing short of a total rebirth. You may not think it to be so right now, as the situation you are in at the moment is rather extreme, but when the current situation is resolved, you will be wiser and stronger for the experience. The transformation you are going through could be such a major life event you may very well succumb to an illness. This illness could manifest itself physically, as you suffer from a string of conditions that are exacerbated by stress. Alternatively, you could suffer from depression, neurosis, or even psychosis, which has been euphemistically termed a 'creative illness'. In order to come to terms with what you are experiencing, you may develop obsessions, compulsions, or phobias, which you may need outside help to overcome. Rest assured, you are not crazy, but merely going through a metaphysical rebirth, which is necessary for you to continue along your earth walk with a heightened awareness of the greater workings of the universe. Although we have been conditioned to believe that mental illness is a reflection of one's weakness of mind, it is important to realise that many great thinkers in our past, such as Sigmund Freud and Carl Jung, have succumbed to mental health problems at least once in their life. It is interesting to note that these episodes of illness occurred after a period of intense mental activity, and usually occurring around their 4th decade. Perhaps these beings needed to go through a period of inner turmoil so they could gain greater empathy and understanding for the suffering of other souls.

XIV Temperance   If Temperance has appeared in the Querent position, this is one instance where you are being guided by the angel of time. It is important that you maintain a good sense of humour and try to keep a sense of balance and harmony during a turbulent period in your life. You are protected in all that you do, provided you conduct your affairs morally and honourably in this incarnation. This is a period of transition where you are going through the healing process by the passage of time. Time really does heal all wounds, and can transform a boiling rage into an inner wisdom of the injustices that are so much a part of our existences. Although wisdom and truth will not solve all of your problems, they will give you greater clarity to view the world in a different light.

XV Devil   If The Devil has appeared in the Querent position, you are in the process of experiencing what are considered to be the more negative aspects of our physical existence. Instead of being happy and carefree, you are weighed down with the responsibilities of this world that effactually give you a sombre disposition. The macabre fascinates you, as you delight in exploring the unknown. You have gone beyond subtle manipulation as indicated by The Magician, and have progressed into deeper realms of the magical arts, sometimes even partaking of what is known as black magic. Manifesting your own existence through the use of mental imagery and your thoughts no longer appeal to you, as you prefer to dabble in the dark arts. Lest you proclaim in righteous indignation that you would never engage in such practices, it must be emphasised that even something as tame as negative thinking can bring about malefic effects. Even if you are a regular churchgoer and consider yourself devout, if you pray to God that misfortune befall anyone of your fellow men, you are in fact guilty of dabbling in the dark arts. In addition to your predilection for the exploration of the darkness of our souls, you have a secret you don't want anyone to know about. Nothing remains closeted forever, and what has been shrouded in mystery will become public knowledge in time.

XVI Tower If The Tower has appeared in the Querent position, you are going through a period of inner upheaval, which could manifest itself as anger. You are angry with people and organisations for what you feel is their inability to deal with you fairly. Your home life may be up in arms because you are having difficulty communicating your needs to those close to you. This failure to communicate has had the knock-on effect of causing tension, and you may feel alienated, as if you somehow are not welcome in your own home. What you need is a change of scenery; either a holiday or a new job, anything to jolt you out of the complacency that has set in. If you are not able to find a suitable outlet for the anger that is welling up inside of you, you could turn your rage inward and consequently develop any one of the many depressive illnesses. Depression is, after all, anger that is directed toward oneself rather than others.

XVII Star If The Star has appeared in the Querent position, you are a person who remains hopeful even during the bleakest of times. You have a friendly disposition, which makes you quite a likeable person. You are also somewhat balanced, effectively harmonising your ability to reason with your intuition, which gives you an innate understanding of other individuals. Because you have so much empathy and the ability to communicate to others tactfully, many people are likely to come to you and ask for advice about their personal problems. You have a higher awareness and are in touch with celestial beings that guide you in your day-to-day activities and ensure you are far from adversity. Although you have chosen to reside in the earth plane to experience the physicalities of the universe, you are not from this world. Your true home is a place, galaxies away, where beings are composed of light, each light allocated to a star. In this world, beings cannot comprehend the concept of density and therefore cannot understand how a being on earth could be weighed down with a cumbersome, physical body. Those beings freely exist, going anywhere they wish merely by using their thought processes. These beings are able to manifest alternate realities merely by wishing it so. These beings are what our ancestors, in awe of souls more highly advanced than ours, called Gods.

XVIII Moon If The Moon appears in the Querent position, you are somewhat of an illusive soul, not quite in touch with reality. You know in your heart you have difficulties coping with the harsh realities of the here and now, but somehow you get by. Although you are intuitive, sometimes you do not exercise good judgement because you allow what you desire to overrule what really is. You are a dualistic individual because part of you is still very feral in a domestic world. Although you can be co-operative, no one can really tame you. You are so emotional that many people are able to offend you when they did not intend any malice at all. This intense sensitivity can make you appear bristly to others, which means you have difficulties maintaining relationships. When you learn to harness the psychic abilities that are within, you will be satisfied with yourself when you use them to help others for the good of mankind.

XIX Sun If The Sun has appeared in the Querent position, you have a very happy disposition and have many childlike qualities. You have an affinity for children, animals and the outdoors. You enjoy being the centre of attention and will therefore do things to attract attention to yourself, either positively or negatively. There is an element to your personality that makes you want to be the life and soul of the party, and as a result you tend to be somewhat of an exhibitionist. You are also a very me-centred individual, which can pose difficulties in your personal relationships because any successful partnership entails give and take on both sides, something you are not prepared to do.

XX Judgement If Judgement has appeared in the Querent position, you are going through a period of inner transformation that can only come about through a deep, inner cleansing and healing. You may have suffered an injury in this incarnation, a previous life, or even a lateral existence that occurs simultaneously to the one you are currently conscious of. This injury must heal before you can carry on in your soul growth. If left untreated, you will behave and react in manners that can best be described as coping mechanisms, but such activities are not necessarily synchronous with how you would prefer to be. This healing process can occur in an environment of recuperation, analysis, or intense introspection, applied to retrospective thought of how a certain sequence of events have transpired to bring you to your current station in this life. If all else fails, it is important to keep in mind that time really does heal all wounds. Therefore, given the right amount of time and patience, you will emerge healed and reborn, with a greater understanding of yourself and others.

XXI World   If The World has appeared in the Querent position, you have reached a point in your life where some important issues have come to a resolution. You have completed a major cycle in your life and are therefore ready to begin a new endeavour to preoccupy your mind. This sense of completion has given you the confidence to begin new projects. In addition, if you have been involved in any unsatisfying relationships, now may be time to either re-define or dissolve them if you feel it would be necessary for your soul growth.

Wands/Rods/Fire

Ace   If the Ace of Wands has appeared in the Querent position, you are flowing with creativity, bubbling with new ideas that can benefit yourself and others. You are also receptive to new influences, which makes you highly psychic and able to attune yourself to what is going on with other individuals. You have leadership qualities, which instils in you a great deal of self-confidence. You are probably a very popular person because people sense there is something special in your aura, and they wish to be a part of it, hoping some of your essence will spill over into their auras. You have some very strong healing abilities the weak and infirm are able to intuitively pick up on, and for this reason much lesser beings would like to be around you.

Two   If the Two of Wands is in the Querent position, you are a very caring person who likes to build relationships with other individuals. You prefer to form solid bonds with those people who you must work closely with, thereby instilling you with a fair amount of popularity amongst your contemporaries. Although you are quite dynamic in your own right, you prefer to operate within the confines of an established partnership, thereby doubling any prospects of success.

Three   If the Three of Wands has landed in the Querent position, you are somewhat of a team player. You prefer to work within a group, which is where your personality truly shines. In a group, you can accomplish far more than you ever could attempt individually, which allows you to have a sense of achievement that comes only from a job well done. Money is very much a part of your life, and it is for that reason you will find yourself engaged in various business activities, striving to earn as much financial clout as possible. You are also somewhat of a gambler, forever engaging in calculated risks in an attempt to further enhance your wealth and monetary status in this world.

Four   If the Four of Wands appears in the Querent position, you are a very solid, practical and trustworthy person who thinks a great deal of your home, family and that which will give you a sense of stability from which to work. You are somewhat futuristic in your thinking, always making calculated moves you hope will increase your chances of prosperity and success, which will cement your future financial security. You desire to live in a large home and partake of celebrations with your friends and family. When all is well at home, you are at your very best and are therefore more able to go out in the world and make a name for yourself.

Five   If the Five of Wands has appeared in the Querent position, you are having to struggle because it seems you are at odds with the world around you. Because there is a lack of understanding, you seem to spend a great deal of time in conflict. In metaphorical terms, you spend much of your time 'fighting fires', but never really pinpointing the cause of each and every crisis. If you stop and analyse every conflict you are engaging in, you will probably see they all have one specific problem in common.

Six   If the Six of Wands has appeared in the Querent position, you are in many ways a self-righteous person. You see yourself as being very successful, which could pose a problem to your personal relationships. Because you value success and achievement as personal qualities people should aspire to, you could collect a few undesirable elements in your milieu. You could attract hangers-on, those individuals who do nothing but cling onto your success in the hope that some of it will rub off onto them. You may also discover there are some secret enemies in your circle of associates, those people who are outwardly supportive of you but secretly conspire to see your downfall. The case of Julius Caesar who was assassinated by his so-called friends on the Ides of March is an apt representation of this key. It is therefore essential you analyse your motives and behaviour, and strive to maintain an air of modesty with regard to your personal achievements, thereby attracting well-wishers to your circle of friends.

Seven If the Seven of Wands has appeared in the Querent position, you appear to be under a great deal of stress, which is affecting your personality and temperament. Instead of being cheerful, happy and helpful, you are full of resentment, as you struggle to tackle forces that you have no outer comprehension of. You may have found you have difficulty staying on top of your current situation because you do not possess all the skills and facilities necessary to appropriately respond. It is for that reason you may need to seek outside help to better enable you to transcend the difficult patch that you are currently experiencing.

Eight If the Eight of Wands has appeared in the Querent position, you are a forward thinker who would like to go places, especially with regard to work and career. You may feel the need to travel, so if you do not have a vocation that enables you to go to different places on a regular basis, you may go on exotic holidays if it is within your budget. You are very futuristic, as you try to keep up with the latest advances in technology. You need to be in a sunny place because that is where you will have the opportunity to achieve your true potential in this life.

Nine If the Nine of Wands has appeared in the Querent position, you are somewhat defensive. Because of your various life experiences, you tend to be on guard much of the time, fearing the worst in almost any given situation. As a result of this, you may be seen by others to be somewhat pessimistic, if not downright paranoid. An old saying, 'just because you're paranoid does not mean that someone isn't out to get you' is a good motto to live by at this point in your life.

Ten If the Ten of Wands has appeared in the Querent position, it seems you are exhausted from overwork. It may be you have taken on a task you are really not ready for, but have decided to persevere nonetheless. As a result, you are being initiated into a completely new system of thought that has a steep learning curve. You have a long way to go before the goal you have set for yourself is in sight, but if you persevere, even in the face of adversity, you will get what you desire in the end.

King If the King of Wands appears in the Querent position, you are being influenced in a really big way by a man who may have been considered successful at one time in his life. He has much energy in his auric make-up, which he can use to advance through his work, vocation or hobbies. While he can be quite generous and loving, he can also be somewhat self-serving, looking to meet his own needs over those of anyone else. He is always looking for ways to advance his financial standing in this world with minimal effort, and is therefore brimming over with business ideas. He quite often has an unusually high opinion of himself and naturally assumes that everyone adores him as much as he adores himself.

Queen   If the Queen of Wands has appeared in the Querent position, you are being influenced in some way by a woman who has a great deal of vibrancy and personal magnetism. She generally needs to stay active in order to be at her best, either working or pursuing hobbies and other creative activities. While she has much love to give, she can be very me-centred, which can cause her to become rather melodramatic when life doesn't go the way she desires.

Knight/ Prince   If the Knight of Wands has appeared in the Querent position, a young man is strongly influencing your overall wellbeing. He has a great deal of energy, which he may or may not be using to his best advantage. He has a generally sunny disposition, which makes him well liked by others. Because he lacks the maturity to see prospects through to completion, he is not yet ready for a great deal of responsibility. It is for that reason he still needs a fair amount of mentoring before he is ready to tackle the world head on as an adult would.

Page/ Princess   If the Page of Wands has appeared in the Querent position, there is a person who is very close to you and has a great deal of energy at her disposal. She is somewhat egocentric because she has not yet learned to think of people other than herself. She has a lively personality and needs to be engaged in a variety of activities in order to temper the energy within her.

Pentacles/Disks/Earth

Ace   If the Ace of Pentacles has appeared in the Querent position, you are materialistic in the fact that you would like to have enough money to enable you to aspire to a reasonable standard of living and possess nice things you and those close to you may enjoy. You may work with your hands, which gives you the practicality necessary to live in this physical world. Sensibility and groundedness are attributes that are necessary to successfully navigate through the earth plane, so this should hold you in good stead as you go about your daily activities. The serenity and freshness of the outdoors, possibly within the confines of a well-kept garden, will give you the meditative clarity of thought to work through any difficulties that you find yourself presented with.

Two   If the Two of Pentacles has appeared in the Querent position, you seem to always have difficulties managing your money. Although you know very much how much money is available to you, you tend to stretch the limits as far as possible, often committing yourself to resources that you anticipate receiving, but do not yet possess. You quite likely rely heavily on credit, which is fine, as long as you have enough money coming in to pay off your creditors. The situation you have found yourself in, constantly worrying about your variable income, has begun to affect your mental and physical wellbeing. You may need to seek outside assistance to enable you to better manage the money that you do have, which should give you a little more peace of mind with regard to your future security and prosperity.

Three   If the Three of Pentacles has appeared in the Querent position, you are skilled at what you do, having learned your trade through experience. In your chosen vocation you are well respected and well paid well for the service you provide. Because you are so valued, you may have a relatively high standard of living and are able to enjoy many of the nice things of this world. You are a reasonable and well-balanced individual, which should help your personal relationships run smoothly.

Four   If the Four of Pentacles has appeared in the Querent position, it seems there are many areas of your life where you keep things to yourself. You tend to hold on tightly to your money, even to the point of being miserly. In addition, you may be somewhat closed minded, refusing to open yourself up to new ideas, which will consequently close the door to many opportunities made available to you. Your reservations are not without merit, however, as you have good reason to use discretion when inviting people into your home or personal space. While you should exercise prudence in your activities, especially when dealing with finances, if you allow yourself to be a bit more receptive to others, you will find many more good things will come to you.

Five   If the Five of Pentacles has appeared in the Querent position, it seems you lack confidence and have a very low self-esteem. You see people around you who are more affluent than yourself, and you secretly feel you could never aspire to their level of success. Your circumstances may be more modest than you would like, which can lead to a considerable amount of frustration on your part. You may have been made homeless or vulnerable at least once in your life, which further adds to the feelings of insecurity and anxiety that only make your situation that much worse. You may have had some severe financial difficulties at least once in your life, which were of such an extreme nature that you were not able to obtain food, clothes and adequate shelter for yourself. These rather harsh conditions you have experienced have served to influence the attitudes you have developed about people and life in general, which can be rather dour at times.

Six If the Six of Pentacles has appeared in the Querent position, you need to carry an air of co-operation and mutual trust if you would like others to approach you. The reason for this is because you may be in a position to accomplish all that is necessary, and you need the assistance of others. By the same token, other people may need your help from time to time in order to achieve important goals, and it would be in your best interests to make yourself available to others when they are in need. It is this feeling of philanthropy that will help you to weather the turmoil that comes to all of us from time to time, and ensure there will be people who would like to lend a helping hand whenever you need it.

Seven If the Seven of Pentacles has appeared in the Querent position, you need to take a 'wait and see' attitude because there are forces at work that are beyond your control. The best you can do is to put your best foot forward at all times, get whatever qualifications you need to assure success, and prepare yourself for the time when you will be called upon to perform the role you were destined for.

Eight If the Eight of Pentacles has appeared in the Querent position, you need to take things slow and easy, and pay particular attention to detail. The reason for this is because you are in a situation that is totally alien to you. You do not yet possess all the skills necessary to accomplish the task that is soon forthcoming. You will therefore have to learn through experience what it is you need to do, learning by trial and error. It is likely you will make some mistakes along the way, as you attempt to hone your skills and possibly learn a new trade. The problem is particularly perplexing because there is no suitable mentor to teach you what you need to learn. As a result, you will find yourself in a position where you must accomplish this most crucial task on your own, and you will discover there will be nobody suitable to help you overcome any obstacles that are thrown in your path. Once you have accomplished what it is you need to do, however, you will possess a deep satisfaction, realising once and for all exactly what you are capable of.

Nine   If the Nine of Pentacles has appeared in the Querent position, you have reached a point in your life where your physical and material needs are being taken care of, thus enabling you to spend more time in leisure activities. This pursuit of enjoyment should not be seen as frivolous because we all need to take a break from the pressures of the world from time to time. You may receive money you did not actually go out and earn at least once in your life, which should give you the financial security you need to relax a little and enjoy the good things this earth has to offer.

Ten   If the Ten of Pentacles has appeared in the Querent position, you are very heavily involved with your family, particularly when dealing with property, finances and other material matters. Because you are involved with members of your family financially, social elements are likely to come into play as well. You may have received, or are expecting to receive, an inheritance from someone related to you, which further complicates the issue. It is in your best interests, therefore, to stay on good terms with other members of your family regardless of how you feel about them personally.

King   If the King of Pentacles has appeared in the Querent position, you are being influenced in some way by a man who has a high standing in society. He may be somewhat affluent, but even if that is not the case, he is well thought of in his community. This man is a very ethical person and has a healthy respect for the lawful order of the universe. He has some practical advice to give you, if you would only listen.

Queen   If the Queen of Pentacles has appeared in the Querent position, there is a very sensible woman who is influencing you in some way. This person is not prone to flights of fancy, and will therefore stabilise you during the more tumultuous periods of your life. While she can be sensitive and caring, there are times when she appears somewhat stern. Because she is so level headed, she is not likely to allow her heart to rule her head. It is for that reason she can afford you some sound advice, if you choose to talk to her about what is on your mind.

Knight/ Prince   If the Knight of Pentacles has appeared in the Querent position, you are being influenced by a young man who has a great deal of practicality about his aura. He has a very grounding influence over you and tries to see reason in every situation. Although he is slow and methodical at times, he usually accomplishes what he sets out to because he is persistent and has a very determined spirit.

Page/ Princess If the Page of Pentacles has appeared in the Querent position, the moves you are currently making are highly dependant on the feelings of a young person who is heavily involved in the situation that prompted you to consult the oracle. This person is very grounded and therefore not easily swayed by the meagre affairs of man. There is a sense of modesty to this humble, yet stubborn individual, who can teach you much about the significance of residing here on the earth plane.

Swords/Air

Ace If the Ace of Swords has appeared in the Querent position, you have a great deal of information you need to communicate to others. It is for that reason you will be writing letters, memos, emails, faxes and other documents, trying in earnest to get your point across. Alternately, you need to take in a great deal of information from other sources, which means you will need to read literature, attend lectures, visit galleries, and even go to concerts in order to absorb as much data as you possibly can. Legal issues figure prominently, so it is important you and those around you ensure any data you are involved in disseminating is well within the boundaries of ethics and good taste.

Two If the Two of Swords has appeared in the Querent position, you have been receiving information from separate sources that are at variance to each other. It is for that reason you are in such a quandary. It is very important that you look at the associations you form at this time because some individuals may be feeding you incorrect information, which will only harm your prospects and reputation in the long-run.

Three If the Three of Swords has appeared in the Querent position, your heart is breaking over one specific incident that has plagued your thinking processes for quite some time. This event has affected your whole outlook on life, and permeates through your entire being, so much so that you are not able to separate yourself from it. People who you come into contact with instantly recognise that there was a deep-seated tragedy you were forced to endure at a critical time in your life. They can perceive the sadness that is such a part of you, a sense of melancholia that never goes away, even at times when celebrations and gaiety are at hand.

Four If the Four of Swords has appeared in the Querent position, you are currently in a period of stasis. The situation you are in is not moving forwards, backwards or laterally, but has come to a standstill. It is therefore a propitious time for you to regain your energy by getting the rest you have not been able to get previously due to a rather hectic lifestyle. It is also a good time to take stock of your existing circumstances by engaging in self-analysis by meditation and introspection.

Five   If the Five of Swords has appeared in the Querent position, you may be feeling somewhat quarrelsome because you are at odds with those around you. It seems you do not see eye to eye with several people who you are close to, and this is affecting your quality of life. Perhaps you need to take a breather from those individuals who you are in disagreement with because it will enable you to acquire a fresh perspective on the situation once you have had some time apart.

Six   If the Six of Swords has appeared in the Querent position, you have some relationship issues to work on, which is having the effect of giving you a less than gay disposition. You may be going through a personal crisis which you have little control over. Therefore, in order to improve your circumstances, you may find you need to move away from a relationship or situation. It is a difficult decision for you to make, hence the sadness you will feel when you make the decision to walk away from the situation you have no ultimate control over. You will be able to make a new life for yourself and things will improve, eventually.

Seven   If the Seven of Swords has appeared in the Querent position, you seem to have a rather fertile imagination and therefore can engage in a type of creativity that many people are not able to readily appreciate. You have the ability to think laterally, which in essence enables you to come up with alternatives to situations that others might perceive to be hopeless. Because you have such an active imagination, you may have a tendency to embellish far beyond the truth. It is for that reason you will need to exercise logic and rationality in your day day-to-day dealings with others so you do not develop a reputation as a fantasist. You are a very clever individual who is able to turn almost any crisis into an opportunity. The problem you may find, however, is that you could take someone else's ideas as your own, which could cause you to lose credibility if you ever get caught.

Eight   If the Eight of Swords has appeared in the Querent position, you are in somewhat of a rut. You may be either physically or mentally incarcerated, which is affecting your ability to think clearly to resolve any issues that may arise. In addition, you may not be in possession of all the facts, which further hinders your ability to focus on the issues affecting you today. Worse yet, someone could actually be misleading you, which will in effect cause you to make totally inappropriate decisions based on the misinformation you have received. It is for that reason you need to analyse and critique every shred of evidence that is presented to you, thereby better enabling you to successfully navigate through many of the distractions that will inherently be a part of your earth walk.

Nine If the Nine of Swords has appeared in the Querent position, you have much to worry about, which is consequently causing you to lose sleep, and you will eventually make yourself ill if you are not able to get your concerns under control. Whether or not the worries you have are legitimate is not that important because your concerns are very real to you, thereby giving them a great deal of significance in your life. As a result, you may find yourself becoming depressed, anxious or phobic, trying to cope with a situation that is becoming more and more untenable. You may need to seek outside help for your troubles, which will do a great deal to relieve the sense of foreboding you are currently experiencing.

Ten If the Ten of Swords has appeared in the Querent position, it seems you are at a low point in your life. You feel let down for a variety of reasons, and will need time to recover from the experience. Unfortunately, as much as you would like for someone, anyone, to help you in your hour of need, there will be no outside assistance forthcoming. It is for that reason you will have to pick yourself up from the depths of despair all on you own. After you have recovered your composure, you will be able to see the underlying reasons behind certain incidents you have been unsure of. With this clarified hindsight, you will be able to carry out your day-to-day affairs with greater confidence.

King If the King of Swords has appeared in the Querent position, you are being influenced in some way by a man who can be quite vociferous in his views. He is quite knowledgeable on a wide variety of subjects, but for whatever reason may not be disseminating his knowledge using the most appropriate vehicles of communication. He has something important to tell you, but he may relay this message in a less than orthodox manner. It is essential, therefore that you watch this individual carefully to glean the true meaning of his actions.

Queen If the Queen of Swords has appeared in the Querent position, you are being influenced by a woman who is has an extremely sharp intellect. Although she has a wide breadth of knowledge, she may not necessarily have had the energy necessary to put it to good use and effectively use her swaying power. As a result, she may not be as happy as she would like to be, which would have the result of affecting your personality. If you listen to her with interest, her demeanour may change positively and she could impart some knowledge of value to you.

Knight/ Prince If the Knight of Swords has appeared in the Querent position, you are being influenced by a young man who is quite vociferous when relating his opinions. Because he is so communicative, you are often in no doubt about how he feels about certain situations. He does, however, have difficulties expressing his emotions, which could pose difficulties at times. It is therefore essential you ask probing questions of this individual in order to get a better idea of who the person behind the mask is. Once you have a greater clarity of his true feelings, you will be able to take appropriate action with the situation that prompted you to seek the advice of this oracle.

Page/ Princess If the Page of Swords has appeared in the Querent position, you are being influenced by a young person who is chatty, witty and a good communicator. She has something very important to show you or tell you, which will help you to better focus on your priorities in this life. Her innocent inquisitiveness will be refreshing to you, as you are able to relate on more simplistic terms to her and other individuals.

Cups/Water

Ace If the Ace of Cups has appeared in the Querent position, you have a great deal of emotional depth, which makes you highly psychic and intuitive to the needs of others. You have much love to offer those who are receptive to you. You have also been blessed with an abundance of good fortune, which is something that has been awarded to you through your good deeds in past, present, future and even parallel existences. You will find that places where there is an abundance of water will leave you rejuvenated and refreshed, ready to successfully deal with the pressures ahead.

Two If the Two of Cups has appeared in the Querent position, you have the ability to make people who you come into contact with feel special, which has the effect of endearing you to others. Because people skills are so important, it is likely you will be successful in just about anything you set out to achieve. You have a pleasant, approachable disposition, which is a definite asset to your personal relationships. You will be shortly engaged with another individual who will enable you to experience some of the more positive feelings that are within the realm of our human existence. With this person, you will have the opportunity to experience true happiness and fulfilment, which only comes from a pure soul-mate union.

Three   If the Three of Cups has appeared in the Querent position, it seems you are going through a period where you are engaging in more socialising than you have in the past, thereby fulfilling your need to feel part of a group. You have a need to bond with other individuals at this time, which is one of the reasons why you will be attracted to places where other people gather together to meet. You will therefore tend to accept invitations to attend parties, celebrations, and other functions that will assure you the opportunity to blend into a crowd and meet with other like-minded souls. You have a lot to be happy about and others will sense the contentment in your soul, which will have the effect of attracting them to you. At this time in your life you will find you have no shortage of company, which should provide you with some happy memories in years to come.

Four   If the Four of Cups has appeared in the Querent position, it may be there are some aspects of your life in which you lack confidence. You may be uncertain of where your true direction in this life lies, and it is for that reason you tend to waiver, reluctant to make any concrete decisions that will affect your true path in this life. This matter is further complicated by the fact that you are hearing whispers from others, which makes it all the more difficult to make your mind up. The best way to successfully navigate through a period where you are fraught with uncertainties is to only place your trust in those individuals who have proven themselves to be reliable and trustworthy associates. You should also rely upon your intuition, because how you feel about the situation is often a good indicator of the best way to respond. Once you have resolved the uncertainties you have been confronted with, you will become better equipped to deal with and escalate your future actions to bring about your desired goal.

Five   If the Five of Cups has appeared in the Querent position, you have somewhat of a melancholy disposition because you do not feel you have all you would like out of a certain situation. It is for that reason you feel let down. People around you are able to instantly pick up on your feelings because they can read your body language quite easily. While it is important to allow yourself to grieve and ultimately heal yourself of the disappointment you have faced, little by little, the pep in your step will pick up and the smile on your face will return. You will also be able to see with clarity that while the circumstances that led to certain avenues have been closed to you, there are other opportunities you may never have previously considered exploring. Things will definitely pick up because the universal flow indicates the wheels of change must forever be in the motion.

Six   If the Six of Cups has appeared in the Querent position, you are heavily linked to situations that have occurred in the past. You may be thinking about childhood experiences, which are affecting you as an adult. Children figure prominently, and you may have chosen a vocation that enables you to have contact with young people. Your childhood home means a great deal to you, as you try to think about the good times you have had in the past. You may have contact with people who influenced you in your more formative years, which could be a rewarding experience for the both of you.

Seven   If the Seven of Cups has appeared in the Querent position, you seem to be unsure of which path you would like to be on. There are many opportunities that are being made available to you, but it seems you are not being presented with all of the pertinent facts. It is for that reason it is essential you take it upon yourself to properly research any choices you are considering undertaking. While some of the options you are considering are viable and will give you the sense of fulfilment you desire, other alternatives will lead you nowhere, and you would consequently be wasting your time. If you are unsure, perhaps you should seek counsel from someone you trust. Above all, you should rely upon your intuitive processes because your higher self will never let you down.

Eight   If the Eight of Cups has appeared in the Querent position, you are somewhat unsure of what the future has in store for you. The reason for your uncertainty is because you have vested a great deal of your emotional energy into one particular situation and you have received nothing in return. Having carried on like this for quite some time, you have finally had to face the fact that there is nothing you can do to alter the situation in your favour. If the situation changes in a positive direction, it will be as a result of forces you have no control over. For your own emotional wellbeing, it would be best if you stand back and observe the situation with impartiality. This objective watching, however, will reveal to you insights you had been previously unaware of, insights that will reveal to you certain factors you had previously been blind to. Although you are somewhat disquieted at the moment, the situation will improve, and you will be given other more propitious opportunities that are far more advantageous to your soul growth. The situation you are so preoccupied with may very well rectify itself, but only if you stand back and let the universal flow work in the manner that is destined.

Nine   If the Nine of Cups has appeared in the Querent position, you have very good reason to be pleased with yourself. You may enjoy the culinary pursuits, which involves cooking for others and entertaining. If you have no one to dine with, you do not mind eating and drinking on your own. The fact that you enjoy the pleasurable oral sensations you experience when eating good food and drinking fine wine means you may develop somewhat of a weight problem. It is for that reason you may need to stick to a healthy eating plan and only indulge in the more fattening foods and drinks during special occasions. If you only treat yourself occasionally to the sinful indulgences we all enjoy, your health will be significantly improved as you minimise the effects of arthritis, diabetes, hypoglycaemia, heart problems and other physical ailments that are exacerbated by excess weight.

Ten   If the Ten of Cups has appeared in the Querent position, you are very happy and content with yourself, but need a partner in order to feel completely fulfilled. What would give you the greatest amount of happiness would be to become involved in a loving relationship with another person, and possibly a family.

King   If the King of Cups has appeared in the Querent position, you are being strongly influenced by a man who, although he may try to hide it, is quite emotional. He is very perceptive to the feelings around him and often tries to adapt this behaviour to the needs of others. He can be stern, when he has to be, but this is merely a façade for a soft, inner core that is wounded very easily. He can be quite petty, however, and may seek retribution for any wrongs that may have been inflicted upon him. His home and family are very important to his self-identity, so he will try to maintain ties with family members, even if they are not worthy of his affection.

Queen   If the Queen of Cups has appeared in the Querent position, you are being influenced by a highly perceptive woman. This person has a very high degree of emotional intelligence and therefore uses her intuition with a much greater capacity than her reasoning ability. This person is very visual, and therefore relies on the symbolism of pictures to a much greater degree than the written word or numbers. She is highly imaginative and may be able to see auras, and may even be clairvoyant at times. She has something to show you that is highly significant to the current situation you are involved in.

Knight/ Prince

If the Knight of Cups has appeared in the Querent position, you are being influenced by a young, emotive man in some way. He is highly articulate and has the ability to motivate others into his way of thinking, and it is for that reason he usually gets what he wants out of life. He is somewhat emotional and can easily become hurt by the words and actions of others when none was intended. It is for this reason he will often become embroiled in petty squabbles when more enlightened souls would simply walk away. In order to maximise your relationship with this individual, it is important to watch him carefully. Quite often, his actions will speak louder than his words.

Page/ Princess

If the Page of Cups has appeared in the Querent position, there is a young person around you who is influencing certain aspects of your life in some way. This individual is very emotional and has a vivid imagination, which she uses to occupy her active mind. She may have had imaginary playmates when she was growing up, as she found them to be more amenable than real ones. She is also very perceptive and is therefore able to suss out people's true intentions with very little effort. The downside is this individual is not averse to making up stories and telling the odd white lie, especially if she thinks it will help her to achieve her goals.

8 The Environment

0 Fool   If The Fool appears in the Environment position, you have recently undergone a change in your life, which has had the result of affecting your immediate environment. You may have changed jobs, home or friends to propel you into a totally new scenario. As a result of this, you will undergo new experiences that will enhance your present perspective in life. You may have decided to join a club or other social setting that will bring you in touch with different types of people, individuals who have the ability to influence your way of thinking. Ideas that in the past would have been alien to you are now quite plausible in their own unique sort of way. These new people who you will be put in touch with will help you to entertain more progressive ideas, which is a necessary component to your continuing soul evolution.

I Magician   If The Magician has appeared in the Environment position, you are in somewhat of a learning situation. You need to acquire some very important skills before it will be possible to successfully manoeuvre through the web of physicalities of our life. The situation you are enquiring about contains certain elements for which you have no past experience. You may very well need to attend a school to pick up valuable tools of the trade you will soon be undertaking. College or university is not an option that should be ruled out because it is quite likely you will be embarking upon a course of study that will give you an important qualification to practice a particular trade. There are some very subtle influences at work you should be cognisant of because what you don't know definitely can hurt you. Of note, there is at least one individual around you who has an eloquent manner of speaking and behaving. Positively, he can influence people to opt for a particular course of action. Negatively, he can manipulate people to serve his own needs. The Magician is representative of magic, the magic that is produced from one's mind or mental imagery. Our thoughts are able to manifest themselves in the physicalities of this world if we are aware of and are in tune with the ebb and flow of the universe, which is the past, present and future all rolled up into one. We should also not discount parallel universes that exist in the same space, yet at different vibrational overtones than our present plane of existence. We can catch a glimpse into these lateral worlds during that twilight time when we are dreaming. If we perceive things out of the corners of our eyes instead of looking directly ahead, we will also be able to glimpse elements of our conscious awareness that are not readily apparent. If you attempt to see the world through the corners of your eyes, you will begin to perceive animals, people and objects that are apparently near you, but not physically near you in the manner you would normally imagine. Another way you can become more enlightened as to the potentialities of the people around you is to carefully scrutinise dress, appearance and mannerisms. What costumes and jewellery have individuals decided to adorn themselves with? What do you see in people's eyes and facial expressions? These are all clues that will reveal the personality behind the mask. And lastly, The Magician can be seen as Lucifer, when he acted as God's most glorious creation before he fell down to earth and became Satan. It is for that reason you need to guard yourself against secret enemies, who will make their presence known to you at the most inopportune of times.

II High Priestess

If The High Priestess has appeared in the Environment position, you tend to be surrounded by people who are very perceptive without appearing obtrusive. You may have become involved with a group of people who are quite spiritual and have a quest for the higher meaning of life, which is quite different from religious people, who merely focus upon the simple, more basal, demonstrative elements of one's spiritual beliefs. You may very well have a secret admirer who would love to get to know you on a more intimate level. In addition, there is a person around you who can show you how you can receive alternative realities and thereby gain a greater understanding of the universal ebb and flow of the world we have chosen to incarnate into.

III Empress

If The Empress has appeared in the Environment position, you are surrounded by people who are highly perceptive. Someone in your immediate milieu may be expecting or trying to conceive a baby, which will bring to her a great amount of joy. One of your friends has a very calming influence on you because she has the wisdom, self-confidence and maturity that is necessary to see beyond the petty squabbles that are an inherent part of our day to day living. Some people in your surroundings are also very territorial, which means you will need to tread carefully and establish protocol in order to ensure people around you are co-operative and attentive to your needs.

IV Emperor   If The Emperor appears in the Environment position, you are surrounded by powerful people who have the ability to make or break your reputation in this world. It is for that reason you need to tread very carefully to ensure you don't step on anyone's toes, because you need as many allies as you can get to help you to succeed in this world. In addition, you may have peers who are destined for high places, so it is important that you stay on friendly terms with all of the people who you come into contact with.

V Hierophant   If The Hierophant has appeared in the Environment position, you are close to some individuals who are considering making some very important life changes. Whether it is a marriage, divorce, christening, funeral service or decision to enter into a specific vocation, the choice at hand is one that isn't to be taken lightly. You may be close to individuals who are heavily involved in church or some other religious organisation, and their religious convictions may or may not lie in accordance with your own mythological primary certitude. This liaison, however, is not without difficulties because there needs to be a balance between the exoteric principles portrayed by The Hierophant and the esoteric doctrines as depicted by the High Priestess. If anyone steers toward the exoteric, the problem that can arise is that the individual taking this path in life may be prone to rote memorisation of religious dogma with no real understanding behind the scriptures that are being studied so ardently. If one leans too far on the side of the esoteric, the problem will arise where people are not sufficiently grounded to the earth plane, which is essential for living harmoniously in this plane of existence. It is for this reason, therefore, that a balance needs to be achieved in order to receive the abundant riches available to those who are able to master their environment through an understanding of its complexities.

VI Lovers   If The Lovers has appeared in the Environment position, you are surrounded by individuals who presently are, or soon will be, engaged in a love affair. You may not even be aware of the intricate workings of the subtle sexual chemistry that pervades us all from time to time, and it is for that reason you need to attune yourself to the body language of others, which will emit valuable clues. Ancient Tarot decks depict a young man who is presented with the elements of vice and virtue, and he must select only one as his true path in this life. It is for that reason the people around you may be involved in a love triangle of sorts, but only one person can be chosen as the life-long partner.

VII Chariot   If The Chariot has appeared in the Environment position, you may find the people around you are perpetually on the go, either through vocation or lifestyle. These individuals who are around you may be successful, which is a result of the drive and ambition they have allowed to manifest in their lives through their positive mental attitude. These individuals tend to possess self-confidence, and a correspondingly large area of personal space to go with the self-assuredness that comes only through victorious personal achievements. You may very well be invited to go on such a jaunt with one of your up and rising peers, and it would be wise to accept such an invitation so you can observe him and gain a greater understanding of his secret of success.

VIII Strength   If Strength has appeared in the Environment position, you are surrounded by individuals who are animal lovers. They have much love to give, but animals, specifically cats, seem to be the main recipients of their adoration. These individuals possess charm and grace, and therefore have the ability to make complex tasks seem easy. They are natural leaders, often the star of the show, able to convince people they really want to do whatever it is they would like. These individuals possess an inner reserve of will power, which gives them the strength to carry on under the weight of insurmountable odds, thereby giving other less durable souls something to strive for in the never ending cycle of life.

IX Hermit   If The Hermit has appeared in the Environment position, you seem to be spending a great deal of your time in solitude. Even if you find yourself in the midst of a crowd, it seems the people who you normally come into contact with on a daily basis are giving you space so you can work through some very important issues that have been troubling you. They have decided to stand back for the time being, because they know the direction you are taking is not necessarily the direction they would like to be on. It is for that reason these people will tend to detach themselves from your auric web and allow you to pass through their space unhindered. You may not particularly enjoy this important quest you are embarking upon, but such an endeavour is necessary for your inner enlightenment and soul growth.

X Wheel of Fortune   If The Wheel of Fortune has appeared in the Environment position, it seems that all around you things appear to be in a state of flux. It is not the natural order of the universe for our lives to remain in a perpetual state of stasis, and it is for that reason we will continually be presented with choices that serve to keep the wheel of cause and effect constantly in motion. If your immediate surroundings have gone through a period of affluence, then expect to go through a period where a sense of frugality will be necessary. Alternatively, if your immediate surroundings have been somewhat austere, then expect the situation to improve so you can rest a little easier. This is also a period of magical opportunities, a time that will enable you to advance your position in life by what many would consider to be a mere coincidence. It is therefore essential not to discount any opportunities that come your way because they very well could change your fortune for the better.

XI Justice   If Justice has appeared in the Environment position, the universe is in the process of harmonising any imbalances that may have been inherent in the situation that prompted you to consult the oracle. If you or someone in your immediate circle has been hard done by in some way, events will come into play in order to effect a retribution, thereby changing what you had initially believed to be a certain outcome. If, however, you or somebody close to you has found yourself to be at an unfair advantage, you will soon find your circumstances will change in order to balance out the situation. You, or someone close to you, may be involved in litigation and it is therefore important to ensure your affairs are conducted in a judicious manner to ensure you are happy with the outcome. You may also find other people are judging you for one particular reason and you are not entirely happy with their sentiments. The reason for these unwavering, judgmental attitudes, however, is reflected in the fact that those individuals have not had the same life experiences you have and therefore have no basis for understanding what you may be experiencing.

XII Hanged Man   If The Hanged Man has appeared in the Environment position, it seems the things going on around you are at a standstill, neither going forward nor going backward. During this period of stasis, however, you can accomplish a lot inside your head. You can use this period productively as a time of reflection, introspection and retrospection. You can gain a greater understanding of why certain incidents occurred as they did, thereby enabling you to gauge your future actions accordingly. It is also a time for you to rest and regain much of the energy you have wasted engaging in petty squabbles with other individuals who really are not in a position to affect your true path in this life. It may also be beneficial for you to use this time to explore your own inner spirituality, to look deeper into the true essence of your being, and to find the true spiritual path you were destined for.

XIII Death If Death has appeared in the Environment position, your immediate surroundings are going through some profound changes of such magnitude that nothing less than an eventual total renewal is expected. You, or someone close to you, may sustain a loss that will inevitably change your lifestyle. It will take you and those around you time to gather your composure, and until that time you will in all likelihood find yourself at a loss as to what to do with yourself. There is a long held philosophical belief that what doesn't kill you makes you stronger, and this is one of those instances where you will emerge stronger and wiser from any incident you must endure. In times of extreme stress, it is important to maintain an element of hope because, as in the nature of the continuous cycle of life, things can only get better.

XIV Temperance If Temperance has appeared in the Environment position, your immediate surroundings are in the process of becoming more balanced in accordance with the natural flow of the universe. If you have gone through a period of frenetic activity, things will slow down so you can catch your breath and evaluate recent circumstances. If, on the other hand, you and those close to you have gone through a period of idleness and boredom, certain situations will come into play to give you something to do to keep your mind occupied. It is important, therefore, to stay busy and engage yourself in productive activity. During the course of your duties, you will be able to gain much more insight into why destiny has unfolded in the manner that it has, thereby helping you to decide the best way to navigate through future scenarios. This is also a time of healing and convalescence, a time where you will gain greater insight into what makes you ill and what improves your state of being.

XV Devil If The Devil has appeared in the Environment position, you may feel as though you are surrounded by some dour individuals, persons who tend to look on the dark side of life and bring other people down. The fact that these individuals are so depressive does not make them bad people, it is just that they have chosen to deal with life experiences in a more sombre manner than you would prefer. It is important, however, to keep in mind your thoughts are in fact forms of energy, and if we focus our thoughts intently enough, they will manifest in material form. It is for that reason that if we tend to allow negative thought patterns to enter into our conscious awareness, we will continuously be bombarded with unpleasant situations and may truly believe we are the victims of bad luck. Alternatively, if we try to maintain a positive mental attitude during the most extreme of situations, we will find that we will encounter more positive than negative influences. Because thoughts can very well manifest themselves in the physical world, if we think good thoughts about others, they will experiences an uplifting sensation that can only come from the positive thoughts directed by us, which is one of the reasons why praise is so important in our lives. On the same note, if we think negative thoughts and direct those impressions towards another being, he will feel the malefic influences we have directed at him and can even succumb to illness if enough harmful vibrations are able to penetrate his psychic web. Lest you believe you have found the perfect vehicle to harm others with your negative thoughts, which in itself is a form of black magic, it is important to keep in mind that whatever thoughts you inflict on another soul will boomerang and come right back at you. It is therefore prudent to endeavour to think positive, uplifting thoughts, regardless of how difficult it may be, because there is simply too much negativity in our physical world, and we really don't need any more.

XVI Tower   If The Tower has appeared in the Environment position, it appears that the people around you have taken a conspiratory attitude with regard to one specific issue. There has been a great deal of whispering about, but as of yet, nothing concrete has been established. It is time, therefore, to dispel any rumours that have been circulating and establish the truth, which must inevitably emerge. If you personally are not in a position to dispel any myths that may be surrounding you, it is best to approach the source of the problem, which will be either the originator of the rumours or the person who has the power to affect you and your way of living. During the course of the division between fact and fiction, you will be quite surprised and possibly dismayed to discover some very pertinent pieces of information that will have a direct impact on your particular situation. As a result of the chaotic events that are occurring all around you, you may find yourself in a different home or vocation, with possibly a whole new set of friends, thus putting an end to the complacent position you have previously been residing in.

XVII Star   If The Star has landed in the Environment position, you are in an environment of hope and inspiration, where new ideas are coming forth with a great fluency. There is much friendliness surrounding you, but you need to be aware of insincerity in certain individuals, especially those persons who you don't know very well. There may be someone around you who has something to teach you, although she is likely to use some rather unorthodox teaching methods. You may have a close friend who needs someone to talk to about a particular issue in her life, so it would be a good idea to make yourself available for a friendly one to one chat.

XVIII Moon   If The Moon has appeared in the Environment position, it seems that you are not in total control of your surroundings. Your sense of perception is veiled in some way, which makes it difficult for you to clearly see your situation in the true light of day. It is for that reason some individuals who you believe to be your friends are actually working at cross-purposes to you, trying to achieve a goal in variance to yours. There are also some feral aspects to your current environment, as some individuals have not learned the correct way to conduct themselves in a civilised society. This failure to conform also poses problems, as you are uncertain how to deal with those individuals who do not behave in a manner that you would traditionally expect them to. You do have friends who you can count on, but because they have chosen to reveal themselves directly to you, it will take you quite some time to realise their true value as allies.

XIX The Sun   If The Sun has appeared in the Environment position, you may be in a situation where people try their best to put on a happy face, even under the most trying of circumstances. It is for that reason if something is amiss in paradise, you will need to look for less obvious clues, such as feet and eye movements. Someone you know may be thinking of having a child, and it would be a very propitious time to do so because a baby would bring much happiness to an otherwise dull world. There may also be someone around you who needs to be the centre of attention or his self-esteem will suffer. In order to stay in the limelight, he may resort to attention seeking antics, which could only serve to show him in a bad light amongst his contemporaries. It is for that reason he may need some support to help to resolve those crucial issues that affect him so.

XX Judgement   If Judgement has appeared in the Environment position, the circumstances that you are involved in represent retrograde movement throughout your particular evolutionary development. You will continuously find yourself encountering people and situations from the past, who prompt you to re-think some crucial issues you thought had been resolved. While you may think to yourself, 'My, what a coincidence!', the rationale behind these carefully orchestrated scenarios is to allow you to face your problems from the past by encountering them all over again. Hopefully, in the interval between first facing the obstacle and subsequent occurrences, you will have taken the time to reflect on what brought the situation to your attention. What circumstances prompted you to take action? How did you feel your action or intervention affected the outcome of the situation? How did you feel about the outcome of the situation? What, if any, lessons did you learn? After careful analysis by yourself, or with the help of a trusted friend, you should be able to gain at least a fair degree of enlightenment through the process of hindsight and introspection. With this information at hand, when you do find yourself revelling in a déjà vu type scenario, think carefully about how you will handle the situation this time around. While it is true you cannot recreate the past in the normal laws of the physicalities we have chosen to live under, you are being given the opportunity to make amends for any errors you have made long ago. Unfortunately, because of the laws of cause and effect that are a part of our karmic existence, if you are not able to successfully resolve the dilemma you are being presented with this time around, the universe will assign you the same karmic lessons over and over again until you are finally successful in the major objective. Because that is the true nature of things, it is important you think very carefully about how your actions and reactions will affect others.

XXI World   If The World has appeared in the Environment position, it seems the people around you are entering a cycle of completion in some way. This sense of finality may very well have come about as a result of finishing a lesson or course of study, ending a job or major project, moving house, getting a promotion, graduating to a higher level of study, or moving on from a relationship. Whether this change is positive or negative, a period of grieving is nevertheless a necessary healing component in the transition from one mode to another. It is for that reason tempers may flair, as individuals test the water of their new environs. Patience will therefore be necessary to ensure those close to you can adequately adjust to their new position in life and the upcoming tasks they will be expected to face.

Wands/Rods/Fire

Ace   If the Ace of Wands has appeared in the Environment position, you are surrounded by creative persons who prefer to express themselves via the artistic forms they produce, rather than the spoken or written word. You may be close to people who work in the world of art, music, theatre or films because these avenues allow people to make statements through means much more vast than the more traditional ways of expression. You may also be in an environment where business transactions are taking place because some people like to use their abundance of energy in the wheeler-dealer world of business, thereby creating wealth and abundance for themselves and others. Because there is a huge potential for great things being accomplished, you would be prudent to watch your contemporaries carefully to see if you can pick up things from them that will be useful to you. Your contemporaries will also be keeping an eye on you, trying to discover how you are able to accomplish some crucial tasks seemingly effortlessly.

Two   If the Two of Wands has appeared in the Environment position, you may be approached by another person to work with him on an endeavour that has the potential to yield profitable results. It is important you work to build relationships with the people who you come into contact with in your normal day-to-day activities because they have the ability to help or hinder you along your way to enlightenment. How you feel about someone personally is not the issue here, because what is important is for you to put your personal differences aside to work towards a common goal that will be beneficial for the both of you.

Three   If the Three of Wands has appeared in the Environment position, you have found yourself to be surrounded by a group of people who have a great deal of energy. It is likely you know this circle of people through your work, as you all must work together to achieve a certain goal. There is also the possibility, however, that the people who you come into contact with could be related to a team sport, where you must co-operate with the entire group if you would like to succeed. Whatever the nature of this get-together, in order to come out a winner, it is essential you appear to be an excellent team player. If your contemporaries feel your alliance has not been given 100% to the team, it will become very difficult for you to work effectively with other people.

Four   If the Four of Rods has appeared in the Environment position, you may be spending much time at home, engaging in numerous activities.

People around the home or your immediate family may very well be vibrant, dynamic individuals, who have a great deal of initiative, which you find to be quite appealing. As a result of this, they tend to keep the family together, concentrating on the financial aspects of the small, close knit unit as well as much more practical aspects of any liaisons. In addition, people close to you have a strong need to feel secure and therefore plan for their future meticulously in order to help ensure their prosperity is established even in later years.

Five If the Five of Wands has appeared in the Environment position, it seems everyone around you is quarrelling over one topic or another. While you may not personally be in dispute over any of the issues that seem to be oh so important to those closest to you, you seem to be caught in the middle, a situation that makes you feel somewhat uncomfortable at the very least. You do not want to appear to take sides because whichever side you take will only alienate you from other individuals. The best you can do, therefore, is to remain impartial when individuals are pouring their hearts out to you, telling you their version of events that have caused them so much anguish. You will find, however, that there is one root cause of the troubles of those near you. When the crux of the problem is resolved, everything else will fall into place and make sense to you in what is becoming with each day an ever increasingly nonsensical world.

Six If the Six of Wands has appeared in the Environment position, you seem to be surrounded by people who are positive thinkers. These individuals are very ambitious, and subsequently try to surround themselves with equally ambitious and talented individuals. They are great networkers, building relationships with people who they feel have the potential to help them to excel in this life. Although there is the smell of success in the air, in any climb up a social or career ladder, only one person can reach the pinnacle at any one given time. It is, however, how an individual approaches his escalation to the top that counts. If he steps on the little people on his climb upward, they will no doubt remember his ruthless behaviour on his way down and react by repaying him in kind. If the same individual is thoughtful of those less fortunate than himself whilst becoming upwardly mobile, those same individuals will be thoughtful and helpful when times are not so good for him. It is also important to keep in mind that in virtually any endeavour, the air of hypocrisy will prevail in some areas. It is therefore essential you do not place your trust wholeheartedly in any individuals who have not proven themselves to be trustworthy because some individuals who make your acquaintance could have insincere intentions. An apt scenario is the case of Julius Caesar, where he was warned to beware of the Ides of March. It was his supposed closest friends who assassinated him in the halls of the senate, and not his enemies, as one would have supposed.

Seven   If the Seven of Wands has appeared in the Environment position, you seem to be under pressure to perform under rather austere conditions. You may very well have reached a pinnacle in your career or social ladder, but it is important to keep in mind that unless you are extremely lucky or astute, you cannot stay on top of the situation forever. Therefore, you will experience other people who are vying for the position you now hold. It is important, therefore, to keep your composure and sense of grace even under the most trying of circumstances, because you will need as many allies as you can get when times are not so opportune. You will also need to keep your wits about you in order to hang onto all the things you have worked so hard to attain.

Eight   If the Eight of Wands has appeared in the Environment position, you are surrounded by people who are going places in this world. They may be very ambitious, striving to get as far up their career or social ladders as possible, and are therefore eager to mix with the right types of individuals on their climb to the top. If you consequently feel left out, don't take it personally. It is nothing you have said or done, but the fact that certain people around you don't feel you are in a position to make a viable contribution to their success, and have therefore decided not to waste their time trying to cultivate a meaningful relationship with you. You may feel their actions are rather snubbing, which they are, but you should not take it as a reflection of you, but merely an example of their lack of maturity and insight into the complicated world we live in.

Nine   If the Nine of Wands has appeared in the Environment position, you are in a situation where everyone seems to be on their guard and are defensive for one reason or another. You may be in a rather precarious economic environment, which will leave people vulnerable about their own position in this world. It is for that reason they may appear a bit snappy, so it is a good idea not to take the insulting things they may say or do personally.

Ten   If the Ten of Wands has appeared in the Environment position, you are surrounded by several people who have been visited with a great deal of responsibility, but are unsure of exactly how to use it. They may very well be inept at the task they have been assigned, but unless you personally have the power to assign or de-assign work, there is not much you can do about the situation, no matter how frustrating it may be at times. If you bicker with those individuals, it will only show you in a bad light. The best you can do, therefore, is to either lend a helping hand when you can, or stand back and allow them to muddle through, unhindered by you.

King If the King of Wands has appeared in the Environment position, there is a powerful man around you who has the ability to influence the situation one way or another. For the time being he is observing the unfolding of events as they transpire, but the time may come when he will decide to intervene. He can at times appear stern, but this is merely a façade he uses because he feels he can be more successful if he puts on a serious front. Because he has a fiery temper and an active mind, he may change his opinions quite quickly, which can be exasperating for those who need a firm decision so they can take appropriate action.

Queen If the Queen of Wands has appeared in the Environment position, there is an active woman who is trying to exert her influence over you. Whether or not she is successful will depend on how resolute you are in your own mind with regard to the situation that prompted you to consult the oracle. While she very often may mean well, she does have ulterior motives that may or may not be to your liking. She may also have some problems of her own that she needs to resolve in her mind, which will consequently affect the accuracy of what she relates to you. It is therefore best to trust your own intuition in this matter because you alone will know what is correct and proper with regard to your particular situation.

Knight/ Prince If the Knight of Wands has appeared in the Environment position, you are close to a young man who has some very dynamic qualities. He possesses a great deal of energy in his auric make-up, which means he needs to stay active physically as well as mentally in order to be happy and at ease with himself. The Fire in his astrological make-up means he can be impulsive, acting on the spur of the moment. While making impromptu plans can be fun for a while, he needs to learn to carry his projects out to completion if he is to receive full benefit of his active intellect and reasoning ability.

Page/ Princess If the Page of Wands has appeared in the Environment position, you are close to a young person who is having an influence on the successful resolution of the situation that prompted you to consult the oracle. This person has a great deal of energy and likes to stay busy. It is for that reason she needs a fair degree of supervision to ensure she is given direction and does not find herself in trouble during more turbulent times in her development.

Pentacles/Disks/Earth

Ace If the Ace of Pentacles has appeared in the Environment position, you have found yourself to be in a situation where you are surrounded by money or assets that give others the impression of material wealth. While you personally may not be financially solvent, the circumstances you have found yourself in indicate you have access to those items that belong to others. These possessions you personally don't own could come to you through a partner, family member or employer who allow you to use their belongings at their pleasure. It is for that reason you need to exercise care when considering any radical moves that could upset the status quo, because the nice things that you currently have around you could be taken away as a result of any rash moves on you or another's part.

Two If the Two of Pentacles has appeared in the Environment position, you are in a situation where everyone around you seems to be worried about money. It appears that no one you know has enough money to pay for all of the things they need in order to comfortably exist in modern day society. Some people will try to live frugally and make sacrifices, which means forgoing expensive holidays and trips abroad. Others, however, will run up huge debts, leaving them wondering how they will ever meet their financial obligations. Somehow, the bills will be paid, but it may mean either giving up some not so essential items or taking on more paid work. The important thing, however, is not to allow yourself to be lulled into a sea of never-ending debt because one day you will be expected to repay what you owe to others.

Three If the Three of Pentacles has appeared in the Environment position, you may very well find yourself in the midst of some very successful souls. These individuals may very well work with their hands in some way, creating something of value where none previously existed. Certain individuals in your social or professional circle may consider moving, and this move will be seen as a progression of their material standing amongst their contemporaries in our very physical world.

Four   If the Four of Pentacles has appeared in the Environment position, you are surrounded by several people who, for whatever reason, are quite cloistered in their own little world. These individuals are somewhat insular in their outlook on life, and do not feel comfortable when they find themselves out of their element, an environment they have not set up for themselves. As a result of this, they tend only to go to places and associate with people who they know well and feel safe in the company of. Certain individuals may even suffer from phobias, such as claustrophobia, agoraphobia and social phobias, which will further inhibit their ability to get out and about. You need to ascertain exactly why those around you would prefer not to venture out into the big wide world.

Five   If the Five of Pentacles has appeared in the Environment position, you seem to be in an environment where there is never enough money to meet your physical and emotional needs. Those around you must live on modest incomes, which means they are not necessarily in a position to splash out and treat themselves to the real luxuries in this life. Because the people around you never seem to have enough money to enjoy a reasonable standard of living, they could very well succumb to depression, as they struggle to make ends meet in an ever increasingly complex world. While some people close to you may be able to weather the economic storm, others will be forced to admit defeat and surrender their assets to more powerful authorities.

Six   If the Six of Pentacles has found itself to be in the Environment position, you are surrounded by philanthropic individuals. You may know people who perform unpaid work, engaging in the activities for the sheer satisfaction of completing a task, with little or no monetary reward. You may also know other individuals who, for whatever reason, are down on their luck and therefore need a helping hand in the form of favours or charity. There is an aura of gifts given and received, as people work to fulfil their karmic obligations that have been acquired from actions in past, present, future and parallel existences.

Seven   If the Seven of Pentacles has appeared in the Environment position, it seems certain individuals around you are in contemplation about a certain issue, waiting with great trepidation for a successful outcome to a situation they are not sure of. Not all things in this world can come to a quick resolution, as some rather crucial events may take days, weeks, months or even years to come to fruition. For example, craftsmen must often study for years before they can even be allowed to leave the apprenticeship phase of their vocation. In the same vein, some students study academic subjects for years before they are even qualified to take on a position as a trainee, only to struggle for several more years before they are trusted enough to work unsupervised. Major projects in government and business sectors also must take time, and are very rarely achieved overnight. The situation you have found yourself in, therefore, is one of those occasions when you and those around you must work tirelessly to bring about an end result that will occur in the not so near future.

Eight   If the Eight of Pentacles has appeared in the Environment position, you have found yourself in a situation where you are amongst a group of individuals who are in a learning environment. You, or those close to you, may be in a period of training, which is very much of a hands-on nature, as you must become qualified through experience. In the process of honing your skills, you must learn by trial and error, trying out various methods before you find one that is most suitable to you.

Nine   If the Nine of Pentacles has appeared in the Environment position, you are surrounded by people who are fairly satisfied with the position they have worked hard for in this life, and have therefore decided to take some time out to enjoy it. Because their finances are relatively secure and they have made provisions for their future prosperity, they have decided it is time to relax and experience the pleasure of just being, enjoying the world as it is. As a result, they may decide to spend more time vacationing with family and friends, recharging their batteries after a time of hard work and dedication to their chosen profession. These people have the confidence that comes only from having made significant achievements and earned enough money to be able to relax. In addition, there may be some individuals among your group of associates who have acquired wealth through means other than effort, such as having been given an inheritance or having married into money. These individuals have the luxury of enjoying the nice material things of this world without having had to go out and earn them. Because of these special circumstances, their attitude is much more flippant because they do not have true understanding of the sacrifices others have had to make so they could pursue a life of luxury. Because these individuals have not had to work for their money, they have no appreciation of its true value, and as a consequence they may tend to spend it unwisely or even squander it.

Ten   If the Ten of Pentacles has appeared in the Environment position, you are heavily involved with certain members of your family, particularly the ones who control the finances. While you personally may not command a great deal of wealth, certain members of your family may have possessions that you stand to have a share in if you maintain ties with those persons. The problem arises, however, that if you would like to share in the good fortune of others, you may be expected to make certain personal sacrifices. Certain members of your family may not approve of your choice of partner or friends, and could therefore put pressure on you to associate with individuals of their choice. The message is clear, if you tow the family line and behave in a manner that is suitable to what they would expect of you, then you stand to gain a lot from them. If, however, you exert your own free will, which is your right as a member of the celestial universe, you may risk being ostracised from the very ones who are able to give you a semblance of physical security. Because this oracle only reveals to you what is likely to transpire if you carry on in the same fashion as you have been previously, it would be inappropriate for the oracle to direct you to a specific course of action. The choice of which direction you take in this life, therefore, is yours and yours alone.

King   If the King of Pentacles has appeared in the Environment position, there is a powerful man who is influencing the situation that has prompted you to consult the oracle. He is a man of independent means, having ensured his physical needs will be met well into old age. Because he is secure in his position in this world, he is able to impart sound knowledge and advice to others, with no ulterior motives. He is therefore able to act impartially on matters that concern those who are close to him. Because he is not worried about money and other material assets many lesser souls contemplate on a daily basis, he has the ability to lavish presents on the objects of his desire. Knowing this, he is never short of company, as there are always those longing to benefit from his good fortune.

Queen   If the Queen of Pentacles has appeared in the Environment position, you are being influenced by a woman who is practically minded and has wealth in her own right. She has the confidence that comes from the security of knowing her physical needs are being met. It is for that reason she will usually speak her mind and will not be terribly bothered if she offends anyone who may be within earshot. Because she is so forthright in her manner of speaking, she may not have a great many friends: casual acquaintances usually prefer to be around someone with a little bit more tact. This is a pity, however, because if she were to put forth a little more effort to speak with a modicum of diplomacy, she would be able to form more powerful alliances.

Knight/ Prince

If the Knight of Disks has appeared in the Environment position, you are close to a young man who is very deliberate in all that he does. He analyses his actions and weighs out the possible pros and cons of every move he makes, taking into consideration factors of each and every move. His methodical nature may lead people to believe he is slow, but they could not be further from the truth. What they perceive to be a reluctance to take action is merely a dedicated effort on his part to do the right thing. This young person is interested in his status in this life, and will therefore attempt to enter a vocation that will enable him to acquire the acclaim he so desperately needs to build what is in actual fact a very fragile ego. This person needs to be pampered and made to feel special, even though he would never admit to it.

Page/ Princess

If the Page of Disks has appeared in the Environment position, you have a young person close to you who has a huge impact on the situation that has prompted you to consult the oracle. This person is very grounded and is not prone to flights of fancy. Although she is likely to be spiritual in her own way, this is something that is deeply private to her, so private in fact that she would never even consider thinking in terms of esoteric matters that preoccupy the minds of so many others. She tends to think intuitively, but does not see it as such, preferring to attribute her keen perceptions to being able to read body language and being able to attune herself to other clues that would be apparent to others, if they would only look. This person has a logical reason for everything, and if she does by chance come across an aspect of the world at large that she cannot explain rationally, she would prefer to dismiss it from her mind. It is not that she is not open to metaphysical matters, but she already knows pursuing such things are not her path in life and therefore prefers not to waste any of their precious time dabbling in such matters.

Swords/Air

Ace

If the Ace of Swords has appeared in the Environment position, you are in a situation where a great deal of mental activity is prominent in your mind, which will bring about some rather complex thought processes. Books, computers, libraries and correspondence predominate your life, as you need access to valuable information if the situation that prompted you to consult the oracle is to be resolved satisfactorily. This is also one of those situations you have been karmicly destined to face, a dilemma you are obliged to successfully resolve before you can embark upon the next phase of your soul evolution. You need to have all the facts at hand in order to determine your next move, so it is essential you take a critical look at any and all data presented to you. If you are misinformed, it could adversely affect the outcome of your particular circumstances.

Two If the Two of Swords has appeared in the Environment position, you are in a situation where people seem to be at odds with one another. There is likely to be two differing schools of thought, and you are being induced to take sides in the matter. The problem is that if you side with one individual or group, you will effectively alienate yourself from the differing set of people, which is something you don't wish to do. The situation is further complicated because you are not in full possession of the facts, which makes it difficult for you to make any type of educated decision on the matter. It is an emotional situation close to the heart of the quarrelling parties. The best you can do is to refuse to allow yourself to become entangled in the ensuing web of deceit because it is highly unlikely that any of the concerned parties will achieve a desired outcome. It will be difficult for you to detach yourself, however, because those individuals who are trying in earnest to get you to adopt their point of view won't allow you to. You may have to resort to agreeing to disagree, but that is not a necessarily a desirable option either.

Three If the Three of Swords has appeared in the Environment position, you seem to be surrounded by strifeful individuals who have gone far beyond the point of merely disagreeing on a few important points. These individuals have totally and utterly uncomplementary personalities, which has made it difficult for them to agree on any one issue so there could be at least something they could have in common. To make matters worse, you seem to be stuck in the middle, which has made it all the more difficult for you to view the situation in a detached manner and thereby make objective life choices. Because there is such a conflict of personalities, someone will have to go, which will result in an element of heartache for all concerned parties. Only you can decide how best to resolve this situation, but it is not going to be an easy decision to make. No matter what you do, someone will be hurt.

Four   If the Four of Swords has appeared in the Environment position, you have entered into a period where those around you are in a time of reflection. They have expended a great deal of mental energy, thinking and plotting, and now it is time to rest their weary minds and achieve enlightenment through the process of retrospective introspection. The people around you are spending a great deal of time thinking of the past, considering how their actions and reactions have brought them where they are today. They are also thinking of themselves, wondering exactly what it is that motivates them and why they feel the way they do. During this time of reflection, a time when they can be still and quiet their minds, they will receive insight by remembering events of past, future and parallel lives that have a direct impact on their world growth at this point in time. They will also attain clarity of mind as they receive illumination from higher, more knowledgeable powers, which will help guide them along this earth walk.

Five   If the Five of Swords has appeared in the Environment position, you are in a situation where there appears to be a great deal of tension and strife. The reason for this is a clash of personalities combined with different ideas about how things should be accomplished. The result of differing viewpoints is a great deal of tension, which does not seem to be subsiding any time in the near future. While a bit of friendly rivalry is always a good thing because it gives people the motivation to try to perform just that little bit better, too much competition can erupt in bitter disputes and sometimes even all-out war. If the situation you find yourself in is too worrying, you may find the best course of action is to walk away and leave the conspirators to their own devices. Those who you are in dispute with are unlikely to change their views any time in the near future, so it is useless trying to sway them.

Six   If the Six of Swords has appeared in the Environment position, either you or someone close to you is intending on making a major move sometime in the near future. It appears things have not been going so well, your life path has not transpired in the sequence of events you had originally envisaged, and you may very well have a bitter taste in your mouth about it. You may have had some disputes, and although you tried to utilise your best powers of persuasion to make others see your point of view, those in a position to lessen the stress you had been experiencing were not necessarily sympathetic to your cause. While you could very well stay on and struggle in the face of adversity, it would be prudent to know when you are fighting a losing battle, and to know when to walk away. Choosing to walk away does not necessarily make you a loser; it makes you astute to the signs of the times. You may have to leave a relationship, job or a home, but the hope of a brighter future ahead is what will give you the will to leave an untenable situation and enter into the unknown.

Seven   If the Seven of Swords has appeared in the Environment position, you have found yourself in a situation where you need to keep your wits about you. The reason for this is because things are not always as they seem. The people around you are quite duplicitous, which will make it difficult for you to try to establish any kind of meaningful relationship with them. It is also important to keep in mind there are a great deal of surreptitious activities going on behind the scenes you may be totally unaware of. The clues may have presented themselves to you, but in your desire to see and hear only what you wanted, you have either blocked or repressed the sensations that would rattle the status quo, thus further embedding your deep denial-induced psychological slumber. More specifically, there is a thief in your midst, and he is likely to steal ideas and relationships more readily than material objects. It is essential, therefore, that you be vigilant and observe the acts of those around you.

Eight   If the Eight of Swords has appeared in the Environment position, you and those around you are stuck in a rut. For reasons known only to you, you are in a physical or conceptual incarceration that is preventing you from taking any concrete steps to improve your situation in this life. Even if you are physically unable to do anything about the austere predicament you have found yourself in, you can free your mind and experience other aspects of our existence just by sheer mental imagery. Once you experience new insights with a positive mental attitude, other aspects of your living will begin to improve as well because nothing can stay in a state of stasis forever. The 20th century psychic, Edgar Cayce, stated that everything is dreamed before it manifests in the physicalities of this world, so maybe it is time to open your mind to your dreams and see what happens next.

Nine   If the Nine of Swords has appeared in the Environment position, you are in a position where there are many people around you who are not well. The illness is such that the sufferers should not be working, but should be trying to take it easy and recuperate. There is the feeling people are not getting enough sleep, as they spend a great deal of time tossing and turning, worrying about all their problems. This lack of sleep and seemingly endless sense of worry is further exacerbating any real or imagined health problems that may be in existence. Mental difficulties should not be discounted during this time of distress, as psychological disorders tend to increase in direct proportion to how civilised a society becomes.

Ten   If the Ten of Swords has appeared in the Environment position, you are in a situation where those around you are at a low point in their life. The people around you tend to be despondent, as their hopes have been dashed in some way. They may have placed their faith in the wrong people, and this misplaced trust has caused well-laid plans to completely go awry. This sense of betrayal has been intensified because it was committed by someone who they had imagined to be a friend, a person who they believed they could trust with all their heart. If such an act of deception had been committed by an enemy or someone they were indifferent to, the sense of grief would not be nearly so bad. The very act of disloyalty by someone they had assumed to be an ally makes the situation ten times worse. It is for this reason you need to take special care of the sensitivities of others because they are at an all time low and have pretty much lost their will to live in what sometimes can be a very wicked world.

King   If the King of Swords has appeared in the Environment position, you are being influenced by a man who has a very sharp mind. He is well read and tends to use his intellect when dealing with people. He is a very good at conceptualising and is therefore able to make long range plans to affect the futures of himself and those around him. Because he spends so much time in thought, he has a tendency to brood when he could be just as easily doing something constructive with his time. This sense of introspection can lead to a desire for retribution for real or imagined wrongs. This quest for retribution could cause him to spend even more time in thought, which quite often results in scheming, which can lead to neurosis, and then ultimately psychosis. In order to stop what can often become a never ending circle of inward thinking, which can ultimately lead to mental illness, he will need to stop using his intellect for a while and do something constructive with his hands. After a period of cerebral rest, he should be able to think with restored clarity of mind.

Queen   If the Queen of Swords has appeared in the Environment position, you are being influenced by a woman of some considerable intellect. She may have been fortunate enough to have received a good standard of education, but even if that is not the case, she is able to live by her wits.

She is a logical person who uses reason to solve the dilemmas she finds herself needing to resolve. She is perceptive because she watches people closely, determining the various personalities and temperaments through subtle observation. She is an apt communicator and will therefore tend to enter vocations that will allow her to present to people the information she feels they will need to progress onto the next level of their evolution.

Knight/ Prince If the Knight of Swords has appeared in the Environment position, you are being influenced by a young man who is very cerebral in nature. There is a great deal of mental activity going on with this person, and you can never be quite sure exactly what is in his head. He is extremely quick-witted and tends to think his way out of difficulties, often fabricating stories if it is in his best interests to do so. It is therefore best to take whatever this individual says with a grain of salt, since he cannot be relied upon to give an honest account of the events which have prompted you to seek a reading.

Page/ Princess If the Page of Swords has appeared in the Environment position, you are influenced by a young person who is quite inquisitive. She is very chatty and tends to use her reasoning ability to help her to manoeuvre around life's obstacles. She may have a learning disorder that will need to be addressed before she can successfully progress to her next level of education. Because she is so chatty, she may unwitting reveal to others subjects told to her in confidence, so it is therefore essential you exercise discretion in whatever you reveal to her.

Cups/Water

Ace If the Ace of Cups has appeared in the Environment position, you are in an environment of happiness and emotional wellbeing. There exists within you the need to bring about the fulfilment of many of your hopes and dreams, which will have the effect of making those close to you happy as well. This is a time of dharma, where you and those close to you are experiencing the karmic gifts you have received from good works performed in past, present and future incarnations.

Two If the Two of Cups has appeared in the Environment position, it appears your personal relationships at this point in your life are taking precedence over more mundane endeavours. You may very well have come into contact with one special someone who was in many ways destined to meet you. The both of you find you are in awe of each other, as you attempt to create a bond that will withstand the test of time and endure through each incarnation.

Three   If the Three of Cups has appeared in the Environment position, you are in a situation where those around you tend to be gay and cheerful. There are several social invitations being given, so it is likely to be a lively time. The one thing to keep in mind is the vast majority of people will only want to be around you when you are cheerful and upbeat, so it would be wise to put on a happy face and smile if you want to be included in any merry-making activities.

Four   If the Four of Cups has appeared in the Environment position, you are in a situation of uncertainty, as those around you are unsure of exactly where to turn next. There are many whispers abounding, some true and some not so true. The best you can do, therefore, is to rely on your gut instinct, because your inner guidance will direct you onto the path that is right for you and those around you.

Five   If the Five of Cups has appeared in the Environment position, you seem to be surrounded by people who seem to be disappointed and let down in some way. Perhaps certain individuals have disappointed them, and they need time to work through the resulting problems in their own way to come to terms with what has transpired. While there is a fair degree of despondency in the air, in time people will see the resulting situation was not as dire as they had supposed it to be. They will eventually be able to adjust to the new arrangements, looking for alternative solutions to any problems they may have. This will be a good time to think laterally and explore possibilities that have never before been pondered.

Six   If the Six of Cups has appeared in the Environment position, you may be in a situation that reminds you of the past, a situation that enables you to relive many of your childhood memories, whether they are pleasant or something you would rather forget. You may also come into contact with children on a daily basis, which will have the effect of provoking you to reflect on children in general. Children are such innocent, trusting beings who take pleasure in the simplest things in this life. They express unabashed wonder at the things we take for granted and help us to take a renewed interest in the world around us. It is for that reason children should be treasured because they truly are a gift from God. They will grow up soon enough, so the memories they have should be pleasant.

Seven   If the Seven of Cups has appeared in the Environment position, you are surrounded by mystery, wondering what the future has in store for you. There is an element of change that must take place, but the problem is it is difficult to make a choice. There are so many options, but which direction will yield the most beneficial results? You must beware of charlatans, people who make fabulous claims and distorted promises that will rarely come to fruition. It is for that reason you should use a great deal of caution when considering getting involved with someone who would make such outlandish promises. Even if you do get what you want from these people, you may be expected to make a sacrifice that is wholly out of proportion with what you will actually be receiving. While it is often advantageous to take a risk, it is best to seek advice beforehand so any chances you take will be calculated, and success would be a more reasonable possibility.

Eight   If the Eight of Cups has appeared in the Environment position, it seems people all around you are sad for one reason or another. It seems certain people around you have invested much emotional energy into a specific project or relationship, and after careful deliberation have decided to abandon something that had at one time held so much promise. Could it be that you unwittingly had a part to play in the situation that someone close to you has decided to abandon? If so, you may want to contemplate how you can resolve any issues that will affect your relationship with that person, because it is clearly evident that communication will be strained at the very least. If you act now, you may be able to salvage what is lost, especially if the people in question mean a great deal to you.

Nine   If the Nine of Cups has appeared in the Environment position, you may be close to an individual who likes to eat, drink and make merry. He has a very jovial personality, but it is important to look beneath this outward persona and then you will discover more clues to the person behind the mask. What you perceive to be joviality may be anxiety or despair, as it is a well-known fact that people will tend to laugh when nervous. Whilst it is nice to have a drink, smoke or bite to eat to unwind, too much of a good thing is unwise because it wreaks havoc on one's health. It is therefore essential to carefully scrutinise your friends' habits because they could very well misuse or abuse substances in an attempt to self-medicate. Your friend may very well be using food, drink or cigarettes as a coping mechanism, which in essence inhibits him from becoming a whole human being.

Ten   If the Ten of Cups has appeared in the Environment position, it seems you are in an environment of happiness and harmony. Your personal relationships are satisfying and you are quite happy with your home life. You may very well have been united with your one true soul mate in this life, which means you would very much like to form a more permanent bond with this individual, possibly by adding to what the two of you have by having children or pets.

King   If the King of Cups has appeared in the Environment position, you are being influenced by a thoughtful man who is concerned about the happiness and wellbeing of others. He can give you some sound advice, if you are prepared to listen to what he has to say.

Queen   If the Queen of Cups has appeared in the Environment position, you are close to a woman who has many benevolent characteristics. She takes an interest in helping those who are not in a position to help themselves, and may therefore take in stray animals and people who cross her path. She is, however, prone to depression when things do not go exactly as she had planned, which could cause further health problems. It is therefore essential she take steps to remain firmly grounded, concentrating on the task at hand. If she is about to success-fully complete one project at a time, it will go a long way to allaying any feelings to self-doubt that she may experience.

Knight/ Prince   If the Knight of Cups has appeared in the Environment position, you are in close proximity to a young man who is quite sensitive to the needs of others. He has a great deal of feeling, which he expresses to those individuals he is close to. He may, however, suppress some of his more tender emotions, which could have the effect of bringing them out in explosive force at the most inopportune times. It is therefore necessary to take measures to make time for rest and relaxation even during hectic times.

Page/ Princess   If the Page of Cups has appeared in the Environment position, you are close to a young person who is sensitive, caring and quite emotional. She has an influence over the situation that prompted you to consult the oracle. Because she is so sensitive, some things will upset her that would not upset sturdier souls, and it is for that reason you need to tread carefully when criticising her because her feelings can become hurt very easily.

9 For and Against

0 Fool   If The Fool has appeared in the For and Against position, you will have an opportunity to make a fresh start and carve out a new life for yourself. If you have been stuck in a rut, bored and complacent about what has become a routine monotony of a life you no longer have enjoyment in, this will be a perfect opportunity for you to begin afresh, living the life you have always wanted to pursue. For a time, anyway, you may not have as much money and may therefore not be able to afford things you previously had taken for granted. The sense of exhilaration you will feel at having the freedom from the chains that had formerly bound you will far outweigh any financial boundaries you may find yourself temporarily constricted by.

I Magician   If The Magician has appeared in the For and Against position, you will have the opportunity to receive training, which will be an initiation into higher levels of awareness. You may have decided to enter into a new profession, which would ultimately involve learning new skills, either in a formal classroom setting or a more informal training scenario. You may also decide you would like to progress in your chosen career, which will involve more learning and possibly exams to test your competency. Any time you try something new, there will always be a learning curve that you must overcome before you reach your desired level of competency. In order to achieve maximum results in any endeavour, you must learn to focus your thinking into a clear and distinct pattern. If your thought processes are scattered, you will not achieve great success, it is therefore essential you learn to focus your thinking patterns, which may mean you have to give up some extraneous activities that are hampering your progress. You can do anything you like with a positive mental attitude, and that little known fact is something you need to keep in mind when you go about fulfilling your dreams. What is important to keep in mind is that 'if you think it to be so, it will be'.

II High Priestess If the High Priestess has appeared in the For and Against position, you need to be aware that if you continue along your present path you will be initiated into some of the many secrets of the universe. This knowledge is likely to be revealed to you while sleeping, during meditation, or during a religious ceremony where you must remain silent and attuned to the 'now'. In the New Testament, Jesus spoke to the masses in parables, but revealed the true universal secrets to his selected disciples. The reason for this was because the masses would not be able to comprehend many laws of our universal existence, and therefore had to be taught within the framework of a story, or analogy. In the same manner, you have a perfect opportunity to learn valuable secrets that have only been revealed to a select few. The downside of all this, however, is the masses will not be receptive to your new-found revelations because they are not ready to revel with you in your new knowledge. It is for that reason you will have to keep what you have learned to yourself, sharing it with only a select few individuals who you see eye to eye with, and you know you can trust.

III Empress If The Empress has appeared in the For and Against position, there is a likelihood that you could add to your present family because this is a very fertile time for you. Your relationships will be highly significant, and you will have the opportunity to bring your hopes and dreams to fruition with the help of one specific person. You will have the opportunity to form a very solid foundation, in particular a relationship, which will bear fruit and allow you to leave quite a substantial legacy.

IV Emperor If the Emperor has appeared in the For and Against position, you have the ability to carve out a rather powerful base for yourself. You will have the opportunity to build a firm foundation for any business, government or family, which will hold you in good stead for years to come. You may, however, be somewhat authoritarian and strong-willed, thinking of your personal gratification before the needs of others. Such egocentric practices, however, will not hold you in high esteem amongst those around you, and they could secretly wish to see you fall. It is for that reason you will be much happier with your lot in life if you take the time to learn a few people skills and take the needs of others into consideration when making important decisions.

V Hierophant If The Hierophant has appeared in the For and Against position, you will have the opportunity to carve out a niche for yourself in the world of business and commerce. It is a high area of professionalism, and you will be afforded the chance to gain respect through your knowledge and expertise in certain areas. You will be exposed to the formalities of education, religion and the professional sector. What you gain in standing amongst your contemporaries, you must sacrifice spiritually. Because you will be surrounded by people who need to operate within the framework of tradition and superb organisation, they will not normally be receptive to the more esoteric aspects of our soul's existence. It is for that reason if you decide to follow the path of traditional religious and business ethics, you would be wise to follow the exoteric path, focusing on the here and now. Whilst you may yearn to explore the unseen possibilities that make up the conceptual aspects of our awareness, those whose support you need are not open to such ideas. Jesus spoke in parables to the masses because they could not fully comprehend the true secrets of the universe. In the same vein, you would be wise to keep your conversations with the general public on a very practical, general level, because they will not generally be receptive to topics that involve any significant depth.

VI Lovers If The Lovers has appeared in the For and Against position, you will be given the opportunity to make a major choice in your life. You are on a path that will soon come to a metaphorical crossroad. You can either proceed, taking one of the two paths that are available to you, or you can stop where you are. If you stop, the development of your soul will effectively stand still, eventually withering from the self-imposed inertia. The downside of this failure to act is that sooner or later you will have to face the dilemma that has stopped you dead in your tracks, if not in this life, in another. It therefore would be in your best interests to confront the dilemma in this life, preventing any reactive consequences. If you choose to take a path, you will have to select one or the other avenue that is being made available to you. Both may look equally appealing, but unfortunately you can choose only one. The direction you elect to take will take your life on a completely different route, one that you possibly hadn't dreamed could occur. During times of heightened psychic awareness, you may actually be able to glimpse the alternate reality of the path you could have chosen, enjoying it for a time, experiencing the multiple nature of our souls. In addition to the soul growth you are destined to make, you also will be given the chance to come into contact with your one true love in this life. In order to capture the eternal bliss you might have with such an ultimately compatible soul, you may have to give something up, something you believe you cannot live without. The choice is yours.

VII Chariot If The Chariot has appeared in the For and Against position, you will have the chance to embark upon a journey that will serve to enhance your promotional capabilities and expand your level of awareness. It seems people will look to you for direction because you will be given a certain level of responsibility, which you really should use wisely. It is highly likely that you will be a success in whatever you set out to do because the energy you exert will be enough to see the project through to completion even when your interest has begun to wane. It is important that you carefully observe all around you because it is in your immediate scenery that you will gain clues to the prevailing climate.

VIII Strength If Strength has appeared in the For and Against position, you will have the opportunity to learn new skills, especially with regard to tact and diplomacy. In order to achieve a positive outcome to what you desire, you need to develop the art of subtle persuasion, such as the enchantress did when she was able to tame a ferocious lion. You need to be able to use a fair amount of guile to convince others that they actually want to help you achieve your aims, because they will not assist you if they do not believe they will ultimately gain something personally from their collaboration. In addition, if you do not show the appropriate demeanour, it is highly unlikely you will receive the assistance you require. A fair and amiable outlook will go a long way towards endearing yourself to others and taming the wild beast within us all.

IX Hermit If The Hermit has appeared in the For and Against position, you may be expected to spend time in solitude, which is not necessarily what you would like. You would rather be in the company of others because they keep your mind occupied, thereby assisting you in not thinking about what is really important right now. If you stay busy and surround yourself with people, you will not have many opportunities to reflect on your past experiences and gain a greater understanding of how they formed you into the person you are today. With time on your own, you will have the chance to reflect upon your problems. The process of enlightenment through self-analysis can be an emotionally painful endeavour, as you must re-experience many more traumatic experiences that have caused so many blockages in your psyche and have kept you from being the person you were destined to be. After the pain comes healing, which will repair the emotional wounds that are clearly evident and have marred certain aspects of your personality so.

X Wheel of Fortune   If The Wheel of Fortune has appeared in the For and Against position, you will have the opportunity to expand your level of awareness by experiencing what it is like to be on the other end of the spectrum of your spatial awareness. If things have been going well for you lately, you may find a few hiccups in your best-laid plans, which will serve to slow down your progress. Expect a change of fortune that will effectively lift your spirits and restore your faith in the world. The Wheel corresponds with the zodiacal wheel, which refers to the whole person in the horoscope. It is therefore expected you will be given the opportunity to become a whole person through your various life experiences.

XI Justice   If Justice has appeared in the For and Against position, the universal flow you are a part of will balance out your situation so no inequalities will exist any longer. If you have been hard done by, you can expect a change in circumstances so you receive retribution for any injustice that has transpired. On the other hand, if you have treated someone unfairly, you can expect your actions to be revealed in the light of day, which will at the very least cause you some embarrassment. It is for that reason you need to ensure all of your activities are ethical and honourable, because any surreptitious activities will be uncovered sooner or later.

XII Hanged Man   If The Hanged Man has appeared in the For and Against position, you can expect to attain a fair degree of spiritual enlightenment by certain events in your personal life. While everything around you seems to be in a state of inertia, there is much activity going on in the more etheric realms of your existence. You will have greater understanding of the world around you, and with such knowledge at your disposal, you may very well have decided you would rather take a break from the hustle and bustle of such a busy lifestyle, and enter into a hiatus of sorts. While your outer world may very well be perceived to be less than satisfactory, there is much going on in your mind.

XIII Death   If Death has appeared in the For and Against position, you can expect to go through some changes of such magnitude that things will never again be the same. You may experience a loss that is so dramatic that you feel you can no longer carry on, but carry on you must. Any birth process is an arduous journey. You are drastically yanked from the cosy existence you had once known, taken through a passage that could be quite traumatic, and then you are thrown into a new existence that is totally alien to you. It is only natural that you would want to recoil in horror at this new world you have found yourself in, but it is important you take note of all of your experiences. The point is, however, that you can't go back to the way things were no matter how hard you try. You have mastered whatever lessons you have been assigned and you must move onto the next step of your soul's evolution.

XIV
Temperance

If Temperance has appeared in the For and Against position, you will be given a chance to balance out any existing inequalities in your life. If you have been rushed off your feet, things will slow down, so you will be able to catch your breath and observe with a renewed clarity the sequence of events that has recently occurred. Conversely, if you have been idle, things will pick up so that you will be given a renewed sense of purpose in a world you thought had been passing you by. Balance is the key here because any time one area in your life is out of proportion with other areas, you will feel a sense of uneasiness, or dis-ease. If this tension exists for any length of time and is not resolved, you could very well make yourself ill. Any illness, after all, is merely a physical manifestation of imbalances that have existed in our psyche for quite some time.

XV Devil

If The Devil has appeared in the For and Against position, you will have the opportunity to be brought in touch with the more basal aspects of our existence. You may be given a great deal of responsibility, which means you must work hard to make any significant accomplishments. You may have found yourself in a situation that is dubious at best, and it is up to you to either extract yourself or come to a satisfying resolution to the problem. You may find yourself engaged in an inappropriate relationship, which will only drag you down in the end. You will need to use your best judgement to resolve this dilemma and emerge with your reputation intact.

XVI Tower

If The Tower has appeared in the For and Against position, you will have the opportunity to go through some interesting times, as your best laid plans may not necessarily turn out as you had originally planned. You may end up losing something of importance, and the reason for this is because you may have been in a period of stasis, not moving forward, which is what we all must do if we wish to progress onto the next step of our soul evolution, and not moving backwards either. In order to recover what has been lost, you will need to keep your wits about you and think laterally, pondering alternatives you may have previously deemed unsuitable. You need to take extra precautions not to have an accident because it could prove to be injurious and debilitating to your health.

XVII Star   If The Star has appeared in the For and Against position, you will have the opportunity to make new friends, thereby expanding your level of awareness with regard to the intricate workings of a certain personal relationship. You will be afforded the opportunity to receive higher knowledge from beings who have transcended the need to operate within our concept of space and time. Because you have received what can best be described as enlightenment, you are able to think laterally and will be able to come up with unique solutions to complex problems. You may even find yourself aware of the fact that there are other entities that co-exist in your world, only invisible to us because we are not tuned to their specific wavelength. Often, when we congratulate ourselves on what we consider to be a really fabulous idea, it is in fact merely an idea has been relayed to us by those opaque, other-worldly beings.

XVIII Moon   If The Moon has appeared in the For and Against position, you will have the opportunity to explore your psychic abilities because nothing you come into contact with will be as it seems. Friends, family and colleagues will become elusive to you, as you can never be sure of their true intentions. It is for that reason you must look for other clues as to their sentiments because the words they speak cannot be relied upon. It is best, therefore, to observe their body language and tonal inflections, where you will gain valuable insight. This is a time where you will be able to cultivate the untrained part of yourself, a part that has been lying dormant for quite some time because you have been deterred from using it. It is also a time where you cannot rely on others because there are some individuals who have motives that are contradictory to your own, which will be rather frustrating when you discover what these individuals have been surreptitiously involved in. You will find out who your true friends are, but not before you realise that some individuals who you thought were your friends, are not.

XIX Sun   If The Sun has appeared in the For and Against position, you will have the opportunity to achieve a great deal of happiness and abundance in your life. Children are featured highly, so if you were planning to have children or work with children in some capacity, it will be a propitious time to achieve this goal. The outdoors is also signified, and you will have an opportunity to go outside and enjoy the marvellous wonders of plant and animal life, which were created by God for humans to enjoy and experience. While this is a period where you can feel quite self-confident and successful, it is important you do not allow yourself to become smug or arrogant. The reason for such a cautionary note is

213

because we all must go through cycles in our lives, experiencing the highs and lows of a fruitful existence. When the good fortune that has been depicted by The Sun has waned and the inevitable darkness has descended upon you, you need to make sure you have people sympathetic to you during less fortunate times.

XX Judgement If Judgement has appeared in the For and Against position, you will be able to see many aspects of your life with renewed clarity. In the past, your perceptions had been shielded, which prevented you from fully understanding many things that had been going around you and have affected you. With a fresh perspective, you will be able to see people and situations in a new light, which will give you insight into why certain events transpired as they did. You will also be given a chance to begin a new life for yourself, having gained much wisdom through your various life experiences. A deep inner healing will go through the various layers of your auric make up right through your core being, the aspect of yourself that makes you unique amongst all the other souls. Having been given a chance to start afresh, you will learn from past mistakes and move onto a higher level of your spiritual evolution.

XXI World If The World has appeared in the For and Against position, you will have the opportunity to complete a major cycle in your life. After having finished such an important event, you will have a feeling of unity, knowing you have taken care of any loose ends that have kept certain aspects of the situation lingering indefinitely. When you have accepted the fact that you have concluded a major life event, such as a job, training programme, relationship, or other vocation, you must also accept the time will come for you to make a fresh start. Opportunities will come to you when you least expect them, so you must keep your eyes open for any new ventures from the most unlikely of sources. You may also suffer a loss, which is necessary for you to go on to your next stage of spiritual evolution.

Wands/Rods/Fire

Ace If the Ace of Wands has appeared in the For and Against position, you will have the opportunity to come up with new ideas that have the potential to yield fruits at a much later date. The possibility exists for you to enjoy your life and bask in the Sun as it shines down on your soul. You may very well enter into an enterprise that has the possibility to be a great success if you follow the appropriate procedures and liaise with other like-minded souls.

Two   If the Two of Wands has appeared in the For and Against position, you will have the opportunity to work with another person on a venture that could relate to work, social engagements or love. You will come together with this individual for the sole purpose of completing the task you both have taken an interest in, and it is therefore not likely the foundation of this relationship will be strong enough to endure after the specific project has reached its completion. It is for that reason you should enjoy the liaison while it lasts and not allow yourself to become too upset when it doesn't withstand the test of time.

Three   If the Three of Wands has appeared in the For and Against position, you will have an opportunity to gather together with a group of like-minded individuals to accomplish a specific task. The project you will engage in could be business, professional, social, religious or family oriented, but it is necessary to enable those involved to express their own creativity in some capacity. You must be aware, however, that at least a few of the people you will relate to during this endeavour are only using you in an attempt to further their own ambitions. Even though you are being taken for granted, you can still benefit from this enterprise because you will be given the opportunity to accomplish what you would not otherwise have been asked to achieve. You will also emerge with a sense of achievement, a feeling that will only come from a job well done.

Four   If the Four of Wands has appeared in the For and Against position, you can expect to encounter a situation that will help you to feel more secure and settled in what is often a highly unstable world. You may have landed a job, finished a course of training, received a substantial sum of money through a legacy, or even married well. Whatever the actual event, you have cause for celebration because many aspects of your future prosperity and security are being looked after. You may have become involved in a family get-together, and it is important that you participate because you need the backing of your friends and family to assure your future successes.

Five   If the Five of Wands has appeared in the For and Against position, you cannot expect to make any substantial progress in this matter. It seems all parties involved are not able to focus, which will prevent them from achieving their goals. In may ways, it is as if they are striking out, trying to hit anything, but not sure exactly what their target is. Even in their quarrels, they do not appear to be particularly effective because they are not sure exactly what it is they are battling against. The problem is that the cause of such discord is rooted much deeper than any of the parties involved realise, and they are merely fighting the symptoms of a much greater issue. The only way you can resolve this issue is to undertake a deep analysis of the situation to try to ascertain exactly when and where the crisis actually began. You may meet an individual who will act as a catalyst, which will help to speed up a process that has been delayed for quite some time.

Six   If the Six of Wands has appeared in the For and Against position, you may be successful in what you set out to do. You will, however, need to make sure you don't take any shortcuts and follow all established procedures. In addition, it would be in your best interests to cultivate as many relationships as you can because you will need your allies at this time. At one point in time you may find yourself laid bare for the entire world to see. It is for that reason you need to make sure you do not have any skeletons in your closet because your enemies will be more than happy to expose any foibles you may be embarrassed about.

Seven   If the Seven of Wands has appeared in the For and Against position, don't expect to make a great deal of progress in this matter. You will encounter obstacles, and in your effort to combat the problems that have come your way, you will not have time to focus on the initial enquiry that prompted you to consult the oracle. It will take a concentrated effort on your part to stay abreast of the situation, so it would be in your best interests to streamline your activities and concentrate on the things that are really important to you.

Eight   If the Eight of Wands has appeared in the For and Against position, you may very well make significant advancements during this period. You may even find yourself travelling, which will serve as a rejuvenating experience. While you may be expected to work hard for any successes you make, the rewards will far outweigh any sacrifices you may be required to make.

Nine   If the Nine of Wands has appeared in the For and Against position, you may find yourself needing to take a defensive stance in a certain situation. Your best-laid plans may have gone somewhat awry, thereby leaving you with a feeling of tension about your present circumstances. You may very well get what you want in the end, but the situation that occurs as a result of obstacles you had not planned for will take away the feelings of elation you had initially hoped for. As a result of this, you are likely to feel you must always be on your guard, which will have the effect of eventually wearing you down.

Ten   If the Ten of Wands has appeared in the For and Against position, you must be warned that if you continue on your current path, you are at risk of taking on too many obligations. You may be trying to spread yourself too thin, which means if you do not relinquish a few of your responsibilities, you stand the chance of doing all of them very badly, which will do your credibility no good. If you continue to work relentlessly with no respite, you will wear yourself down, which will eventually adversely affect your health. You need to stop, take a breath, and ask yourself if you have taken on other people's problems in your quest for single-handedly taking care of the woes of the world. If there are any tasks that are more appropriately handled by someone else, it would be in your best interests to leave it to them. As diligently as you endeavour, you can't do it all, and trying to will only bring misfortune.

King   If the King of Wands has appeared in the For and Against position, the situation is to a large extent determined by an older man who has much wisdom for his years. He may very well take on the role of family man because he enjoys the adulation he receives from his spouse and children. He can be somewhat egocentric, which means he expects other people to defer to his needs, and not the other way around.

Queen   If the Queen of Wands has appeared in the For and Against position, a woman who has a very dramatic disposition will come into the picture to influence the situation in some way. She is somewhat egocentric and therefore enjoys any attention she can get. If she is lacking in admirers, she may actually stir things up a bit so people will be distracted enough to pay attention to her. She needs desperately to be loved, and it is for that reason she will enter into relationships where she is the object of another's adoration. If the loving attention she desires is not forthcoming, she will either seek retribution for what she believes to be unrequited love, or move onto another more deserving love interest. How she responds will be determined by her psychological make-up and past experiences.

Knight/ Prince   If the Knight of Wands has appeared in the For and Against position, you will come into contact with a young man who will have a very strong influence over the situation that prompted you to consult the oracle. He is likely to have a great deal of confidence to convince people, specifically women, to see his way of thinking. He may very well have a great deal of charisma he uses to his advantage. Although he may be loving and sincere in his declarations of affection, he has not yet experienced enough of life to understand that exclaiming his adoration should be reserved only for the special people in his life, and not anyone who he may fancy in one specific week. It is best, therefore, to tread carefully when dealing with this person because you may be one of many who have been let down by him.

**Page/
Princess** If the Page of Wands has appeared in the For and Against position, you will come into contact with a young person who is full of energy and therefore hard to keep up with. If she has not been damaged by the many irregularities that come to us in this life, she is likely to be happy, lively and full of love. This individual needs a great deal of attention, and for that reason she can be somewhat of a handful. She needs a great deal of supervision in her more formative years to ensure she doesn't get into any serious mishaps while she ponders her experience of life.

Pentacles/Disks/Earth

Ace If the Ace of Pentacles has appeared in the For and Against position, you will have the opportunity to make money or other material wealth out of a venture you are considering. There is the very definite possibility of financial gain, even if it will give you ideas for other ventures you could pursue at a future date.

Two If the Two of Pentacles has appeared in the For and Against position, it is likely you will experience a fluctuation of fortunes and other material wealth. Because your physical world is in such a stage of instability, it could very well be an anxious time for you, as you ponder whether you will be able to afford to take care of what you consider to be the bare necessities of life. If you must organise your finances with another individual, this could very well lead to quarrels, which would further exacerbate your worries.

Three If the Three of Pentacles has appeared in the For and Against position, you can expect to either move house or engage in some form of renovation of your present accommodation. You will likely move in with another person, which will give you great satisfaction. There is a strong possibility you will have more money to spend and will be respected in your work, thereby intensifying your self-esteem.

Four If the Four of Pentacles has appeared in the For and Against position, you can expect to spend significantly more time at home, almost as if you are in a self-imposed isolation of sorts. You will need to be very careful what types of people you allow into your personal space because some of those individuals are not who they seem to be. The best thing to do in this respect is to take your time to get to know people before you invite them into your home. You will also need to save your money because in the not too distant future, you will need it for something special.

Five   If the Five of Pentacles has appeared in the For and Against position, it is highly unlikely you will get your heart's desire if you continue on your present path. In addition, you may find yourself in a position where you are on the outside looking in. You could very well be envious of others because you feel they have much more material wealth than you. In addition to the financial difficulties you may find yourself embroiled in, you may find yourself succumbing to a depression you have been working diligently to keep at bay for quite some time. The depression could start out as prolonged states of anxiety or worry, which could escalate into panic attacks, which could then progress into a full blown depression that could last for six months to a year, or longer. It is for that reason you need to stop and think very carefully about your next course of action because the current venture that has prompted you to consult the oracle may not be the most suitable move for the prosperity of your soul.

Six   If the Six of Pentacles has appeared in the For and Against position, you are likely to get out of this venture exactly what you put into it. You may be expected to perform some favours or other unpaid work for another person or organisation, but you will be remembered indirectly. As payment for the effort you put in, you may learn some valuable skills you otherwise would not have acquired. In addition, you will receive the satisfaction of knowing you have done something for someone other than yourself, which can only be beneficial to your soul growth. You may also find yourself in the position of needing help or assistance from more fortunate individuals. The assistance you need will be given to you, provided you perform good works for other individuals less fortunate than yourself, thereby balancing the karmic debt that is so very much a part of the universal flow.

Seven   If the Seven of Pentacles has appeared in the For and Against position, everything you do for the time being will come to fruition at a later date. You may feel as if life is passing you by and you are metaphorically spinning your wheels, but everything you do has a purpose, even though you may not see the results for quite some time. It may take as long as five or more years for your efforts to come to fruition, so do not despair as you carry on carrying on.

Eight   If the Eight of Pentacles has appeared in the For and Against position, it is very likely you will learn new skills that will help you in the ventures you will soon be undertaking. What you will learn will be something you cannot pick up in a normal training environment, but is a skill you must pick up by doing it until you have perfected the process. Therefore, you will become qualified in your trade by experience, rather than studying for and sitting academic exams. Because you must learn by experience, it is probable that you will make a few mistakes before you become proficient at your craft. You may also be expected to work on a small salary or even take a cut in pay, but the monetary sacrifices you make now will be rewarded at a later date when you have acquired the competence to command a higher salary.

Nine   If the Nine of Pentacles has appeared in the For and Against position, you may experience a respite from the pressures of this world. You may enter into a hiatus, holiday or convalescence, which will give you time to reflect upon the quality of your life. Your physical needs will be met during this period of transition, so money is not necessarily a problem. What you need to do at this time is to concentrate on yourself because a deep, inner healing needs to take place before you can enter into the next stage of your development with regard to the physicalities of this life.

Ten   If the Ten of Pentacles has appeared in the For and Against position, you need to be prepared to become engaged in family business, which may or may not be to your liking. This has both positive and negative aspects because while there will be a great deal of interaction with other family members, those outside the family may not receive all the attention they need or deserve. This situation could be a bit difficult if money is involved because you may be obliged to have more dealings than you would like with certain family members for financial reasons. The key here is to strike a balance between family and friends, because your friends are not likely to hang around if they feel neglected.

King   If the King of Pentacles has appeared in the For and Against position, you will come into contact with a man who places a great value on his possessions. He enjoys the finer things in this world and goes out of his way to make sure he is surrounded by them. He can be generous and thoughtful because he does not mind sharing his good fortune with those he is close to. He can, however, be unwavering in his opinions, so if he has taken a dislike to you for any reason, it is highly unlikely he will change his views.

Queen
If the Queen of Pentacles has appeared in the For and Against position, you will come in contact with a woman who has a great deal of self-confidence. The reason for this is because she accepts her limitations and only engages in activities she knows she can do well. In matters of social standing, she would rather be a big fish in a little pond than a little fish in a big one, and will therefore select her path in this life accordingly. In matters of love, she is more inclined to logically weigh the odds of her financial status of such a partnership, and therefore is more likely to engage in unions if she believes they will benefit her in some way.

Knight/ Prince
If the Knight of Pentacles has appeared in the For and Against position, you will encounter a young man who is very fastidious and pays a great deal of attention to detail. Even at a young age, he is very money and status oriented, which will set him apart from his peers. He is therefore driven to make his mark in this world in order to achieve the good things that life has to offer. He prefers to live nicely, and therefore enjoys luxurious cars, prestigious homes and glamorous girlfriends.

Page/ Princess
If the Page of Pentacles has appeared in the For and Against position, you will come into contact with a young person who is quite practical in her approach to dealing with day to day activities. Even at a relatively young age, she is quite sensible and therefore has a good head on her shoulders. Combined with her stability is a great deal of drive that will manifest itself as ambition in later years.

Swords/Air

Ace
If the Ace of Swords has appeared in the For and Against position, you will begin a period of intense communication with other individuals, which is necessary for you to evolve to the next phase of your spirituality. There will be correspondence in the form of letters, emails, faxes, phone calls and meetings. It is important, therefore, that you keep close guard over any information you have in your possession because if it falls into the wrong hands, it could be detrimental to your welfare.

Two
If the Two of Swords has appeared in the For and Against position, you may find you will fall out with another person on an issue that is of great significance to you. The problem may very well be one of semantics, but it is of such a delicate nature that you need to tread carefully on this issue. The problem is that you really do care about the individual who you are in disagreement with, which makes the dilemma all the more

difficult for you to successfully resolve. If the person who you could not see eye to eye with did not mean a great deal to you, it would be very easy for you to just wash your hands of the situation and walk away. The sheer fact that this person is important to you makes it difficult for you, as the only way the two of you can realise your own individual realities is to do so separately and not as a team effort.

Three   If the Three of Swords has appeared in the For and Against position, it is very unlikely the situation that prompted you to consult the oracle will yield the results you desire. You may experience a period of heartache, and it will take a very long time to heal the psychological and emotional wounds that remain. You need to ask yourself if the benefits of such a venture are going to outweigh any sacrifices you may have to make. It may be better to walk away now before you invest any more emotional energy into a dubious situation, only to wind up getting hurt in the process.

Four   If the Four of Swords has appeared in the For and Against position, this will be a propitious time for you to ask the universe to send you higher cognition of the situation at hand. It is a time of quiet reflection and meditation, and the answers you seek will come to you in time. What is important is not to make any hasty decisions until you receive sufficient guidance to enable you to make informed choices.

Five   If the Five of Swords has appeared in the For and Against position, you may find yourself to be in disagreement with a person or a group of people with regard to the specific reason that prompted you to consult the oracle. This could be somewhat frustrating because you do not want to find yourself at odds with others, but the situation is so critical it must be addressed. You need to ask yourself whether the venture you are on is worth the aggravation it will potentially cause because it does not seem as if you or the other individuals involved will be happy with the outcome.

Six   If the Six of Swords has appeared in the For and Against position, you will find you will move away from a situation that has caused you a great deal of difficulties. This problem may have arisen due to a relationship, so this issue must be resolved before you can progress mentally and spiritually. The problem lies in the fact that the difficulties you experience may be a result of a much deeper underlying problem that needs to be addressed. If the root experience is not properly integrated into your psyche, you will eventually begin to manifest symptoms of the problem, which are merely coping mechanisms. To correct the symptom but not the root experience that caused the trauma is, metaphorically speaking, putting a psychic bandage on a deep, gaping wound that is inherent in your auric make-up. What you need is psychic healing and self-analysis to help to wash away the residue from the event that distressed you in the past. Then, and only then, will you be able to walk away from a difficult situation and not be confronted with similar situations at a later date that will ultimately act as stumbling blocks to your soul growth.

Seven If the Seven of Swords has appeared in the For and Against position, you need to be very careful who you speak to. The reason for this is because some other people will take advantage of any opportunity to advance themselves, even if such activities are of a dubious nature. You may encounter a theft of sorts, which means you will need to take adequate precautions to secure your valuables. Information is also valuable, so you will need to safeguard any data you hold in your possession. Alternatively, you may find you are the one doing the stalking and stealing. If that is the case, you need to ask yourself what you hope to gain from such activities because such acts are destructive to both you and the object of your conquest. There may be more orthodox ways to get what you want and you would be wise to explore such alternatives. It is important to keep in mind that if your activities are unethical, you will be found out sooner or later.

Eight If the Eight of Swords has appeared in the For and Against position, it is not envisaged that you will benefit from the situation that has prompted you to consult the oracle. You are not in possession of all the facts, which makes it difficult for you to make any appropriate decisions. You or someone close to you may be experiencing a confinement of sorts. This may be self-imposed or inflicted by someone else, but it poses a very restrictive influence if you are not able to get out and about. Your sphere of awareness of the physicalities of the world you have incarnated into will be severely limited, which will ultimately affect your attitude to the world around you. There will be some situations, such as in matters of health or incarceration, where it will be more difficult for you to achieve a normal degree of mobility. Other instances, such as those inflicted by yourself, can be just as difficult to manoeuvre because you do not have a positive mental attitude, and you will need to break free from the thought-induced chains that hold you down. Because it is such a difficult situation to be in, you need to carefully consider whether you wish to carry on in the present path of your soul's exploration. You possess within yourself all the skills to begin a new path, if that is what you desire.

Nine   If the Nine of Swords has appeared in the For and Against position, it seems you will spend a great deal of time in a state of high anxiety. You have a great deal on your mind and spend a fair amount of time worrying and fretting over real or imagined problems. As a result, you could lose much needed sleep, which will further exacerbate the problem and hinder you from thinking reasonably and resolving any issues you are facing. You may therefore need to take a break from those things that are causing you tension. If you get away from such a stressful situation, you will be given the space to think more clearly and make reasoned choices about your life direction.

Ten   If the Ten of Swords has appeared in the For and Against position, it is highly unlikely that you will achieve the satisfaction you desire from this particular venture. It is highly likely that you will be let down badly by one particular person, a person who you had previously trusted. It is very difficult for someone to betray you when you have not regarded them as a confidant because they are not privy to your hopes, dreams, desires, and what motivates you in this world. If someone who has little meaning to you does something to harm you, it is not nearly so hurtful because such an act would not seem so out of character. When you allow someone into your confidence, however, you let him or her into your life to certain degree. When they take the trust you had in them and use it in a way that is harmful to you, you feel the destructive forces that manifest themselves through such a betrayal tenfold, as they sear through your auric web into your soul. After such a psychic assault, you will need time to recuperate and pull together your energies. After you have gathered your composure, you will emerge much wiser to the ways of certain individuals who are close to you.

King   If the King of Swords has appeared in the For and Against position, you will come into contact with a man who is knowledgeable on any subject he takes an interest in. He takes his time to study any given subjects in an in-depth fashion, making him an expert of his chosen field. Because he has a superior intellect, he is able to use his wit to his advantage in any debate. The problem is, however, that if it suits his purposes, he can use a false rationale to sway any uncertain thinkers in his direction, thereby becoming the propagator of misinformation. If he is not able to direct his immense intellect through appropriate channels, he can be quite cruel, thereby gaining a few enemies. .

Queen   If the Queen of Swords has appeared in the For and Against position, you will receive some valuable insight from a woman who is quite knowledgeable on a variety of subjects. She possesses a great deal of wisdom she has gleaned from observing others and her personal experiences. If life has not been kind to her, she may tend to soften the blows of missed opportunities by embellishing stories to make her situation seem more favourable than it actually is. It is therefore essential to listen carefully to her words for any contradictory meanings in order to get the true content of her story.

Knight/ Prince If the Knight of Swords has appeared in the For and Against position, you will be influenced by a young man who is very ambitious. He is an astute individual and is able to think quickly on his feet. Because he does have such a sharp mind, he can use his intellect to reason his way out of difficulties. He can be very unrealistic in his expectation of others, which can cause him to fall into a depression when he discovers we are all only human, and therefore fallible. He is also somewhat dualistic because although he expects perfection in the people around him, he does not see why he should have to adhere to the strict standards he sets for others.

Page/ Princess If the Page of Swords has appeared in the For and Against position, you will be strongly influenced by a young person who is witty, communicative and quite sociable in her desires. She uses her intellect as a means to manoeuvre through what at times can be a difficult existence. She has a very active mind, which can be her friend or her foe. Positively, she can use her imagination to play games or make up stories when she is bored. Negatively, she could find herself living in a fantasy world if she is not getting enough stimulation from her immediate environment.

Cups/Water

Ace If the Ace of Cups has appeared in the For and Against position, the likelihood of you finding happiness and emotional well-being is quite strong. You will experience emotional happiness, which is something that may very well have been missing in your life for quite some time. If you continue on the path you are presently on, you will be well on your way to experiencing a deep satisfaction and finding things to be ticking along more smoothly than they ever have before.

Two If the Two of Cups has appeared in the For and Against position, it is envisaged that you will receive much emotional happiness and a sense of wellbeing with respect to the situation that prompted you to consult the oracle. Your personal relationships should be particularly satisfying, and you may even come into contact with that one special person who can fill you with the happiness and excitement that can only be achieved through living in this material world in harmony with another being. You may begin a courtship with another person, which will enable you to experience the heights of ecstasy that can only come from working closely with your one true soul mate in this life.

Three   If the Three of Cups has appeared in the For and Against position, it appears your social life will improve dramatically. You will be invited to significant gatherings and nights out, which will add meaning to what may have become a dull existence. This renewed interest in other people indicates it is likely to become a happy time, where you have the opportunity to engage in light banter and exchange experiences with other like-minded souls. Because you will be given the chance to let your hair down and enjoy yourself, it is probable other areas of your life will improve as well. You will find that you are not quite so serious about those areas in your life that are not transpiring in the manner you would have preferred. Having total control over every aspect of your life will not seem so important, as you allow a sense of spontaneity to become a part of your sphere of awareness.

Four   If the Four of Cups has appeared in the For and Against position, you are going through a period of trepidation, wondering exactly what the future holds for you. You have your doubts about the situation that prompted you to consult the oracle, and your concerns are clearly visible for the entire world to see. To confound the issue, you are receiving contradictory information from various sources, which makes it difficult for you to decide the most appropriate course of action. Since you are in so much doubt as to the correct path to follow, you will probably want to hold off on making any major irrevocable decisions for the time being. The truth will be revealed soon enough if you are prepared to wait for it.

Five   If the Five of Cups has appeared in the For and Against position, it is highly unlikely the situation you are enquiring about will produce a result that is satisfactory to you. A major point you had not anticipated will hinder the progress that you had hoped to make, thereby negating any benefits you had hoped to achieve by following the current path. You will emerge from the whole scenario a bit emotionally dishevelled, but your basic perspective will remain intact. You will learn a valuable lesson that will stay with you for some time to come. In addition, there may be a certain aspect of your personality you had hoped to conceal, but it has been revealed to show you in a less than positive light. In order to save face, the best that you can do is apologise and resolve to change any negative personality traits. The question is, however, are you a big enough person to acknowledge your own shortcomings and then work to change them?

Six   If the Six of Cups has appeared in the For and Against position, the situation that prompted you to consult the oracle is one that is reminiscent of the past. You may recall some childhood experiences that have had a direct impact on your current situation. You may also recall events that had long been repressed that will serve to clarify many unanswered questions that have lingered dormant in your psyche literally for years. You may also find children figure prominently, and they can teach you to embrace the world with a type of innocence that has long lain sleeping in your soul.

Seven   If the Seven of Cups has entered into the For and Against position, you will enter into a period where all is not as it seems, which is going to make it difficult for you to make any well reasoned life choices. There are some individuals who hope to further their own aims by persuading you to make a particular decision that will affect one specific course of your life. It is for that reason this person will be seen to manipulate the facts, which will in effect alter the course of your life if you choose to allow this individual to influence you. There is another situation where you are not in possession of pertinent pieces of information that will help you decide your future, and as a result, you may appear to be misguided. You are so full of hope for the future that every option available to you seems to be the golden opportunity you have been seeking your entire life. The problem is, however, except for very rare instances, there are no quick fixes in this life. The vast majority of us only make progress through slow, methodical toil, which is necessary for our soul growth. We only see improvement little by little, as we struggle to adapt to each new karmic lesson we are presented with along our evolutionary journey. If something seems too be good to be true, it probably is.

Eight   If the Eight of Cups has appeared in the For and Against position, it appears that you will enter into a period of sadness with regard to the situation that prompted you to consult the oracle. It looks as if you will endeavour to make an awkward situation or relationship tenable, hoping in the end you will be able to achieve an element of satisfaction, and even happiness. This is one of those instances where you are operating on nothing short of blind faith, and such sentiments are passé at the very best. While it is more than appropriate to place your bets on a long-shot where there is at least a slim chance of benefiting, hanging onto a situation or relationship that even you know is pointless is nothing less than pure folly. You really need to ask yourself whether you want to invest any more of your valuable energy in a venture that is doomed to fail. If you look around, there may be more viable alternatives open to you that will yield far greater rewards.

Nine   If the Nine of Cups has appeared in the For and Against position, you may very well find you are content with yourself, but underneath that smile lies a sadness that is not easily discernible by the more shallow observer. If you carry on in the path you are currently taking, you may find yourself on your own, even amongst a crowd, which is not something you would necessarily like. You may feel the need to compensate for the sense of enforced solitude by overindulging in drink or food, which could then exacerbate your dilemma by giving you a weight problem as well. It is for this reason you need to think very carefully about whether or not you would like to continue on your current venture because it may not give you the sense of solidarity and togetherness that you would have originally presumed. There may be another way for you to get what you want without leaving you feeling so all alone in the world.

Ten   If the Ten of Cups has appeared in the For and Against position, it is quite likely that you will find the happiness and fulfilment you deserve if you continue on your present karmic path. It is envisaged that you will unite with your one true soul mate in this incarnation, which will give you the emotional fulfilment you need to progress and grow in your karmic journey. It is difficult to spiritually evolve when your life is in constant upheaval. The mere fact that you are in a satisfying supportive relationship will give you the security and stability you need to ponder the more profound concepts that are part of the laws of the universe.

King   If the King of Cups has appeared in the For and Against position, a mature man will have an influence on the situation that prompted you to consult the oracle. He is highly emotive, and as a result, can be somewhat impulsive. He is a considerate individual who takes other people's feeling and opinions on board before making important decisions. Because he is highly perceptive, he is able to pick up thought forms from the universal mind, and uses this knowledge in his day-to-day activities. As a result, he can employ some rather unorthodox techniques that less enlightened souls may not fully appreciate. Because he is open to new ideas, he embraces alternative concepts of living in an increasingly civilised and stressful society wholeheartedly. He understands the need to progress technologically, spiritually and mentally if our kind is to enter the next step of the soul evolution for which we are destined.

Queen   If the Queen of Cups has appeared in the For and Against position, you will have dealings with a woman who is highly emotive. She lives her life based upon how she feels. Unless she has learned through past experience to utilise the reasoning ability that is very much a part of her, she will tend to allow her emotions to stay on her sleeve instead of reserving them for individuals who are worthy of such honesty and clarity of emotions. If she has had difficult earlier experiences she has not been able to properly integrate into her personality as a whole, she may develop a type of neurosis, which is a coping mechanism that helps her to survive many of the difficulties life sometimes puts in our path. The problem this poses, however, is that if she is not helped to come to terms with some of her more traumatic life experiences, she can develop personality disorders and will not be able to effectively face the karmic task she was put in this world to complete.

Knight/   If the Knight of Cups has appeared in the For and Against position,
Prince   there is a young man who has a part to play in the scenario that prompted you to consult the oracle. He is highly intuitive, but has not yet developed his powers of perception into a skill he can use to assist him in his life travels. It seems he can pick up feelings and thoughts from various directions, but has not yet learned how to zone in on one particular impression and determine exactly who it is coming from. At times he can be totally unaware that he is picking up another being's emotions, and believe these feelings belong to him, which is totally incorrect. It is for that reason he can at times appear moody and inconsistent. When he finds a suitable mentor, he will learn how to focus his perceptions and therefore concentrate on what is important, and filter out what is unimportant to him.

Page/   If the Page of Cups has appeared in the For and Against position, a
Princess   young person will play a significant role in the successful resolution of the issue that prompted you to consult the oracle. This individual is

highly intuitive and is sympathetic to the needs of others. Although she does not have the vocabulary to express many of her sentiments, she has a deep awareness of what motivates other people. If she is allowed to live in an environment where she is nurtured, she will thrive and grow into a compassionate, sympathetic person. If, on the other hand, she finds herself in a cold and abusive environment, she will suffer developmental delays and can adapt coping mechanisms that can become clearly destructive to herself and others.

10 The Next Half Year

0 Fool If The Fool has appeared in the Next Half Year position, you will soon embark upon a new path that will aid you in your karmic evolution. In many ways, you will experience a rebirth because you will come across people and situations that are totally alien to you, thereby allowing you to build upon your current skill base. You may suffer a loss of some kind, but this too is necessary for you to gain an understanding of the ebb and flow of universal trends. Although you will be unsure of your footing in some of the situations that you find yourself in the midst of, it is important to remember that you will be protected in whatever you do, as long as your intentions are honourable.

I Magician If The Magician has appeared in the Next Half Year position, you will soon be entering into what can only be described as a magical time in your life. You will soon begin a course of study that will reveal to you knowledge that you have previously been totally unaware of. This knowledge will instil in you the competence to create a better future for yourself, which is something you would definitely like to have. You will also encounter a young person who is a very astute individual. This person is educated and can show you different ways of looking at things, which will ultimately enhance the creative impulses you have within yourself. The tools The Magician has at his disposal are the four elemental archetypes of the Wand for creation, the Pentacle for manifestation, the Sword for thought formations, and the Cup for one's ability to perceive emotions.

II High Priestess If The High Priestess has appeared in the Next Half Year position, you will soon be made privy to a secret that will enable you to go about your daily activities with greater clarity about your life purpose. The information that will soon be revealed to you will have such a profound impact on you that you will never view the world in the same ordinary way. You will begin to see new meaning in the most mundane things, which will begin to take on a whole new spiritual significance to you, as you ponder your purpose in this life. It is quite likely you will begin to see auras, but if not, you should take note of the messages that people will send through the clothes they wear or the body language they unconsciously project.

III Empress If The Empress has appeared in the Next Half Year position, you will soon be influenced by some maternal instincts, which could be referring either you or someone close to you. You may consider planning a family, which will be of great importance to you. In addition, a female figure may decide it is time to wield her influence over her offspring, which may or may not be to your liking if you do not happen to be part of her family.

IV Emperor If The Emperor has appeared in the Next Half Year position, you will soon encounter some karmic influences, and you may wonder exactly who is in control of your destiny. You may have dealings with a powerful person who has much control over many aspects of your wellbeing, which means you will need to tread carefully when dealing with this person so you do not interrupt the very fragile make-up of the universal forces that are so much a part of our existence. The time coming is one of the making or breaking of your destiny, so it is propitious to conduct your affairs soberly to ensure you are successful in your endeavours.

V Hierophant If The Hierophant has appeared in the Next Half Year position, you will soon come to a major crossroad in your life. You need to make an important decision of such magnitude that things will never be the same again. It is important that you think very carefully about your next move because once your mind is made up, you cannot go back to the way things were without great difficulty.

VI Lovers If The Lovers has appeared in the Next Half Year position, you will soon meet an individual who is one of your soul mates, who you are destined to come into contact with in your many incarnations to help you with your soul growth. In many ways, you will feel a true connection with this person, possibly not even recollecting the deep psychic bond the two of you have had throughout the ages. Although you will feel you have met your one true love in this world, there are some choices the both of you will need to make on the path to true enlightenment. In order to achieve eternal bliss with your one true soul mate in this life, you must first be okay with yourself, which will in all probability be one of the most difficult tasks you will ever be asked to accomplish. In addition, you may be asked to give something up in order to balance out the universal forces that have deemed it appropriate for you to find happiness with your one true love in this incarnation.

VII Chariot   If The Chariot has appeared in the Next Half Year position, you will soon be making a journey that will be worth your while and give you a fresh perspective on your current situation. Your travels are likely to be successful and you will be wiser for the experience, thereby enabling you to lead your life with much greater clarity of purpose.

VIII Strength   If Strength has appeared in the Next Half Year position, you will soon be put in a situation where many of your resources will be drained. You may have some health problems, which are a result of the many stresses in your life. It is for that reason you need to put your best foot forward and show the world you can still shine under pressure. Animals will be a huge help to you, as they will help to restore harmony in what is otherwise a rather hectic life. These beings can give you the pure, simplistic love that only an animal can give.

IX Hermit   If The Hermit has appeared in the Next Half Year position, you will be spending some time on your own. This time of solitude will enable you to reflect on your current situation in this life so you will know what it is you need to do so you can continue on your path to true enlightenment. It is important you develop an inner calm, which you can achieve through meditation, thereby allowing you to open your mind up to possibilities you would not have otherwise perceived. If possible, it would be in your best interests to attend a sanctuary or retreat, as you will be put in touch with like-minded souls who have the potential to become friends in time.

X Wheel of Fortune   If The Wheel of Fortune has appeared in the Next Half Year position, you will soon encounter a change in fortunes. If your circumstances have been difficult in recent months, you should find that by some fluke, you will be given some good news, which will enable you to embark on activities that were previously not available to you. If certain situations in your life have been going well for you, you can expect a hidden glitch to shake up your stability, which will ultimately keep you from becoming too complacent in the universal ebb and flow of the eternal flame of life. The Wheel has within it the four fixed astrological signs of Taurus, Leo, Scorpio and Aquarius, which correspond with the four elemental forces of Earth, Fire, Air and Water respectively, and give it a sense of stability and equilibrium to maintain the everlasting revolution of life. Because the four signs form a square to each other, a feeling of tension needs to be released if good fortune is to be achieved. It is also important to keep in mind that most 'luck' is not luck at all, but in fact hard work, which has shown a profit. Therefore, if you have put in the required effort, you will reap the final rewards of your labour.

XI Justice   If Justice has appeared in the Next Half Year position, you will soon encounter equilibrium of forces where there has previously been an imbalance, which has had the effect of creating havoc in the environment around you. The reason for this balancing of power is because in order for the universe to continue the never-ending cycle of renewal and regeneration, it must operate in a state of co-existence, striving to balance the positive and negative forces that are an inherent part of life. You may find yourself engaged in legal proceedings, which could be an anxious time if you are relying on an outcome in your favour. In order to assure fair dealings, it may be possible to bring your grievance to an impartial party who will be able to mediate for you and help you come to a decision suitable to all concerned parties.

XII Hanged Man   If The Hanged Man has appeared in the Next Half Year position, you will soon find that you will have to make a sacrifice, which will mean that you will have to give up something that is of great importance to you. You will realise you cannot force those situations that are destined to transpire because as soon as the pressure is removed, what you have desired will leave you of its own accord. It is for that reason you must forgo force, which will get you nowhere, and instead endeavour to use subtle influences to bring that which you desire into your sphere of existence. Because gentleness is the key here, you may have to wait for that which is your utmost goal. In the process of waiting and slowly manipulating the cosmic forces in your favour, you may consequently find that what you thought you wanted is not what you really need for your soul's development. When you come to this realisation, you will achieve a fair degree of enlightenment with regard to the forces of nature, thereby allowing what you need to be given to you with little or no effort on your part.

XIII Death   If Death has appeared in the Next Half Year position, you will shortly encounter a situation that will cause such a massive change to your psychic development that it will seem you will experience a loss of some kind. This will be a transformative time for you because you will have experiences of such an extreme nature that when the dust has settled, you will have been through nothing short of a total renewal. When a woman gives birth to a child, it is in many ways a traumatic experience like nothing she has ever endured, leaving her in a temporarily weakened state, which has resulted from the birth crisis. In the same vein, when Death appears, a rebirth will occur, which in all probability will entail a similar level of pain and anguish before the realisation of the new life has been acknowledged. It is therefore important to remember the beautiful butterfly must first emerge from a cocoon, and in the same vein, you to must endure a time of darkness before the brilliance of your new identity will slowly emerge.

XIV Temperance If Temperance has appeared in the Next Half Year position, you will soon be entering a period where all appears to be in a period of stasis. This is not a time where you can make any magnificent achievements because the universe is in the process of harmonising and achieving a balance between positive and negative forces. Because it seems there is nothing productive you can do during this time of waiting, you may assume the best you can do in situations such as these is to do nothing. Abstaining from action, however, is in effect taking action, albeit passively. The best action you can take, therefore, is to ensure all of your affairs are in order for the more propitious time that will occur sometime in the future. It would be in your best interests to work diligently to achieve moderation in all aspects of your life.

XV Devil If The Devil has appeared in the Next Half Year position, you will soon be given much responsibility, which will subsequently cause you to think more often about the practicalities of the earth we have incarnated into. Because you will be preoccupied with work, money and responsibilities, you may not feel as carefree as you have felt in earlier times, which may give you somewhat of a dour disposition. You will focus more on the physical and material side of our existence, which will in many ways weigh you down to the earth plane. Because you are concentrating your energies on the more basal elements of life, you will be more susceptible to the lower, darker influences that can pervade your soul when you are thinking negatively. It is for that reason you may find yourself more sombre in temperament, perhaps even possessing a dark, sardonic type of humour, which many people cannot readily comprehend.

XVI Tower   If The Tower has appeared in the Next Half Year position, expect a fair amount of upheaval in your life to occur. You may very well have made sure all your i's were dotted and the t's were crossed to ensure there was as little confusion as possible, but there is one crucial element to the complex web you have woven that you may have missed. Because everything in your life may have seemed to have been ticking along so smoothly, you have developed an attitude of complacency, feeling you have done all you possibly can to achieve a stable, secure, and even possibly boring life. There are, however, some things in this life you have absolutely no control over. Although you have free will over your own destiny, you do not have free will over the destiny of others, whose lives may very well overlap with yours. This interconnecting of individual destinies that are at cross purposes to one another could very well bring about a sense of karmic confusion, as all parties involved try to restore equilibrium in the resulting chaos. In addition, you may need to come to terms with the fact that the life you have carved out for yourself may not necessarily be the life that is going to afford you maximum soul growth, which is why your subconscious has decided to shake things up a bit. You may therefore see the upcoming period of transition as a time of loss, but this is also a time of opportunities that will come at the most propitious of times. It is also a time when you can explore choices that you may not otherwise have been open to. It is always important to keep in mind that when the universal forces close a door, they will always open a window.

XVII Star   If The Star has appeared in the Next Half Year position, you will soon be entering a period of optimism and hope for what lies in the future. You will possess a happy disposition, as you try to think positively and hope your dreams will come to fruition. It is likely you will develop a friendship with another person, and this liaison will be satisfying for the both of you. This is a time of Aquarian ideals, where science and technology will figure prominently in your day-to-day activities. If you have been considering becoming more involved in information technology, the timing would be auspicious. If your intentions are honourable and you only desire is to serve mankind, you cannot fail in your endeavours.

XVIII Moon   If The Moon has appeared in the Next Half Year position, you will soon be entering a period of confusion, as you will realise that all is not as it appears. There are forces at work that are occurring simultaneously and are at cross-purposes to the life you are currently living. You are aware that things are occurring that are simultaneous and parallel to your own life, but you cannot pinpoint exactly what it is that is transpiring. Whilst in the dream state, you will be able to glimpse those worlds that are similar, but not identical to your own, making you discover there are other realities that co-exist on the earth plane, just beyond your mental grasp. There are times when you are daydreaming or lost in thought, when you will get mental flashes of lost worlds, which will make you wonder if the imagery you were presented with was a glimpse from this or a parallel existence. All of those intrusions from other realities can make you question your own sanity, but sanity is not an issue as long as you reveal those impressions you have received only to your most trusted friends. Your friends, however, can be deceptive, as you will come to realise who your true companions in this life are. Just because a person is friendly and polite does not make that individual a friend, which you will soon discover. You will be quite surprised to learn that those you had believed to be your friends will pass you by, but the people you had not previously given much note to will become worthy of merit.

XIX Sun If The Sun has appeared in the Next Half Year position, you will go through a period of happiness and gaiety. It seems you will possess a high level of self-confidence that you have not had before. Animals and children will figure prominently in your sphere of awareness because they love unabashedly and are not terribly concerned about a person's outward appearance. This will be a time of high exposure, so you will therefore need to make sure you are at your best when under public scrutiny.

XX Judgement If Judgement has appeared in the Next Half Year position, you will soon be undergoing a deep cleansing process, and the faith you had lost in humanity will eventually be restored. You may decide to embark upon a type of therapy, which will go a long way to heal many of the wounds that still remain in your auric web. You may meet someone along your earth walk who can help you to meet the many demands that are placed upon you, thereby giving you a feeling of unity, which you have not experienced for quite some time.

XXI World If The World has appeared in the Next Half Year position, you will soon be completing a major cycle in your life, which will bring you closer to the unification of your soul's twin flame. You may complete a course of study, which would end your sojourn as a student of life and hopefully propel you into the arena of work and professionalism. You may have decided it is time to take a personal relationship one step further in its evolution, which could be a commitment of some sort. Alternatively, if the relationship is non-productive, or even destructive, a dissolution of the relationship may be deemed more appropriate so all involved parties can further progress in their soul development. The body plays a significant theme in the symbology of the world so matters relating to the body will also take precedence.

Wands/Rods/Fire

Ace   If the Ace of Wands has appeared in the Next Half Year position, you will shortly enter into a period of creativity that may possibly yield financial results. You may begin to think about what you can do to expand your professional standing amongst your contemporaries, and therefore explore new ideas as they are presented to you. You may decide to expand upon what you already know, or decide to embark upon an altogether new path, which may entail a learning curve before you find that you are able to undertake any new endeavours.

Two   If the Two of Wands has appeared in the Next Half Year position, you will soon be approached by another individual to partake of an activity that would theoretically yield profits for the both of you. The reason for this is because you both possess skills independent of each other, and when these assets are used in conjunction, they have the potential to produce far more than both attributes separately. What you are planning is likely to be a creative endeavour, but was ultimately designed as a profitable venture so that the both of you could enjoy the fruits of your labour.

Three   If the Three of Wands has appeared in the Next Half Year position, you will shortly find yourself amongst a group of people who are engaged in achieving one common goal. This group may be comprised of work colleagues because business enterprise is often associated with the element of Fire, which governs the magical nature of the Wand. The group could also be comprised of friends and acquaintances who have gathered together to join a sporting or social activity. It could also be comprised of family members, who are tied together in a business venture. It is unlikely the alliances you form during this time will be lasting, as the group was formed only in pursuance of a specific goal. Nevertheless, it would be in your best interests to form this union because you will find it to be a satisfying experience and should help to build your self-confidence.

Four   If the Four of Wands has appeared in the Next Half Year position, you will soon have cause for celebration. Events will transpire that will make you feel more secure than you have been in a very long time. You may have received a professional position that would enable you to fulfil some of your personal goals, thereby enabling you to feel less vulnerable in what can often be a rather volatile world. Your family and home will be of paramount importance to you, as you will feel greater solidarity towards those who you are close to.

Five If the Five of Wands has appeared in the Next Half Year position, you will soon discover you are struggling over one particular situation that is causing you a great deal of angst. This situation has been a huge source of trouble for you, and you are not able to put your finger exactly on what the root cause is. Because you are in the dark about the precise dilemma that is causing many of your difficulties, you are striking out in all directions, trying to solve one crisis after another. You are probably thinking to yourself, 'just as soon as I get over this one hurdle, everything will be okay and I will be able to live normally'. The problem is that just as soon as you get over that one hurdle, another one of even greater magnitude will present itself to you, thereby allowing you to continue to attempt to resolve the issues that are thwarting your soul growth. It will take much soul searching on your part to try to come to terms with the root trauma responsible for your problems, but when you have, many thought patterns that had previously been inaccessible to you will seem to fall into place. If you are not able to find out what the root cause is on your own, you may want to consider outside help.

Six If the Six of Wands has appeared in the Next Half Year position, you will accomplish a significant achievement in the future. This accomplishment will be of such magnitude that you will feel the need to reward yourself for a job well done. There is much to do, however, to secure your future prosperity and happiness, so it is not appropriate to sit back and relax after what is in reality only a minor victory. It is also essential you make appropriate preparations for any proposed activities because one mistake could negate all previous successes.

Seven If the Seven of Wands appears in the Next Half Year position, you will have to work very hard to maintain any successes that you may have had in the past. If you have recently been promoted to an elevated position, you will have a steep learning curve to overcome, and those around you will not be prepared to wait for you to catch up to their speed. It is for that reason you should keep any insecurities you have close to your heart. If you confide your doubts to inappropriate individuals, you will merely be perceived as weak and not up to the job that you have been given overall responsibility for.

Eight   If the Eight of Wands appears in the Next Half Year position, you will soon be taking a trip that will expand your level of awareness in some way. You will go somewhere that, to you, is quite far away. You may find that you will advance academically, professionally, or even spiritually, as you aspire to self-actualise through a progressive and consistent attainment of your goals.

Nine   If the Nine of Wands has appeared in the Next Half Year position, you will soon have reason to feel as if you are on the defensive for some reason. You will find that you will have opposition from the most unlikely of individuals, which will further influence your outlook on life. People may not see you as you really are, which could cause them to discredit you in some way. Because you feel threatened, you will tend to behave differently and people will not see the 'you' that is relaxed and would like to enjoy life.

Ten   If the Ten of Wands appears in the Next Half Year position, you will soon find yourself in a position where you are totally overwhelmed by events that will soon be taking place. You may take on a role you are not quite ready for, and because you do not possess all the skills necessary to see the task successfully to completion, you are filled with a sense of foreboding. Although you work tirelessly to try to complete the tasks you have been presented with, you are spinning your wheels, not accomplishing a great deal of anything. Before you reach a level of total exhaustion, you need to take a good look at the problem that is causing you so much anguish. You may need to go out and acquire the skills you need to see the project to completion, either in the form of a formal classroom environment or additional life experiences. Alternatively, you may decide it is in your best interests to abandon the pursuit altogether, leaving such endeavours to more able souls.

King   If the King of Wands has appeared in the Next Half Year position, you will soon be influenced by a man who has a flair for business and enterprise. Whenever he happens upon a new thing, he instantly wonders how he can exploit the situation and use it to his advantage. He has much love to give, which he will lavish on children, animals, partners, or anyone else he feels worthy of his attention. This individual will stand out in a crowd, and the colours yellow and red will be significant to him.

Queen   If the Queen of Wands has appeared in the Next Half Year position, you will soon be influenced by a woman who is very shrewd and astute about the ways of the world. She has much vibrancy about herself, which makes her the life and soul of any gathering. She is very wise and can impart wisdom to you metaphorically, using parables to get her message across. She is not, however, one to relate to those who do not wish to listen, and will therefore wait until she is asked to speak frankly on any given subject.

Knight/ Prince   If the Knight of Wands has appeared in the Next Half Year position, you will soon become involved with a young man who possesses a great deal of energy. He has much charisma within himself, which makes him very attractive to others. It is important to note, however, that because he has not yet experienced many of the facets of this life, he needs time to explore the world and learn from what he has been exposed to. It is for that reason he may be an able paramour to dally in the waters of romance and the fleeting feelings of love, but he is not ready for commitment and therefore an unsuitable candidate for any kind of enduring relationship.

Page/ Princess   If the Page of Wands appears in the Next Half Year position, you will soon come in contact with a young person who has much energy and needs to stay busy, or she will get into mischief. She is a very loving individual, but needs a great deal of attention, or she will feel neglected and could react inappropriately as a way to draw attention to herself.

Pentacles/Disks/Earth

Ace   If the Ace of Pentacles has appeared in the Next Half Year position, you will soon be thinking of money and material possessions, because those are the very things you need to live in this very physical world. You may be considering beginning a venture that has the possibility of bringing you greater wealth and prosperity, which would definitely improve your standard of living. Alternatively, you may be thinking of making a major purchase that will bring more responsibility with it because you will have to organise exactly how you will pay for the item that you would like to possess.

Two   If the Two of Pentacles has appeared in the Next Half Year position, you will soon have some financial or material concerns that will need to be resolved before you can progress any further in your current endeavour. It appears that you will need to learn how to take greater control over your financial situation because it will be necessary for you to manage your resources more effectively so you do not find yourself swimming in a sea of debt. You may find it necessary to take another job in an attempt to pay the people you owe money to. You may also need to ask people to repay debts they owe you, which could be somewhat of an awkward exercise in tact and diplomacy.

Three   If the Three of Pentacles has appeared in the Next Half Year position, property and possessions will soon mean a great deal to you. You may consider moving into a new home, which you hope will be an improvement over your present living situation. You may also consider making a major renovation to your property, which will entail considerable investment and expertise on your part. A marriage, engagement or other type of commitment is likely, but this union would in all probability be based just as much on material concerns as the concept of true love. It is important, therefore, not to allow yourself to fall prey to any illusions that you may have with regard to the partnership you are considering.

Four   If the Four of Pentacles has appeared in the Next Half Year position, your possessions specifically relating to your personal security will shortly become vital to you. You need to prepare for lean times ahead by living simply and keeping your expenditures to a minimum. It is not a propitious time to invest your money in any risky ventures because it is unlikely you will receive a return on your initial investment. You need to take a discriminating look at who you allow into your confidence and into your home because some individuals who wish to get to know you better have interests at cross-purposes to your own. It is important, therefore, that you keep your doors locked because intruders will use any opportunity to profit from the smallest lapse in your own personal security.

Five   If the Five of Pentacles has appeared in the Next Half Year position, you would be wise to prepare for lean times ahead, where you will need to pull in your belt and live as frugally as possible. You will very likely go through a period of depressive illness because there are certain aspects of your life you are unhappy with. You have a strong desire to belong, so when certain individuals who you perceive to be popular snub you and deny you membership to their particular clique, you will feel the full force of such a rejection. The fact that you are not exactly where you would like to be in your career and social standing is not necessarily a failing on your part, but merely a phase you must undergo in the cycle of transformation and change that affects us all in at least one point in our lives. The best you can do is save your money, live simply, and prepare yourself for more prosperous times, which will inevitably come back to you.

Six   If the Six of Pentacles has appeared in the Next Half Year position, you will soon undergo a karmic balancing act. A sense of harmony in the universe is necessary to enable it to run smoothly, and it is for that reason the positivities and the negativities of this world must co-exist in a state of equilibrium to establish harmony in the universe. It is for that reason you may be asked to do something that would have no apparent benefit to you. You will, however, reap the rewards of your unrequited gift at a later date, so you do not need to worry about giving without the benefit of recompense. By the same token, you may find yourself in the position where you need to ask for assistance from a power higher than yourself. You should not be ashamed or embarrassed at having to receive any kind of help from others because it is merely a part of the universal cycle that has a never-ending rotation. You will, however, be expected to repay in kind any gifts you receive so the universe will continue to attain a harmonious balance.

Seven   If the Seven of Pentacles appears in the Next Half Year position, you are undergoing a period of waiting, especially with regard to the situation that prompted you to consult the oracle. You may very well have put in a fair amount of effort to see a certain project to completion, but the forces that prevail indicate there is nothing you can do to influence the situation for the time being but wait. Because Pentacles represents the physical aspects of ourselves, if you have been hoping to start a family, you will soon find you are very fertile and receptive to the influences that come about to make such an objective reality. If, however, you do not want to add to your existing family, it would therefore be wise to take adequate precautions with regard to that matter as well.

Eight   If the Eight of Pentacles has appeared in the Next Half Year position, you will soon learn some new things either in your current vocation or a different line of work altogether. These skills you will soon be acquiring will in all probability relate to working with your hands, which can go a long way to healing some of the emotional or mental blocks that continue to reside in your psyche.

Nine   If the Nine of Pentacles has appeared in the Next Half Year position, you shall soon be entering a hiatus, which is something you desperately need in order to recuperate from what has been a rather stressful situation. During this time of rest, your physical needs will be taken care of, which will enable you to spend time in reflection so you can determine exactly what direction it is you would like to follow.

Ten If the Ten of Pentacles has appeared in the Next Half Year position, it is anticipated that very soon you will find yourself involved with your family in a matter that concerns property or money. It is a distinct possibility that you will be asked to work closely with older members of your family circle, which should instil in you more responsibility than you currently have at the moment. The increased duty you may be asked to take on promises to yield greater wealth and prosperity in later years, thereby lessening some of the resentment you may feel at being denied the carefree existence you feel you deserve.

King If the King of Pentacles has appeared in the Next Half Year position, you will soon come into contact with an influential man. He is somewhat of a self made man, and even if he is not instilled with a great deal of material wealth, he is a valued member of his community because his opinions are sound and considered worthwhile. This individual has a solid personality and is not prone to rash behaviour. He can be generous when it is in his best interests, but he needs to exercise caution not to become miserly in later life.

Queen If the Queen of Pentacles has appeared in the Next Half Year position, you will soon come into contact with a woman who has much self-confidence and has money of her own. She is an independent woman because she has wealth in her own right to enable her to do the things she would like. She can be kind when it suits her to be so, and helps those who are less fortunate than herself, which ultimately makes her a leader in her own community. She is very practical and level-headed, and is therefore not inclined to whimsical behaviour. When asked, she can impart sound advice to the querent, but is not prone to asserting her opinions without first being asked for them.

Knight/ Prince If the Knight of Pentacles has appeared in the Next Half Year position, you will soon have the opportunity to come into contact with a young man who is stable and level headed. He has a good head on his shoulders and is not one to act hastily. Although he is somewhat slow and methodical, he usually gets what he wants through persistent effort. Material possessions are important to this individual whose self-esteem is often determined by what he owns and how much money he earns. For that reason he will work hard so he can amass wealth and strive towards self-actualisation through his career achievements.

Page/
Princess

If the Page of Pentacles has appeared in the Next Half Year position, you will soon come into contact with a young person who has the potential to be affluent, but has not yet made her mark in this life. She is very practical, methodical and steadfast in her opinions, and can be somewhat obstinate until she has learned the art of tact. She is determined to achieve material prosperity because wealth and possessions are very important to her sense of self and wellbeing.

Swords/Air

Ace

If the Ace of Swords appears in the Next Half Year position, you will soon enter into a period of correspondence with regard to one specific issue. The initial sparks of an idea will flow, but this should not to be confused with the creative energies inherent in the Ace of Wands. Rather than the concept of building something new, which is in the creation principle of Fire, you and those associated with you will have an intense desire to make your ideas and opinions known via the spoken and written word, which is the intellectual principle behind Swords. This is a time of deep karmic significance, where you will be forced to come face to face with the obligations you have built up over various incarnations, and must face before you can progress along your soul evolution.

Two

If the Two of Swords has appeared in the Next Half Year position, you will soon find you are in disagreement with another individual about one crucial issue. The both of you are not in possession of all the facts and therefore are not in a position to make an accurate assessment of the situation, thus making what you are involved in all the more frustrating. As a result of you not being able to see eye to eye with this person, you may decide that, for the time being anyway, the best thing you can do is to part company until the truth of the matter is revealed in a more coherent fashion. If this individual meant nothing to you, you would have no difficulty whatsoever walking away from him. The fact is, however, that much emotional energy has been cultivated between the two of you, which makes it all the more difficult to leave the anguishing situation behind. When all the facts become known, it may be possible to try for a reconciliation, but a cooling off period is necessary if equilibrium and harmony are to be restored.

Three

If the Three of Swords has appeared in the Next Half Year position, you will soon go through a very emotionally tumultuous period. It seems there are individuals who mean a great deal to you, but they are not treating your relationship with the respect it deserves. Their total disregard for you and your feelings is causing you a great deal of emotional pain, as you cannot understand what you have ever done to this individual to cause him or her to treat you with such blatant disregard. The fact is you didn't do anything to bring such emotional pain to yourself, it just happens to be one of those occurrences that have nothing really to do with you. The problem lies with the other person, who must find his own way in this life before he can wholly relate to you, and has not yet learned to treat his relationships with the maturity and care that ultimately comes from mutual respect and love. Although you are in anguish at this point in your life, it is important to keep in mind that you were merely caught in the crossfire of the antics of misguided souls. The person who has hurt you so is merely not ready to be loved by you, which is why he or she has behaved in such a hurtful manner.

Four   If the Four of Swords has appeared in the Next Half Year position, you need to get as much rest as possible so higher guidance will be revealed to you. Reserve your energy for a time when things will become much busier than they presently are. This period of rest should be used as a time of meditation and inner reflection, a time where you allow your mind to wander so new ideas can come into your head, undeterred by the hustle and bustle of an active lifestyle. New thoughts that enlighten you will come, if you let them. If you take the time to quiet your mind and open yourself up to new and wonderful impressions of other worlds that await you and anyone else who is ready for such inner adventures, you will realise there is so much more to what you perceive in what you thought was a three dimensional universe.

Five   If the Five of Swords has appeared in the Next Half Year position, you will soon find yourself at odds with a person or group of people who you had originally felt to be your friends. There seems to be much banter going on, and a significantly large proportion of it appears to be malicious gossip, which is intended to harm the reputation of involved participants. While some of this activity can be viewed as lively debate on the ethics of a particular topic, some of it is merely stories that have been made up in an attempt to slur the characters of others. It is not envisaged that you will stay in this environment for any length of time because you will soon tire of such destructive behaviour from other individuals. Since you will find yourself mixing with people who are morally and ethically inferior, the best you can do in such a situation is to exercise caution in all you say or write. It would be in your best interests, therefore, to keep copies of any documents relating to the situation you will soon be entering into. These documents will become useful in the future if there are any intentional or accidental lapses in your or another individual's memories.

Six   If the Six of Swords has appeared in the Next Half Year position, you will soon be leaving a difficult time, hoping to make a new life for yourself. You may have been involved in a relationship or vocation that was not healthy for you, and consequently brought you a great deal of sadness. After much soul searching and reflection, you will decide the best you can do is to walk away from a situation that has been causing you so much grief, even if it means you will have to give up a great deal in the process. The decision to build a new life for yourself will come about with some melancholia because the fact is that you would have preferred to see the situation you are leaving turn out more positively. Because you will need to make new acquaintances in the environment you will soon be entering, you will need to practise discretion so you can select only positive people who will be able to afford you harmonious relationships in your upcoming milieu. The time coming will be a time where you will need to learn from your mistakes, so you need to exercise attention to detail so you can keep any errors to a minimum. All you have experienced in the past will have been of no value to you if you cannot learn from it and then move on to better, more fulfilling relationships and situations.

Seven   If the Seven of Swords has appeared in the Next Half Year position, you need to be guarded in your activities because there are individuals around you who are claiming your ideas as their own. You need to guard your possessions because you may unknowingly invite someone into your home who may decide to take something of value from you without your knowledge. Even if you take adequate precautions not to invite dubious characters into your space, an opportunist could always take it upon himself to take advantage of any unlocked doors or windows. Alternatively, you may find yourself in a situation where stealth and secrecy is necessary. You will therefore need to ask yourself whether what you intend to do is honourable and ethical. If it isn't, maybe there is something more worthy of your efforts that you can engage yourself in to achieve the same goal.

Eight   If the Eight of Swords has appeared in the Next Half Year position, you will soon enter into a period of entrapment that has in many ways been caused by your own sense of tact and diplomacy. You may find you have become involved in something that is not beneficial for your soul growth, and this has consequently taken you off your true path in life to such an extent that you will not know the correct course of action to take. You will find yourself to be in a period of confinement, which may be self imposed or caused by forces more powerful than yourself at this moment in time. During your isolation you will not be made privy to vital pieces of information that are important to your own wellbeing and safety, which will thus compound the problem that you will soon be involved in. Although it is difficult to see it at the moment, there is a way out of this predicament, but you may be required to make some tough decisions with regard to your future. The best you can do at this time is to keep your affairs legitimate and above board, thereby lessening any negative influences that will inevitably come your way.

Nine   If the Nine of Swords has appeared in the Next Half Year position, you will soon go through a period of mental confusion, which will cause you to feel very anxious. You may find you have difficulty sleeping because you have so much on your mind that it is difficult for you to relax enough to get a good night's sleep. You may also find you are prone to falling prey to one of the many mental illnesses, such as depressive disorders, personality disorders that are a result of past, unresolved experiences, obsessive/compulsive disorders, anxiety, panic, addictions that have come about as a result of your attempt to self-medicate, neurosis, and even psychosis. While there are many things in your present life you have no control over, there are some qualities you have within yourself the ability to take command of. It is for that reason the best you can do to navigate through this difficult patch is to live simply and honestly, steering clear of those individuals who will only drag you down. Above all, you need to eat properly and get plenty of rest, which will give you adequate reasoning power to decide what is best for your particular life path.

Ten   If the Ten of Swords has appeared in the Next Half Year position, you will soon feel quite unhappy about a particular situation. It seems you have placed your trust in inappropriate individuals who have only let you down when you were the most vulnerable. Unfortunately, there is nothing you can do but lick your wounds, nurse your damaged ego, and take stock of the situation that has caused you so much anguish. Upon reflection, you may see that the signs of dissent were there, but you did not want to see them. It may be a good time to decide to mix with a different crowd of people who would be more appreciative of your company, thereby lessening the chance of any future betrayals.

King   If the King of Swords has appeared in the Next Half Year position, you will soon be influenced by a man who has a significant command of the power of words. He has the ability to express himself eloquently, which instils in him the ability to speak poetically and metaphorically. He needs the company of other people, which makes him a witty and pleasant conversationalist most of the time. Although he is intensely loyal to people while he is with them, when they leave his sphere of awareness, he can easily forget all about the friendship he had developed. It is for that reason this individual has had many relationships, much to the dismay of his present partner, who is also at risk of being a figment of his past as well.

Queen   If the Queen of Swords has appeared in the Next Half Year position, you will soon be widely influenced by a woman who is very articulate and able to express herself well. She is knowledgeable about many subjects, but fame may have alluded her, leaving her with the feeling that life has passed her by in some way. It is for that reason she may carry an air of importance she has not really earned, thereby leaving some people perplexed by her behaviour. She is knowledgeable about a wide variety of subjects and would like to impart the wisdom she has gleaned to others, but only wants an audience who will listen.

Knight/ Prince   If the Knight of Swords has appeared in the Next Half Year position, you will soon be influenced by a young man who has some very high ideals and aspires to great things in life. He has somewhat of a temper, however, which manifests itself through explosive outbursts and insulting remarks. He has the potential to one day be a great thinker and communicator, but until that time he needs to mature and grow through his life experiences. Because he is able to freely express himself, he will never be short of admirers.

Page/ Princess   If the Page of Swords has appeared in the Next Half Year position, you will soon be influenced by a young person who is quite chatty. She has an inquisitive mind and therefore asks many questions that less astute individuals would overlook. She can also be quite nervous and may be prone to biting her nails or engaging in a frenzy of activity, as she tries to release much of the energy inside of her. As she matures, many of the frenetic activities she pursues will wane, but until that time it is important she stay busy through hobbies or educational pursuits so she does not become involved in any negative activities.

Cups/Water

Ace   If the Ace of Cups has appeared in the Next Half Year position, you will soon enter into a situation that has the potential to bring you great happiness and fulfilment. This situation could be a job, school, holiday or relationship, but you will know when you come across it because it will feel right to you.

Two   If the Two of Cups has appeared in the Next Half Year position, you will soon become involved with an individual who can bring you a great deal of happiness just through your contact with him or her. There will be a unique bond that will keep the two of you together, as you form a partnership that is likely to be a lasting one.

Three   If the Three of Cups has appeared in the Next Half Year position, you will soon find you have a lively social life, full of parties and get-togethers. There is likely to be much merry-making, as the people in your social circle would like to have a good time and enjoy themselves. You will receive invitations to social events, and it would be in your best interest to accept them because you never know what opportunities might be presented to you in any chance encounter. Because there will be so many social outings, you may find you are eating and drinking more than usual. It is for that reason you may want to prepare for this period of intense social activity by watching your weight and getting into shape.

Four   If the Four of Cups has landed in the Next Half Year position, you will soon be entering into a period of uncertainty and doubt. While all outward signals appear normal, you cannot help but get an inner feeling that something is amiss in paradise. You may suffer from nervousness or anxiety, which gives further rise to the misgivings you have with regard to the situation you will soon be involved in. To further confuse the issue, you will be receiving conflicting stories from various sources, leaving you rather perplexed about what the truth actually is. It is for that reason you should only be swayed by factual evidence and allow your inner voice to guide you to the direction you should be taking.

Five   If the Five of Cups has appeared in the Next Half Year position, you will soon be entering a period of melancholia because what you had hoped would happen has not transpired in the manner that you would have liked. You may have had your hopes up high with regard to one particular issue, and never really believed things could turn out differently than what you had previously envisaged. When the unexpected occurs, it seems you will be caught totally off guard, which will only serve to add to the uncertainty you will soon be feeling. It is understandable that you will be disheartened, but with the new knowledge you possess, you have within yourself the ability to create a new life for yourself.

Six   If the Six of Cups has appeared in the Next Half Year position, you will soon enter into a situation that reminds you of past times. You may be reunited with someone from your childhood, thereby enabling you to relive those experiences. You may also find yourself working with children in some capacity, which will enable you to grow as an individual, as you are able to recapture some of your lost youth. If you live far away from where you were in your more formative years, you may find yourself travelling back to that place, which will help to renew your sense of self. You will soon be able to see with clarity where you have been, and this should help you to determine where you would like to go from there and then to visualise what your ultimate goal is.

Seven   If the Seven of Cups has appeared in the Next Half Year position, you will soon find yourself in a situation where several options will be made available to you. You do not, however, know which option will yield the greatest results, and that is precisely where your challenge lies. The point to remember is that some choices will be positive, while others will get you nowhere, and still others will be detrimental to your emotional wellbeing. It is for that reason you should not become bamboozled by a highly developed sales pitch, which has been presented by no less than a confidence artist. If you are unsure about a particular decision you need to make, it would be best to ask for a second opinion and shop around until you find something that feels right for you. It is crucial you do not allow others to force you into a decision you are not fully prepared to commit yourself to because you could find yourself wasting valuable time and energy on a path that is not destined for you.

Eight   If the Eight of Cups has appeared in the Next Half Year position, you will soon be entering into an unknown realm of existence. There is one particular area of your life you have held onto relentlessly. Even though you know deep down in your heart this person, situation, or way of life was not a positive experience, you nevertheless clung on, hoping circumstances would change and you would feel happy at last. After a great deal of soul searching, you will come to the reluctant decision that you must walk away from that which has caused you so much heartache. The decision to leave will be difficult because you will have to sacrifice some long-term goals that have fuelled your dreams. Better, more worthwhile experiences will come to you, but in the meantime, you must go through the grieving process for what you have given up.

Nine   If the Nine of Cups has appeared in the Next Half Year position, you will soon enter into a period where you are happy and content with yourself. You may, however, spend a lot of time on your own, so you should use this time to get to know yourself better, a time of inner reflection and attunement to your spiritual awareness. On the down side, you may find you are eating or drinking more than is necessary for the healthy functioning of your body, and this could consequently lead you to put on weight, which is not necessarily a good thing. It would be wise, therefore, to rest, eat sensibly and exercise regularly so you do not gain unwanted pounds.

Ten   If the Ten of Cups has appeared in the Next Half Year position, you will soon find yourself in a situation that has the ability to give you a great deal of happiness and harmony. You may come face to face with your soul mate in this life, the person who you love and want to share a home and family with. It is likely you will bask in the simplest pleasures this world has to offer, such as walking in the countryside and spending time with the one you love.

King   If the King of Cups has appeared in the Next Half Year position, you will soon find yourself under the influence of a man who is a very sensitive individual. He is quite knowledgeable about a variety of subjects and may even be psychic. He is very perceptive, assessing any situation before deciding whether he would like to involve himself. He is somewhat introverted, preferring to keep his thoughts and opinions to himself, not wishing to offend anyone with any views that might be considered controversial. He does, however, have many secrets, which you will need to uncover before you decide just how involved you would like to become with this man.

Queen   If the Queen of Cups has appeared in the Next Half Year position, you will soon be influenced by a woman who is quite emotive at times. It is easy for her to display her true feelings, whether good or bad, thereby making it difficult for her to lie. It is easy to tell when she is saying something that is not true because she will tend to avert her eyes from the recipient of her communications. She does, nevertheless, have something very important to impart to you, but you will need to watch her closely to glean the true meaning of the message she is trying to impart.

Knight/
Prince
If the Knight of Cups has appeared in the Next Half Year position, you will soon come into contact with a young man. He can be very caring because he is such an emotive soul. Because he is so sensitive, he appeals to the opposite sex, as they feel an affinity for his more intuitive side. The dark side, however, is not something most people would like to explore because he has a depth that even he may not be aware of. When slighted, he can be petty and spiteful, which detracts from what is otherwise a delightful personality.

Page/
Princess
If the Page of Cups has appeared in the Next Half Year position, you will soon come in contact with a young person who is very sensitive to the moods of others. She is somewhat emotional and wears her heart on her sleeve, often becoming affected by the subtle motives of others.

11 The Unexpected

0 Fool   If The Fool has appeared in the Unexpected position, quite by chance you will be given the opportunity to begin a new path in this life. This means you will need to tie up any loose ends in your existing sojourn so you will be sufficiently able to take up the new venture that will be presented to you sometime in the next year. It will involve doing things you have never before done, so you need to prepare yourself by reading books and taking courses on anything that piques your interest. The road ahead may be somewhat rocky, so you will need to ensure you have the proper spiritual foundations to ensure you can see such a task through to completion. Whatever your endeavour, however, if it is ethical you will be protected whatever course you decide to embark upon.

I Magician   If The Magician has appeared in the Unexpected position, you will come into contact with a young, clever man who is quite astute and has the tools available to him to create the future he would like. It is highly likely he has been endowed with a good standard of education and a reasonable family background that will enable him to get ahead in a world where 'who you know' is just as important, if not more so, as 'what you know'. You must however, tread carefully with this individual because as nice as he may appear to be on the outside, he is extremely self-serving and acts to get what he wants out of life, and is therefore not too particularly concerned about the feelings of others. Alternatively, you may be given the opportunity to begin a course of study. If at all possible, you should endeavour to attend to such a course because the intensified programme of study will endow you with skills that will enable you to advance in this world. In the Biblical sense, this person can be best described as Lucifer, God's favourite angel before he fell down to earth. Lucifer is Latin for the light bearer, and The Magician is depicted as The Light One, which is in contrast to The Devil, who is depicted as The Dark One. The Hebrew prophet Isaiah used the term in a satirical allusion to the king of Babylon, describing the frustrated ambition of the morning star to rise higher than all the other stars: 'How art thou fallen from heaven, O Lucifer, son of the morning'.

II High Priestess

If the High Priestess has appeared in the Unexpected position, you will encounter a young, single woman who is spiritually inclined. She has a great deal to teach you about the universal flow and will reveal to you many aspects of human nature that you had not previously been aware of. Some of these character traits that she will make known to you are quite unpleasant, but she must show you this because it is what keeps mankind in this third dimensional reality and prevents him from moving on to higher dimensions. In many ways, she will act as a mirror to you, showing you those aspects of yourself that you may not necessarily be aware of. If there is something you don't like about her, it is merely because she presents an aspect of yourself that you have denied the existence of. It is for that reason you should endeavour to correct the character defects in yourself before attempting to remedy those in others. Was it not Jesus who said, 'Cast out the beam out of thine own eye, and then shalt thou see clearly to cast out the mote of thy brother's eye'?

III Empress

If The Empress has appeared in the Unexpected position, you will come into contact with a woman who either has children or is ready to start a family. She is somewhat possessive of what she considers hers, and this can be quite a substantial list of possessions. Among her domain are partners, lovers, friends, children, her personal possessions, and the possessions of her partners, just to name a few. The Empress is not one to get into a dispute with because she is stubborn and unreasonable in any disagreement, which makes it very difficult to come to any kind of compromise. She also does not like to fight her battles single handedly, and therefore uses any and all means to illicit sympathy for her cause. If for any reason you are not able to get this woman on your side, it is best to tread carefully and not openly do anything to upset her, because she doesn't make a very good friend, and an even worse enemy.

IV Emperor

If The Emperor has appeared in the Unexpected position, you will come into contact with a very powerful man who has a great deal of control over your destiny. It is for that reason you must tread carefully with this individual. He is a very me-centred person who thinks of his needs over those of others. He is relatively wealthy and is very respected among his community, which is a result of the clout he has amassed through his diligent efforts. He has many professional and social contacts that he will call upon whenever the need arises. He is ruthless and will take whatever he wants, regardless of whether it has belonged to anyone else in the past. If this man is your ally, he can help you to advance in your chosen vocation, but on the other hand, if he has taken a dislike to you for whatever reason, he can make life very difficult indeed. To be on the safe side, reveal nothing to this person unless it is absolutely essential that you do so, therefore shielding yourself from any possible retribution.

V
Hierophant

If The Hierophant has appeared in the Unexpected position, you or someone close to you may become involved in a religious ceremony or become more active in the church. The event in question is of a major significance, and could be a christening, marriage or funeral and will need many preparations. If you or someone you know has been having marital difficulties, they may decide to formalise the lack of a cohesive union by initiating either a separation, divorce or an annulment. The important thing to remember is the event in question will be of such magnitude that your life will not be the same afterwards. It is also likely to involve a religious official or church ceremony, which further illustrates the seriousness of the event in question. It will be a life-changing event, for which it will be very difficult to return to former times. It is for that reason you will need to think very carefully about what you do next in relation to this matter.

VI Lovers

If The Lovers has appeared in the Unexpected position, you or someone close to you is likely to come into contact with an individual who you are very attracted to. This bond is likely to be destined, as you have met an individual with whom you have had contact in past, future and alternate realties. The feelings you have for this individual will be of such an intense nature that they will shake up your existing opinions of love, romance, marriage and commitment. Whereas in the past you may have viewed your partnerships more rationally, that is as a means to help you get what you want out of life, this new person you will meet will teach you that love is not like that. You will learn that love cannot be defined within the boundaries of age, sex, social standing, education or profession, and you may be required to make a major decision regarding this person, who you will come to view as one of the major loves in your life. You may be required to leave an existing relationship in order to be with this person, but that is a choice only you can make.

VII Chariot If The Chariot has appeared in the Unexpected position, you will find that you or someone close to you will embark upon a journey that will be a life-changing experience. This trip will be essential to your future prosperity, so you will need to take it even if it poses an inconvenience to you. You may have to struggle with one particular issue that is very important to you, but it is likely your drive and ambition will see you through any difficulties you will encounter along the way. Your perceptions will be expanded, which will broaden your mind and show you there are many avenues one can take to accomplish the same goal.

VIII Strength If Strength has appeared in the Unexpected position, either you or someone close to you is going to have contact with animals. These animals are quite possibly feral or very close to wildness because they do not appear to be very domesticated. Animals have very therapeutic qualities because they do not possess the more narrow-minded human attributes that inhibit a free flow of love and affection. The one thing that esoterically sets animals apart from human beings and brings them closer to the God in heaven is that animals must kill for survival, while humans kill for sport or fun. Animals such as cats and dogs, however, have a social structure similar to that of humans, which makes them ideal companions in this life. Although they have their own unique personalities, they are able to love unconditionally, which transcends the human imposed boundaries of sex, race, social class, education or profession.

IX Hermit If The Hermit has appeared in the Unexpected position, you can expect to spend some time on your own. You may initially balk at the prospect of having nobody but your own self for company, but the solitude that has been forced upon you is as much necessary for your soul growth as it is for the development of those around you. It may be somewhat daunting for you to be a lone individual in what can sometimes be a cruel world because you would so much like to be a part of a couple or a group of people. Even if you are in a relationship, you will find yourself in a situation where you nonetheless feel all alone much of the time. You should use this time of quite solitude to reflect upon your life so you can decide where you would like for it to go from this point in time. After having spent enough time in your own company, you may realise you don't need to be part of a relationship as much as you had previously supposed. It is important to remember that while we humans are social creatures and need the company of others, our personal relationships can at times serve as distractions and prevent us from facing the more crucial issues that are a part of our psychological make-up. It is for that reason you should use this period of quiet reflection to work on your soul.

X Wheel of Fortune If The Wheel has appeared in the Unexpected position, you are going to be quite surprised that you will undergo a sudden change of fortune. You will complete a minor cycle in your life, which will open the door for new opportunities to come to you. Because The Wheel is composed of the four zodiacal signs that represent the four elemental forces, you need to prepare yourself for somewhat of a rejuvenated existence because new alternatives will be presented to you that will have the potential to change your lifestyle. The only thing for you to do is to make well-reasoned choices as they come to you, and your future prosperity will be particularly secured.

XI Justice If Justice has appeared in the Unexpected position, you can expect to deal with a legal problem that has arisen quite out of the blue. While the case may not actually make its way to the courtroom, a fair degree of mediation will be necessary for you to see a successful resolution. Because Justice is only concerned about what is fair and equitable, you need to ensure all of your dealings with other individuals are ethical and beyond reproach. The reason for this is because the universe is not particularly concerned about who is right or wrong, but will ensure any imbalances are restored to harmony, regardless of the wishes of human beings. Even if you find yourself at an unfair advantage, when you least expect it, any inequalities will be restored, with little regard to your personal feelings.

XII Hanged Man If The Hanged Man has appeared in the Unexpected position, you will undergo a profound experience that will completely change your thinking patterns. What is important to you today will seem totally insignificant after you experience an event that is so profound you may even undergo a complete personality change. For all outward appearances, you may be at what can be considered a standstill, not going forward and not going backward. What is going on in your perceptions is a completely different matter, however. When we are firmly grounded to the earth, concentrating on making money and building our future prosperity, it is almost impossible to still our minds to the point where we can consciously listen to the subatomic particles that collide in such a fashion as to gently whisper the secrets of the universe. It is when we stop, look and listen, that the secrets of the universe will be revealed to us, and it is then we will know the truth of our reality.

XIII Death If Death has appeared in the Unexpected position, you or someone close to you will suffer a loss of some kind. It doesn't matter how insignificant the loss actually is, because to you it will be a major cataclysm, and it is how you feel that is important. You may sustain a loss in the form of a relationship that is very important to you, which could bring you a period of grieving. The universe has a way of balancing things out, so you will be presented with new opportunities to fill the void left by the departure of something dear to you. Perhaps you had unrealistic expectations with regard to a particular person or situation, and the false perceptions you have will be brought to your attention with a resounding clarity and leave you in no doubt as to the reality of the situation. After an appropriate period of mourning for what you have lost, it is important to remember that you will go on.

XIV Temperance If Temperance has appeared in the Unexpected position, you will decide to make plans with regard to a certain issue that will involve a specific period of time. You may decide to engage in a course of study, training programme or apprenticeship that is a very lengthy process. In addition, you may decide to host an event or celebration some time in the future that will require extensive planning and preparation. Because what you are about to become involved in is such a lengthy process, the only thing you can do is to plan what you would like to happen in the future and carry out preparatory measures with precision. In addition, there are things that will be occurring in your life for the duration of this reading that will not become relevant to the master plan of your life purpose for quite some time. It is for that reason you will find it useful to keep an accurate hand-written diary of all that you experience so you can refer back to it in the future. Your thoughts, feelings and perceptions will become an accurate record in time when the importance of the situation you will soon be entering will be revealed to you.

XV Devil If The Devil has appeared in the Unexpected position, you will find yourself in a position where you must focus on the physicalities of this world. Your immediate priorities will be work, career, finances and property, and as a result, you may have to put the spiritual side of your being on hold as you concentrate on acquiring those material possessions you need to adequately exist in this physical world. You may also come into contact with an individual who appears to have all the answers to the dilemma you are in. He may make many promises to you with regard to what he can do for you or how successful you will be in this life. Even if you do what he asks, it is highly unlikely anything he says or does will significantly improve your lot in life. If anything, if you take this person's advice, your circumstances are likely to significantly degrade to the point where you will wonder how you ever allowed yourself to be lulled into such a psychological stupor and find yourself in such a mess. In the Biblical sense, the individual who you will come into contact with will be nothing less than a false prophet, wrecking havoc in the lives of those he meets. This person will promise you the earth, but the fact is he simply hasn't got the wherewithal to give it to you. The only way you can make any progress is through steady methodical effort on your part. There are no quick fixes this time. This individual can be best described as Satan, the fallen angel of the Bible.

XVI Tower   If The Tower has appeared in the Unexpected position, you will encounter a sudden change of circumstances that will shake you up a bit. You may find that events have arisen that have forced your need to look for a new job, living accommodation, or friends, and this will ultimately propel you into a whole new environment. You may meet someone just by chance, and this encounter could lead to new opportunities that will serve to change your life completely. You or someone close to you could also have a mishap either around the house or while out and about, and this in itself could provide you with a whole new set of circumstances that need to be worked around. The key here is to take extra precautions to avoid any accidents, thereby helping to prevent or minimise any calamities that may befall you.

XVII Star   If The Star has appeared in the Unexpected position, you will acquaint yourself with an individual who will help you to see some of your long held dreams become reality. This person will in all probability become a friend to you, and this relationship will help to open you up to new potentialities in this life. You will be able to relate to this person and confide things that you would not reveal to other souls. Such an encounter will have the effect of restoring your faith in humanity, which you may very well have lost at a much earlier stage in your life.

XVIII Moon   If The Moon has appeared in the Unexpected position, events will occur that will leave you in a state of perplexity. You will be somewhat confused and in the dark about some aspects that will affect your well-being. You will come to realise that you really don't know the people you thought you knew, which will lead to further disenchantment about certain aspects of your life. Your friends will turn out to be unreliable because, lacking understanding of the situation that you will soon be in, they will not be entirely sympathetic to your cause. Some people who you had assumed to be empathetic and on friendly terms with you will turn out to either intentionally or unintentionally cause you more harm than good. This will be a time when you cannot rely on others because they are either not interested or do not have the capability to understand your particular situation in this life. The only thing you can do is get plenty to rest and relaxation so you will be able to trust your higher guidance when you are unsure of what to do.

XIX Sun If The Sun has appeared in the Unexpected position, something will occur that will bring you much happiness and joy. You may have an addition to your family in the form of a child or a pet, and this will help you to see the world from a completely new perspective. You may also go to a sunny place, where you are able to relax a bit and enjoy yourself, basking in the glory of The Sun. You will also receive renewed clarity about one particular situation, and be able to see it in a new light. While this new understanding may not be positive, the sheer fact that you are in possession of pertinent facts will equip you to more effectively carry on with your day-to-day activities and give you a renewed sense of purpose.

XX Judgement If Judgement has appeared in the Unexpected position, you will come face to face with a person or a situation from the past that had been long forgotten. The fact is that you really did not forget the incident, no matter how much you would have liked to. Because you were not fully equipped to deal with the issue in a conscious, rational way, your subconscious shoved it to the back of your mind, waiting for a time when you would be sufficiently ready to remember it. These long repressed memories can bring you an inner psychic healing of a wound that has been embedded so deeply in your soul that you were almost able to overlook it. If nobody brought it to your attention and you looked around the area that scarred you so, you could almost deny its existence. Now is the time to face your demons from the past so you can emerge reborn, a renewed individual, much wiser for the experience.

XXI World If The World has appeared in the Unexpected position, you will come to realise that one specific area of your life has come to its natural conclusion. It may be difficult for you to accept this, especially if you wanted the situation to carry on, so you may need to go through a period of grieving. This ending may be seen as a loss of sorts, but with every ending there is always the potential for a new beginning. You may have found yourself in a vocation that had become outmoded and stale, so to leave it may very well be the best action you could take. Of course, you may find it is not you, but the other party who wants to conclude the situation, and in that case you will need time to reflect upon the reasons why and the events that led up to the metaphorical ending in your life. When you have had time to think about the situation reasonably, you will begin to notice new opportunities will open up to you so you can embrace the next step of your soul's evolution.

Wands/Rods/Fire

Ace   If the Ace of Wands has appeared in the Unexpected position, you will find yourself in a situation where you will have many opportunities to advance creatively, professionally and spiritually. You may find yourself in a new job, neighbourhood, school or group of friends, and this new scenario will be enough to spur you to new ideas so you will begin to ponder alternative solutions to problems so you can improve your future prospects.

Two   If the Two of Wands has appeared in the Unexpected position, you will come together with another person to accomplish an objective that could benefit the both of you. This could be a partnership in a business, educational or social setting, where you are expected to work as part of a team to achieve a common goal. It is very likely that an exchange of money or property will be involved because most business is engaged in the processing of goods and services. Alternatively, you may come together with another individual in a religious setting, possibly deciding to go to a church ceremony. You would benefit greatly from exploring the spiritual side of yourself, and you may meet someone to help you to discover it.

Three   If the Three of Wands has appeared in the Unexpected position, you will find yourself amongst a group of people who you must co-operate with socially or professionally. The job you do may change so that you find you have to work together with other people in a team type setting, which may require you to learn a few people skills so you can effectively persuade people to your line of thinking. You may also engage in a sporting or social activity where you must co-operate with others so you can achieve a common goal. The archetypal symbol of

Wands typically represents business and commerce, so expect an exchange of money to take place. You may also find yourself involved in a religious ceremony, which will give you a new sense of meaning in this life.

Four If the Four of Wands has appeared in the Unexpected position, you will be pleasantly surprised to find yourself engaged in a celebratory event. You may have achieved a milestone in your life, which has the effect of securing your professional, financial or material security, thereby enabling you to feel more settled in your own status in this world. If your immediate material or security needs are met, it will be much easier for you to concentrate on less immediate, yet just as crucial dilemmas you may very well have had to put on the backburner of your mind for quite some time. Once you are able to resolve those less urgent issues that have caused you considerable anxiety, you are well on your way to becoming a more well-rounded and adapted individual.

Five If the Five of Wands has appeared in the Unexpected position, you may find you have some troubles you cannot quite put your finger on. You will discover many symptoms to your problem, which will manifest as disagreements with other people. Since you have not yet discovered the root cause of the difficulties, you will experience problems that will become progressively worse until you are left with no alternative but to try to identify what the crux of the problem is, and correct it before your life gets totally out of hand. You will be very surprised to find the root cause of the problem is not what you had originally supposed, but that is something you will need to figure out for yourself, and when you do, you will have greater understanding of your purpose in this life.

Six If the Six of Wands has appeared in the Unexpected position, you will find you have won a minor victory in the battle of life. You will not be expecting to achieve such success, but by a sudden turn of events, things will turn out in your favour. It is important to keep in mind that, metaphorically speaking, you may have won the battle but you haven't won the war. Not everybody is happy about your good fortune because it is quite possible someone may have had to give something up in order for you to get your heart's desire. It is for that reason you must remember you have achieved only one small victory on a constant uphill struggle that will only end when you have completed your last lesson in this incarnation.

Seven If the Seven of Wands has appeared in the Unexpected position, you will encounter some difficulties at your work that will delay you in making the advances in this life you would like. You may discover you have some competitors you had previously not taken into consideration, and this will force you to develop alternate strategies to achieve the same goal. You may also find the economic climate has changed, which will pose some difficulties to you, as you try to carry on as if everything is normal during what can be considered austere conditions. You will ultimately arrive at your desired destination, but it may take a little longer and be a little more difficult than you had originally planned.

Eight   If the Eight of Wands has appeared in the Unexpected position, you will be quite surprised and possibly even delighted to find that you will go on a journey, either physically or mentally. This trek can be seen as an excursion that will take you away from your daily activities, which can at times be quite boring. You may have worked very hard and have received either a promotion or a new position that is seen as a step up the career ladder. Things will be looking up for you, as you will have an opportunity to meet new people and places, and as a result broaden your awareness in this world.

Nine   If the Nine of Wands has appeared in the Unexpected position, you will find that you are on the defensive for some reason. Perhaps some individuals are jealous of your good fortune and have therefore decided to attempt to thwart it. You may have some competitors who would like to achieve the same goal as you, and it is for that reason you will need to make sure you are the best at what you do. This will have the effect of putting added stress onto an already overloaded situation, so you need to prepare yourself by taking care of your body and looking after your personal and professional affairs. You may find the climate around you has changed, which will make it all the more difficult for you to accomplish your goals. While you may very well achieve what you set out to do, it will be somewhat more difficult than you had originally hoped and you will need to work diligently to hang onto any successes that come you way.

Ten   If the Ten of Wands has appeared in the Unexpected position, you will find you have taken on more work than you are physically capable of handling, and this has the effect of wearing you down. If you are offered a new position that would entail increased responsibilities, you need to think very carefully about accepting it because you may discover that you do not have all the skills necessary to complete the task at hand. You may need to undertake a training course or get some more life experience before trying to take on such an ambitious task.

King   If the King of Wands has appeared in the Unexpected position, a man is going to come into your life who will change it dramatically. He may be in a position to help you with your current dilemma, either by giving you sound advice or helping you out in some way. He is a loving person and likes to share his love with other people by showering them with affection and gifts whenever the opportunity arises. He can impart sound knowledge to those who would open themselves up to listen.

Queen   If the Queen of Wands has appeared in the Unexpected position, you will encounter a woman who has an element of flair to her demeanour, which makes her stand out in a crowd. She has somewhat of a dramatic personality, which means she is never boring. She enjoys the company of other people, and often entertains so she can be around the company she would like. This individual has something to relate to you, so you would be wise to listen carefully to her words for any hidden clues.

Knight/ Prince   If the Knight of Wands has appeared in the Unexpected position, you will come into contact with a young man who has a great deal of passion and flair in his aura, which endows him with a dynamic personality that people like to be around. Because he is so passionate about what he believes in, it is easy for him to be swept away in a flood of emotion, which unfortunately can fade just as easily as it can begin because this individual is such a fickle soul. It is for that reason you need to take your time to get to know this person before you commit yourself to him because he is likely to change his mind many times before he settles on one particular vocation or relationship.

Page/ Princess   If the Page of Wands has appeared in the Unexpected position, it is highly likely that a young person will soon enter your life. Unless she has lived in an austere environment, she will have a sunny disposition and therefore love to be around people and animals. She is somewhat possessive of that which she adores, however, so this can pose problems if she becomes jealous. She likes to stay active, and therefore needs hobbies and other interests to keep her mind occupied. She is happiest when she is in a warm, bright, sunny place.

Pentacles/Disks/Earth

Ace   If the Ace of Pentacles has appeared in the Unexpected position, you will come into some money, which you will find to be a huge surprise.

You may receive a bonus, rebate or inheritance that will come to you totally out of the blue. In addition, you may win a sum of money that was gained by pure speculation. Because the universe has decided to give you extra wealth, you will have the wherewithal to improve your standard of living in some way. You may decide to buy new clothes or something more substantial, such as a car, computer or home. You may also decide to take the money and re-invest it, hoping that in time it will incur even greater financial rewards.

Two   If the Two of Pentacles has appeared in the Unexpected position, you may acquire some debts you had not anticipated. This will have the effect of putting a strain on your finances because you had not budgeted for such expenses. As a result of your financial obligations, you may have to take on a part-time job to keep your current standard of living. Alternatively, you may decide there are some things you really don't need after all, and therefore choose to forgo them. Because your financial situation is in a state of fluctuation, it would be wise for you to carefully consider any commitments before you make them. You will come to realise that you don't really need what you thought you just couldn't live without.

Three   If the Three of Pentacles has appeared in the Unexpected position, you may quite unexpectedly move house or make much needed changes to your living situation. This move will be seen as a progression, because it will be nicer, more affluent accommodation than you have previously been living in. It may also be that you decide to set up house with a particular person, which will give you the stability you will need to perform well on the job, and subsequently advance in your chosen vocation. If you are content with your living situation, other things will fall into place with little or no effort on your part.

Four   If the Four of Pentacles has appeared in the Unexpected position, you will be taken by surprise with regard to matters of your home or other assets. You may decide to invest money into your home by making repairs or redecorating. You may be asked to invest money in a financial venture that, although it promises to yield results, guarantees nothing concrete. It is for that reason you need to exercise caution and act prudently when spending any of your hard-earned wealth on this endeavour. Unless your investment is promised in the form of a return via a contractual agreement, it would be best to refrain from involving yourself in such a scheme.

Five   If the Five of Pentacles has appeared in the Unexpected position, you will discover that you, or someone close to you, will experience some financial difficulties. As a result, you may not be in a position to pay for all the material items you need in order to successfully live in our physical world. You may have been presented with a large bill, which is very difficult for you to pay, thereby putting pressure on you in other areas. Because your material problems are weighing heavily on your mind, you may fall prey to worry, anxiety and depression. The important thing to remember is this difficult phase in your life will pass. If you are prudent in your dealings with others, you will be able to weather the financial and emotional dry spell you will soon be encountering.

Six   If the Six of Pentacles has appeared in the Unexpected position, you will be asked to make a philanthropic contribution of some kind so that you can repay humanity for the good things you have been given in this life. You may be asked to make a charitable contribution or to perform some unpaid work that will benefit someone other than yourself, which will in many ways be more beneficial to you than to those you are assisting. In addition to the favours you are being asked to perform for others, you may need help from someone else. The universe has a way of balancing things out, so any good deeds you perform will be repaid in kind through the cosmic laws of the universe.

Seven   If the Seven of Pentacles has appeared in the Unexpected position, you will find yourself involved in a situation that is not likely to yield any positive results for quite some time. The important thing to do is to analyse the situation carefully and make sure your involvement is open and above board. When the time comes for these events to be accounted for, you will have an accurate record of your specific experiences with regard to the matter. This will be a period of waiting, waiting for a time where it will be more propitious to act and to reap the rewards of your labour.

Eight   If the Eight of Pentacles has appeared in the Unexpected position, you will find that you will be working with your hands in some capacity. It is also envisaged that you will need to undergo a learning curve, using trial and error, and becoming qualified in your trade through experience. You will find it to be very rewarding for you to engage in this new activity because you will learn valuable skills that will better equip you for future employment and projects that you will be given in this life.

Nine   If the Nine of Pentacles has appeared in the Unexpected position, you may suddenly find the universe has given you enough material assets to meet all of your financial obligations in this three dimensional, physical world. As a result, you will have more free time to enjoy the God-made gifts that have been given to us to enjoy. You will also have time to reflect upon your life, and such a period of deep self-analysis will help to give you a greater understanding of human nature and how certain incidents have affected your outlook on life.

Ten   If the Ten of Pentacles has appeared in the Unexpected position, you will be involved in family matters through a sudden turn of events which you have no control over. Property and finances are likely to be highlighted, as you are involved with certain family members in a venture that involves the distribution of wealth amongst the other parties. You may or may not actually desire to be so heavily involved with certain family members, but you are tied to them through blood and money, and would therefore find it difficult to extricate yourself from any such alliances without causing offence. It is for that reason you stay in the alliance, quite possibly at the expense of your own worldly hopes and dreams.

King   If the King of Pentacles has appeared in the Unexpected position, a man will influence the situation you are currently in, in some way. He is extremely money oriented, and is usually wealthier than he lets on. He has many possessions, which he wants to keep hold of, and will therefore take steps to preserve what is his, and ultimately attempt to acquire even more wealth. Although he can be quite genuine and caring, he is also greedy and is therefore not above using unscrupulous methods to manipulate others. Although this individual may claim poverty, he is actually quite well off and there is no need to add to the riches he has already accumulated.

Queen   If the Queen of Pentacles has appeared in the Unexpected position, a woman of means is likely to influence you in some way. She has wealth of her own, which instils in her a sense of confidence in the future that more vulnerable creatures do not have. She may be able to help you in some way and is therefore a good person to befriend when in need.

Knight/ Prince   If the Knight of Pentacles has appeared in the Unexpected position, you will be influenced in some way by a young man who is motivated to a large extent by material wealth. It is for that reason he will endeavour to enter into a vocation he feels will promise material security. He enjoys nice things and therefore aspires to opulence in this life. If for whatever reason he is not up to acquiring wealth on his own, he will strive to gain it through his partner. In that respect, he is a very shrewd individual because he knows how to use people to get what he wants out of life.

Page/ Princess If the Page of Pentacles has appeared in the Unexpected position, a young person will influence the situation in some way. She is quite practically minded and is methodical in how she pursues certain activities. She can be quite opinionated, and is therefore stubborn in her viewpoints until other evidence is presented to her in a reasonable manner.

Swords/Air

Ace If the Ace of Swords has appeared in the Unexpected position, you will receive an item of correspondence that will take you quite by surprise. You may receive a letter, fax or email out of the blue that will contain information of such a profound nature that you will be forced to take action. You may receive legal correspondence you were not expecting, and it will involve an issue that you had previously felt was concluded and you therefore had no further reason to be involved in. Alternatively, you could very well find yourself as the originator of some very important correspondence or literature, which will involve other individuals. You may very well decide to write about an actual or fictional experience, which could very well be cathartic to your soul, as the very act of expressing your thoughts and feelings will lead to a deep inner healing that would not otherwise occur.

Two If the Two of Swords has appeared in the Unexpected position, you will have a disagreement with someone who you had supposed you got on really well with. This will tend to serve as a double blow to your ego, because not only will you be at odds with a particular individual, but the person you are in disagreement with is someone whose opinion you value a great deal. If you were in dispute with someone you did not care for, the matter would not be so crucial to you because you would expect such behaviour from a person who is not your friend. Because you think a lot of the individual in question, it poses an even greater feeling of turmoil in your psyche. The disagreement may be of such a grand nature that you may not be able to continue the alliance any longer, which will be a quite upsetting experience. The problem lies in the fact that you and the other person involved are not in possession of all the facts, which will make it difficult for the both of you to make sound decisions.

Three   If the Three of Swords has appeared in the Unexpected position, you will experience some heartache brought about by the actions of another person, and this experience will have the affect of colouring your whole outlook on life. You are feeling especially vulnerable because the person who has wounded your soul was someone you did not believe could be capable of inflicting such emotional pain. After having seen a totally different aspect of this person, you will come to realise that absolutely anything is possible. You may also find it difficult to trust again because, after someone who you believed to have been totally trustworthy has let you down in such a tumultuous way, you will have a great deal of difficulty believing anyone again could be worthy of your trust. If you think about it carefully, you will come to realise the person who hurt you so was not acting out of character, but behaving in accordance with his true personality, which is markedly different from the temporary character attributes you wanted to see. The fact is there were clues to his true personality long before you were so abruptly shaken up, it was just that in your desire to live in an ideal world, you allowed yourself to overlook his character flaws in preference to his outer persona.

Four   If the Four of Swords has appeared in the Unexpected position, you may be given occasion to take a much needed rest. You may find yourself in a church or other religious setting, which would restore your sense of self and clarify any religious or spiritual questions you may have. When you quiet your mind, you will be given higher guidance as to what the next step in your soul evolution should be.

Five   If the Five of Swords has appeared in the Unexpected position, it seems you will re-evaluate a situation that is less than satisfying, and decide there is nothing that can be productively achieved by continuing on in the same vein. You will therefore decide it would be best to cut your losses and walk away from what appears to be a no-win situation with your reputation intact. There may be some harsh words said as a parting shot, but it really is in your best interests to have nothing more to do with people or organisations that are either consciously or unconsciously hindering your soul growth. When you have eliminated such negative influences from your life, the door that can bring positivity will open up to you.

Six   If the Six of Swords has appeared in the Unexpected position, you will find you will move away from a situation that was very difficult for you. This move could be an actual journey, but it could just as well be a change in your thinking patterns with regard to situations and people. There is a specific part of your life circumstances that has caused you a great deal of emotional tension, if not heartache. After careful reflection, you will decide to distance yourself from the situation, either physically or mentally. Ideally, it would be in your best interest to physically move from the person or situation that is a source of grief for you, but if that is not possible, you can use a positive mental attitude to psychologically remove yourself from what bothers you. In time, your life circumstances will improve and more positive opportunities will be made available to you, but the whole sadness of the incident will stay with you for quite some time, hopefully preventing you from becoming embroiled in other similar scenarios.

Seven   If the Seven of Swords has appeared in the Unexpected position, there is an element of secrecy that surrounds your milieu. You may be asked to keep a secret because the disclosure of a vital piece of information could be detrimental to either you or someone close to you, which will inevitably put you in an awkward position. You need to therefore keep your ideas and even your possessions close to your heart, revealing little even to those who you feel to be trusted friends. Someone close to you, a person who you suppose to be a confidante, could be the very person who proves to lack discretion, so it is very important you exercise care in your dealings with all individuals, including those whom you have faith in.

Eight   If the Eight of Swords has appeared in the Unexpected position, you will find yourself in a relationship or other situation where you feel there is no way you can possibly go forward. The reason for this is because you are not in possession of all of the facts because someone close to you is intentionally keeping vital information from you. This could very well serve as a mental block on your part because it will be difficult for you to decide the best way forward if you are not being presented with the situation as it realistically is. When we are presented with information we do not want to know, our minds have a way of processing that information in a way that is less painful to us. We will sometimes repress or deny that information, which helps us to carry on in our existence, but in the long run is really not good for our emotional wellbeing. When we repress information, our minds will shove the memory of the incident to the back of our consciousness, where it stays dormant until the time comes when we are ready to deal with it in a reasonable, mature fashion. When we are in denial, a much more complex psychological process occurs where our minds distort that information so we honestly believe everything is fine when really it isn't. Denial is trickier because we have interpreted information differently than the way it was actually presented to us, and it will take a major shock to wake us from our psychological slumber.

Nine   If the Nine of Swords has appeared in the Unexpected position, you will find yourself in a situation where you are full of worry and fear. For whatever reason, you may not feel entirely secure in your situation in life, which will predispose you to anxiety attacks. Anxiety in itself is bad enough, but the problem is that if it is not tempered with a good dose of common sense, it can escalate to phobias, panic attacks, depression, bipolar disorder, neurosis, and even psychosis. If you feel the stresses of this world are getting on top of you, perhaps it would be wise to consult a medical professional, who could determine the most appropriate treatment available to you. You may need a break from the pressures of this world, and this could give you a clearer perspective on your current situation so you can resume your activities with restored enthusiasm.

Ten   If the Ten of Swords has appeared in the Unexpected position, you will be quite disappointed to discover someone who you trusted has disappointed you in some way. Perhaps an individual made you a series of promises they could not or would not keep, which had the effect of dashing your hopes. It can be so disappointing when someone lets you down, and it can take a very long time for you to trust again after such a violation of trust. You may confide something to someone, only to discover that the person betrayed your confidence, which had the effect of negatively altering your circumstances in some way. It is for that reason, therefore, that you really need to be careful who you speak to because some people who you had supposed to be your friends could unknowing or unwittingly become your adversaries though the smallest slip of the tongue.

King   If the King of Swords has appeared in the Unexpected position, a man will figure prominently in the successful resolution of the problem that has prompted you to consult the oracle. He is an intellectual and strives to better himself by reading extensively on the subject of his interest. He does, however, have a sharp tongue he will use to disarm or harm anyone who he does not feel is worthy of his respect. Much of his activity is in his mind, and he may have conquered nations and won wars within the confines of his vivid fantasy world. The problem arises, however, when he allows his dissociated states of fantasy to override his waking consciousness. It is important, therefore, that his thoughts are tempered with a fair amount of reason to ensure he does not end up making up stories that would only fuel any disorders he may have.

Queen If the Queen of Swords has appeared in the Unexpected position, a woman will come into the scene who in many ways holds the key to the answers you seek. She is very logical and spends a great deal of time pondering the greater issues of this life, trying to formulate suitable theories that meet her primary certitude. She has a desire to communicate, and therefore will go to great lengths to reveal the truth, even if it causes embarrassment to herself or others. As a result of this, some people may perceive her as harsh, which is not an accurate reflection of her true personality. More appropriately, she seeks balance in all her dealings with others, and retribution when necessary.

Knight/ Prince If the Knight of Swords has appeared in the Unexpected position, a young person will figure prominently in the situation that prompted you to consult the oracle. He has an active mind, and unless he has learned to control his impulses, he will tend to say what he thinks with little or no regard as to who he may offend in the process. While he desires a relationship, he may not be willing to put forth the effort to maintain one, and would therefore prefer to think about how lovely it would be in a relationship, as opposed to actually being in one.

Page/ Princess If the Page of Swords has appeared in the Unexpected position, a young person will play a significant role in the successful outcome of the situation that prompted you to consult the oracle. This individual is very much thought oriented and will attempt to rationalise the world using logic and reason. When it is not possible to use intellect to solve problems, that is when problems arise in the form of anxiety and other coping mechanisms that normally manifest as neurosis.

Cups/Water

Ace If the Ace of Cups has appeared in the Unexpected position, much to your surprise, you will find happiness and fulfilment in an area that you never before thought of. You may also find the people around you are very sensitive to your moods, so you therefore need to endeavour

273

to keep your emotional state on an even keel, not allowing yourself to express an overabundance of positive or negative emotions. When you have been able to achieve an inner harmony, you will be quite surprised to discover the environment around you will attain a balance. The premise, you will eventually discover on your own, is that your surroundings are merely a reflection of what is going on inside of you. Therefore, if everyone and everything around you is in a state of chaos and disarray, it is merely a reflection of your inner self, which is also quite probably in a state of chaos and disarray. In the same vein, if your environment is orderly, your inner emotions are likely to be orderly as well. Therefore, if you would like your current situation to evolve to a point of tranquillity then it would be in your best interests to develop an inner calm, even amongst outer turmoil.

Two   If the Two of Cups has appeared in the Unexpected position, you will be quite surprised to meet one special person who you can relate to on a highly personal basis. In a world full of superficiality and insincerity, it is so nice to be able to intimately relate to another person who will instinctively understand you without your having to go into elaborate explanations. Maybe you have been drifting along, becoming complacent in your less than satisfactory personal relationships, assuming you would be obliged to carry on indefinitely tied to people who you simply cannot relate to on a holistic level. When you least expect it, you will meet someone who you are compatible with, someone who you do not have to work at getting along with. The sense of renewal you will feel at having met one of your soul -mates in this life will be enough to restore your faith in the order of the universe and the part you play in its intricate web.

Three   If the Three of Cups has appeared in the Unexpected position, you will be surprised by a sudden uplift in your social life. You will receive invitations to parties, concerts, company functions, and other occasions where you will be able to look forward to a good night out. Even if you are a religious person, you can still find times to socialise, such as church gatherings, revivals, and special ceremonies. This period of activity will be good for your soul, as it will give you a break from the day-to-day activities that can become somewhat boring, if other elements are not put in place to lessen the tedium.

Four   If the Four of Cups has appeared in the Unexpected position, you will reach a period of indecision that will leave you somewhat perplexed. The reason for this is because you are being offered something that may be of value of you, but you are reluctant to accept what will be fully given to you if you should decide to accept it. Although you are not consciously aware of the developing situation, your subconscious is highly attuned to the subtle clues the logical part of your mind has refused to acknowledge. In circumstances such as these, it is entirely appropriate to take your time deciding. It would be best to gather all of the relevant facts before deciding on one definitive course of action.

Five   If the Five of Cups has appeared in the Unexpected position, it appears you will be disappointed and hurt over one particular situation in your life. Perhaps you allowed yourself to exist in a state of denial because the truth was simply too painful for you to bear. In his state of self-induced ignorance, you allowed yourself to carry on; completely unaware of what was going on all around you. You cannot carry on forever, believing in people who are not worthy of such acclaim and getting your hopes up high, because the universe simply will not allow it. Part of the purpose of our existence in this world is that we grow, evolve and develop, thereby enabling us to progress along to the next phase of our soul evolution. It is for that reason if we refuse to see the truth on our own, the universe will set up a scenario that will force us to see the reality of what can often be a surreal situation. When you recover your composure, after having seen for yourself you did indeed have unrealistic expectations of certain individuals and organisations, you will be able to re-evaluate the role you played in a situation that was not wholly satisfactory. It will take some time, but you will be able to pick up the pieces and move on, much wiser for the experience.

Six   If the Six of Cups has appeared in the Unexpected position, you will be quite surprised to come into contact with someone from the past, and this person is quite possibly a link from your childhood. You will consequently spend a great deal of time thinking about the past and reflecting on how it has moulded you into the person you are today. You may also have occasion to spend time with children, and this could be a valuable experience for you, as you re-learn to think on more simplistic terms.

Seven   If the Seven of Cups has appeared in the Unexpected position, you will be presented with a series of options that are available to you. Some of them are viable opportunities that stand to yield a positive result, while others will yield nothing. At least one of these alternatives could even be detrimental to your wellbeing. It is for that reason you will need to think very carefully about anything you do; this is not a time to act hastily because you may need to go on a completely divergent path than the one you are currently on. You need to weigh all the pros and cons before endeavouring to make any irrevocable decisions. You may be quite surprised to find you are in a position that is entirely different from what you had originally supposed.

Eight   If the Eight of Cups has arrived in the Unexpected position, you will encounter a period of sadness and desolation, as there is a relationship or an endeavour you will have to give up. It is not a decision you will make lightly, but after having expended a great deal of energy in trying to turn the situation around to something that is beneficial for your development, you will reluctantly come to the realisation that you are fighting a lost cause. This is not to mean that you will never get your heart's desire in relation to that one specific issue, but in the foreseeable future it is not envisaged you will get a great deal of satisfaction from what you have been involved in. You and possibly the other persons involved need to complete more soul work, which is why what you desire is not possible at the moment.

Nine   If the Nine of Cups has appeared in the Unexpected position, you will have occasion to be very happy with yourself. You may come into a sum of money, which means you will be able to go out and enjoy yourself more. Because you have more expendable income to spend on eating, drinking and being merry, you may develop a weight problem an unfortunate consequence of a better standard of living. It is for that reason it would be in your best interests to begin a healthy eating and exercise programme so you don't find you can no longer fit into your clothes. You may find it beneficial to share your good fortune with others because it will not be much fun celebrating all on your own.

Ten   If the Ten of Cups has appeared in the Unexpected position, you will in all likelihood be quite surprised to find that you will experience happiness and contentment, which is largely due to the fact that you are satisfied with your personal relationships. You may have met that one special person who you want to spend your life with. The contentment of knowing you have met your one true soul mate in this life is enough to experience a type of euphoria that makes you happy to be a participant in such a physical reality in order to satisfy your more sensual needs and desires.

King   If the King of Cups has appeared in the Unexpected position, the situation that prompted you to consult the oracle will be influenced by a man in some way. He is quite sociable and therefore goes out of his way to get to know the people who he is surrounded by. He is often a caring, considerate person, but at times can be somewhat self-serving, focusing on his needs before the needs of others. At times he needs to be given direction about what the common good is because his sense of priorities can be completely different from what other people would expect. He does, however, have good intentions and can be kind-hearted, which is one of his qualities that are endearing to others.

Queen If the Queen of Cups has appeared in the Unexpected position, the situation that prompted you to consult the oracle will be influenced in some way by a woman who is highly emotional. If she has not learned to direct the physical manifestation of what she feels in a positive way, she can become highly strung, engaging in a wide variety of activities so she is so busy she will not have any possibility to think about the problems that plague her. If she does happen to slow down, she could very well fall into a depression because she is not able to reconcile herself with the elusiveness of her perceptions. If she has learned to integrate her instincts with her day-to-day activities, she will be able to intuitively select the most promising opportunities that are presented to her and therefore effectively steer clear of hidden pitfalls.

Knight/ If the Knight of Cups has appeared in the Unexpected position, you
Prince will come into contact with a young man who has a great deal of sensitivity and feeling. Because he is quite emotional, he can be somewhat explosive if other stabilising factors are not present. Because he has not matured and become grounded in his sense of self, he may not know how to direct his emotional tendencies in a positive manner, which could be detrimental to his personal relationships. Once he learns to focus his feelings into a positive outlet, he will be able to achieve much and contribute to this world.

Page/ If the Page of Cups has appeared in the Unexpected position, you will
Princess be introduced to a young person who has a great deal of sensitivity, which might not be readily apparent to the casual observer. It is for that reason you may need to probe into her psychological make-up to find out what makes her tick. The influence she plays could be positive or negative, so it would be wise to watch her carefully.

12 The Unknown

0 Fool   If The Fool has appeared in the Unknown position, there is someone operating in the background who is somewhat of a prankster. He may be a practical joker, playing tricks on others for his own personal amusement. If he is an unbalanced person, he may derive a sort of sadistic pleasure in the demise of others, and may therefore set about creating folly in the lives of people who really don't need any more distress. It is therefore essential to keep your affairs private and secure, revealing little to those who you have not developed a trusting rapport with. If any of your personal details were to get into the wrong hands, at the very least you could suffer an element of embarrassment amongst your contemporaries.

I Magician   If the Magician has appeared in the Unknown position, there is a very clever individual who is manipulating the situation in some way. He is quick-witted and is able to think swiftly on his feet, which enables him to successfully manoeuvre his way through life's little scrapes. He in all probability has a good standard of education; even if that isn't the case, he will endeavour to learn as much as he possibly can by utilising the many learning tools that may be made available to him. One problem he has is with the truth. This individual does not see the truth as factual evidence that he can use to make informed decisions that will affect him and those close to him. He sees the truth as something he can shape in order to fit into the elaborate web that makes up the existence he would like to create for himself and others. If you happen to be favoured by him, he can conjure elaborate tales that will show you in a good light. If, on the other hand, you have fallen out of favour over some real or imagined slight, he will use your name disparagingly in his lengthy yarns, slandering you and tarnishing your reputation without your knowledge. It is for that reason you need to keep your ear to the ground and listen intently to any gossip that may be circulating, because some of it may be about you.

II High Priestess   If The High Priestess is found in the Unknown position, you are not aware of this, but there is a young woman who is influencing the situation that prompted you to consult the oracle. The person in question is in all probability single, but if it transpires that she is in a relationship, it is not likely that it will be giving her the satisfaction she desires. The relationships this young woman forms with men are not likely to fulfil all of her needs, and she therefore looks for other things to fill the void in her life. She may undertake hobbies as a therapeutic pastime and may attempt to build a satisfactory social life that will put her in contact with a variety of people. She may also throw herself into her work and become the consummate career woman. She may even become the other woman in a heated affair with a married man, thereby allowing her to enjoy all the passion of marriage, but none of the commitment.

III Empress   If The Empress has appeared in the Unknown position, there is a woman who is working behind the scenes to play a significant role in the situation that prompted you to consult the oracle. She would like to have power, and therefore uses whatever influence she has to control whoever she can, such as children, husbands, friends and lovers. The problem lies in the fact that this woman is not necessarily content to allow them to live their own lives and make their own decisions. She prefers to use subtle manipulation to get people to do what she would like   them to do. When her covert manoeuvres fail, she is not above using overt tactics. When all else fails, she will resort all out warfare, engaging in a feud type mentality and forcing those people who she holds dear to take sides, risking any love and respect she may have acquired over the years. She believes that one way or another she will get what she wants in the end because her offspring would not dare to disobey her. She may very well succeed in what she wants, but the emotional blackmail she uses will only show her in her true light, which is not necessarily very pleasant.

IV Emperor   If The Emperor has appeared in the Unknown position, there is a very powerful man who is working behind the scenes to influence the situation that has prompted you to consult the oracle. He has such great drive and ambition that he will be successful in whatever he sets out to do, whether it is business, property development, the military, the police, or even the religious sector. He is somewhat authoritarian in nature and may not necessarily be well liked. Although he is about as individualistic as they come, he expects those who are subordinate to him to operate as a cohesive team to successfully accomplish the objectives he sets. It is for that reason he is somewhat of a paradox. This individual is a good person to have on your side because he can make or break your reputation and therefore affect any vocational ladder you choose to climb. It is best not to anger him because he is not the sort of person who you would like to have a battle with.

V
Hierophant

If The Hierophant has appeared in the Unknown position, there are some very important issues you need to be aware of before you can make any reasonable decisions regarding the future of the situation that has prompted you to consult the oracle. Although you are not aware of it, it appears that individuals close to you may have formed an alliance that will affect you in some way. These people could have entered into a contractual agreement, totally unknown to you. They may be at great pains to keep you from realising the truth, perhaps even hiding important documents or artefacts. Alternatively, someone close to you could have some very strong religious convictions, which will have an effect on you in some way. It is therefore essential you look for any clues to a person's religious beliefs or marital status before you pursue the issue further.

VI Lovers

If The Lovers has appeared in the Unknown position, it seems there are some individuals close to you who may very well be in love. They may be involved in a clandestine affair because they do not want to hurt others. The problem will occur, however, when the relationship progresses to the point where a decision will need to be made. The truth will come out sooner or later, and someone could be hurt if the decision that needs to be made will be a choice between one person or another. The best thing you can do is to look for any surreptitious clues as to the nature of the affair and then organise your life accordingly.

VII Chariot

If The Chariot has appeared in the Unknown position, there is an individual working in the background who has a very ambitious nature. He is quite driven to succeed and will therefore put all of this energy into getting what he wants out of life. He has a wide domain and prefers to travel extensively to view what he has or what he aspires to have. He is a courteous, polite individual, which will endear him to others so he has the ability to work his way to the top in his chosen field. It is important to keep in mind that underneath his friendly demeanour is a steely determination to succeed, and if he has to, he will step on people who get in his way.

VIII Strength If Strength has appeared in the Unknown position, there is a woman in the background working behind the scenes to effect the successful resolution of the situation that has prompted you to consult the oracle. She has an affinity with animals and especially can identify with the regal qualities of cats. She has a great deal of charm, which endears her to others, especially members of the opposite sex. She is a very gentle soul who has gained a great deal of experience that has been gleaned through her subliminal awareness of her past, present and future lives. She is highly psychic and is therefore able to access the Akashic records of others at will, knowing their destiny. This woman is such a wise, knowing soul that she has many admirers, and some of them may very well have commitments elsewhere to other people.

IX Hermit If The Hermit has appeared in the Unknown position, you may not be aware of it, but there is someone close to you who is feeling somewhat lonely. Even when in a crowded room, he does not feel as if there is anyone he can confide in. He may have put out feelers, dropped hints, and even suggested social outings, but no one has picked up on his desire and/or need for human company. As a result of this, he may spend a lot of time going deep within himself, reflecting upon the circumstances that brought him to the point where he finds himself in need of company. He may very well have people who he can spend his time with, but for some reason they do not fill the void within his soul. Perhaps there is something you can do to relieve the deafening silence he is feeling right now. Perhaps a phone call, a friendly chat, or even a social outing is all that is needed to ease the loneliness that has pervaded the depths of this lost soul's being.

X Wheel of Fortune If the Wheel of Fortune has appeared in the Unknown position, it seems the karmic wheels are set in motion and there is not a lot you can do about it. Although you have free will to decide your own personal destiny, you are also part of a group of individuals that has what can be best described as group karma. Groups, organisations and nations have their own karmic influences that they must work through in order to progress and develop along the evolutionary path they are destined for. This is precisely why groups, organisations and nations have certain characteristics that are stereotyped and caricatured throughout the physical universe. Sometimes during an intense karmic spell, we must forgo our own karmic and dharmic desires in order to fulfil the destiny of the greater good. This does not mean to imply that our own hopes, dreams and ambitions will be thwarted as a consequence of our group destiny, but it does mean that what we personally desire and need will have to take a back seat to the desires and needs of the group we are in. For example, when the area that we live in is encountering an economic recession or depression, it is quite likely we will feel the knock-on effect of such influences by experiencing a depressed financial situation as well, even if our natal horoscope indicates that in theory we should be financially well off. In addition, during times of famine, disease and war, young souls who are so full of promise for the future may have to give up their own personal dreams and ambitions to fulfil the karmic obligations of the group they belong to in order to enable that specific group to grow and develop as a unit in its own right. It is also for that reason souls have a tendency to incarnate together into groups and specific periods of time, thereby enabling that spiritual circle to fulfil its karmic destiny, as depicted in the Akashic records.

XI Justice If Justice has appeared in the Unknown position, you may not be aware of this, but the wheels of balance are in motion. Someone you know may be involved in litigation, but for reasons known only to them, they have decided not to broadcast the situation. The universe is in a constant state of motion and flux, correcting any imbalances that may exist within it. It is for that reason you need to ensure that your affairs are in order because even if you are able to keep any deceptions secret, the higher powers of our super-consciousness will ensure any deceptions come to light and are made public knowledge.

XII Hanged Man If The Hanged Man has appeared in the Unknown position, there is someone around you who is very depressed and does not know how to adequately express his feelings to other people. He perhaps feels very misunderstood, and for that reason does not feel as if he fits into the normal scheme of things. The reason for this is because he has not yet discovered his true path in this world. All the same, this knowledge does nothing to allay his feelings of being a fish out of water. Perhaps he needs a friend, and perhaps that friend could be you.

XIII Death If Death has appeared in the Unknown position, you are not aware of it, but all around you people are going through major transformations. These changes may at first be seen as massive upheavals, which is the universe's way of effecting transition when people do not want to make the necessary adjustments on their own. As a result of this, people around you may suffer job losses, difficulties at home, problems with school, losses of relationships, and in some cases, even death. You may not be aware of what is going on around you because many people are reluctant to discuss their difficulties, often considering it socially unacceptable to 'air one's dirty laundry' in public. It is for that reason that you must look for subtle clues that will keep you abreast of hidden agendas. The best course of action is to keep your mouth shut, and your eyes and ears open, and people will open up to you when they find you a worthy confidante. It is important for you to attune yourself to what is going on in the lives of others because any changes in their circumstances will eventually have a knock-on effect on you.

XIV Temperance

If Temperance has appeared in the Unknown position, the Universe is in the process of balancing and adjusting any areas where there is a lack of harmony. What is transpiring is of such a subtle nature that you and those around you are not aware of the transformation taking place. The opportunities that are being presented to you and those close to you are apparently so minor that you will not automatically give them any credence for making major life changes. However, those chance encounters today are what will influence your future, so it is essential to make the most of every opportunity, no matter how insignificant it may appear at the time.

XV Devil

If The Devil has appeared in the Unknown position, it seems that some individuals are undertaking a few nefarious activities behind your back, and you will not be too pleased to find out what is going on under your very nose. Perhaps someone close to you is embarking upon a path that is not suitable to what you desire and need for your soul growth. The fact this individual is taking on what you would perceive to be a more sinister outlook on life is an indicator that you may very well be entertaining company that is not suitable to your spiritual development. It is important to think carefully about the associations that you keep. If your relationships are not giving you the happiness and fulfilment you deserve as a celestial being, maybe it is time to sever those ties so more suitable individuals can enter into your sphere of awareness.

XVI Tower

If The Tower has appeared in the Unknown position, people around you are going through some major upheavals in their life. They may find they suddenly have to move house, which will be a somewhat stressful ordeal. Someone close to you may have an accident, which will deeply affect you because you are close to that person. You will no doubt lament about the unfairness of life, as you must eventually see people around you going through difficulties, which you are powerless to do anything about. During your observations you will receive clarity of mind and a unique awareness of the laws of cause and effect. It is then that you will more fully understand that every action has a reaction, and some individuals who seem unlucky are not total victims in the unfoldment of their destiny. Perhaps they had to move house because they did not pay their rent or damaged the property. Possibly an accident occurred because they did not follow adequate safety precautions. It could be that they lost their job because they were not doing it properly. There is a reason for everything and it is up to you to ask probing questions and analyse the situation before making any biased assumptions.

XVII Star If The Star has appeared in the Unknown position, it seems people around you are on very friendly terms and are making plans for the future. They are full of hope because they have not yet been affected by the knocks life gives us all. They may work closely in an educational setting because there is a strong desire to learn and disseminate the information they have been given from higher sources. It is possible you have not been included in the happy gathering because they feel you would not be interested. It is for that reason you should put on a happy face and try to be a bit friendlier if you would like to be included in group social activities.

XVIII Moon If The Moon has appeared in the Unknown position, you really need to take care to protect your assets because nothing truly is as it seems. Everything is in a muddle and your auric vision is being blinded, thereby preventing you from seeing things as they actually are. Because we all have certain tasks we are obliged to perform whilst we are incarnate in the earth plane, certain ethereal filters have been incorporated into our biological bodies, which prevent us from seeing the world as it really is. If we were to perceive the complexity of our world beyond our five physical senses, it would simply be too much for our three dimensional bodies to be able to incorporate into our information processes. We would see a spectrum of colours that reach far beyond the three primary colours and various hues, tones and shades that are composed of their combination. We would see shapes and dimensions far beyond what we normally can perceive, and we would realise the mansions Jesus spoke of in his father's house, are composed of a crystalline foundation amongst vapours and mist, almost like glass, except for the fact that they are shatter-proof. We would also be able to hear with a clarity we have never before experienced, as we are able to perceive the angels speaking to us, filling us in on little known karmic truths. The reason why filters are in place is because if we were able to experience the sensation of oneness of the universe, we would be so engrossed in the many mysteries of the universe that we would forget to remember our mission in this life. Although we are weighed down by our three dimensional bodies in a three dimensional physical world, we have been given the gift of auric vision, which enables us to intuitively perceive that which we have no conscious reason to know. It is this sixth sense that helps us in our life and prevents us from seriously injuring ourselves during mishaps. There are times, however, when our auric vision becomes blocked, and it is these times when we are not even able to use the logical reasoning ability that we all have to make adequate life choices. When we are under tremendous stress or under the influence of cigarettes, drugs alcohol, and even food, we are clogging up our bodily processes and therefore unable to accurately perceive people and situations as they truly are. This is one of those times when you are not aware of what is going on underneath your very nose.

XIX Sun

If The Sun has appeared in the Unknown position, it seems love is in the air, but you are totally unaware of it. You, or someone you know, may be in the process of starting a family, but for reasons known only to you, it has not become apparent to anyone else. An animal may soon be coming into your life, and this can be seen only as a positive thing. Animals are able to give a pure, wholesome love that is uncomplicated by the intricate web of human life. Their love shows no bounds, and this may be something you need to restore your faith in the world around you. Exhibitionism is likely, as someone close to you may be showing off, either to get attention or to add an element of shock to people unprepared for such displays. It is for that reason you need to look around your immediate environment. Is there someone close to you who craves attention? If so, then this individual may need to be reminded there are other more orthodox ways to make his presence known.

XX Judgement

If Judgement has appeared in the Unknown position, you or someone close to you may be in need of healing, but are totally unaware of it. Physically, you could be without symptoms, and you will not be aware of the illness until it has entered into its more advanced stages. Emotionally, you may have endured a trauma, and not knowing how to handle the experience, you repressed or denied it. During repression, you simply push the incident to the back of your mind, where it resides until you feel safe enough to recall it and process how you feel about it on a healthy level. When you deny something, however, your mind twists the experience around so you are able to make yourself believe something entirely different altogether. While you may be totally unaware of your need for healing, your auric make-up is composed of each and every psychic wound that you have encountered that has not been properly dealt with and integrated into your core being. The key here is to stop, look, listen, and keep your mind as quiet as possible, and it is then you will awaken from your slumber of eternal forgetfulness.

XXI World If The World has appeared in the Unknown position, there is something in your life that has reached a natural conclusion, but perhaps you have not realised it. You may have been involved in a relationship, vocation or hobby you have outgrown, but since it is so much a part of your day to day activity, it may be difficult for you to see that you really need to move on in your life. The best way to gauge whether something has outlived its usefulness is to ask yourself how bored you are. If you are bored, ask yourself what you need to do to alleviate the boredom. It may mean you need to change jobs, begin a course of study, or start a hobby. In relationship matters, you will need to have a heart to heart discussion with your significant other to think of ways you can to renew a relationship that is on the verge of going stale.

Wands/Rods/Fire

Ace If the Ace of Wands has appeared in the Unknown position, it seems there is a great deal of creativity going on around you, but for some reason you are not utilising such energy to your fullest potential. You are not using your psychic potential and for that reason are missing out on much spiritual insight and knowledge of the Akashic records. In order to tap into the psychic elements that are a part of your environment, it would be best for you to begin to engage in creative endeavours, such as drawing, painting or design. There is universal knowledge you can attune yourself to, you just need to make yourself an appropriate channel for the information.

Two If the Two of Wands has appeared in the Unknown position, there are two individuals who have come together to form a partnership, but for some reason have decided to keep it quiet. These people may be involved in a working relationship, but there might be more to the situation than meets the eye. They may meet together for a sporting, academic or even religious event, and for whatever reason, they need the mental stimulation this other person affords them. Their relationship, however, is of interest to you because you need to be aware of it so you can make your own choices with regard to the situation that prompted you to consult the oracle. It is for that reason you need to keep your ear to the ground and look for any subtle clues as to the nature of this major life lesson you are being presented with.

Three   If the Three of Wands has appeared in the Unknown position, there is a group of people who have gathered together to accomplish a common goal. It may be social, sport, business, academic or religious, and for some reason you have not been included in the group. The reasons for your exclusion could vary; you may not have the necessary skills to compete with your contemporaries, you may have a different belief system that would keep you from harmonising in the group, or more negatively, you could be under a great deal of stress that prevents you from interacting with your peers in a positive manner. If you are feeling left out, you need to ask yourself if the reason is because of something you or the group has done. If it transpires it is because of something you have done then maybe you can take actions to remedy the situation.

Four   If the Four of Wands has appeared in the Unknown position, there is a family gathering that you are totally unaware of. It may concern a family celebration or other important event, but for some reason you have not been included in the organisation of it. The reasons for your exclusion can vary, but it is important you are aware of it because it will affect you in an indirect fashion. It is for that reason you need to be on the lookout for clues to the nature of other people's involvement. When you become aware of exactly what this group of people is involved in, you will be able to make your reasonable life choices accordingly.

Five   If the Five of Wands has appeared in the Unknown position, there are people around you who are at odds with one another. The reason for their strife is because they are not happy with themselves. If these individuals were content, they would have no need to bicker amongst themselves. The simple fact of the matter is some people just love a good fight because it is the only way they know how to relate to other people. Perhaps they did not receive enough positive attention during their more formative years, and as a consequence lack the supportive emotions that arise from hugs and cuddles given for the sheer sake of showing love and emotion to someone they are fond of. If the only attention a young person receives is a smack or verbal admonishment then he in turn will become conditioned to show that kind of attention to others, which is a very negative way to relate. It is important for you to astutely determine exactly where this backbiting is coming from so you can make sure you don't allow yourself to become drawn into it.

Six   If the Six of Wands has appeared in the Unknown position, there are people around you who are making plans for their future success and prosperity. If the nature of their venture is professional, their success could possibly mean you will be required to defer to them in some way. Because the world we live in is so fickle and people's tastes change quite rapidly, you need to stay abreast of such interesting times and adapt yourself accordingly. Because you will never know precisely when you will need someone as an ally, it would be in your best interests to cultivate positive relationships, no matter how irrelevant they may appear at the time.

Seven   If the Seven of Wands appears in the Unknown position, someone you know may be having some difficulties, which could very well indirectly affect you. You may be close to an individual who is under a great deal of stress in his personal or professional life, which is affecting how he conducts his affairs. There may also be a difficult economic climate, which means there may be less money to purchase much-needed products or services. It is for that reason you need to remain sensitive to the needs and desires of those around you. When the situation improves, as it inevitably will, those who you helped or did not hinder along their way will remember your acts of humaneness and repay you in kind.

Eight   If the Eight of Wands has appeared in the Unknown position, it seems some people close to you will be making a journey, probably in respect to their duties or obligations. This individual may be given a promotion or more responsibilities at work, which will have an indirect impact on you. You may find yourself in a subordinate position, when in the past, you were regarded as a peer. Possibly, because of the personal circumstances going on in your own life, it is difficult for you to take an interest in other people. As a result, you may appear to be unapproachable to those who would otherwise be friendly to you. Therefore, if you would like to know what is going on with others, you will need to take an active interest in them, even if it means allowing your own problems and concerns to take a backseat, for a little while at least.

Nine   If the Nine of Wands has appeared in the Unknown position, there are some individuals around you who feel as if they have been put in the defensive position. Perhaps they lack confidence in their ability to perform well, and as a result see any comments made by you or anybody else as an affront, which will automatically make them feel as if they must defend themselves. Such feelings will result in you not receiving all of the information that you need to carry out your day-to-day activities. The important thing is to try to cultivate an environment of mutual trust and acceptance, which will give other individuals the feeling they can freely relate to you on all manner of subjects.

Ten   If the Ten of Wands has appeared in the Unknown position, the circumstances you are in are tense at best. The reason for this is because those around you have made commitments they are having difficulties keeping. As a result this is putting a great deal of stress on all parties involved. The economic climate may not be right for growth in a profitable capacity, and this means it is highly improbable that any significant advances will be made. The situation will affect you because you could lose out on employment prospects, which would affect your financial situation. Therefore, even though you personally may not be responsible for the austere environment you and those around you have been enveloped in, you will in all likelihood be made to suffer for the mistakes of others. It is for that reason a team effort to work in a positive, proactive direction is what will be needed to overcome the difficult times ahead.

King   If the King of Wands has appeared in the Unknown position, there is an older man who is influencing the situation that prompted you to consult the oracle. He might work in a professional capacity, giving advice to people who he feels need it. He also has a great deal of personal magnetism, which makes him a very attractive individual indeed. Because he has so much influence amongst his contemporaries, he either knowingly or unknowingly is working behind the scenes to effect some major changes in your life, which could include a change in job, home, vocation, religion or partner.

Queen   If the Queen of Wands has appeared in the Unknown position, there is a woman who can be quite animated, and she works behind the scenes in some capacity. She may not even be aware that she has such a major influence over you, but she does, nevertheless, play an important role in your life. To find out who this woman is and what role she plays, it is important to ask astute questions that are designed to feel out people's values and intentions. It is also important that you look for any hidden meanings in the conversations you have with others, because much can be gleaned from simple Freudian slips the speakers may not even be aware of making.

Knight/ Prince   If the Knight of Wands has appeared in the Unknown position, there is a young man who is working behind the scenes to influence the situation in some way. He may be totally unaware of the part he is playing in the resolution of the situation that has prompted you to consult the oracle, but he could also be surreptitiously working to influence the situation in his favour. It is for that reason you need to become a careful observer with regard to the activities and subtle nuances of others, because the non-verbal cues are the ones that will lead to you an insightful awareness of this person who has become an interloper in your current circumstances.

Page/ Princess   If the Page of Wands has appeared in the Unknown position, there is a young person who is influencing the situation in some way. Whether you are aware of her presence or not, her mere association with the situation that prompted you to consult the oracle will have an impact on the successful resolution of any problems you may encounter. She has a cheerful disposition and enjoys having a good time. She likes to be the centre of attention and will engage in attention seeking tactics of either a positive or negative ilk to get a reaction from others.

Pentacles/Disks/Earth

Ace   If the Ace of Pentacles has appeared in the Unknown position, it seems a new set of economic forces will come into the climate to shake things up a bit. It is for that reason you may be asked to invest in a venture of some sort. You will, however, need to think very carefully about any financial arrangements you make because there is no guarantee you will receive a return on your investment.

Two   If the Two of Pentacles has appeared in the Unknown position, someone close to you is just beginning to have financial difficulties. They may have to juggle their finances, often waiting until they get their final reminder before paying their bills. This could inadvertently affect you because if you lend this individual money it will take you a long time to get it back, and you will have to be the one to instigate any requests for reimbursement, which will undoubtedly put a strain on your relationship with that individual.

Three   If the Three of Pentacles has appeared in the Unknown position, some-one close to you will be undergoing a change in his or her finances, which is likely to be for the better. They may move house, which will be seen as a step up the material ladder. They will have more money, which means their living circumstances and standard of living will improve considerably. This will indirectly affect you because you stand to benefit from this person's prosperity, especially if you are intimately involved with him. If the person in question is your partner then it would be assumed that you would be able to share in his increased material wealth. In the same vein, because he has greater wealth, it would not be unreasonable to assume he would become more attrac-tive to others. It is for that reason that if this individual means a lot to you, you would need to exercise the necessary precautions to ensure he stays with you.

Four   If the Four of Pentacles has appeared in the Unknown position, there is someone close to you who is quite frugal. He does not like to spend his money and prefers to keep it stashed away, hopefully in a safe place. Correction: while he does not necessarily mind spending money on himself, he is loath to spend money on other people. While this does not necessarily pose a problem at the moment, what would happen if you should decide to become intimately involved with this person? If you do enter into an alliance with this person, you would be expected to contribute your fair share financially to keep the relationship on an even keel. What you consider being fair and equitable might not neces-sarily be what he considers to be a fair share, and that is where the problems will arise. In addition, if you were to decide to marry and start a family with this individual, more difficulties will present them-selves. If this individual is not prepared to share what he has with you, could you possibly expect him to provide for any children that might arise from the union? These are serious questions you need to ask your-self about this person. If you are prepared to spend your life putting more into such a relationship than you might receive, then such a liai-son may be worth pursuing. If, however, you would prefer to be with someone who is going to be generous with you then you might want to consider looking around some more for a more giving soul.

Five   If the Five of Pentacles has appeared in the Unknown position, some-one close to you is having difficulties in the physical world we live in. These problems could very well be financial in nature because one of the biggest worries we have is our ability to provide adequately for our families and ourselves. It has become a well-established fact, however, that worries about money can often lead to depression. Therefore, the very nature of the problem will become twofold because when a person is depressed, they lose confidence, which will ultimately affect their earning ability because they would be reluctant to take on the more high profile, financially rewarding jobs. When people have financial difficulties there are other areas of their life that suffer as well because they may not be able to attend schools, participate in social activities, and even attend church services.

Six   If the Six of Pentacles has appeared in the Unknown position, someone may be helping you out in some way and you do not even realise it. You may be receiving subsidised housing, food, clothing or transportation from a benevolent soul. You may also have been helped along your career path by someone who feels you deserve a break. It is important, therefore, to never look a gift horse in the mouth because benevolence does not come into our lives often. The important thing to remember is the universe is in a constant state of flux, balancing out any inequalities that may exist. For that reason it is your duty as a celestial being in a physical world to perform your share of good deeds in order to give back to the universe what has been given to you.

Seven   If the Seven of Pentacles has appeared in the Unknown position, you and those around you are engaged in a waiting game. There are individuals around you who are working in preparation for a big event you may not even be aware of. The effects of these activities will not become apparent until much later, but when you finally are to be made privy to the events that are going on under your very nose, everything will fit in with a renewed clarity that would not have been possible before. Because the individuals involved are not likely to go out of their way to fill you in on their long-term hopes, dreams and ambitions, you will need to take it upon yourself to act as a sleuth and uncover pertinent details using your own higher cognition.

Eight   If the Eight of Pentacles has appeared in the Unknown position, someone close to you will very likely begin a new job or take a course that will enable them to learn new skills. The hands are paramount, as this individual will be required to work with them. There will be a learning curve that needs to be overcome, but when he becomes proficient at this new task, he will be highly skilled at what he does. This re-training may come about through necessity, as circumstances may arise where he must find a new job or vocation in life. He may also decide to take up a hobby, which is likely to be a very rewarding experience. You will in all probability be affected by this new experience, as he will relay to you the events that brought about his transition onto this new path in life.

Nine   If the Nine of Pentacles has appeared in the Unknown position, someone you know may need a period of rest and convalescence, possibly spending time in a quiet, serene environment to enable him to recuperate and recharge his batteries. He may have acquired a sum of money, which will allow him to take time off work to spend time on himself. Even if he hasn't received money through benevolent sources, he may need to live off of his savings, which could pose a source of frustration for him. This is a time where he needs to rest and reflect on the consequences of his actions and inactions, because when his equilibrium is restored, he will be able to view the world with renewed clarity and make appropriate life decisions, which could very well affect you.

Ten   If the Ten of Pentacles has appeared in the Unknown position, it seems someone close to you is heavily involved with their family, so much so that it is affecting your personal circumstances. You may not be aware of it because discussions and negotiations are going on without your knowledge, but it is very likely the conversations that are taking place concern you. It is crucial you maintain your integrity at all times, even when you have every right to be angry. If you are romantically involved with this person, you need to ask yourself if you would like to continue in a relationship with an individual who will potentially put his family before you.

King   If the King of Pentacles has appeared in the Unknown position, there is a man influencing the situation from afar. He may be able to wield considerable influence because he either controls finances or business endeavours, which will affect your standard of living considerably. He may also be able to influence the people around you, which will ultimately have an impact on how comfortable you will feel with certain people and situations. It is therefore important you tread carefully with this individual and follow established protocol when dealing with him.

Queen   If the Queen of Pentacles has appeared in the Unknown position, there is a woman who is playing a significant role in the situation that has prompted you to consult the oracle. Because she is so level-headed, she has acted appropriately to ensure her physical needs are being taken care of. She may have wealth and prosperity in her own right, which instils in her a level of confidence that is not evident in other less fortunate souls. She is a sensuous person and has a healthy appetite for food, wine and sex. It should therefore come as no surprise to find she has no shortage of admirers who will help to share these good times with her. She does, however, guard what she sees as her possessions fiercely, and is therefore not one to become tangled in any disputes with regard to money, property, or even friendships.

Knight/ Prince If the Knight of Pentacles has appeared in the Unknown position, there is a young man who is playing a significant part in the situation that has prompted you to consult the oracle. He is generally a very stable individual who can act as a grounding influence during those more uncertain times. He is headstrong because he knows what he wants. Although he has not yet figured out how he would like to go about getting that which he desires, he has a strong, rational intellect that he can use to plan his agenda. He is somewhat sensual because he enjoys the luxurious things this material world has to offer. If for some reason he is not in a position to go out and get all of those nice things he desires, he does not mind asking his friends and partners to help him out, sometimes even if it means other people will have to do without so he can live the lifestyle he feels he is worthy of.

Page/ Princess If the Page of Pentacles has appeared in the Unknown position, a young person is playing a paramount role in the situation that prompted you to consult the oracle. She has a very practical mind and therefore has a sensible approach to life, even at a very young age. As a grounded individual, she is highly focused on whatever tasks she is presented with, whether it is a hobby, schoolwork, or vocation in life.

Swords/Air

Ace If the Ace of Swords has appeared in the Unknown position, the universal laws of balance are at work to remedy any inequalities or injustices that are inherent in your current situation. There are some circumstances that have an evolutionary path that transcends far beyond the affairs of mere mortals, which indicates there are some things we humans have very little control over. For instance, in the last century human beings have placed a tremendous stress on the earth by polluting it and using mass farming techniques. So much harm to an already fragile ecology could not go on indefinitely, and such abuses of power have resulted in the phenomenon called global warming, which will have a major impact on the structure of the earth as we know it. On a more ordinary level, if a person abuses his power in any way, shape or form, his activities will come to light sooner or later, showing him for the person he actually is. The Ace of Swords shows no sympathy and cannot be biased one way or another. Being dual edged, it sees things as right or wrong, and will use the magnificence of its archetypal energies to set about correcting any inequalities. It is for that reason you really need to ensure all of your affairs are ethical and above reproach because any surreptitious activities will eventually be revealed to any relevant parties.

Two   If the Two of Swords has appeared in the Unknown position, certain individuals are intentionally keeping you in the dark with regard to some issues that will have a very definite impact on your wellbeing. At the very best they are simply withholding information from you because they consider it to be a private matter. At the very worst, they are intentionally giving you misinformation, which will affect your ability to carry out your day to day activities. Because you are not aware of all of the facts, it will be very difficult for you to make any appropriate long-range plans for yourself. It is for that reason now is not the time to engage in any permanent agreements with individuals who you do not know inside and out.

Three   If the Three of Swords has appeared in the Unknown position, it seems there are some nefarious activities going on behind your back. You may not be aware of it, but there are individuals associated with your milieu who are quite definitely mean and spiteful. The hidden activities ave come about because the persons perpetrating harm on others have character defects that are a result of psychological wounds that have never properly healed. As a result of these injuries that are quite obvious in the auric make-up of the person, their personalities have not properly developed, and they consequently have a desire to harm others in the same manner they were harmed. The problem that presents itself is the fact that every time they knowingly and premeditatedly inflict pain on another soul, it does not relieve the pain they feel within themselves, but only intensifies the self hatred and self loathing they feel. Some souls who are not inclined to lash out at others in an attempt to ease the searing anguish that permeates their being will resort to self harm, which acts as a temporary catharsis, but never truly heals the aching inside. The recurring problem, however, is the pain never goes away because the wound has not been healed. As a result of this, they must inflict pain on themselves and others repeatedly so they can achieve a temporary release of the tension within, thus creating a never-ending cycle of abuse on themselves and others. It is for that reason you may have found yourself to be the target of such unwarranted abuse, but instead of despising the perpetrator of such acts, you should pity him. It is he who needs healing, not you.

Four If the Four of Swords has appeared in the Unknown position, there is someone close to you who has uncertainties about a particular situation, and for that reason he seems to be hesitant about forming a more formalised relationship with you. There is the possibility he has heard whispers from others who do not have your best interests at heart. Because he trusts these individuals who are so earnestly trying to manipulate him, he does not want to see the harm they are perpetrating. These individuals have their own personal agendas and may not necessarily have his best interests at heart. There is nothing you can do to influence this person's opinions because he is not receptive to anything you have to say in the matter. The only thing you can do is to ensure your own actions are above reproach. Eventually, he will see those individuals who had been whispering in his ear had agendas at cross-purposes to his own. Until that time, the only thing you can do is weather the psychological storm ahead.

Five If the Five of Swords has appeared in the Unknown position, there are acrimonious negotiations going on behind your back, which will have an impact on you. It seems you are unknowingly surrounded by an air of slander, libel and deliberate misinformation. People around you are in dispute, and whether you like it or not, you have been caught up in idle gossip. When all is revealed, which it inevitably will be, you will not want your name to be included amongst those who will be reputed to have been trying to stir up angst.

Six If the Six of Swords has appeared in the Unknown position, there are some individuals close to you who are considering moving on in their lives. It seems there is a particular relationship or situation they are not happy with, and although they may not have expressed their dissatisfaction in a manner that has been readily apparent to you, they have, metaphorically speaking, come to the end of their tether. The problem may arise in the fact that because you have not been receptive to the verbal and non-verbal cues that have been presented to you, it will seem to be a decision that has come totally out of the blue. The problem that may also arise is the departing of this individual will leave a void in your life that will not be so easy to fill. Therefore, it would be in your best interests to become more alert to the signals people are sending out, and ask probing questions to ascertain the true intentions of others.

Seven If the Seven of Swords has appeared in the Unknown position, there are surreptitious and possibly even wicked activities going on under your very nose. People who you had supposed to be your friends are taking advantage of your good nature by taking things from you that they have no right to appropriate. If you have told one particular person something in confidence, it is very likely that individual will repeat what you thought you were confiding in the strictest of privacy, which could cause considerable embarrassment to you if the wrong persons were to find out that information. If you have entrusted someone with property or finances, it is possible that person has decided to appropriate some of it for himself. Some people who you know in a professional capacity may take your ideas and work, and pass it on as their own, which will help them to promote themselves. With these factors in mind, it would be prudent to handle your affairs personally, thereby preventing any wickedness from opportunists who you might meet.

Eight If the Eight of Swords has appeared in the Unknown position, someone close to you is experiencing a mental block, which is preventing him from acting and speaking freely. It could be that he is experiencing a high level of dissatisfaction with regard to one particular aspect or relationship in his life. Because he does not possess the vocabulary to adequately express his feelings on the matter, not knowing precisely which words to use, he chooses to say nothing, thereby prolonging the inner paralysis he feels. He may also be much too tactful to express any negative sentiments, so he chooses to say nothing about the issue, thereby denying both of you the opportunity to grow as individuals within the relationship. With this knowledge in mind, perhaps it would be wise for you to consciously use your powers of perception and look beneath outward appearances to try to gain a greater understanding of exactly what is making this person reluctant to speak openly.

Nine If the Nine of Swords has appeared in the Unexpected position, there is someone close to you who is suffering from worry and anxiety, and is losing sleep in the process. He may suffer from a mental illness, such as any one of a number of depressions, psychosis, neurosis, obsessive-compulsive disorders, or an addiction. Because things are not right in his head, his behaviour can be quite erratic, which can be somewhat confusing for individuals who are not able to pinpoint the problem. This individual may be experiencing symptoms of a mental illness due to a chemical imbalance, which could be the result of food intolerances, a hormone imbalance or digestive problems, which would adversely affect the body's ability to absorb essential nutrients. Because this person who is exhibiting such problematic behaviour is close to you, it can be a perplexing time because you are not certain exactly what the problem is. It is therefore essential that you help this individual to get the appropriate medical attention in order to ease his suffering.

Ten   If the Ten of Swords has appeared in the Unknown position, you are surrounded by an atmosphere of betrayal and letdown. Someone you know has been harmed in a big way by the activities of others, and you may have unwittingly played a part in his demise. It is for that reason you may not be very popular because some individuals may hold you responsible for the downfall of others. The best way you can lessen the impact of what appears to be a rather unfortunate situation is to make sure all of your activities are ethical and strictly business. You really need to be careful what you say because other more malevolent souls may take any statements you utter and twist them around to mean something entirely different. It is also important to be aware that if the individual who has been badly let down holds you responsible for his demise in some way, he may seek retribution, which could cause further problems for you.

King   If the King of Swords has appeared in the Unknown position, there is an intellectually powerful man who is operating behind the scenes in a certain capacity to affect the situation that prompted you to consult the oracle. He has a mind that is capable of processing large quantities of information to come up with logical conclusions, which indicates he may work in a professional capacity, dealing with large quantities of data. Because he has such rapid deductive ability, he is capable of manipulating information so it appears to be something that it really isn't, thereby persuading more impressionable souls to do his bidding. It is therefore essential you listen critically to the message this man attempts to impart to others. In addition, it is essential you double-check all of the information he presents to you for accuracy, seeking outside help if necessary. He is a master manipulator, capable of bamboozling people with an overwhelming logic.

Queen   If the Queen of Swords has appeared in the Unexpected position, there is a woman operating behind the scenes to influence the situation that has prompted you to consult the oracle. She is thoughtful and considerate, and for that reason is often well liked by others. She spends much time in deep thought, however, which could cause her to lose sight of her true purpose in this life. She is very knowledgeable on a wide variety of subjects and tries to impart what she knows to others. Because she is always searching for the perfect relationship, she may find that one person is often not enough to satisfy all of her needs. It is for that reason she will need several people in her life to fulfil the needs of her multifaceted personality.

Knight/ Prince If the Knight of Swords has appeared in the Unknown position, there is a young man working behind the scenes to effect the object of your enquiry. He has an active mind and therefore needs to stay mentally stimulated or he could have difficulties functioning in a productive capacity. While he desires a happy partnership, most of his affairs and relationships are more a part of his elaborate fantasy world than what is actually transpiring in the material world. The reason for this is that he is such an idealist that few, if any, mere mortals will be able to live up to the high standards he sets. For that reason if he is able to settle down in a formal relationship with one individual, he will need other outlets in the form of people outside of the relationship, or a highly developed fantasy world. In his fantasies his perfect partner will exist and never let him down.

Page/ Princess If the Page of Swords has appeared in the Unknown position, there is a young person who is operating behind the scenes to influence the situation in some way. She is quite communicative and is therefore able to establish a rapport easily with many people. She also enjoys one to one relationships, and treats everyone as if they are special. Because she is so personable, she rarely has a shortage of friends and acquaintances, and she needs these people to be near her because she has a very strong desire to fit into a group.

Cups/Water

Ace If the Ace of Cups has appeared in the Unknown position, there exists within you the capability for everlasting happiness, but you first need to clear away a few blockages you do not even know exist at this time. It is not so much a fact that you are not aware of the blockages in your auric make-up, but you have allowed yourself to be lulled into an eternal forgetfulness, similar to Homer's epic poem. In Odyssey, Odysseus and his group of men where almost lulled into opium-induced indifference and thereby temporarily lost their way home during the course of their journey. In the same vein, you have allowed yourself to live in an indefinite state of self-induced narcosis, and thereby allowed yourself to lose consciousness of the traumas that have brought about the blockages in your psyche. Now is the time to wake up from your self-induced state of indifference so you can begin to feel the intense happiness and elation that is in fact your birthright.

Two   If the Two of Cups has appeared in the Unknown position, there is someone around you who seems to be extremely happy, as he or she has found someone with whom they are highly compatible. This sense of contentment they feel is likely to spill over into other areas of their life, as they will see the futility of squabbles over supposedly important issues, which, if the truth is known, are not that huge in the grand scheme of things. They are likely to become somewhat introverted, as they would prefer to spend their free time with the one person who they feel they are truly compatible with. This newfound love and harmony may be wonderful for the participants involved, but if one of the players happens to be someone who you are committed to and rely on on a daily basis, it could pose problems. It is essential, therefore, that you delve deeper into the absences of someone dear to you if you feel they may be sharing their affections with another.

Three   If the Three of Cups has appeared in the Unknown position, there are some individuals around you who are engaged in an abundance of social activities. These festivities are likely to be somewhat prolonged, as they eat, drink and make merry on a regular basis. These social activities can be quite positive, except for the fact that since you are not being made aware of these activities, there is the possibility you are being excluded for one reason or another. While you may receive some insight if you go right out and ask why you are not being included in these social activities, a more subtle approach may reveal more pertinent information with less embarrassment. It would therefore be best to use a more intuitive approach by observing body language and the non-verbal clues one unconsciously lets out. While you may very well be hurt by the exclusion you feel, even if you were invited to such social activities, you may very well not enjoy the company. Alternatively, it may be in your best interests to make friends who have personalities you are more attuned to because in reality you would glean much more enjoyment from their company.

Four   If the Four of Cups has appeared in the Unknown position, there is someone close to you who may be having doubts about his relationship with you, even though you may very well be totally unaware of any reservations he has. The reason for this is because you have allowed yourself to become so mentally embroiled in how you perceive the relationship to be that you have lost touch with how it actually is. The clues of his uncertainty are there if you look closely, but if you are having a relationship in your mind, it will be significantly more difficult for you to perceive what is really going on between the two of you. It is for that reason you need to dissociate yourself from the relationship and look at it with a critical mind, thinking logically rather than emotionally, and it is there that the true nature of your liaison will slowly dawn on you.

Five   If the Five of Cups has appeared in the Unknown position, it seems there is someone close to you who is disappointed in a recent turn of events. This individual may very well be going through a depression, as he attempts to come to terms with the fact that his ideals have not matched reality. It could be this person is disappointed in you because you have not lived up to the expectations he had of you. He may not have openly expressed his disappointment to you, but if you observe his demeanour, it is likely he will express an anger that wells up just beneath the surface of his conscious awareness, and can be seen as a dichotomy of what appears to be a placid demeanour. This can take the form of sarcastic comments, veiled jokes, or passive aggressive actions. Is there a promise you have made you have not kept? Have you not met specific obligations to a specific person? Those are questions you need to ask yourself because although you may have forgotten all about it, the person close to you hasn't.

Six   If the Six of Cups has appeared in the Unknown position, children figure prominently in the situation that has prompted you to consult the oracle. Someone close to you may be mulling over events from the past, revelling in the idea of the good times he had, and wishing to recreate those times. What is important to remember is the fact that as universal beings, we are all in a process of evolvement, changing subtly with every second of every day. Therefore, even if one manages to get in touch with friends from the past to re-create those good times, the reunion will never be the same as it was in past times. It is also important to note that children will figure prominently in some capacity, and it is therefore important to search for clues to exactly whose children they may be.

Seven   If the Seven of Cups has appeared in the Unknown position, there is someone close to you who is contemplating making a change in his life that will very likely have an effect on you. The problem will arise in the fact that this individual will not be in possession of accurate information, which will result in his inability to make an appropriate decision that will be beneficial for the both of you. It is for that reason that if someone close to you is going to be making decisions that will have an effect on you, it would be in your best interests to take it upon yourself to research the appropriate information, using whatever means available to you, thereby assisting in the decision making process.

Eight   If the Eight of Cups has appeared in the Unknown position, it seems someone you know has been experiencing a high level of dissatisfaction with one particular relationship or situation for quite some time. This individual may very well have tried his best to adapt to an environment that was not necessarily to his liking. He may very well have verbally and non-verbally expressed his ambivalence to a situation that was becoming increasingly untenable. The fact is, however, that this particular situation or relationship has not been suitable to his soul growth, and he has begun to feel the pull of his psyche to move on to more rewarding endeavours. This person has truly tried to make a go of the situation and has felt he has failed. He has therefore decided to accept the fact that there are some things in this life he is not destined to have, and has made the decision to walk away. What you need to be concerned about is that this individual may be walking away from you in the process, which may or may not be to your liking. It is for that reason you need to proactively ascertain exactly what the problem is so you can take corrective actions to resolve any inequalities, if necessary.

Nine   If the Nine of Cups has appeared in the Unknown position, there is someone close to you who appears happy on the outside to those who can see this individual at a passing glance. This individual needs to be observed with somewhat more depth and with a critical mind in order to realise there is a lot more to this person than meets the eye. This person may appear to be happy on the outside because he has learned maladaptive coping mechanisms to stressful situations that are rooted deeply in his subconscious, as a consequence of events he has had difficulty coming to terms with. Although the events that prompted these coping mechanisms have been long forgotten, buried somewhere with the hidden recesses of his mind, the mechanisms have become so much a part of him that he continues with these habits without any apparent knowledge of why. It is for that reason this individual may tend to take things to excess, such as overeating, over-drinking, or over-smoking, just to name a few of the vices that prevail in the society we are currently a part of. It is for that reason you need to take a careful look at those around you to see if they have adopted any unhealthy habits. If it is the case, maybe you can lend a helping hand to assist them in overcoming what is bothering them.

Ten   If the Ten of Cups has appeared in the Unknown position, there is a couple close to you who have found everlasting happiness together, as they are destined to perform karmic work together to aid their soul growth. It could be you are involved with the individual in question, and it is therefore essential you attune yourself to the subtle signals people in love send out to each other.

King   If the King of Cups has appeared in the Unknown position, a man is working behind the scenes to influence the situation in some way. He is highly intuitive and uses the animalistic instincts he was born with to suss out people and situations. When he has been able to integrate his life experiences in a positive direction, he can be a caring, compassionate person who takes the needs of others into consideration when making decisions. If, however, he has not been able to channel his life experiences in a productive, growth-provoking manner, he can become somewhat eccentric and unstable, abusing the power he has been given. It is for that reason you need to look carefully at the men in your life to see if there is something they may be hiding from you.

Queen   If the Queen of Cups has appeared in the Unknown position, there is a woman working behind the scenes, subtly endeavouring to influence the situation in her favour. You may be in competition with her over a relationship, job or other similar interest. She has therefore decided that if she keeps her perceived level of involvement to a minimum, she has the possibility of effecting the greatest change. Because she will not openly declare to you her true intentions, it is therefore important you stay vigilant to keep your affairs away from prying eyes and in scrupulous order. You never know what opportunist may be lurking around the corner, waiting to take immediate action at your first falter.

Knight/   If the Knight of Cups has appeared in the Unknown position, there is
Prince   a young man who is influencing the situation. He may or may not be aware of the significant role he plays but he nonetheless exerts a huge influence by his mere presence. He is quite considerate of other people and as a result has wide circle of friends who appreciate his thoughtfulness. As a result of his friendly demeanour, he will not be short of admirers. It is for that reason he could become involved with more than one paramour simultaneously because he is loath to offend anyone by choosing one lover over the other.

Page/
Princess
If the Page of Cups has appeared in the Unknown position, there is a young person who is influencing the situation in question, although she may be totally unaware of the role she is playing. She is quite emotional and tends to cry easily because she has not learned to keep her emotions in check. Because she is such an emotive individual, she may not be able to channel her feelings positively and may learn maladroit coping mechanisms that can be dangerous for herself and others. If her past experiences have been negative and of a nature that inhibited her soul growth and maturity, she could become very self absorbed and demanding. It is for that reason she needs to be in a supportive or nurturing environment, thereby enabling her to become a productive member of society.

13 The Best Course Of Action

0 Fool   If The Fool has appeared in the Best Course of Action position, the oracle is telling you that you need a fresh perspective on the situation that has prompted you to consult the oracle. This means you will need to initiate a new start in one particular area of your life. You may need to move house, change jobs, change schools, even change relationships, which will give you a change of scenery and therefore a new outlook on life.

I Magician   If The Magician has appeared in the Best Course of Action position, you need to embark upon a course of learning, which could relate to either a formal classroom environment, on the job training, or self-study. You would also do well to adopt a positive mental attitude because the immense power of the mind cannot be discounted when working to resolve critical issues. Even the simple act of adopting a pleasant demeanour and only allowing positive words to be uttered from your lips would be a massive step forward, as you are making yourself approachable to others and dispelling any negative forces that may latch onto you and hinder you from attaining all that you are capable of. You may want to try to reprogramme your mind as a way of dispelling bad habits, such as nail biting, compulsive eating, or other unsavoury addictions. A simple method of reprogramming is a form of self-hypnosis, where you repeat positive affirmations to yourself whilst in a meditative state. And lastly, magic is implied here. You could evoke simple white magic by projecting mental images of the outcome you would like each day whilst in meditation. You can also perform a type of Sigil magic, which is merely making a drawing composed of all the letters of a word that accurately reflects the outcome you seek.

Alternatively, you can write in very specific detail all the things you would like to transpire on a sheet of paper, and hide it away, only to be looked at on a predetermined future date. You need to be careful what you ask for, however, because you just might get it.

II High Priestess If the High Priestess has appeared in the Best Course of Action position, you need to spend some time on your own, reflecting on the hidden secrets of the universe that keep the stars in the sky and the earth revolving around the Sun with apparent ease. You would also do well to stay away from men for the time being because the energy they emanate is not necessarily what you need to advance in your soul growth at this point in time. You will know what you need to do when you have spent some time alone with yourself, utilising the aspect of yourself that needs to be further developed before you will be made aware of the secrets of the universe, as referenced in the Akashic records.

III Empress If The Empress has appeared in the Best Course of Action position, you need to use the feminine aspects of yourself in an attempt to effect the changes that need to be made to bring about a successful resolution to any dilemmas you may have. It is for that reason you need to adopt a pleasant attitude because people will be more inclined to help you if you are amenable. It is important that you focus on the practicalities of life, such as taking care of your immediate physical needs, and the other areas of your life that are less than satisfactory will fall into place all by themselves. If you were thinking of starting a family, now would be a propitious time to do so.

IV Emperor If The Emperor has appeared in the Best Course of Action position, the Tarot is telling you that you need to take control of your life. This means you need to take proactive steps to correct any areas of your life that are less than satisfactory. If you have found yourself abusing food, cigarettes, drugs or drink, then it is time for you to face the issues that caused you to turn to those things for comfort. If you are having financial difficulties then it is time to take proactive steps to budget your money, even if it means making a few sacrifices. If you are having relationship difficulties then it is time to take a long hard look at the reasons why your interpersonal relationships are less than satisfactory, even if it means dissolving some liaisons that are no good for your spiritual growth. The point is you must take proactive steps to resolve any recurrent issues because they will not correct themselves without any intervention on your part.

V Hierophant If the Hierophant is found in the Best Course of Action position, you are being urged to follow the traditional path to get what you want from this life. If you are contemplating entering into a marriage, it may be a propitious time to do so because the union is more likely to withstand the test of time if it is initiated within a formalised structure, such as a wedding service. On the other hand, if your marriage has not been going so well and you are contemplating a divorce then that may be the best course of action as well, but only you know the answer to that dilemma. The Hierophant represents practicality and tradition, so you may find the answers you seek within a church, possibly during a religious ceremony. It is best to keep your affairs open and above board because any secrets will be uncovered sooner or later.

VI Lovers If The Lovers has appeared in the Best Course of Action position, you are being presented with a choice that needs to be made before you can develop and grow as an individual. The choice will not be easy to make, as you will be presented with conflicting paths and will not be sure which one is best for you to follow. In the ancient Tarot depictions, a young man being presented with the choice of vice and virtue, which indicates he will need to decide whether he wants to take the path of lust and avarice, which is gratifying in the short term, or the path of prudence, which will yield more long term benefits. It is not an easy decision to make, but one that you must decide upon all on your own.

VII Chariot If The Chariot has appeared in the Best Course of Action position, you will need to take proactive action to ensure a successful outcome to the situation that prompted you to consult the oracle. You may be required to travel, such as making a trip for your work. You may even need to move to another part of the country to be near certain people who play an important part in your life. If you are given an opportunity to make a trip, it would be propitious for you to do so to enhance your chances of success in this life.

VIII Strength If Strength has appeared in the Best Course of Action position, you need to draw upon an inner reserve to be able to carry on carrying on in the face of adversity. Even during the most hectic of times, if you try to maintain a serene demeanour, you will be able to accomplish all that is required of you, and then some. If you have been thinking of getting a pet, it would be a wise course of action because pets can love you in a simplistic fashion that very few humans are capable of. Animals do not exhibit the same boundaries that humans tend to, and do not discriminate against sex, race, religion, age or creed. It is the pure naivety of the unconditional love that these beings present that brings them much closer to God.

IX Hermit   If The Hermit has appeared in the Best Course of Action position, you need to spend some time on your own to reflect on the situation that prompted you to consult the oracle. It could be you do not really enjoy your own company and will therefore spend time with anyone and everyone who will dull the inner voices in your head that are stirring you to pursue a certain path in this life. Perhaps the people who you have chosen to share your time with, although rather innocuous, are hindering you from embarking upon the true path that will lead you to the happiness and fulfilment you so earnestly desire. It is for that reason you need to spend time on your own, such as a weekend retreat or solo holiday, where you will have the quiet solitude you need to listen to the inner voice, which will direct you on the path you were meant for in this life.

X Wheel of Fortune   If the Wheel of Fortune has appeared in the Best Course of Action position, the oracle is telling you that you need to take a chance in this life. Although it would not be prudent to throw all caution to the wind and begin anew, there are some calculated risks you can take that have the potential to improve your life circumstances significantly. If there is anything you have been considering undertaking, but lack the self-confidence to attempt, you will never know how successful you could have been unless you give it a try.

XI Justice   If Justice has appeared in the Best Course of Action position, you are being urged to make sure all of your affairs are legal and above reproach. This is not the time to become involved in any nefarious activities because sooner or later such endeavours will be found out, much to the embarrassment of everyone involved. If you are involved in any disputes, it may be necessary to seek mediation as a means to resolve any issues amicably. You may be forced to have your problem resolved through the courts, but this is an avenue you will need to carefully broach. It is important to keep in mind that in any legal disputes, the biggest winners will always be the lawyers.

XII Hanged Man   If The Hanged Man has appeared in the Best Course of Action position, you are being urged to let go of the situation that has been bothering you, and allow the higher forces of the universe to resolve the issue that prompted you to consult the oracle. The reason for this is because there are some things that are not meant for you, and this may very well be one of them. Even if you put every last bit of energy and capital in a venture that means a lot to you, it may not be the path you should be on at this point in time. If you carry on, trying to evoke a particular course of events that you feel you are destined for, you will just become disillusioned at your failure to make sufficient progress to see any kind of a gain. You would fare better if you focused your energies in the pursuance of more worthwhile projects, which will be made apparent to you at a later time.

XIII Death If Death has appeared in the Best Course of Action position, you are being urged to let go of the situation that is bothering you. The reason for this is because major forces are at work that you have little, if any, control over. While you may have free will over your own personal destiny, you do not have power over the lives and destinies of others, which will have an effect on the course of your life. We are all involved in an intricate web that is of such a complex nature there are many souls that need to work harmoniously together in order to achieve a common group goal that most people are not aware of on a conscious level. It is also important to keep in mind that you may desire a relationship, job, vocation, or family setting with all your heart, but if the individuals involved do not want you, there is very little you can do. Unfortunately, this is one of those situations where you have very little influence, so it would be prudent to sit back and allow the universal forces take effect until a more propitious time approaches that will enable you to use your influence to change the affairs of humankind. You would do better to just focus on the things you can improve within your own personal circumstances in this life.

XIV Temperance If Temperance has appeared in the Best Course of Action position, you need to adapt a calm outlook on life because it is not going to do you any good to get excited about things you have very little control over. There are powerful forces at work, effecting a series of synchronous chain events that will transpire over a set period of time, thereby ensuring that the meagre affairs of man amazingly come to order. The only thing you can do is wait for the time to come when your true destiny in the world is revealed to you. In the meantime, the best you can do to ensure the outcome occurs in the manner that you would like is to make sure all of your affairs are in order. If you exercise moderation in all aspects of your life, you will thereby prepare yourself for the day your true destiny is revealed to you.

XV Devil   If The Devil has appeared in the Best Course of Action position, the best thing you can do is to focus on the practicalities of the issue that prompted you to consult the oracle. It is for that reason you need to concentrate on working hard and making money because the capital you acquire through these endeavours will come in handy for other investments you would like to make. You may find yourself in a relationship, job or other situation that does not meet your ideals, but for the time being, is the best you can hope to achieve and it would be wise to stick with it for a little while longer. Even if your personal relationships are not giving you the satisfaction you desire, if you persevere and work through the issues causing you concern, they are likely to improve and eventually become more rewarding endeavours.

XVI Tower   If The Tower has appeared in the Best Course of Action position, you really need to slow down and exercise caution because you very well could have an accident that is brought about through your own or another's negligence. It is for that reason you need to slow down and exercise appropriate safety precautions. You also need to ensure all of your financial obligations are met, otherwise you could put your living conditions at risk. The important thing for you to do is to communicate with others to ensure you know what they want and they know what you want, thereby ensuring all involved parties are operating on the same wavelength.

XVII Star   If The Star has appeared in the Best Course of Action position, you need to adopt a friendly attitude even whenever you are under extreme stress. The reason for this advice is because many people who you meet on a day-to-day basis are not aware of, and cannot imagine, the personal problems you may have. Therefore, even if you have every reason to be sad and miserable, the people around you will not necessarily be sympathetic to the situations in your life that are causing you pain. If you try to be friendly to others, even when you do not particularly feel like being sociable, you will be amazed that other people will return your amenability with kindness and will slowly develop a compassionate understanding of your dilemma. Your friends will be able to help you by showing you compassion and giving you sound advice, thereby helping you to put your problems in perspective.

XVIII Moon   If The Moon has appeared in the Best Course of Action position, it is best if you trust your own inner guidance on this matter because you cannot rely on other people to provide you with accurate information. You are entering into what can best be described as interesting times.

Although you will not realise it for a while, those who you believe to be your friends will let you down, while those who you had never really noticed will be the ones who rally round you during difficult times. Because the veils that allow you illumination and clarity of mind have not yet been lifted, it is best if you keep your own counsel and place very little trust in others until they have proven themselves as true friends.

XIX Sun   If The Sun has appeared in the Best Course of Action position, the best thing that you can do is to don a sunny disposition, even in the face of adversity. The reason for this is because it will only serve to alienate you from other people if you adopt a dour expression, even if you have every reason to be melancholy. If you try to look on the bright side of any difficult situation, you will find that you will have a greater chance of boosting your immune system and protecting yourself from illnesses, which often occur as a result of trauma in our lives. If you have been thinking of adding to your family, it would be a propitious time to do so because additions are likely to bring you much joy and happiness. It may also be wise to go to a place that is sunny and warm, as such an environment has many rejuvenating qualities. After a break in a warm, sunny place, you will be refreshed so that you can again competitively resume your day-to-day activities.

XX Judgement   If Judgement has appeared in the Best Course of Action position, you need a deep, inner cleansing to clear out the psychic debris that is the result of past traumas you have endured and may not even be conscious of. You may need to see a doctor or have a complete medical check-up that will uncover any hidden illnesses that have not been previously diagnosed. You may also wish to try one of the many alternative therapies, which will help to uncover and heal any of the many psychosomatic illnesses you may have adopted as a means of integrating past experiences into your psyche. You may also meet a person who will be able to help you to work through any unresolved issues from your past just by the sheer nature of your relationship with him. The important thing to remember is that you do need healing and should therefore spend time on yourself to repair the wounds that have been deeply embedded in your aura for a very long time.

XXI World   If The World has appeared in the Best Course of Action position, the most appropriate thing for you to do would be to tie up any loose ends holding you back from reaching your fullest potential. There may be several minor aspects of your life you have let slide, convincing yourself those little things don't matter in the grand scheme of things. The fact is, however, everything you say, do or think does matter. You may neglect a little item here, a little item there, until you have amassed a lot of little items that have not been resolved and have therefore been left dangling in thin air. The fact is that all those small, supposedly insignificant items you have been meaning to take care of but thought you never had the time, added up to a huge mess that will sooner or later get out of hand. All of these areas in your life that have been left unresolved will therefore leave your life in a state of disarray until you endeavour to take care of any and all unfinished business that is preventing you from moving on to other activities that can aid you in your development. What you need to do is make a list of all of the unfinished tasks that need to be concluded in your life. You then need to go down the list and complete each and every item you have written down. When you have completed all of items on the list, you will have completed a major cycle of your life and will therefore be ready for new karmic assignments and dharmic gifts that will aid you in your soul growth.

Wands/Rods/Fire

Ace If the Ace of Wands has appeared in the Best Course of Action position, you need to begin thinking of things you can do to enhance the creativity within your psyche. You may have allowed yourself to become lulled into an attitude of complacency by doing the same things each and every day, and seeing the same people each and every day. As a result, you may have become bored and complacent, and the creative aspects of your personality have lain dormant for quite some time. If you take up a new hobby or a sport, it will do wonders for your overall health and wellbeing.

Two If the Two of Wands has appeared in the Best Course of Action position, it would be in your best interests to enter into an enterprise with another person because you could accomplish much more as a couple or team than you can individually. You may decide to get married, accept a position, join a church, or enter into a business arrangement with another person, which is likely to yield profitable results that will serve to enhance your position in the universe and develop your ability to work co-operatively on a one-to-one basis.

Three If the Three of Wands has appeared in the Best Course of Action position, you would be in a good position to try to work together with a group of people to achieve a common goal. There are some things that would be very difficult for you to accomplish on your own, such as building a house or writing one of the many elaborate computer programs used in scientific and business sectors today. It is for that reason there are some instances where one must forego their own personal sense of independence and individuality for the sake of the common good of the universe.

Four If the Four of Wands has appeared in the Best Course of Action position, you would be wise to make any future decisions based upon your potential security and prosperity if you are offered a position or accommodation that allows you to feel more secure in your place in this world. You would be wise to accept any such invitation even if it does not meet your ideal. It may be wise to participate in a family celebration or reunion, which will help you to reaffirm the bond that holds you together with certain people you are related to. Even if you do not see eye to eye with certain family members, it would be in your best interests to try to get along with them because the mutual co-operation you can achieve will come in useful when times are not so affluent.

Five If the Five of Wands has appeared in the Best Course of Action position, it seems you are involved with a group of people who like to bicker just for the sake of it. The reason for this is because they are bitter about many unfulfilled ambitions in their lives, but instead of working to actualise their dreams they would rather lament their many lost opportunities to others. There is nothing you can do to alter the behaviour of these individuals because they will only change when they are ready, and it does not appear this is going to occur for quite some time. If you are not able to find another group of people to associate with, it would be wise if you distanced yourself as much as possible from their activities because others are likely to look on them with disdain.

Six If the Six of Wands has appeared in the Best Course of Action position, you need to adopt a positive, can-do attitude and take proactive steps to achieve your dreams. In order to get what you want out of this life, it may be necessary for you to travel. Any sacrifices you make will be well worth it because the rewards you will receive will be immense. It is important to remember, however, this is one of those times when you will need to adopt an independent attitude because you cannot rely on your friends to come to your aid during times of distress. If anything, some people who you suppose to be your friends will become jealous of your good fortune, and will therefore take whatever steps they feel necessary to hinder you from achieving your objectives.

Seven   If the Seven of Wands has appeared in the Best Course of Action position, you are advised to continue carrying on even in the face of adversity. This is not the time to give up, because if you persevere in your efforts, you will eventually achieve your ultimate goal. The individuals who have agendas at cross-purposes to your own are not really worthy opponents, although you may not realise it right when they are competing with you.

Eight   If the Eight of Wands has appeared in the Best Course of Action position, you are being advised to take a trip, as it will help you to achieve your goals in this life. This journey you need to take may very well be a place you consider to be far away because in the grand scheme of things, all distances are really very subjective. What may be a long journey to you may be considered a short trip by someone else, so this trip you will make needs to be put into perspective as to what the achievable goal is. If for some reason you are not in a position to leave your immediate surroundings, you can broaden your perspective by reading books, watching television, going to movies, or using the internet. There is a wide world out there; you only need to find it.

Nine   If the Nine of Wands has appeared in the Best Course of Action position, it would be in your best interest to maintain an attitude of vigilance in your dealings with others. The reason for this is because the position you are in is somewhat volatile and has the potential to change quite suddenly, leaving you in a rather difficult position. This is not a time to trust others because you really do not know who your friends are. It is best to maintain a pleasant disposition even amongst your enemies, thereby ensuring your relationships will remain intact even during less prosperous times.

Ten   If the Ten of Wands has appeared in the Best Course of Action position, the best thing you can do to resolve the situation is to carry on with your work. If you mind your own business and focus on your obligations in this world, eventually the heavy burdens you feel will begin to subside. The many pressing issues you face will resolve themselves through your unremitting determination to carry on with your duties. If you focus on the work that needs to be accomplished, it will be completed and you will be able to relax and enjoy yourself when the situation that you will soon be involved in becomes less arduous.

King   If the King of Wands has appeared in the Best Course of Action position, you would be wise to cultivate a relationship with a man who is quite knowledgeable on a wide variety of subjects. He is self-absorbed, however, and tends to think of his own desires above those who he claims to care about. This can pose problems because those close to him may have a hard time believing he does actually love them when they see him thinking only of his own concerns.

Queen   If the Queen of Wands has appeared in the Best Course of Action position, you need to develop a relationship with a woman who has a great deal of energy and possesses much insight into the ways of the world. She is very astute and directs her energy in a positive way, which enables her to achieve her heart's desire. Because she has so much energy, she needs to maintain interests to help her to stay active and thereby dissipate any anxiety she may feel. She has much love to give, but it is important she gives her love to deserving people so she can remain happy and well balanced in life.

Knight/   If the Knight of Wands has appeared in the Best Course of Action posi-
Prince   tion, you would do well to spend some time with a young man. He is intuitive and uses his senses as a creative outlet, such as composing music, writing poetry, gardening, and spending time with those he is attracted to. This person is involved in the situation that prompted you to consult the oracle, and holds the key to the successful resolution to some of your problems.

Page/   If the Page of Wands has appeared in the Best Course of Action posi-
Princess   tion, you will get a great deal of reward from spending time with a young person who has the ability to influence the situation just by her mere presence. She has a great deal of energy and therefore needs to channel her exuberance into activities so she can stay focused on progressing along the path that she was destined for.

Pentacles/Disks/Earth

Ace   If the Ace of Pentacles has appeared in the Best Course of Action position, you need to take into consideration your future material and financial prosperity. This may involve investing in yourself, which could involve purchasing property or paying tuition on a course of study. If you thoroughly research any investment you intend to make, you will be well on your way to achieving the material prosperity you deserve in this life.

Two   If the Two of Pentacles has appeared in the Best Course of Action position, the best thing you can do is to ensure your financial affairs are in order. The reason for this is because you may have made so many financial commitments that it would be very easy for you to fall into a debt that would be very difficult for you to repay if only one small variable were to change in your financial situation. The financial strain you have put yourself under has had the effect of making you unusually nervous and other people have noted a change in your personality. In order to resolve this problem that you really don't need in your life, it would be in your best interests to streamline your living expenses, striving to live simply. It may mean you must live in modest surroundings, but you will feel so much better knowing you do not have enormous debts hanging over your head. You may also need to see a financial adviser, who will be able to help you to consolidate your debts into more affordable payments.

Three   If the Three of Pentacles has appeared in the Best Course of Action position, you would be wise to hone your skills in your present occupation. If you are very good at what you do, you will be in greater demand and will be able to command a higher income. If you have been considering moving house, it may be propitious to make the move, as you would probably be happier in a new home. Before making any major decisions with regard to such a move, however, it would be wise to check the structure of the house so you do not uncover major problems at a later date.

Four   If the Four of Pentacles has appeared in the Best Course of Action position, you would be wise to save your money for a rainy day, because you don't know when it will come in handy. It could be you are being somewhat extravagant, spending your money on things you really do not need. It could also be you are letting certain individuals into your life who, in the long run, will only hinder your development in the physical plane you have chosen to incarnate into. You need to think very carefully about the money you are spending and the people who you are allowing into your life. You will find you will be able to conduct your affairs in a more efficient manner if you think about it.

Five   If the Five of Pentacles has appeared in the Best Course of Action position, you would be wise to begin living simply and cutting out any unnecessary expenses. The reason for this is because the economic climate is in a state of flux, always adhering to the ebb and flow of universal influences. It is for that reason times may not have been as affluent as in the past, and the only way you will be able to weather the economic dry spell is to keep your expenses to a minimum. The situation will improve, but you will need to do your part to improve your financial circumstances before you can begin to live prosperously again.

Six   If the Six of Pentacles has appeared in the Best Course of Action position, you would be wise to work in an area of mutual trust and co-operation. The reason for this is because you are not in a position to do everything on your own, and it is for that reason you need to accept help and assistance. In the same vein, there are some individuals who need your help. In order to balance out the law of cause and effect, it would be in your best interests to help others so people will help you when you are in need.

Seven   If the Seven of Pentacles has appeared in the Best Course of Action position, you would be wise to wait to see how the situation you are currently involved in develops. The universe is in the process of balancing and harmonising any inequalities that may exist, and it is for that reason a certain sequence of events must occur before all is revealed to be true. You may not feel what you are engaged in at this point in time is worthwhile, but you will eventually be able to see the relevance of the recent course of events with a renewed clarity.

Eight   If the Eight of Pentacles has appeared in the Best Course of Action position, you would be wise to stay active. If you keep your mind on your work, it will be easier for you to weather the more difficult emotional and material crises that will come your way. You may also need to upgrade your existing skills in some way, and this will serve to improve your employment prospects if you find yourself needing to change jobs. The important thing to remember is to keep your hands busy, and the other problems that arise will sort themselves out automatically.

Nine   If the Nine of Pentacles has appeared in the Best Course of Action position, you would be wise to take a much-needed rest from your day-to-day activities. A spell in the countryside would do you a world of good, as you would be put in touch with the natural forces that make-up our earth. Your material needs will be taken care of, so it would therefore be a propitious time to take care of your emotional and mental needs.

Ten   If the Ten of Pentacles has appeared in the Best Course of Action position, you would be wise to enter into an arrangement with other family members so your future prosperity and success can be assured. Because there is much more a group of people can achieve together than you personally could hope to accomplish on your own, a union to accomplish one specific task would be appropriate to help ensure your material security and prosperity in future years.

King   If the King of Pentacles has appeared in the Best Course of Action position, you need to communicate with a man who has a great deal of common sense and much insight into the practical aspects of life. Because he is not one to act impulsively, he has been able to amass much in his many years of experience. This individual can offer you some good advice and steer you on the straight and narrow.

Queen   If the Queen of Pentacles has appeared in the Best Course of Action position, you need to approach a woman who is stable and can offer some practical advice. She is very level headed and it is for that reason she is able to maintain a grounded perspective, even when it appears her world is falling down around her. Her no-nonsense approach to life will help you to maintain equilibrium during those more turbulent times.

Knight/ Prince   If the Knight of Pentacles has appeared in the Best Course of Action position, you would be wise to develop a relationship with a young man who is very down to earth in his dealings with others. He is practical and methodical, and tends to keep his long-range goals in mind when conducting his affairs. He is analytical and can provide you with sound advice on a matter that is important to you, but you need to exercise caution when approaching him, ensuring you do not engage in conversation with him when he is under stress.

Page/ Princess   If the Page of Pentacles has appeared in the Best Course of Action position, you would be wise to develop a relationship with a young person who is quite methodical in her approach to life. She avidly pursues the physicalities of this world and therefore enjoys eating, sleeping and drinking, not particularly worrying about other more esoteric aspects of our existence. She knows the physical universe is her destiny, and therefore pursues materiality to make her living circumstances more pleasant during this incarnation.

Swords/Air

Ace   If the Ace of Swords has appeared in the Best Course of Action position, it would be in your best interests to keep accurate documentation on those matters that are very important to you. You may need to generate certain items of correspondence of your own, but you need to ensure everything you produce is accurate and relevant. Because this card is representative of our karmic obligations in this life, you will need to be prepared for the fact that anything you say or do can come back and haunt you.

Two   If the Two of Swords has appeared in the Best Course of Action position, there are some issues in this life you will simply have to agree to disagree on. The problem will arise that you are not aware of all of the facts, which will make it difficult for you to make an accurate decision on the matter. It would therefore be prudent for you to refrain from making any important decisions until the true facts of the situation are made known to you. You may find it necessary to part company with one person who means a great deal to you, but this separation is necessary for your spiritual development, so you should not dwell too deeply on this separation.

Three   If the Three of Swords has appeared in the Best Course of Action position, you would be wise to cut one particular relationship or aspect of your life out. The reason for this is because you are involved in a situation that can be very destructive, and in order for you to progress along your spiritual evolution, you must forego something that is hindering your growth. Although you will inevitably suffer from the very difficult decision you will have to make, newer, better opportunities will open up to you.

Four   If the Four of Swords has appeared in the Best Course of Action position, you are being urged to rest your mind and wait for higher guidance that will come to you during your meditations and reflections. At the moment there is nothing you can do to sway the situation in your favour, so it would be propitious for you to wait for the higher forces of nature to act. During dreams or meditation, you will know what is right for you to do.

Five   If the Five of Swords has appeared in the Best Course of Action position, it seems highly unlikely there is anything you can say or do to effect a successful resolution to the situation that prompted you to consult the oracle. Because you can't win, so the best you can possibly do is to walk away from the person or situation that is causing you so much angst. It will be a difficult decision for you to make because there is much you would like to say and do with regard to the situation. You would be wise, however, to save your breath because those individuals who you would like to speak to are not interested in listening to your words.

Six   If the Six of Swords has appeared in the Best Course of Action position, you are leaving a situation that has caused you to become bitter about the world. You feel let down because circumstances have not transpired in your favour. The best you can do with regard to this situation that has caused you so much unhappiness is to walk away from it. Although there are many misplaced emotions you will be forced to deal with, those whom you would like to relate to are not interested in anything you have to relate. Time will heal all wounds, but in the meantime, you need to concentrate on improving your own circumstances in this life.

Seven   If the Seven of Swords has appeared in the Best Course of Action position, you would be wise to keep a very low profile. It would be in your best interests to reveal very little to those people around you. The less they know, the better, because that will enable you to carry out your affairs with the least opposition. An element of stealth is indicated here, which means it really would be in your best interest to be more secretive about your activities to those who really do not need to know.

Eight   If the Eight of Swords has appeared in the Best Course of Action position, you are in a situation that you are not easily able to extricate yourself from. There are many factors that keep you tied to a less than satisfactory situation, which includes financial, geographical, emotional and physical, just to name a few. Because you are not in a situation in which you are free to move around in the manner you would like, the best you can do is to stay where you are. In time your circumstances will change to allow you more freedom to do as you wish.

Nine   If the Nine of Swords has appeared in the Best Course of Action position, you may very well find yourself in a tense situation that is leaving you feeling very stressed. As a result of this, you may find yourself losing sleep or falling prey to one of the many stress related illnesses. There really is not a great deal you can do to effect any positive changes at this time, so there is no point in endlessly worrying. As difficult as it may seem, you really do need to try not to suffer about things you have no control over, because you will just make yourself ill in the process. If you are not able to calm down using one of the many relaxation techniques, you may need to consult outside help to ease some of your many anxieties.

Ten   If the Ten of Swords has appeared in the Best Course of Action position, it appears you are in what can best be described as a no-win situation. There really isn't anything positive you can do to influence this situation. Anything you do attempt may only make matters worse, so you need to think very carefully about any actions you intend on taking. Since anything you do may only wreak more havoc on an already precarious situation, the best that you can do is to do nothing at all. Instead of focusing your energies in an outward direction, you would be wise take care of your own interests. You need to take on such a selfish attitude because you will soon discover the only person who you can really count on in your hour of need is yourself.

King   If the King of Swords has appeared in the Best Course of Action position, you need to consult a knowledgeable man about the situation that prompted you to consult the oracle. He is very intelligent, and for that reason may be in one of the professional disciplines, a cleric or an academic. While he is in a position to provide sound advice, he may not necessarily relate it in a sympathetic fashion. This individual does have a sentimental side however, but it is shrouded in logic and reason, thereby making it difficult to perceive.

Queen   If the Queen of Swords has appeared in the Best Course of Action position, you need to liaise with a woman who is very knowledgeable in many subjects. She has a quick mind and uses it to relate to others on a wide variety of topics of conversation. She is very interested in higher education, and it is for that reason she is well read on the subject of her interest. Because she has experienced much in the years since her birth, she has sound advice to impart. Whether or not you choose to listen to her is up to you.

Knight/ Prince   If the Knight of Swords has appeared in the Best Course of Action position, you need to speak to a young man who is involved in the situation that prompted you to consult the oracle. It may, however, be difficult to relate to this person at times because he has a rather high opinion of himself. Because he has not yet matured to the point where he has the relevant communicative skills to express himself thoroughly, he may lose his temper when he is not able to effectively relate his thoughts to others. This loss of rationality is merely a frustrated attempt to get his message across the only way he knows, which is by using brute force. When he has matured and is further educated, those outbursts will become less conspicuous because he will be able to relate in an adequate fashion so people will know his thoughts through discussion.

Page/ Princess If the Page of Swords has appeared in the Best Course of Action position, you need to incorporate a young person into your sphere of awareness because such contact will be beneficial to you. This individual is very talkative and is an imaginative thinker, thereby coming up with unusual answers to usual everyday problems. Although she is quick-witted, she may have some emotional difficulties that need to be addressed so she can use her personality holistically and not fragmentally, which is so often the case when individuals become unbalanced through life's more tragic experiences.

Cups/Water

Ace If the Ace of Cups has appeared in the Best Course of Action position, you need to put on a happy face and try not to worry about those things you have no control over. If you send out love and harmony to others, the universe will pay you back tenfold. In every dark cloud lies a silver lining, so you do have something to look forward to even during what may appear to be dismal times.

Two If the Two of Cups has appeared in the Best Course of Action position, you need to work to cultivate happy and harmonious relationships with others. You will be much happier with yourself and with the world at large if you are able to live within the confines of a stable relationship. Even if you do not believe the person who you are with at this point in time is what you would consider to be a soul mate, if you work at getting along better with this person, you will see just how much happier you can be with your life circumstances.

Three If the Three of Cups has appeared in the Best Course of Action position, you are being urged to go out and socialise because you will be rewarded for your efforts to meet other people. When you go out and meet different people, your sphere of awareness will increase and new opportunities will open up to you. You will have the opportunity to make new friends, develop business contacts, or even meet your one true love in this world through your social contacts. None of this will happen, however, if you are content to stay home.

Four If the Four of Cups has appeared in the Best Course of Action position, you are being urged to proceed with caution. You have a few inner reservations that are keeping you from forging ahead with regard to one specific venture, and you are right to trust your intuition and to be wary of what you feel could be a dubious situation. There are some hidden pitfalls that have not been revealed to you, but your subconscious is well aware of what is going on. If you are in doubt, it is perfectly acceptable to wait until you feel more secure and ready to move in a positive direction. If something is meant for you, it will come to you.

Five   If the Five of Cups has appeared in the Best Course of Action position, you need to go through a period of grieving before you can go forward in your life. You have every reason to be unhappy, and to try to cover up your feelings of despair with a false sense of bravado will only result in you repressing or denying such a sad time in your life. It is important you allow yourself to be sad and go through the grieving process so you can continue to grow and evolve in the direction that was meant for you. Better times will come to you when you have let go of the emotional anguish from your past unpleasant experiences.

Six   If the Six of Cups has appeared in the Best Course of Action position, you are being urged to return to a time when life was much simpler. While you may have conned yourself into believing you must have a fast-paced, hectic lifestyle, the fact is the path you have chosen is one of your own creation. It is for that reason you have within yourself the capability to streamline your activities. You may find it beneficial to spend some time with children because their innocence can rekindle a genuine aspect of trusting that has lain dormant in your mind for quite some time. If you know children who are feeling neglected, you might want to pay attention to their needs because the children of today are the adults of tomorrow.

Seven   If the Seven of Cups has appeared in the Best Course of Action position, you are being urged to think carefully about all the options available to you. The reason for this is because some opportunities will be presented to you, but not all of them are viable for your own personal life circumstances. It is therefore essential that you research every available option thoroughly before deciding upon the correct course of action. You should also not allow your heart to rule any decisions you make because what you want at this point in time is not necessarily what is best for you. If in doubt, you may want to ask someone you trust for advice in order to help you make this very important decision that will be coming your way.

Eight   If the Eight of Cups has appeared in the Best Course of Action position, the best thing you can possibly do is to walk away from a situation that is causing you at least a fair amount of discomfort. The reason for this is because not all relationships and opportunities are for you to pursue in this life. You will learn through trial and error what you are good at and what you are not. It is therefore pointless to try and pursue a relationship, job or vocation that you have struggled with, only to fail. Rather than waste any more of your valuable time, energy and emotion on a situation that is leading you nowhere, you would be wise to withdraw from it and focus your energies on those areas you have an aptitude for. If you use your inner guidance, you will know what path you need to follow.

Nine   If the Nine of Cups has appeared in the Best Course of Action position, you need to try to be happy with yourself, even if you find you are on your own. It is also important you save your money and other material possessions for a time when there is not so much wealth and abundance available to you. You need to get out and about, even if it is on your own, because you do not want to miss memorable events just because you do not have anyone to share the moment with.

Ten   If the Ten of Cups has appeared in the Best Course of Action position, you have the opportunity to achieve happiness and fulfilment through one particular person or situation. Perhaps you have come into contact with your one mate in this life, and you are being invited to grasp the opportunity and unite with this person who will come to know you better than any other person in this world. Perhaps your one true partner is not who you think he is, but in time you will come to understand the part he or she played in your life to assist in the unfolding of the most positive aspects of your personality.

King   If the King of Cups has appeared in the Best Course of Action position, you need to cultivate a relationship with a caring man who can help you to solve some of your problems. He is compassionate and thoughtful of others, but at the same time has enough self-centredness to ensure his needs are met before he even begins to consider the needs of others.

Queen   If the Queen of Cups has appeared in the Best Course of Action position, you need to cultivate a relationship with a woman who will be of assistance in resolving the situation that prompted you to consult the oracle. She is quite sensitive, so you should be careful how you speak to her, ensuring you do not inadvertently upset her in some way. Because she holds the key to the answers you seek, you need to ensure she is interested in helping you. The problem may arise if, for whatever reason, she has taken a dislike to you, because she may be inclined to embellish the truth so no one will be interested in coming to your aid in a time of need.

Knight/ Prince   If the Knight of Cups has appeared in the Best Course of Action position, there is a young man who holds the key to the successful resolution to the situation that prompted you to consult the oracle. He is quite sensitive and is even psychic, although loath to admit it. Most of the time he would prefer to rely on his logical perceptions and therefore uses rational terminology to describe the intuitive hunches he periodically receives. He has a strong desire to belong, and it is for that reason he will be reluctant to show the more sensitive side of himself.

Page/ Princess   If the Page of Cups has appeared in the Best Course of Action position, you need to spend some time with a young person who will help you to grow and evolve in your present path in this life. She is quite emotive and has not learned how to mask her true feelings in a socially acceptable façade the world at large is prepared to accept. If she has been raised in a healthy environment, she can be quite giving and considerate of others.

14 The Solidifier

0 Fool   If The Fool has appeared in the Solidifier position, you will soon embark upon a new path that will aid you in your karmic evolution. In many ways, you will experience a new beginning because you will come across people and situations that are totally new to you, thereby allowing you to build upon your current skill base. You may suffer a loss of some kind, but this too is necessary for you to gain an understanding of the ebb and flow of universal trends. Although you will be unsure of your footing in some of the situations you find yourself in the midst of, it is important to remember you will be protected in whatever you do as long as your intentions are honourable. If you have been offered the opportunity to do something you have never before tried, it would be a propitious time to embark upon something new.

I Magician   If The Magician has appeared in the Solidifier position, you will soon be entering into what can only be described as a magical time in you life. You will soon undertake a course of study that will reveal to you knowledge you have previously been totally unaware of. This knowledge will instil in you the competence to create a better future for yourself, which is something you definitely need at this time in your life. You will encounter a young person who is a very shrewd individual and is wise to the ways to the world even at a young age. This person is endowed with a good standard of education and can show you different ways of looking at things, which will ultimately enhance the creative impulses you have within yourself. The tools The Magician has at his disposal are the four elemental archetypes of the Wand for creation, the Pentacle for manifestation, the Sword for thought formations, and the Cup for one's ability to perceive emotions. It is with these tools he is able to manifest his own future. He is able to manifest reality merely with his mind, which is a rare skill indeed.

II High Priestess If The High Priestess has appeared in the Solidifier position, you will soon be made privy to a secret that will enable you to go about your daily activities with greater clarity as to your life purpose. The information that will soon be revealed to you will have such a profound impact on you and you will never view the world in the same ordinary fashion again. You will gain a new understanding of the most mundane of things in this world, which will begin to take on a whole new spiritual significance to you, as you ponder your purpose in this life. It is quite likely you will begin to see auras, but if not, you should take note of the messages people will send through the clothes they wear or the body language they unconsciously present. This is a time to go within yourself to understand the basic universal secrets, which are available to anyone who would only ask. What you need to learn you cannot glean from books, lectures or mentors. It is something you can only be given from the higher powers of the universe.

III Empress If The Empress has appeared in the Solidifier position, you will soon be influenced by some maternal instincts, which could be referring either you or someone close to you. You may consider planning a family, which will be of great importance to you. In addition, a female figure may decide it is time to wield her influence over her offspring, which may or may not be to your liking if you do not happen to be part of her family. If you have children or grandchildren of your own, you will need to use your years of experience to help to guide these individuals on the path they are destined for.

IV Emperor If The Emperor has appeared in the Solidifier position, you will soon encounter some karmic influences, and you may wonder exactly who is in control of your destiny. You may have dealings with a powerful person who has much control over many aspects of your wellbeing. This indicates you will need to tread very carefully when dealing with this person so you do not interrupt the fragile make-up of the universal forces that are so much a part of our existence. The time coming is one of the making or breaking of your destiny, so it is propitious to conduct your affairs soberly at all times, thinking of the higher good. If you find yourself in the position of influencing others, it is essential you use the power that has been instilled in you wisely to ensure no inequalities occur.

| V Hierophant | If The Hierophant has appeared in the Solidifier position, you will soon come to a major crossroad in your life and you will need to make an almost irrevocable decision about the course you would like your life to follow. You need to make a decision of such magnitude that things will never again be the same. It is important, therefore, that you think very carefully about this important choice that you will be confronted with because once your mind is made up, you cannot go back to the way things were without great difficulty. It would be in your best interests to pursue the path of tried and true traditionalism, thereby assuring your chances of success in this life. |

| VI Lovers | If The Lovers has appeared in the Solidifier position, you will soon meet an individual who is one of the soul mates you have been destined to come into contact with in this incarnation. In many ways, when you reunite with this individual, you will feel a true connection, possibly not even recollecting the deep psychic bond the two of you have had throughout the ages. Although you will feel you have met your one true love in this world, there are some choices the both of you will need to make on the spiritual path to what can only be described as nirvana. In order to achieve eternal bliss with another person, you must first be okay with yourself, which in all probability will be one of the most difficult tasks you will ever be asked to accomplish in this physical world. In addition, you may be asked to give something up in order to balance out the universal forces that have deemed it appropriate for you to find happiness with your one true love in this incarnation. |

| VII Chariot | If The Chariot has appeared in the Solidifier position, you will soon be making a journey that will be worth your while and give you a fresh perspective on your current situation. Your travels are likely to be successful and you will be wiser for the experience, thereby enabling you to lead your life with much greater clarity of purpose. You will in all probability be expected to organise such an outing, but you will be well rewarded for any efforts you make. In addition to undergoing a new experience, you will also gain a few leadership skills, which is something you will need if you want to lead others and achieve success in this life. |

| VIII Strength | If Strength has appeared in the Solidifier position, you will soon be put in a situation where many of your resources will be drained. You may have some health problems, which are a result of the many stresses in your life you must encounter on a daily basis. It is for that reason you |

need to put your best foot forward and show the world you can still shine under pressure. Animals will be a huge help to you, as they will help to restore harmony in what is otherwise a rather hectic life. These beings can give you the pure, simplistic love that only an animal can give, and love unconditionally, with no strings attached. If you spend time alone with animals, you will receive their soothing energy so you can face the world refreshed and strengthened from the experience.

IX Hermit   If The Hermit has appeared in the Solidifier position, you will be spending time on your own, pondering what exactly makes people do the things they do. This period of solitude will enable you to reflect on your current situation in this life so you will know what it is you need to do to continue on your path to true enlightenment. It is important you develop an inner calm, which you can achieve through meditation, thereby allowing you to open your mind up to possibilities you would not have otherwise perceived. If possible, you need to attend a sanctuary or retreat, as you will be put in touch with like-minded souls who have the potential to become friends in time. Although you may not necessarily like your own company at this time in your life, you need to spend time in solitude to find the answers you so desperately seek. It is not necessary to engage yourself in total meditation, as you can undertake solitary pursuits, such as walking, jogging, craftwork or any hobby you can do alone in the privacy of your own mind. In time, you will gain greater understanding of what makes you tick and find you are actually a likeable person, given the right circumstances.

X Wheel of Fortune   If The Wheel of Fortune has appeared in the Solidifier position, you will soon encounter a change in fortunes. If your circumstances have been difficult in recent months, you should find that by some fluke of nature, you will come into good news, which will enable you to embark upon activities that were previously unavailable to you. If certain situations in your life have been going well, you can expect a hidden glitch to shake up your stability, which will ultimately keep you from becoming too complacent in the universal ebb and flow of the eternal flame of life. The Wheel has within it the four fixed astrological signs of Taurus, Leo, Scorpio and Aquarius, which correspond with the four elemental forces of Earth, Fire, Air and Water respectively, and gives it a sense of stability and equilibrium to maintain the everlasting revolution of life. Because all four signs form a square to each other, ultimately forming a configuration called the grand square, a feeling of tension needs to be released if good fortune is to be achieved. It is also important to keep in mind that most 'luck' is not luck at all, but hard work, which has shown a profit at a most unexpected time. Therefore, if you have put in the required effort, you will reap the rewards of your labour sooner or later.

XI Justice

If Justice has appeared in the Solidifier position, you will soon encounter an equilibrium of forces where an imbalance has previously taken place. The reason for this balancing of power is because in order for the universe to continue the never-ending cycle of renewal and regeneration, it must operate in a state of co-existence, striving to balance the positive and negative forces that are an inherent part of life. You may find yourself engaged in legal proceedings, which could be an anxious time if you are depending on an outcome in your favour. In order to assure fair dealings, it may be possible to bring your grievance to an impartial party who will be able to mediate and help you come to a decision suitable to all concerned parties.

XII Hanged Man

If The Hanged Man has appeared in the Solidifier position, you will soon find you will be required to make a sacrifice, which will mean you will have to give up something that is of importance to you. You will realise you cannot force those situations that are destined to occur, because as soon as the pressure is removed, what you have desired will leave you of its own accord. It is for that reason you must use subtle influences to bring that which you desire into your sphere of existence. Because gentleness is the key, you may have to wait for that which is your utmost goal. In the process of waiting and slowly manipulating the cosmic forces in your favour, you may find that what you thought you wanted is not what you really need or want for your soul's development. When you come to this realisation, you will achieve a fair degree of enlightenment with regard to the forces of nature, thereby allowing what you need to be given to you with little or no effort on your part.

XIII Death

If Death has appeared in the Solidifier position, you will encounter a situation that will be of such a massive significance that it is likely you will receive a gift disguised as a loss. This will be a transformative time for you because you will have experiences of such an extreme nature that when the psychic dust has settled, you will have been through nothing short of a total rebirth, with a completely different personality than the one before the occurrence. When a woman gives birth to a child, it is in many ways a traumatic experience for both mother and child, unlike anything they have encountered before, leaving them in a temporarily weakened state. In the same vein, when Death appears, a rebirth of sorts will occur, which in all probability will entail a similar level of pain and anguish before the realisation of the new life has been acknowledged. It is important to remember the beautiful butterfly must first emerge from a silken cocoon, and in the same way, you too must endure a time of darkness before the brilliance of your new identity will emerge. Rather than lamenting the loss that you may be expected to suffer, it would be in your best interests to look forward to the newer, better things that will soon be coming to you.

XIV Temperance

If Temperance has appeared in the Solidifier position, you will soon be entering a period where all appears to be at a standstill. This is not a time where you can make any magnificent achievements because the universe is in the process of harmonising and achieving a balance between positive and negative forces that have been in an imbalance. Because it seems there is nothing productive you can do during this time of waiting, the best you can possibly do in situations such as these is to do nothing and wait for the universe to act. Abstaining from action, however, is in effect taking action, albeit passively. The best action you can take, therefore, is to ensure all of your affairs are in order for a more propitious time that will ultimately occur sometime in the future. It would be in your best interests, therefore, to work diligently to achieve moderation in all aspects of your life, thereby giving you a balanced perspective when the time has come for you to reap the rewards of your efforts.

XV Devil

If The Devil has appeared in the Solidifier position, you will soon be given more responsibility, which will subsequently cause you to contemplate the practicalities of the earth we have chosen to incarnate into. Because you will be preoccupied with work, money and responsibilities, you may not feel as carefree as you have felt in earlier times, which may give you somewhat of a dour disposition. You will focus more on the physical and material aspects of existence, which will in many ways weigh you down to the earth. Because you are concentrating your energies on the more basal elements of our physical existence, you will be more susceptible to the lower, darker influences that can pervade your soul when you are thinking negatively. It is for that reason you may find yourself more sombre in temperament, perhaps even possessing more of a dark, sardonic type of human behaviour. You may have a chance meeting with an individual who is rather illusive and has darkness about his aura. Before deciding to involve yourself in any activities he invites you to join, you need to research this person thoroughly. After careful study, you will realise all is not as it seems.

XVI Tower   If The Tower has appeared in the Solidifier position, expect a fair amount upheaval in your life. You may very well have made sure all the i's were dotted and the t's were crossed so there is as little confusion as possible to the situation you will soon be encountering. There is, however, one crucial item that you may have missed, so you need to go back and check and double-check until you have discovered what it is you have lost. Because everything in your life may have seemed to be ticking along smoothly, you have developed an attitude of complacency, feeling you have done all you possibly can to achieve a stable, secure, and even possibly boring life for yourself. There are, however, some things in this life you have absolutely no control over, and you will soon be encountering one such situation. Although you have free will over your own destiny, you do not have free will over the destiny of others, whose lives may very well overlap with yours. This interconnecting of individual destinies that are at cross-purposes to one another could very well bring about karmic confusion, as all parties involved try to restore equilibrium in the resulting chaos. In addition, you may need to come to terms with the fact that the life you have carved out for yourself may not necessarily be the life that is going to afford you maximum soul growth, which is why your subconscious has decided to shake things up a bit. You may therefore see the upcoming period of transition as a time of loss, but this is a time of opportunities that will come at the most propitious times. It is also a time when you can explore choices you may not have otherwise have been open to. It is always important to keep in mind that when the universal forces close a door, a window is always opened.

XVII Star   If The Star has appeared in the Solidifier position, you will soon be entering a period of optimism and hope for what lies in the future. You will possess a happy disposition, as you try to think positively and hope your dreams will become reality. It is likely you will develop a friendship with a new person who will be coming into your life, and this liaison will be satisfying for the both of you. This is a time of Aquarian ideals, where science, technology, and a sense of service to humanity will figure prominently in your day-to-day activities. If you have been considering becoming more involved in information technology, the timing is now auspicious for you to explore such a vocation. If your intentions are honourable and you only desire is to serve mankind, you cannot fail in what you set out to do. Even if you feel you have not succeeded, you will acquire valuable skills along the way that you can use in other areas of your life.

XVIII Moon   If The Moon has appeared in the Solidifier position, you will soon be entering a period of confusion, as you will realise that all is not as it appears. There are forces at work that are occurring simultaneously and are at cross-purposes to the life you are currently living. You are aware that things are occurring simultaneously and parallel to your own life, but you cannot pinpoint exactly what it is that is transpiring. Whilst in the dream state, you will be able to glimpse those worlds that are similar, but not identical to your own, making you discover there are other realities that co-exist on the earth plane, just beyond your mental grasp. There are times when you are daydreaming or lost in thought, when you will receive mental flashes of lost worlds that have been forgotten to mankind but remain in the annals of the Akashic records. These glimpses of lost worlds will make you wonder if the imagery you were presented with was a glimpse from this or an adjacent sphere of existence. All of those intrusions from other realities can make you question your own sanity, but your reasoning ability is not an issue, as long as you reveal those impressions you have received only to your most trusted friends. Your friends, however, can be deceptive, as you will come to realise who your true companions in this life are. Just because a person is friendly and polite does not make that person a friend, which you will soon discover to your dismay. You will be quite surprised to learn that those who you had believed to be your friends will pass you by, while those who you had not previously given much notice to will become worthy of merit.

XIX Sun   If The Sun has appeared in the Solidifier position, you will go through a period of happiness and gaiety, where you can easily become intoxicated by life. With this newfound optimism you will possess a high level of self-confidence that you have not had before. Animals and children will figure prominently in your sphere of awareness because they love unabashedly and are not terribly concerned about a person's outward appearance. This will be a time of high exposure, so you will therefore need to make sure you are at your best when under public scrutiny.

XX Judgement   If Judgement has appeared in the Solidifier position, you will soon be undergoing a deep healing process, and the faith you had lost in humanity will eventually be restored through the new people who will be coming into your life. You may decide to embark upon a type of therapy, which will go a long way towards healing many of the wounds that can still be seen in your auric web. You may meet someone along your earth walk who can help you to meet the many demands that are placed upon you, thereby giving you a feeling of unity, which you have not experienced for quite some time.

XXI World If The World has appeared in the Solidifier position, you will soon be completing a major cycle in your life, which will bring you closer to unification with your soul's twin flame. You may complete a course of study, which would end your sojourn as a student of life and hopefully propel you into the arena of work and professionalism. You may have decided it is time to take a personal relationship one step further in its evolution, which could be a commitment of some sort. Alternatively, if the relationship is non-productive, or even destructive, dissolution of the relationship may be deemed more appropriate. The body plays a significant theme in the symbology of the world so matters relating to the physical vehicle we must use in this world will also take precedence.

Wands/Rods/Fire

Ace If the Ace of Wands has appeared in the Solidifier position, you will shortly enter into a period of creativity that may possibly yield financial or business returns. You may begin to think about how you can expand your professional standing, and therefore explore new ideas that come to you through the most unusual of sources. You may decide to expand on what you already know, or decide to embark upon an altogether new venture, which may entail a steep learning curve before you find you are competent and successful in your new venture.

Two If the Two of Wands has appeared in the Solidifier position, you will soon be approached by another individual to partake in an activity that would theoretically yield profits for the both of you. The reason for this is because you both possess skills independent of each other, and when these assets are combined, they have the potential to produce far more than both attributes individually. What you are planning is likely to become a business or creative endeavour, but is ultimately a profitable venture so the both of you can enjoy the fruits of your labour.

Three If the Three of Wands has appeared in the Solidifier position, you will shortly find yourself amongst a group of people who are engaged in achieving one common goal. This group may be comprised of work colleagues because business enterprise is often associated with the element of Fire, which governs the magical nature of the wand. The group could also be comprised of friends and acquaintances who have gathered together to form a sporting or social activity, so you should not discount any non-professional alliances. It could also be comprised of family members, who are tied together through a financial undertaking, which will ultimately affect the ties you have with these individuals. It is unlikely the alliances you form during this time will be lasting, as the group you will soon be engaging in was formed only in pursuance of a specific goal. Nevertheless, it would be in your best interests to participate in this group because you will find it to be a satisfying experience and should help to build your self-confidence.

Four   If the Four of Wands has appeared in the Solidifier position, you will soon have cause for celebration. Events will transpire that will make you feel more secure than you have in a very long time, which should bolster your self-confidence. You may have received a professional position that would enable you to fulfil some of your personal goals, thereby enabling you to feel less vulnerable in what can often be a volatile world. Your family and home will be of paramount importance, as you will feel greater solidarity towards those who you are close to.

Five   If the Five of Wands has appeared in the Solidifier position, you will soon discover you are struggling over one particular situation that seems quite perplexing. This situation has been a huge source of trouble for you, and you are not able to put your finger on exactly what the root cause is. Because you are in the dark about the precise dilemma causing so many of your difficulties, you are striking out in all directions, trying to solve one crisis after another. You are probably thinking to yourself, 'just as soon as I get over this one hurdle, everything will be okay and I will be able to live normally'. The problem is that just as soon as you manage to get over that one hurdle, another one of even greater magnitude will crop up. It will take a great deal of soul searching on your part to try to come to terms with the root trauma responsible for your problems, but when you have, many thought patterns that had previously been inaccessible to you will seem to fall into place. If you are not able to find out what the root cause is on your own, you may want to consider outside help. It is important to remember your troubles will not cease until you are able to isolate the negativity in your life that has brought about many of your troubles.

Six   If the Six of Wands has appeared in the Solidifier position, you will accomplish a significant achievement in the future. This accomplishment will be of such a magnitude that you will feel the need to reward yourself for a job well done. There is much to do, however, to secure your future prosperity and happiness, so it is not appropriate to sit back and relax after what is in reality only a minor victory in a long succession of obstacles you will need to overcome. It is also essential you make appropriate preparations for any proposed activities because one mistake could negate all previous successes. This is not a time to rely on assistance from friends and acquaintances, because you will discover they will let you down at the most inopportune times.

Seven If the Seven of Wands appears in the Solidifier position, you will have to work very hard to maintain any successes you may have had in the past. If you have recently been promoted to an elevated position, you will find that you will have a steep learning curve to overcome before you are proficient in your role. Those around you will not be prepared to wait for you to catch up to their speed, which you will find to be all the more stressful. It is for that reason you should keep any insecurities you have with regard to accomplishing the task at hand close to your heart. If you confide your doubts to inappropriate individuals, you will merely be perceived as weak and not up to the job you have been given overall responsibility for.

Eight If the Eight of Wands appears in the Solidifier position, you will soon be taking a trip that will expand your level of awareness in some way. You will go somewhere that, to you, is quite far away. You may find that you will advance academically, professionally, or even spiritually, as you aspire to self-actualise through a progressive and consistent attainment of your goals.

Nine If the Nine of Wands has appeared in the Solidifier position, you will soon have reason to feel as if you are on the defensive. You will find that you will have opposition from the most unlikely of individuals, which will further influence your outlook on life, making it a rather sombre time indeed. Because of the depression you feel, people may not see you as you really are, which could cause them to discredit you in some way. Because you feel threatened in what is an austere environment, you will tend to behave differently and people will not see the 'you' that is relaxed and would like to enjoy life. It is for that reason you need to simplify your life, focus on what it is you really need to do, and get as much rest as possible. Your true friends will stick by you in your hour of need.

Ten If the Ten of Wands appears in the Solidifier position, you will soon find yourself in a position where you are totally overwhelmed by events that will soon be taking place to shake your life up a bit. You may take on a role you are not quite ready for, and because you do not possess all of the skills necessary to see the task successfully to completion, you are filled with a sense of foreboding, fear of what lies ahead of you. In some ways you feel like a fraud, and wonder if everyone is able to see through your veneer of confidence down to the insecure being you really are. Although you work tirelessly to try to complete the tasks you have been presented with, you seem to be spinning your wheels, not accomplishing a great deal of anything. Before you reach a level of total exhaustion, you need to take a good look at the problem that is causing you so much anguish. You may need to go out and acquire the skills you need to see the project to completion, either in a formal classroom environment, or by gaining a few additional life experiences. Alternatively, you may decide it is in your best interests to abandon the pursuit altogether, leaving such endeavours to more able souls.

King
If the King of Wands has appeared in the Solidifier position, you will soon be influenced by a man who has a flair for business and enterprise. Whenever he happens upon a new project, he instantly wonders how he can exploit the situation and use it to his advantage. He has much love to give, which he will lavish on children, animals, partners, or anyone he feels worthy of his attention. This individual will stand out in a crowd, and the colours yellow and red will be significant to him.

Queen
If the Queen of Wands has appeared in the Solidifier position, you will soon be influenced by a woman who is very shrewd and astute about the ways of the world. She has much vibrancy about herself, which makes her the life and soul of any social gathering. She has a great deal of inner clarity, and can impart wisdom to you metaphorically, using parables to get her message across. She is not, however, one to relate to those who do not wish to listen, and will therefore wait until she is asked to speak frankly on any given subject.

Knight/ Prince
If the Knight of Wands has appeared in the Solidifier position, you will soon become involved with a young man who possesses a great deal of energy. He has much charisma within himself, which makes him very attractive to others, especially the opposite sex. It is important to note, however, because he has not yet experienced many of the facets of this life, he needs time to explore the world and learn from what he has been exposed to. It is for that reason he may be an ideal paramour to dally in the waters of romance and the fleeting feelings of love, but he

is not ready for commitment and is therefore an unsuitable candidate for any kind of lasting bond.

Page/ Princess　If the Page of Wands appears in the Solidifier position, you will soon come into contact with a young person who has much energy and needs to stay busy, or she will get into mischief and may harm herself or others. She is a very loving individual, but needs a great deal of attention, or she will feel neglected, and could consequently react inappropriately as a way to draw attention to herself.

Pentacles/Disks/Earth

Ace　If the Ace of Pentacles has appeared in the Solidifier position, you will soon be thinking of money and material possessions. You may consider beginning a new venture that has the possibility of bringing you greater wealth and prosperity, which would definitely improve your standard of living. Alternatively, you may be thinking of making a major purchase that will bring more responsibility with it because you will have to organise exactly how you intend to pay for the item you desire.

Two　If the Two of Pentacles has appeared in the Solidifier position, you will soon have some financial or material concerns that will need to be resolved before you can progress any further in your current endeavour. It appears you will need to take greater control over your financial situation because it will be necessary for you to manage your resources more effectively so you do not find yourself swimming in a sea of debt. You may find it necessary to take another job in an attempt to pay the people who you owe money to, which in itself will further teach you the value of money. You may also need to ask some individuals to repay debts they owe to you, which is necessary for you to pay off your own personal debts.

Three　If the Three of Pentacles has appeared in the Solidifier position, property and possessions will soon mean a great deal to you. You may consider moving into a new home, which you hope will be an improvement over your present living situation. You may also consider making a major renovation to your property, which will entail considerable investment and expertise on your part. A marriage, engagement or other type of commitment is likely, but this union would in all probability be based just as much on material concerns as the concept of true love. It is important, therefore, not to allow yourself to fall prey to any illusions you may have with regard to the partnership you are considering. While the union may lack passion, it will be a worthwhile experience nonetheless.

Four   If the Four of Pentacles has appeared in the Solidifier position, your possessions specifically relating to your personal security will shortly become vital to you. You need to prepare for lean times ahead by living simply and keeping your expenditures to a minimum. It is not a propitious time to invest your money in any risky ventures because it is unlikely you will receive a return on your investment. You need to take a discriminating look at who you allow into your confidence and into your home because some individuals who wish to get to know you better have interests at cross-purposes to your own. It is important, therefore, that you keep your doors locked because intruders will use any opportunity to profit from the smallest lapse in your own personal or professional security.

Five   If the Five of Pentacles has appeared in the Solidifier position, you would be wise to prepare for lean times ahead, where you will need to pull in your belt and live as frugally as possible. You will very likely go through a period of depressive illness because there are certain aspects of your life you are unhappy with. You have a strong desire to belong, so when certain individuals who you perceive to be popular snub you and deny you membership to their particular clique, you will feel the full force of such a rejection. The fact that you are not exactly where you would like to be in your life is not necessarily a failing on your part, but merely a phase you must undergo in the cycle of transformation and change that affects us all at least one point in our lives. The best you can do is save your money, live simply, and prepare yourself for more prosperous times, which will inevitably come back to you through the never-ending cycle of the universe.

Six   If the Six of Pentacles has appeared in the Solidifier position, you will soon undergo a karmic balancing act. A sense of harmony in the universe is necessary to enable it to run smoothly, and for that reason the positivities and negativities of this world must co-exist in a state of equality. It is for that reason you may be asked to do something that would have no apparent benefit to you. You will, however, reap the rewards of your unrequited gift at a later date, so you do not need to worry about giving without the benefit of recompense. By the same token, you may find yourself in the position where you need to ask for assistance from a power higher than yourself. You should not be ashamed or embarrassed at having to receive any kind of help from others because it is merely a part of the universal cycle that has a never-ending rotation. You will, however, be expected to repay in kind any gifts you receive so the universe will continue to attain a harmonious balance in its revolutions.

Seven   If the Seven of Pentacles appears in the Solidifier position, you are undergoing a period of waiting, especially with regard to the situation that prompted you to consult the oracle. You may very well have put in a fair amount of effort to see a certain project to completion, but the forces that prevail indicate there is nothing you can do to influence the situation for the time being but wait. Because Pentacles represents the physical aspects of ourselves, if you have been hoping to start a family, you will soon find you are very fertile and receptive to the influences that come about to make such an objective a reality. If, however, you do not want to add to your existing family, it would be wise to take adequate precautions with regard to that matter as well.

Eight   If the Eight of Pentacles has appeared in the Solidifier position, you will soon learn some new things either in your current vocation or a different line of work altogether. These skills you will soon be acquiring will in all probability relate to working with your hands, which can go a long way to healing some of the emotional or mental blocks that continue to reside in your psyche. It is worth noting that many of the obsessive mental illnesses that are such an inherent part in technologically advanced societies are practically non-existent in underdeveloped countries. It is believed the mere act of working with one's hands and performing physical labour heals and strengthens the body simultaneously. Above all, man is a human animal that needs exercise just as much as any other animals that are a part of our earth. Man was not physically designed to live a sedentary life, which is the root cause of a great many of his ailments.

Nine   If the Nine of Pentacles has appeared in the Solidifier position, you shall soon be entering a hiatus after a time of hard work, which is something you desperately need in order to recuperate from what has been a rather stressful situation. During this time of rest, your physical needs will be taken care of, which will enable you to spend time in reflection so you can determine exactly what direction it is you would like to follow.

Ten   If the Ten of Pentacles has appeared in the Solidifier position, it is anticipated that very soon you will find yourself involved with your family in a matter that concerns property or money. It is a distinct possibility that you will be asked to work closely with older members of your family circle, which should instil in you more responsibility. The increased duty that you may be asked to undertake promises to yield greater wealth and prosperity in later years, thereby lessening some of the resentment you may presently feel at being denied the carefree existence you feel you deserve.

King If the King of Pentacles has appeared in the Solidifier position, you will soon come into contact with an influential man. He is a self-made person, quite confident in himself and others, and, even if he is not instilled with a great deal of material wealth, he is a valued member of his community because his opinions are sound and considered worthwhile. This individual has a solid personality and is not prone to rash behaviour. He can be generous when it is in his best interests to do so, but he needs to exercise caution not to become miserly in later life.

Queen If the Queen of Pentacles has appeared in the Solidifier position, you will soon come into contact with a woman who has a great deal of self-confidence and in many respects has money of her own. Because her material security is pretty much assured, she is fiercely independent, preferring to do things in her own way. She can be kind when it suits her to be so, and helps those who are less fortunate than herself, which ultimately endears her to those in her own community. She is very practical and level-headed, and is therefore not inclined to exploring the more esoteric aspects of this life. It is not that she does not find such subjects to be worthwhile pursuits, it is just that she would prefer to concentrate on the realities of the here and now, building upon her physical prosperity here on earth. When asked, she can impart sound advice to the querent, but is not prone to asserting her opinions without first being asked.

Knight/ Prince If the Knight of Pentacles has appeared in the Solidifier position, you will soon have the opportunity to come into contact with a young man who is stable and level headed. He has a good head on his shoulders and is not one to act hastily. Although he may at times be slow and methodical, he usually gets what he wants through persistent and diligent effort. Material possessions are very important to this individual whose self-esteem is often determined by what he owns, how much money he earns, and who he socialises with. It is for that reason he will endeavour to work hard so that he can amass great wealth and strive towards self-actualisation through his career achievements.

Page/	If the Page of Pentacles has appeared in the Solidifier position, you will

Page/ Princess If the Page of Pentacles has appeared in the Solidifier position, you will soon come into contact with a young person who has the potential to be affluent, but has not yet made her mark in this life. She is very practical, methodical and steadfast in her opinions, and can be somewhat obstinate until she has learned the art of tact. She is determined to achieve material prosperity because wealth and possessions are very important to her sense of self and wellbeing.

Swords/Air

Ace If the Ace of Swords appears in the Solidifier position, you will soon enter into a period of correspondence with regard to one specific issue. The initial sparks of a profitable idea will flow, but these impressions should not to be confused with the creative energies inherent in the Ace of Wands. Rather than the concept of building something new, which is in the creation principle of Fire, you and those associated with you will have an intense desire to make your ideas and opinions known via the spoken and written word. Such creative principles are the intellectual principle behind the element of Air, which manifests itself through the suit of Swords. This is a time of deep karmic significance, where you will be forced to come face to face with the obligations you have built up over various incarnations. You must confront these issues before you can progress along the soul evolution, so the sooner you resolve any negativities in your life the sooner you will open yourself up to the positivities you deserve as a celestial citizen of the universe.

Two If the Two of Swords has appeared in the Solidifier position, you will soon find you are in disagreement with another individual about one crucial issue in time. The both of you are not in possession of all the facts and therefore are not in a position to make an accurate assessment of the situation, which is making what you are involved in all the more frustrating. As a result of you not being able to see eye to eye with this person, you may decide that, for the time being anyway, the best thing you can do is to part company until the truth is revealed in a more coherent fashion. If this individual meant nothing to you, you would have no difficulty whatsoever walking away. The fact is, however, that much emotional energy has been cultivated between the two of you, which makes it all the more difficult to leave the anguishing situation. When all the facts become known, it may be possible to attempt reconciliation, but a cooling off period is necessary if equilibrium and harmony are to be restored.

Three   If the Three of Swords has appeared in the Solidifier position, you will soon go through a very emotionally tumultuous period. It seems there are individuals who mean a great deal to you who are not treating the relationship you have with the respect it deserves. Their total disregard for you and your feelings is causing you a great deal of emotional pain, as you cannot understand what you have ever done to this individual to cause him or her to treat you with such blatant disregard. The fact is you didn't do anything to bring such emotional pain to yourself. You were simply unfortunate enough to be caught up in the emotional crossfire that has resulted from becoming acquainted with a person who is not worthy of your love and attention. The problem lies with the other person, who must find his own way in this life before he can wholly relate to you, and has not yet learned to treat his relationships with the maturity and care that ultimately comes from mutual respect and love. Although you are in anguish at this point in your life, it is important to keep in mind you were merely caught in the middle of the antics of misguided souls. The person who has hurt you so is merely not ready to be loved by you, which is why he or she has behaved in such a hurtful manner.

Four   If the Four of Swords has appeared in the Solidifier position, you need to get as much rest as possible so higher guidance will be revealed to you through dreams or the meditative state. You need to reserve your energy for a time when things will become much busier than they presently are. This period of rest should be used as a time of meditation and inner reflection, a time where you allow your mind to wander so new ideas can come into your head, undeterred by the hustle and bustle of an active lifestyle. New thoughts that enlighten you will come, if you let them. If you take the time to quiet your mind and open yourself up to new and wonderful impressions of other worlds that await you and anyone else who is ready for such inner adventures, you will realise there is so much more to what you perceive to be a three dimensional universe.

Five   If the Five of Swords has appeared in the Solidifier position, you will soon find yourself at odds with a person or group of people who you had originally felt to be your friends. There seems to be much banter going on, but a great deal of it appears to be malicious gossip, which is intended to harm the reputation of involved participants. While some of the activity can be viewed as lively debate on the ethics of one particular topic, some of it is merely fabricated stories that have been made up in an attempt at calumny, which would blacken the character of others. It is not envisaged you will stay in this situation for any length of time because you will soon tire of such destructive behaviour from others. Since you will find yourself mixing with people who are morally and ethically inferior, the best you can do in such a situation is to exercise caution in all you say or do. It would be in your best interests to keep copies of any documents relating to the situation that will transpire within the next year. These documents will become useful in the future if there are any intentional or accidental lapses in your or another individual's memories.

Six   If the Six of Swords has appeared in the Solidifier position, you will soon be leaving a difficult time, hoping to make a new life for yourself. You may have been involved in a relationship or vocation that was not healthy for you, and consequently brought you a great deal of sadness. After much soul searching and reflection upon the situation that will soon be transpiring, you will decide the best you can do is to walk away from a situation that has been causing you so much grief and anguish, even if it means you will have to give up a great deal in the process. The decision to build a new life for yourself will come about with a fair amount of melancholia because the fact is you would have preferred the situation you are leaving to have turned out more positively. Because you will need to make new acquaintances in the environment you will soon be entering, you will need to practise the art of discretion so you can select only positive people who will be able to afford you with harmonious relationships in your upcoming milieu. The time coming up will be a time where you will need to learn from your mistakes, so you need to exercise attention to detail so you can keep any errors to a minimum. All you have experienced in the past will have been of no value to you if you cannot learn from it and then move on to better, more fulfilling relationships and situations.

Seven   If the Seven of Swords has appeared in the Solidifier position, you need to be guarded in your activities because there are individuals around you who are claiming your ideas as their own. You need to guard your possessions because you may unknowingly invite someone into your home who may decide to take something of value without your knowledge. Even if you take adequate precautions not to invite dubious characters into your space, an opportunist could always take it upon himself to take advantage of any unlocked doors or windows. Alternatively, you may find yourself in a situation where stealth and secrecy is necessary. You will therefore need to ask yourself whether what you intend to do is honourable and ethical. If it isn't, maybe there is something more worthy of your efforts you can engage yourself in to achieve the same goal.

Eight   If the Eight of Swords has appeared in the Solidifier position, you will soon enter into a period of entrapment that has in many ways been caused by your own sense of tact and diplomacy. You may find you have become involved in something that is not beneficial for your soul growth, and this has consequently taken you off your true path in life to such an extent that you will not know the correct course of action to take. You will find yourself to be in a period of confinement, which may be self imposed or caused by forces more powerful than yourself at this moment in time. During your isolation you will not be made privy to vital pieces of information that are important to your own wellbeing and safety, which will thus compound the problem you will soon be involved in. Although it is difficult to see, there is a way out of this predicament, but you will be required to make some tough decisions with regard to your future. The best you can do at this time is to keep your affairs legitimate and above board, thereby lessening any negative influences that will inevitably come your way.

Nine   If the Nine of Swords has appeared in the Solidifier position, you will soon go through a period of mental confusion, which will cause you to feel very anxious indeed. You may find you have difficulty sleeping because you have so much on your mind it is almost impossible for you to relax enough to sleep through the night. You may also find you succumb to one of the many mental illnesses, such as depressive disorders, personality disorders that are a result of past, unresolved experiences, obsessive/compulsive disorders, anxiety, panic, addictions that have come about as a result of your attempt to self-medicate, neurosis, and even psychosis. While there are many things in your present life you have no control over, there are some aspects of your current situation you have within yourself the ability to take command of. It is for that reason the best that you can do to navigate through this difficult patch is to live simply and honestly, steering clear of those individuals who will only drag you down. Above all, you need to eat properly and get plenty of rest, which will give you adequate strength to decide what is best for your particular life path.

Ten   If the Ten of Swords has appeared in the Solidifier position, you will soon feel quite unhappy about a particular situation. It seems you have placed your trust in inappropriate individuals who have only let you down when you are the most vulnerable. Unfortunately, there is nothing you can do but lick your wounds, nurse your damaged ego, and take stock of the situation that has caused you so much anguish. Upon reflection, you will see the signs of dissent were there, but you did not want to see them. It may be a good time to decide to mix with a different crowd of people who would be more appreciative of your company, thereby lessening the chance of subsequent betrayals.

King   If the King of Swords has appeared in the Solidifier position, you will soon be influenced by a man who has a significant command of the power of words. He has the ability to express himself eloquently, which instils in him the ability to speak poetically and metaphorically. He needs the company of other likeminded people, which makes him a witty and pleasant conversationalist most of the time. Although he is intensely loyal to people while he is with them, when they leave his sphere of awareness, he can easily forget all about the camaraderie he had developed. It is for that reason this individual has had many relationships, much to the dismay of his present partner, who is also at risk of being a figment of his past experiences as well.

Queen   If the Queen of Swords has appeared in the Solidifier position, you will soon be widely influenced by a woman who is a very articulate individual and is able to express herself. She is very knowledgeable about many subjects, but fame may have alluded her, leaving her with the feeling that life has passed her by. It is for that reason she may carry an air of importance she has not really earned, thereby leaving some people perplexed by her pretentious behaviour. She is knowledgeable about a wide variety of subjects and would like to impart the wisdom she has gleaned to others, but needs an audience who will listen so she can feel she is a valued member of society.

Knight/ Prince   If the Knight of Swords has appeared in the Solidifier position, you will soon be influenced by a young man who has some very high ideals and aspires to great things in this life. He has somewhat of a temper, however, which manifests itself through explosive outbursts and insulting remarks. He has the potential to one day be a great thinker and communicator, but until that time he needs to mature and grow through his life experiences. Because he is able to freely express himself, he will never be short of admirers.

Page/ Princess   If the Page of Swords has appeared in the Solidifier position, you will soon be influenced by a young person who is quite chatty and witty. She has an inquisitive mind and therefore asks many questions less observant individuals would overlook. She can also be quite nervous and may therefore be prone to biting her nails or engaging in a frenzy of activity, as she tries to release much of the energy inside of her. As she matures, many of the frenetic activities she pursues will wane, but until that time it is important she stays busy through hobbies or educational pursuits so she does not become involved in any negative activities.

Cups/Water

Ace If the Ace of Cups has appeared in the Solidifier position, you will soon enter into a situation that has the potential to bring you great happiness and fulfilment. This situation could be a job, school, holiday or relationship, but you will know when you come across it because it will feel right to you. Even if you do not particularly feel like it, you need to put a smile on your face and try to make the best of any bad situations you are currently involved in. When you smile at the world, it will smile back.

Two If the Two of Cups has appeared in the Solidifier position, you will soon become involved with an individual who can bring you a great deal of happiness just through your contact with him or her. There will be a unique bond that will keep the two of you together, as you form a partnership that is likely to be a lasting one. You will find that if you put forth the effort to make your personal relationships more satisfying, they will improve and become much more fulfilling to you.

Three If the Three of Cups has appeared in the Solidifier position, you will soon find you have an active social life, full of parties and get-togethers. There is likely to be much merry-making, as the people in your social circle would like to have a good time and enjoy themselves. You will receive invitations to social events, and it would be in your best interests to accept them because you never know what opportunities might be presented to you during any chance encounter. Because there will be so many social outings, you may find you are eating and drinking more than usual, which may mean you find yourself putting on weight. It is for that reason you may want to prepare for this period of intense social activity by watching what you eat and getting plenty of exercise to compensate for any indulgences.

Four If the Four of Cups has landed in the Solidifier position, you will soon be entering into a period of uncertainty and doubt. While all outward signals appear normal, you cannot help but get an inner feeling that all is not well in paradise. You may suffer from nervousness or anxiety, which gives further rise to the misgivings you may have with regard to the situation you will soon be involved in. To further confuse the matter, you will be receiving conflicting stories from various sources, leaving you rather perplexed about what the truth of a certain situation actually is. It is for that reason you should only be swayed by factual evidence because you will find people cannot be reliable sources of information. In addition, you should allow your inner voice to guide you to the direction you should be taking, and you cannot go wrong.

Five   If the Five of Cups has appeared in the Solidifier position, you will soon be entering a period of melancholia because what you had hoped would happen has not transpired in the manner you would like. You may have had your hopes up high with regard to one particular issue, and never really believed things could turn out differently than what you had previously envisaged. When the unexpected occurs, it seems you will be caught totally off guard, which will only add to the doubts for the future you will soon be feeling. It is understandable that you will be disheartened, but with the new knowledge you possess, you have within yourself the ability to create a new life for yourself. You will emerge from this difficult time with a greater understanding of yourself and the nature of others, which will only help you to attain success in future endeavours.

Six   If the Six of Cups has appeared in the Solidifier position, you will soon enter into a situation that reminds you of past times. You may be reunited with someone from your past, thereby enabling you to relive many experiences you had long forgotten. You may also find yourself working with children in some capacity, which will enable you to grow as an individual, as you are able to recapture some of your lost youth. If you live far away from where you were in your more formative years, you may find yourself travelling back to that place, which will help to heal many wounds and renew your sense of self. You will soon be able to see with clarity where you have been, and this should help you to determine with greater clarity where you would like to go from there, and then to visualise what your ultimate goal in this life is.

Seven   If the Seven of Cups has appeared in the Solidifier position, you will soon find yourself in a situation where several options will be made available to you. You do not, however, know which option will yield the greatest results, and that is precisely where your challenge lies. The point to remember is some choices will be positive, while others will get you nowhere, and still others will be detrimental to your emotional wellbeing. It is for that reason you should not become bamboozled by a highly developed sales pitch, which has been presented by no less than a confidence artist. If you are unsure about a particular decision you need to make, it would be best to seek a second opinion and shop around until you find something that feels right for you. It is crucial that you do not allow others to force you into a decision that you are not fully prepared to commit yourself to because you could find yourself wasting valuable time and energy on a path that is not destined for you.

Eight   If the Eight of Cups has appeared in the Solidifier position, you will soon be entering into an unknown realm of existence. There is one particular area of your life you have held onto relentlessly. Even though you know deep down in your heart this person, situation, or way of life was not a positive experience for you, you nevertheless clung on, hoping circumstances would change and you would feel happy at last. After a great deal of soul searching, you will come to the reluctant decision that you must walk away from that which has caused you so much heartache. The decision to leave will be a difficult one because you will have to sacrifice long-term goals that have fuelled your dreams. Better, more worthwhile experiences will come to you, but in the meantime, you must go through the grieving process for what you have given up.

Nine   If the Nine of Cups has appeared in the Solidifier position, you will soon enter into a period where you are happy and content with your-self. You may, however, spend a lot of time on your own, so you should use this time to get to know yourself better, a time of inner reflection and attunement to your spiritual awareness. On the down side, you may find you are eating or drinking more than is necessary for the healthy functioning of your body, and this could consequently lead you to put on weight, which is not necessarily a good thing for your physical well-being. It would be wise, therefore, to rest, eat sensibly and exercise regularly so you do not gain unwanted pounds and damage your health.

Ten   If the Ten of Cups has appeared in the Solidifier position, you will soon find yourself in a situation that has the ability to give you a great deal of happiness and harmony. You may come face to face with your soul-mate in this life, the person who you love and want to share a home and family with. It is likely you will bask in the simplest pleasures this world has to offer, such as walking in the countryside and spending time with the one you love.

King   If the King of Cups has appeared in the Solidifier position, you will soon find yourself under the influence of a man who is a very sensitive individual indeed. He is quite knowledgeable about a variety of subjects and may even be psychic. He is very perceptive, assessing any situation before deciding whether he would like to involve himself. He is somewhat introverted, preferring to keep his thoughts and opinions to himself, not wishing to offend anyone with any views that might be considered controversial. He does, however, have many secrets, which you will need to uncover before you decide just how involved you would like to become with this man.

Queen   If the Queen of Cups has appeared in the Solidifier position, you will soon be influenced by a woman who has a great deal of emotional intelligence. It is very easy for her to display her true feelings, whether good or bad, thereby making it difficult for her to lie to others. It is easy to tell when she is saying something that is not true because she will tend to avert her eyes from the recipient of her communications. She does, nevertheless, have something very important to impart to you, but you will need to watch her closely to glean the true meaning of the message she is trying to impart to you.

Knight/ Prince   If the Knight of Cups has appeared in the Solidifier position, you will soon come into contact with a young man. He can be very caring because he is such an emotive individual. Because he is so sensitive, he appeals to the opposite sex, as they feel an affinity for his more intuitive side. The dark side, however, is not something most people would like to explore because he has a depth that even he may not be aware of. When slighted, he can become petty and spiteful, which detracts from what is otherwise a delightful personality.

Page/ Princess   If the Page of Cups has appeared in the Solidifier position, you will soon come in contact with a young person who is very intuitive and sensitive to the moods of others. She is quite sensitive and wears her heart on her sleeve, often becoming affected by the subtle messages other people unconsciously put out. Because she is so sensitive, she needs a lot of care and attention so she will not lose her way during her walk through the course of her life.

Recommended Reading

Bach, Eleanor 1990, *Astrology from A to Z*, Allied Books, New York, USA.

Blofeld, John 1984, *I Ching*, Harper Collins Publishers, New York, USA.

Comte, Fernand 1991, *Mythology*, Chambers, Edinburgh, England, UK.

Connolly, Eileen 1979, *Tarot: a New Handbook for the Apprentice*, Aquarian Press, England, UK.

Connolly, Eileen 1987, *Tarot: the Handbook for the Journeyman*, Aquarian Press, England, UK.

Connolly, Eileen 1994, *Tarot: the First Handbook for the Master*, Newcastle Publishing Co, California, USA.

Dee, Jonathan 2000, *Tarot*, Parragon, Bath, England, UK.

Di Pietro, Sylvia 1991, *Live your Life by the Numbers*, Signet, USA.

Garen, Nancy 1990, *Tarot Made Easy*, Piatkus, UK.

Godwin, David 1994, *The Truth about Cabala*, Llewellyn Publications, St Paul, Minnesota, USA.

Goodman, Linda 1987, *Linda Goodman's Star Signs*, St Martin's Press, New York, USA.

Grey, Eden 1971, *Mastering the Tarot*, Signet Books, New York, USA.

Johari, Harish 1990, *Numerology*, Destiny Books, Rochester, Vermont, USA.

Jones, Brian 1991, *An Introduction to Practical Astronomy*, The Apple Press, London.

Lind, Frank 1979, *How to Understand the Tarot*, Aquarian Press, England, UK.

Line, Julia 1985, *Discover Numerology*, Harper Collins Publishers, London, UK.

Lyle, Jane 1990, *Tarot*, Mallard Press, USA.

McLaine, Patricia 1991, *The Wheel of Destiny*, Llewellyn Publications, St Paul, Minnesota, USA.

Morse, Dr Eric 1988, *The Living Stars*, Amethyst Books, New York, USA.

Peach, Emily 1984, *Discover Tarot*, Harper Collins Publishers, London, UK.

Philip, Neil 1995, *The Illustrated Book of Myths: Tales & Legends of the World*, Dorling Kindersley, London, UK.

Porter, Tracy 2000, *House Rules*, American Federation of Astrologers, Tempe, Arizona, USA.

Porter, Tracy 2000, *The Tarot Companion*, Llewellyn Publications, St Paul, Minnesota, USA.

Sharamon, Shalila & Baginski, Bodoj 1991, *The Chakra Handbook*, Lotus Light Publications, USA.

Shavick, Nancy 1988, *The Tarot*, Berkley Books, New York, USA.

Shavick, Nancy 1991, *The Tarot Reader*, Berkley Books, New York, USA.

Shavick, Nancy 1992, *Travelling the Royal Road*, Berkley Books, New York, USA.

Shavick, Nancy 1993, *The Tarot Guide to Love and Relationships*, Berkley Books, New York, USA.

Smith, Caroline & Astrop, John 1988, *Elemental Tarot*, Bantam Doubleday Dell Publishing Group, New York.

Waite, A. E. 1993, *The Pictorial Key to the Tarot*, Parragon Book Service, London, UK.

Wing, R. L. 1982, *The Illustrated I Ching*, Doubleday, New York, USA.